GoodFood

The Collection

480+ triple-tested recipes

10 9 8 7 6 5 4 3 2 1

Published exclusively for WHSmith in 2008 by BBC Books, an imprint of Ebury Publishing
A Random House Group Company

The Random House Group Limited Reg. No. 954009

Addresses for companies within the Random House Group can be found at
www.randomhouse.co.uk

A CIP catalogue record for this book is available from the British Library.

The Random House Group Limited supports The Forest Stewardship Council (FSC), the
leading international forest certification organization. All our titles that are printed on Greenpeace
approved FSC certified paper carry the FSC logo. Our paper procurement policy can be found at
www.rbooks.co.uk/environment

To buy books by your favourite authors and register for offers visit www.rbooks.co.uk

Commissioning Editor: Lorna Russell
Project Editor: Laura Higginson
Designer: Annette Peppis
Production Controller: Antony Heller

Printed and bound by C&C offset Printing Co., Ltd., China
Colour origination by Pixel Envy

ISBN: 978 1846 07931 3

GoodFood
The Collection

480+ triple-tested recipes

BBC
BOOKS

Compiled by Helena Caldon

Contents

Introduction

At *Good Food* magazine we like to make your life in the kitchen as easy as possible, so in this collected edition of six of our best-selling 101 titles, we've included hundreds of tempting, delicious and easy recipes in one complete book. Whether you're looking for simple mid-week meal solutions or inspiration for a special occasion dish, every idea you need is right here.

If after-work evenings are busy, make life a little easier by serving up a satisfying one-pot dish that you've prepared ahead. Or, choose a recipe where everything can be cooked in one pan – saving on time and washing up. If you're preparing a meal for two every night, or cooking a cosy, special-occasion meal, there's bound to be something amongst our inspirational meals for two recipes that will suit every situation.

For those who follow special diets, our veggie section includes a range of healthy, balanced meals that are so delicious they will tempt even the hardened meat-eaters amongst you. If you're watching what you eat in a battle with the bulge, take a look at our delicious low-fat dishes that will prove that you don't have to give up the good things in life while you're on a diet.

As we all know, you don't need to use the most expensive ingredients to create a nutritious and appetising meal, so if you're on a budget, or just want to save a few pennies on the shopping, with this book beside you you'll never be short of ideas for quick, low-cost recipes. And if you've got students in the family – what a great way to get them cooking and give you peace of mind that they'll be eating well when they're away from home.

But economising or not, we all need a little treat every once in a while, and life brings with it special occasions, including birthdays and seasonal, festive celebrations that should all be marked with something delicious and indulgent! To that end, we couldn't leave out cakes and bakes. If you've never baked a cake in your life, don't panic! You don't need to be an expert baker to have success with these recipes – and some can even be cooked with the kids.

As ever, the cookery team at *Good Food* magazine have tested all the recipes featured in this book, so they'll work perfectly for you – every time. We've also included a complete nutritional breakdown for each recipe, so you can keep an eye on the fat, salt, sugar and calorie content, if you wish. We've done the hard work for you, so all that remains for you to do now is choose a recipe and get cooking!

Helena Caldon

Conversion tables

NOTES ON THE RECIPES
• Eggs are large in the UK and Australia and extra large in America unless stated otherwise.
• Wash all fresh produce before preparation.

OVEN TEMPERATURES

Gas	°C	Fan °C	°F	Oven temp.
¼	110	90	225	Very cool
½	120	100	250	Very cool
1	140	120	275	Cool or slow
2	150	130	300	Cool or slow
3	160	140	325	Warm
4	180	160	350	Moderate
5	190	170	375	Moderately hot
6	200	180	400	Fairly hot
7	220	200	425	Hot
8	230	210	450	Very hot
9	240	220	475	Very hot

APPROXIMATE WEIGHT CONVERSIONS
• All the recipes in this book list both imperial and metric measurements. Conversions are approximate and have been rounded up or down. Follow one set of measurements only; do not mix the two.
• Cup measurements, which are used by cooks in Australia and America, have not been listed here as they vary from ingredient to ingredient. Kitchen scales should be used to measure dry/solid ingredients.

SPOON MEASURES
Spoon measurements are level unless otherwise specified.
• 1 teaspoon (tsp) = 5ml
• 1 tablespoon (tbsp) = 15ml
• 1 Australian tablespoon = 20ml (cooks in Australia should measure 3 teaspoons where 1 tablespoon is specified in a recipe)

APPROXIMATE LIQUID CONVERSIONS

metric	imperial	AUS	US
50ml	2fl oz	¼ cup	¼ cup
125ml	4fl oz	½ cup	½ cup
175ml	6fl oz	¾ cup	¾ cup
225ml	8fl oz	1 cup	1 cup
300ml	10fl oz/½ pint	½ pint	1¼ cups
450ml	16fl oz	2 cups	2 cups/1 pint
600ml	20fl oz/1 pint	1 pint	2½ cups
1 litre	35fl oz/1¾ pints	1¾ pints	1 quart

One-pot Dishes

Chunky Winter Broth

This hearty winter supper is a great way of getting your daily vitamins.

2 × 400g cans chopped tomatoes
2 litres/3½ pints vegetable stock
4 carrots, sliced
2 × 400g cans mixed pulses, drained
   and rinsed
175g/6oz spinach leaves
1 tbsp roasted red pepper pesto
crusty bread, to serve

Takes 15–20 minutes • Serves 4

1 Tip the tomatoes into a large saucepan along with the stock. Bring to the boil, turn down the heat and throw in the carrots. Gently simmer the soup until the carrots are cooked, about 15 minutes.
2 Add the pulses and spinach and heat for a few minutes, stirring, until the spinach has wilted. Spoon in the pesto and gently mix into the soup. Serve with some crusty bread.

• Per serving 219 kcalories, protein 16g, carbohydrate 34g, fat 3g, saturated fat 3g, fibre 12g, added sugar none, salt 3.16g

Broccoli Soup with Goat's Cheese

This is a great warming lunch or starter. If you don't like goat's cheese, try brie instead.

50g/2oz butter
1 large onion, finely chopped
900g/2lb broccoli, chopped (keep florets and
   stalks separate)
generous grating of fresh nutmeg or ¼ tsp
   ground nutmeg
1 litre/1¾ pints vegetable or chicken stock
600ml/1 pint full-fat milk
100g/4oz medium-soft goat's cheese,
   chopped (rind and all)
croûtons, to serve (optional)

Takes 40–50 minutes • Serves 4

1 Melt the butter in a large saucepan, add the onion, broccoli stalks and nutmeg and fry for 5 minutes until soft. Add the broccoli florets and stock, then the milk. Cover and simmer gently for 8 minutes until the broccoli is tender.
2 Take out about 4 ladlefuls of broccoli, then purée the rest in the pan with a hand blender until smooth. Return the reserved broccoli to the soup and check for seasoning. (The soup will keep in the fridge for 2 days or you can cool it and freeze it for up to 2 months.)
3 To serve, reheat if necessary and scatter with the goat's cheese – and croûtons, if you like.

• Per serving 371 kcalories, protein 22g, carbohydrate 16g, fat 25g, saturated fat 14.5g, fibre 6.6g, added sugar none, salt 1.67g

Smoked Haddock Chowder

To give this simple, healthy soup a kick, add a dash of Tabasco sauce.

1 onion, chopped
2 potatoes, scrubbed and sliced
500ml/18fl oz vegetable stock
2 smoked haddock fillets, about 100g/4oz
   each, cut into chunks
418g can creamed corn milk, to taste
handful of parsley, chopped (optional)

Takes 20–25 minutes • Serves 2

1 Put the onion and potatoes into a large sauté pan. Pour over the vegetable stock and simmer for 6–8 minutes until the potatoes are soft, but still have a slight bite. Add the chunks of smoked haddock. Tip in the creamed corn and add a little milk if you like a thick chowder, more if you like it thinner.
2 Gently simmer for 5–7 minutes until the haddock is cooked (it should flake when prodded with a fork). Sprinkle over the parsley, if using, and ladle the chowder into bowls.

• Per serving 555 kcalories, protein 37g, carbohydrate 84g, fat 10g, saturated fat 3g, fibre 7g, added sugar none, salt 0.3g

TOP: Chunky Winter Broth   BOTTOM LEFT: Broccoli Soup with Goat's Cheese   BOTTOM RIGHT: Smoked Haddock Chowder

TOP LEFT: Autumn Vegetable Soup   TOP RIGHT: Provençal Tomato Soup   BOTTOM: Three Green Vegetable Soup

Autumn Vegetable Soup

A great soup for freezing ahead. Just reheat, make cheese on toast if you like – it's very tasty with edam – and serve.

1 leek, chopped quite small
2 carrots, chopped quite small
1 potato, peeled and chopped quite small
1 garlic clove, finely chopped
1 tbsp finely chopped fresh rosemary
425ml/¾ pint vegetable stock
½ tsp sugar
2 × 400g cans chopped tomatoes
410g can chickpeas, drained and rinsed
3 tbsp chopped fresh parsley
cheese on toast or buttered toast, to serve
    (optional)

Takes 30–40 minutes • Serves 4

1 Put the vegetables into a large saucepan with the garlic, rosemary, stock and sugar. Season and stir well, then bring to a simmer. Cover and cook gently for 15 minutes or until the vegetables are just tender.
2 Whizz the tomatoes in a food processor or blender until smooth, then tip into the vegetables with the chickpeas and parsley. Gently heat through, stirring now and then. Taste for seasoning and serve hot – with cheese on toast or buttered toast, if you like.

• Per serving 151 kcalories, protein 9g, carbohydrate 25g, fat 2g, saturated fat none, fibre 6.9g, added sugar 0.7g, salt 1.14g

Provençal Tomato Soup

Nothing compares with freshly made tomato soup. Wait until the autumn when tomatoes are at their tastiest.

2 tbsp olive oil
1 onion, finely chopped
1 carrot, finely chopped
1 celery stick, finely chopped
2 tsp tomato purée, or to taste
1kg/2lb 4oz ripe tomatoes,
    quartered
2 bay leaves
good pinch of sugar, or to taste
1.2 litres/2 pints vegetable stock

TO SERVE (OPTIONAL)
4 tbsp crème fraîche
small handful of basil leaves

Takes 1½–1¾ hours • Serves 4

1 Heat the oil in a large saucepan and gently fry the onion, carrot and celery for 10 minutes until softened and lightly coloured. Stir in the tomato purée. Tip in the tomatoes and add the bay leaves and sugar. Season to taste. Stir well, cover and cook gently for 10 minutes until the tomatoes reduce down slightly.
2 Pour in the stock, stir and bring to the boil. Cover and cook gently for 30 minutes, stirring once or twice. Remove the bay leaves. Purée the soup in the pan with a hand blender until fairly smooth, then pour through a sieve to remove the tomato skins and seeds.
3 Return the soup to the pan and reheat. Taste and add more sugar, and salt and pepper, if you like, plus some more tomato purée for a deeper colour. Serve hot, topped with crème fraîche and basil leaves, if you like.

• Per serving 124 kcalories, protein 4g, carbohydrate 13g, fat 7g, saturated fat 0.9g, fibre 3.7g, added sugar 0.5g, salt 1.09g

Three Green Vegetable Soup

The just-wilted watercress and mint add a fresh and peppery flavour to this speedy, tasty soup.

knob of butter or splash of olive oil
bunch of spring onions, chopped
3 courgettes, chopped
200g/8oz podded fresh or frozen peas
850ml/1½ pints vegetable stock
85g bag trimmed watercress
large handful of mint
2 rounded tbsp Greek yogurt, plus extra
    to serve

Takes 15 minutes • Serves 4

1 Heat the butter or oil in a large saucepan, add the spring onions and courgettes and stir well. Cover and cook for 3 minutes, add the peas and stock and return to the boil. Cover and simmer for a further 4 minutes, then remove from the heat and stir in the watercress and mint until they are wilted.
2 Purée in the pan with a hand blender, adding the yogurt halfway through. Add seasoning to taste. Serve hot or cold, drizzled with extra yogurt.

• Per serving 100 kcalories, protein 8g, carbohydrate 9g, fat 4g, saturated fat 2g, fibre 4g, added sugar none, salt 0.81g

Moroccan Chickpea Soup

An unusual and tasty dish for vegetarians. For meat-lovers, fry 4 sliced chorizo sausages along with the onions and celery.

1 tbsp olive oil
1 medium onion, chopped
2 celery sticks, chopped
2 tsp ground cumin
600ml/1 pint vegetable stock
400g can chopped tomatoes with garlic
400g can chickpeas, drained and rinsed
100g/4oz frozen broad beans
grated zest and juice of ½ lemon
large handful of coriander or parsley, and
    flatbread, to serve

Takes 20–25 minutes • Serves 4

1 Heat the oil in a large saucepan, then fry the onion and celery gently for 10 minutes until softened, stirring frequently. Tip in the cumin and fry for another minute.
2 Turn up the heat, then add the stock, tomatoes and chickpeas, plus a good grind of black pepper. Simmer for 8 minutes. Throw in the broad beans and lemon juice and cook for a further 2 minutes.
3 Season to taste, then top with a sprinkling of lemon zest and chopped herbs. Serve with flatbread.

• Per serving 148 kcalories, protein 9g, carbohydrate 17g, fat 5g, saturated fat 1g, fibre 6g, added sugar none, salt 1.07g

White Bean Soup with Chilli Oil

The perfect soup to start a Sunday lunch in winter. The chilli oil is the perfect foil to the mealiness of the beans.

500g/1lb 2oz dried butter beans, soaked
    overnight
2 tbsp vegetable oil
1 medium onion, chopped
1 garlic clove, chopped
2 carrots, chopped
2 celery sticks, chopped
1.4 litres/2½ pints vegetable stock
2 bay leaves
2–3 fresh thyme sprigs, plus extra for
    sprinkling
chilli oil, for drizzling

Takes 1½–1¾ hours, plus overnight soaking • Serves 6

1 Drain the beans. Shuck off and discard the skins by pinching the beans between finger and thumb. Put the beans in a colander, rinse and drain.
2 Heat the oil in a pan and fry the onion and garlic for 1–2 minutes. Tip in the carrots and celery and fry gently for 2–3 minutes. Add the beans, stock, bay and thyme with some pepper, and bring to the boil. Reduce the heat, cover and simmer for 20–25 minutes, skimming off any scum, until the beans are soft.
3 Cool the soup for 10 minutes, discard the bay and thyme, then purée in the pan with a hand blender until quite smooth. Check for seasoning and reheat if necessary, then serve with a drizzle of chilli oil and a sprinkling of thyme leaves.

• Per serving 319 kcalories, protein 18g, carbohydrate 49g, fat 7g, saturated fat 1g, fibre 15g, added sugar none, salt 0.89g

Thai Chicken and Coconut Soup

For an even more authentic meal, serve this rich and creamy soup with some ready-cooked Thai fragrant rice.

2 × 400g cans coconut milk
3 tbsp fish sauce
4cm/1½in piece fresh root ginger or galangal,
    peeled and finely chopped
2 lemongrass stalks, finely sliced
6 kaffir lime leaves or strips of lime zest
1 fresh red chilli, chopped
2 tsp light muscovado sugar
500g/1lb 2oz boneless, skinless chicken
    breasts, cut into small bite-sized pieces
2 tbsp lime juice
good handful of fresh basil and coriander,
    roughly chopped

Takes 35–40 minutes • Serves 4

1 Tip all the ingredients except the chicken, lime juice and herbs into a large saucepan, bring to a gentle simmer and cook uncovered in a relaxed bubble for 5 minutes.
2 Add the chicken, cover and simmer for 8–10 minutes or until tender. Stir in the lime juice, then scatter over the herbs before serving.

• Per serving 479 kcalories, protein 35g, carbohydrate 10g, fat 34g, saturated fat 28.3g, fibre none, added sugar 2.8g, salt 2.96g

TOP LEFT: Moroccan Chickpea Soup   TOP RIGHT: White Bean Soup with Chilli Oil   BOTTOM: Thai Chicken and Coconut Soup

TOP: Roasted Ratatouille Chicken   BOTTOM LEFT: Quick Meatball Casserole   BOTTOM RIGHT: Sausage and Leek Hash

Roasted Ratatouille Chicken

A simple method and lovely Mediterranean flavours and colours make this a versatile dish, perfect for either a family supper or a dinner party.

1 onion, cut into wedges
2 red peppers, seeded and cut into chunks
1 courgette (about 200g/8oz), cut into chunks
1 small aubergine (about 300g/10oz), cut into chunks
4 tomatoes, halved
4 tbsp olive oil, plus extra for drizzling
4 chicken breasts, skin on (about 140g/5oz each)
a few rosemary sprigs (optional)

Takes 50–60 minutes • Serves 4

1 Preheat the oven to 200ºC/Gas 6/fan oven 180ºC. Lay all the vegetables and the tomatoes in a shallow roasting tin. Make sure they have lots of room – overcrowding will slow down the cooking. Pour over the olive oil and give the vegetables a good mix round until they are well coated (hands are easiest for this).
2 Nestle the chicken breasts on top of the vegetables and tuck in some rosemary sprigs, if you are using them. Season everything with salt and black pepper and drizzle a little oil over the chicken. Now roast for about 35 minutes until the vegetables are soft and the chicken is golden. Drizzle with oil before serving.

• Per serving 318 kcalories, protein 37g, carbohydrate 13g, fat 14g, saturated fat 2g, fibre 4g, added sugar none, salt 0.25g

Quick Meatball Casserole

Low-fat, delicious and healthy – and all in one pot, too!

500g/1lb 2oz turkey mince
small bunch of parsley, chopped
1 tbsp olive oil
2 large onions, chopped
2 garlic cloves, crushed
450g/1lb carrots, quartered, then cut into chunks
450g/1lb potatoes, peeled and cut into chunks
1 tbsp paprika
500g jar passata (sieved tomatoes)

Takes 45–50 minutes • Serves 4

1 Mix the turkey mince with half the chopped parsley, and salt and pepper to taste, then shape into 12 balls. Heat the oil in a large non-stick pan or flameproof casserole and fry the meatballs for 4–5 minutes, shaking the pan occasionally, until the meat is browned all over.
2 Add the chopped onions, garlic, carrots, potatoes and 300ml/½ pint water to the pan. Bring to the boil, cover and simmer for 15 minutes.
3 Stir in the paprika, passata and half the remaining parsley. Bring to the boil, cover and cook for a further 10–15 minutes or until the potatoes and carrots are tender. Season to taste and sprinkle with the remaining parsley to serve.

• Per serving 330 kcalories, protein 32g, carbohydrate 38g, fat 6g, saturated fat 1.5g, fibre 6g, added sugar none, salt 0.38g

Sausage and Leek Hash

You can use any leftover vegetables for this simple weekend supper.

2 tbsp olive oil
6 plump sausages
6 potatoes, thinly sliced
350g/12oz thinly sliced leeks (or broccoli or cabbage)
1 tbsp creamed horseradish sauce, or more to taste
100g/4oz mature cheddar or gruyère, grated

Takes 30–35 minutes • Serves 4

1 Heat half of the oil in a large, heavy-based frying pan. Add the sausages and fry gently for 8–10 minutes until well browned. Remove the sausages, then slice them on the diagonal and set aside.
2 Turn the heat to medium and add the remaining oil. Add the potatoes and leeks and give everything a good stir. Cook until the potatoes and leeks are tender and beginning to brown, turning them over from time to time. This will take 15–20 minutes.
3 Toss the sausages back in along with the horseradish, to taste, and heat through for a further 2–3 minutes. Take the pan off the heat, sprinkle in the cheese, season well and stir gently to combine. Serve.

• Per serving 534 kcalories, protein 24g, carbohydrate 35g, fat 34g, saturated fat 13.5g, fibre 4g, added sugar 0.3g, salt 2.46g

Chicken with Creamy Bacon Penne

This amazingly quick and tasty dish works well with fresh salmon, too. Just cook for 3 minutes on each side and leave out the bacon.

1 tbsp olive oil
2 boneless, skinless chicken breasts
100g/4oz smoked lardons (chopped bacon)
4 tbsp dry white wine
100g/4oz frozen petits pois
5 tbsp double cream
220g pack 'instant' cooked penne

Takes 10 minutes • Serves 2

1 Heat the oil in a deep non-stick frying pan, add the chicken breasts and scatter with the lardons. Leave to cook over a high heat for 4 minutes while you gather the other ingredients together.
2 Turn the chicken over in the pan, give the lardons a stir, then pour in the wine and let it bubble over a high heat until it has virtually evaporated. Now add the peas, cream and penne, season and stir well. Cover the pan and cook for 4 minutes more until the chicken is cooked all the way through. Serve straight away.

• Per serving 639 kcalories, protein 48g, carbohydrate 24g, fat 38g, saturated fat 17g, fibre 3g, added sugar none, salt 1.86g

Braised Pork with Fennel

You can ensure your family stays healthy with this low-fat feast.

1 tbsp olive oil
500g/1lb 2oz pork tenderloin, cut into chunks
1 large onion, chopped
3 garlic cloves, crushed
2 × 400g cans chopped tomatoes
2 tbsp tomato purée
½ tsp caster sugar
200ml/7fl oz vegetable stock
1 large bulb fennel
grated zest of 1 lemon

Takes 1¼–1½ hours • Serves 4

1 Heat 1 teaspoon of the oil in a large pan. Brown the pork on all sides (you may need to do this in batches). Remove from the pan with a slotted spoon and set aside. Add the remaining oil and the onion and cook over a low heat, stirring occasionally, for 5–6 minutes until the onion is soft. Stir in the garlic, tomatoes, tomato purée, sugar, stock and pork, then season. Bring to the boil.
2 Trim the fronds from the fennel, roughly chop and set aside. Cut the bulb into thin wedges and stir into the pork. Push the fennel under the surface of the sauce, lower the heat and simmer for 35–40 minutes with the lid on, until tender. Stir in the lemon zest, garnish with the chopped fennel fronds and serve.

• Per serving 242 kcalories, protein 31g, carbohydrate 12g, fat 8g, saturated fat 2g, fibre 4g, added sugar 1g, salt 0.83g

Ham and Beans with Orange

One of the joys of one-pot cooking is putting dishes into the oven well in advance and then forgetting about them until serving time.

250g/9oz dried haricot beans, soaked overnight
2 oranges
2 tbsp olive oil
1 large onion, chopped
2 celery sticks, chopped
450g/1lb piece gammon, cut into large chunks
1 tbsp paprika
3 tbsp dark muscovado sugar
1 tbsp black treacle or molasses
2 tbsp white wine vinegar
2–3 tbsp tomato purée
4 whole cloves

Takes 2½ hours, plus overnight soaking • Serves 4

1 Drain and rinse the beans, then tip them into a pan and pour in 1.4 litres/2½ pints boiling water. Bring to the boil, cover and simmer for 30 minutes.
2 Meanwhile, preheat the oven to 180°C/ Gas 4/fan oven 160°C. Grate the zest from the oranges; set aside. Heat the oil in a large flameproof casserole. Add the onion and celery and fry, stirring occasionally, for 8 minutes, until the onion is golden. Add the ham and paprika and stir for 1 minute, then tip in the orange zest, sugar, treacle, vinegar, tomato purée and cloves. Stir well.
3 Tip the beans and cooking liquid into the casserole, cover and cook for 1 hour. Remove the lid and cook for a further hour. Peel the oranges and cut the flesh into chunks. Stir into the beans, with plenty of seasoning.

• Per serving 493 kcalories, protein 37g, carbohydrate 63g, fat 12g, saturated fat 3g, fibre 13g, added sugar 19g, salt 2.85g

TOP: Chicken with Creamy Bacon Penne   BOTTOM LEFT: Braised Pork with Fennel   BOTTOM RIGHT: Ham and Beans with Orange

TOP LEFT: Chicken and Thyme Bake   TOP RIGHT: Summer Pork and Potatoes   BOTTOM: Frying-pan Sausage Hotpot

Chicken and Thyme Bake

Try taleggio, ripe brie, dolcelatte or Le Roulé if you don't like goat's cheese.

4 part-boned chicken breasts
140g/5oz firm goat's cheese, sliced
bunch of fresh thyme
500g pack cherry tomatoes
olive oil, for drizzling
splash of dry white wine
French bread or ready-cooked saffron rice, to serve

Takes 35–40 minutes • Serves 4

1 Preheat the oven to 190°C/Gas 5/fan oven 170°C. Loosen the skin from the chicken breasts and stuff with the slices of goat's cheese and a sprig of thyme. Put in a shallow ovenproof dish.
2 Halve the cherry tomatoes and scatter around the chicken with a few more sprigs of thyme, a drizzle of olive oil and splash of white wine. Season with pepper and salt, if you wish.
3 Bake for 25–30 minutes until the chicken is tender and golden. Serve with crusty French bread to mop up the juices or some saffron rice.

• Per serving 330 kcalories, protein 40g, carbohydrate 5g, fat 16g, saturated fat 8g, fibre 1g, added sugar none, salt 1.24g

Summer Pork and Potatoes

A great dish for everyone to help themselves from. A green salad, dressed lightly with olive oil and lemon juice, is all you need to go with it.

olive oil, for drizzling
750g/1lb 10oz new potatoes, scrubbed and sliced
500g/1lb 2oz vine-ripened tomatoes, sliced
leaves of 3–4 rosemary sprigs, finely chopped
2 garlic cloves, chopped
4 pork chops or steaks
green salad, to serve

Takes 1¼–1½ hours • Serves 4

1 Preheat the oven to 200°C/Gas 6/fan oven 180°C. Drizzle a little olive oil over the base of a shallow ovenproof dish that is wide enough to take the chops in one layer. Arrange rows of potatoes and tomatoes across the dish, seasoning with salt and pepper as you go and sprinkling with half the rosemary and all the garlic.
2 Drizzle a couple more tablespoons of olive oil over the vegetables and bake for 30 minutes, then sit the pork on top, season and sprinkle with the remaining rosemary. Return to the oven for 35–45 minutes, until the pork and potatoes are tender. Serve with a green salad.

• Per serving 527 kcalories, protein 25g, carbohydrate 35g, fat 33g, saturated fat 11g, fibre 3g, added sugar none, salt 0.2g

Frying-pan Sausage Hotpot

Ready-sliced, cooked, long-life potatoes make this a really speedy supper dish.

1 tbsp vegetable oil
6 plump good-quality sausages with herbs
splash of red wine (if you have some)
175ml/6fl oz vegetable stock
3 tbsp ready-prepared caramelised red onions
400g pack cooked sliced long-life potatoes

Takes 25–35 minutes • Serves 3

1 Heat the oil in a medium frying pan (one the sausages will fit in fairly snugly). Add the sausages and fry for 8–10 minutes, turning them often. Preheat the grill to high. Splash a couple of tablespoons of red wine, if you are using it, into the pan, then pour in the stock and stir in the caramelised red onions. Allow the mixture to bubble for 3–4 minutes, so it thickens a little and turns into a rich gravy. Remove from the heat.
2 Spread the potatoes so they roughly cover the sausages and gravy. Put the frying pan under the grill for about 8 minutes until the potatoes turn crisp and golden. Serve while bubbling and hot – there is no need to add seasoning.

• Per serving 578 kcalories, protein 20g, carbohydrate 36g, fat 40g, saturated fat 14g, fibre 4g, added sugar 1g, salt 5.07g

Lamb in Palava Sauce

Palm oil is an authentic African ingredient that adds a rich red colour – look for oil from Ghana or Sierra Leone in ethnic food shops.

1 red chilli, seeded and chopped
2.5cm/1in piece fresh root ginger, peeled and roughly chopped
2 garlic cloves, peeled
1 onion, half roughly chopped and half sliced
1 tbsp tomato purée
400g can tomatoes
6 tbsp palm or vegetable oil
500g/1lb 2oz lean lamb, cut into 2.5cm/1in cubes
300ml/½ pint lamb, chicken or vegetable stock
200g/8oz fresh spinach leaves, roughly shredded
2 eggs, beaten

Takes 1¼–1½ hours • Serves 4

1 Blitz the chilli, ginger, garlic, chopped onion, tomato purée and tomatoes in a food processor until chopped together to make a sauce.
2 Heat the oil in a large frying pan and fry the sliced onion for 2 minutes. Add the lamb and stir fry over a highish heat for 6–7 minutes until starting to brown. Pour the tomato sauce over the lamb and bubble rapidly for 2–3 minutes, then stir in the stock and add seasoning to taste. Cover and simmer gently for 40–50 minutes, stirring occasionally, until the lamb is tender and the sauce has thickened.
3 Stir the spinach into the sauce so it wilts, then simmer for 2–3 minutes. Drizzle in the egg and continue to simmer for 2 minutes until just set. Serve straight from the pan.

• Per serving 421 kcalories, protein 32g, carbohydrate 3g, fat 31g, saturated fat 9g, fibre 1.5g, added sugar none, salt 0.6g

Chicken Biryani

It's so easy to recreate this classic Indian dish that you'll never order a takeaway again.

2 tbsp vegetable oil
6 large chicken thighs, skin on
1 large onion, finely sliced
2 tbsp curry powder (hot if you like it, mild for tamer curries)
350g/12oz easy-cook long-grain rice
700ml/1¼ pints chicken or vegetable stock
250g/9oz frozen peas

Takes 50–60 minutes • Serves 6

1 Preheat the oven to 200°C/Gas 6/fan oven 180°C. Heat the oil in a large sauté pan and fry the chicken thighs, skin side down, for 8–10 minutes until the skin is golden and crispy. Tip in the onion and continue to cook for 5 minutes until the onion softens. Sprinkle in the curry powder and cook for 1 minute more, then stir in the rice and pour over the stock. Bring the stock to the boil.
2 Cover the pan and bake for 30 minutes until all the liquid has been absorbed and the rice is cooked. Stir in the peas and leave the rice to stand for a few minutes before serving.

• Per serving 445 kcalories, protein 32g, carbohydrate 57g, fat 12g, saturated fat 3g, fibre 2g, added sugar none, salt 0.5g

Curry in a Hurry

Look out for jars of ready-chopped ginger and chillies, and pouches of gujarati masala, in larger supermarkets.

1 tbsp sunflower oil
1 red onion, thinly sliced
1 garlic clove
2 tsp ready-prepared ginger from a jar
½–1 tsp ready-chopped chillies from a jar
200g can chopped tomatoes
250g/9oz boneless, skinless chicken breasts, chopped
2 tsp gujarati masala or garam masala
3 tbsp low-fat yogurt
handful of coriander leaves, roughly chopped or torn
garlic and coriander naan bread, to serve

Takes 15 minutes • Serves 2 (easily doubled)

1 Heat the oil in a pan, add the onion and fry until coloured. Crush the garlic into the pan, add the ginger and chillies and cook briefly. Add the tomatoes and a quarter of a can of water and bring to the boil. Simmer for 2 minutes, add the chicken and masala, cover and cook for 5–6 minutes.
2 Reduce the heat to a simmer, then stir in the yogurt, a tablespoon at a time. Sprinkle with coriander and serve with warm garlic and coriander naans.

• Per serving 252 kcalories, protein 34g, carbohydrate 11g, fat 8g, saturated fat 1.3g, fibre 1.8g, added sugar none, salt 0.46g

TOP LEFT: Lamb in Palava Sauce   TOP RIGHT: Chicken Biryani   BOTTOM: Curry in a Hurry

TOP: Sunday Brunch Beans   BOTTOM LEFT: Pork and Apple Braise   BOTTOM RIGHT: Cheesy Chops and Chips

Sunday Brunch Beans

Baked beans are great, cheap comfort food, and they're nutritious, too.

2 tbsp vegetable oil
1 potato, thinly sliced (unpeeled)
200g can corned beef, sliced
400g can baked beans
splash of Worcestershire sauce

Takes 20–25 minutes • Serves 2 (easily doubled)

1 Heat the oil in a frying pan until hot, add the potato slices and fry for 7–10 minutes or until golden and crisp.
2 Push the potatoes to one side, add the corned beef and fry undisturbed for a couple of minutes. Tip in the baked beans, add a splash of Worcestershire sauce and stir gently until the beans are hot.

• Per serving 510 kcalories, protein 37g, carbohydrate 40g, fat 23g, saturated fat 6.4g, fibre 8.1g, added sugar 6.9g, salt 4.93g

Pork and Apple Braise

A low-fat, one-pot dish that's perfect for a family supper. Serve with ready-cooked rice, available from supermarkets.

500g/1lb 2oz pork tenderloin
1 tbsp plain flour, seasoned
2 tbsp olive oil
1 onion, chopped
1 Cox's apple, cored and cut into thin wedges, skin on
300ml/½ pint chicken or vegetable stock
2 bay leaves
1 tbsp wholegrain mustard
2 tbsp chopped flatleaf parsley

Takes 40–45 minutes • Serves 4

1 Cut the pork crossways into 2cm/¾in slices and coat in the seasoned flour. Heat 1 tablespoon of the oil in a large frying pan and fry the pork in small batches, then remove and set aside.
2 Fry the onion in the remaining oil until soft and golden brown. Add the apple and fry until it has slightly caramelised. Slowly stir in the stock, scraping up any bits from the bottom of the pan.
3 Return the pork to the pan and add the bay leaves and mustard. Bring to a simmer and cook for 15–20 minutes, adding a little more water or stock if necessary. Stir in the parsley and season to taste before serving.

• Per serving 248 kcalories, protein 29g, carbohydrate 9g, fat 11g, saturated fat 2g, fibre 2g, added sugar none, salt 0.41g

Cheesy Chops and Chips

Get your protein hit with this all-in-one roast.

1kg/2lb 4oz potatoes, peeled and thickly sliced
1 onion, thinly sliced
splash of cider, wine, water or stock
2 tbsp olive oil
4 pork chops, about 175g/6oz each
100g/4oz cheddar cheese, grated
1 tbsp wholegrain mustard
3 tbsp milk

Takes 1–1¼ hours • Serves 4

1 Preheat the oven to 230°C/Gas 8/fan oven 210°C. Toss the potatoes, onion, liquid and oil together in a large flameproof casserole. Season, if you like, then bake for 20–30 minutes until the potatoes start to brown. Lay the chops on the potatoes and cook for 10 minutes more.
2 Mix the cheese, mustard and milk together. When the chops have had 10 minutes in the oven, spread the cheese mixture over them and switch the oven over to grill. Place the pan under the grill and cook for about 5 minutes until the cheese is bubbling and the potatoes are golden and crispy. Serve straight from the pan.

• Per serving 580 kcalories, protein 42g, carbohydrate 40g, fat 32g, saturated fat 14g, fibre 5g, added sugar none, salt 1.6g

Moroccan Lemon Chicken

Try using a whole preserved lemon from a jar instead of half a lemon.

1kg pack boneless, skinless chicken
   thigh fillets
1 onion, chopped
3 garlic cloves, crushed
1 tbsp pilau rice seasoning
2 tbsp olive oil
½ lemon, finely chopped – the zest, pith
   and flesh
100g pack whole blanched almonds
140g/5oz green olives (the ones with stones
   in taste best)
250ml/9fl oz chicken stock
large handful of coriander or flatleaf parsley,
   chopped

Takes 40–45 minutes • Serves 4

1 Toss the chicken with the onion, garlic,
rice seasoning and oil in a microwave dish.
Microwave on High for 8 minutes until
everything is beginning to sizzle and the
chicken is starting to change colour.
2 Toss the lemon, almonds and olives
over the chicken. Pour in the stock and stir,
keeping the chicken in a single layer.
3 Cover the dish with cling film, pierce a
few times to allow the steam to escape,
then return to the microwave for another
20 minutes until the liquid is bubbling
vigorously and the chicken is cooked.
Leave to stand for a few minutes before
stirring in the coriander or parsley, then serve.

• Per serving 488 kcalories, protein 49g, carbohydrate
8g, fat 29g, saturated fat 5g, fibre 3g, added sugar
none, salt 2.68g

Spiced Pork with Stir-fried Greens

Use a proper stir-fry oil if you can, as it's
infused with ginger, garlic and spices,
giving a real flavour hit.

1 tbsp stir-fry oil or vegetable oil
250g/9oz pork escalopes, sliced into
   thin strips
bunch of spring onions, trimmed and sliced
175g/6oz broccoli, broken into small
   bite-sized florets
3 celery sticks, sliced
2 heads pak or bok choi, broken into
   separate leaves
2 tbsp chopped fresh coriander
finely grated zest and juice of 1 lime
a few thin slices of red chilli or a dash of
   sweet chilli sauce

Takes 20–30 minutes • Serves 2 (easily
doubled)

1 Heat the oil in a wok or large frying
pan, add the pork and stir fry briskly for
3–4 minutes. Tip in the spring onions,
broccoli and celery and stir fry over a high
heat for 4 more minutes.
2 Add the pak or bok choi and cook for
a minute or so until the leaves have wilted.
Toss in the coriander and lime zest, squeeze
in a little lime juice and add the chilli slices
or sauce. Season with salt and pepper and
serve straight away.

• Per serving 260 kcalories, protein 34g, carbohydrate
5g, fat 12g, saturated fat 2.3g, fibre 3.7g, added sugar
none, salt 0.59g

Crispy-skin Chicken Thighs

You can leave the chicken to marinate in
the fridge for up to a day, if you like.

8 plump chicken thighs, skin on
2 lemons
2 tbsp chopped fresh tarragon
2 tbsp olive oil
750g/1lb 10oz new potatoes, scrubbed and
   cut into wedges
2 tsp paprika, sweet or smoked
green salad, to serve

Takes 45–55 minutes • Serves 4

1 Preheat the oven to 220°C/Gas 7/fan oven
200°C. Slash the skin of each chicken thigh
three times. Finely grate the zest from
1 lemon and squeeze the juice from both.
Mix in a shallow dish with the tarragon,
1 tablespoon of the oil and some salt and
pepper. Add the chicken and turn to coat
in the marinade.
2 Spread the potato wedges over the base
of a roasting tin. Toss in the remaining oil and
sprinkle with paprika. Set a rack on top and
arrange the chicken pieces on the rack. Roast
for 30–40 minutes until the chicken is well
browned and the potatoes are tender. Serve
hot with a simple green salad.

• Per serving 917 kcalories, protein 64g, carbohydrate
32g, fat 60g, saturated fat 17g, fibre 2g, added sugar
none, salt 0.74g

TOP: Moroccan Lemon Chicken   BOTTOM LEFT: Spiced Pork with Stir-fried Greens   BOTTOM RIGHT: Crispy-skin Chicken Thighs

TOP LEFT: Roast Chicken and Root Vegetables TOP RIGHT: Oven-baked Risotto BOTTOM: Bangers and Beans in a Pan

Roast Chicken and Root Vegetables

Transform your chicken breasts into something special. As a bonus, this dish is crammed with health-boosting vegetables.

1 small celeriac, peeled and cut into
   2.5cm/1in chunks
400g/14oz swede, peeled and cut into
   2.5cm/1in chunks
2 large sweet potatoes, scrubbed and cut
   into 2.5cm/1in chunks
2 medium parsnips, scrubbed and
   quartered lengthways
2 large garlic cloves, thinly sliced
2 tbsp olive oil
½ tsp cumin seeds
a few sage leaves
4 boneless, skinless chicken breasts, about
   140g/5oz each
4 slices prosciutto

Takes 1¼–1½ hours • Serves 4

1 Preheat the oven to 200°C/Gas 6/fan oven 180°C. Put the celeriac, swede, sweet potato, parsnips and garlic in a large roasting pan. Sprinkle with olive oil and cumin, and season with salt and pepper. Toss the vegetables together so they are lightly coated in oil. Put in the oven towards the top and roast for 30 minutes.
2 Meanwhile, lay a couple of sage leaves on each chicken breast, then wrap each with a slice of prosciutto to enclose.
3 Take the roasting tin from the oven and turn the vegetables over. Now lay the chicken on top. Roast for 30–35 minutes more, until the vegetables are tender and the chicken is done.

• Per serving 420 kcalories, protein 43g, carbohydrate 39g, fat 12g, saturated fat 2g, fibre 12g, added sugar none, salt 1.11g

Oven-baked Risotto

Cook this simple storecupboard risotto in the oven while you get on with something else – the result is still wonderfully creamy.

250g pack smoked bacon, chopped into
   small pieces
1 onion, chopped
25g/1oz butter
300g/10oz risotto rice
half a glass of white wine (optional)
150g pack cherry tomatoes, halved
700ml/1¼ pint chicken stock (from a cube
   is fine)
50g/2oz parmesan, grated

Takes 30–35 minutes • Serves 4

1 Heat the oven to 200°C/Gas 6/fan oven 180°C. Fry the bacon pieces in an ovenproof pan or casserole dish for 3–5 minutes until golden and crisp. Stir in the onion and butter and cook for 3–4 minutes until soft. Tip in the rice and mix well until coated. Pour over the wine, if using, and cook for 2 minutes until absorbed.
2 Add the cherry tomatoes and the hot stock, then give the rice a quick stir. Cover with a tightly fitting lid and bake for 18 minutes until just cooked.
3 Stir through most of the parmesan and serve sprinkled with the remainder.

• Per serving 517 kcalories, protein 22g, carbohydrate 63g, fat 20g, saturated fat 10g, fibre 2g, added sugar none, salt 3.38g

Bangers and Beans in a Pan

Perfect for a quick after-work meal. And it's so easy to double or treble the quantities to feed a crowd.

1 tbsp vegetable oil
454g pack good-quality sausages, each
   sausage chopped into three
1 small onion, chopped
3 carrots, chopped into thick slices
4 celery sticks, sliced into chunks (finely chop
   the leaves if there are any)
2 × 410g cans mixed pulses (or other beans),
   drained and rinsed
400ml/14fl oz chicken or vegetable stock
1–2 tbsp Dijon mustard (or 2 tsp ready-made
   English mustard)
small handful of parsley, chopped crusty
   bread, to serve

Takes 35–45 minutes • Serves 4

1 Heat the oil over a highish heat in a wide shallow pan that has a lid. Put the chopped sausages into the pan and sizzle for 5 minutes, stirring occasionally, until they are browned on all sides.
2 Throw in the onion, carrots and celery (not the leaves) and cook for 5 minutes until the onion looks see-through. Tip in the beans, give a good stir, then pour in the stock and bring to the boil, stirring. Cover and simmer for 10–15 minutes until the carrots are tender.
3 Stir in the mustard and parsley with any chopped celery leaves, then season to taste with salt and pepper. Serve hot, with chunks of crusty bread to mop up the sauce.

• Per serving 479 kcalories, protein 26g, carbohydrate 38g, fat 26g, saturated fat 8g, fibre 10g, added sugar none, salt 3.7g

Parmesan-crusted Fish

This is a delicious way of jazzing up a piece of white fish.

50g/2oz fresh breadcrumbs
grated zest and juice of 1 lemon
25g/1oz parmesan cheese, grated
2 tbsp chopped fresh parsley
4 thick, firm, skinless white fish fillets, such
 as cod, haddock, hoki or pollock
2 tbsp olive oil
50g/2oz butter

Takes 20–30 minutes • Serves 4

1 Preheat the grill to high. Mix the breadcrumbs with the lemon zest, parmesan, parsley, and salt and pepper to taste. Season the fish.
2 Heat the oil in a frying pan. Add the fish, skinned side down, and fry for 2–3 minutes until the flesh flakes easily with a fork. Turn the fish over and sprinkle with the breadcrumb mixture, then slide the pan under the hot grill and toast the breadcrumb topping for 2–3 minutes. Add the butter to the pan in pieces, pour in the lemon juice and let the butter melt around the fish.
3 Serve the fish with the lemony butter poured over.

• Per serving 334 kcalories, protein 31g, carbohydrate 10g, fat 19g, saturated fat 8.6g, fibre 0.4g, added sugar none, salt 0.78g

Cheesy Fish Grills

Even those who don't love fish will like this simple, speedy, foolproof dish.

sunflower or olive oil, for brushing
4 chunky, skinless white fish fillets, such
 as hoki or cod, about 500g/1lb 2oz
 total weight
4 thin, but not wafer-thin, slices of ham
50g/2oz mature cheddar cheese, grated
2 spring onions, sliced at an angle
green salad, to serve

Takes 15–25 minutes • Serves 4

1 Preheat the grill to high and lightly oil a large, shallow, flameproof dish. Arrange the fillets, skinned side down, in the dish, slightly spaced apart, and brush with a little oil. Grill for 2 minutes.
2 Remove the dish from the grill, turn the fish over and top each fillet with a scrunched slice of ham. Mix together the cheese and onions, scatter over the fish and season with salt and pepper. Return to the grill for 5 minutes or until the fish flakes easily with a fork. Serve with a green salad.

• Per serving 179 kcalories, protein 30g, carbohydrate none, fat 6g, saturated fat 3g, fibre none, added sugar none, salt 0.94g

Fish O'Leekie

Accurate microwave timings ensure that everything is cooked together perfectly.

1 leek, finely sliced
100g/4oz smoked lean back bacon, chopped
500ml/18fl oz vegetable stock
300g/10oz American easy-cook rice
500g/1lb 2oz cod or haddock fillet, skinned
 and cut into large chunks
3 tbsp chopped fresh parsley
grated zest and juice of 1 lemon

Takes 20–30 minutes • Serves 4

1 Put the leek and bacon in a medium microwave dish with 4 tablespoons of the stock. Cover the dish with cling film, pierce the film with a knife and microwave on High for 5 minutes.
2 Uncover the dish and stir the rice and remaining stock into the leek and bacon. Microwave on High for a further 5 minutes.
3 Gently stir in the fish chunks, cover the dish with cling film again, pierce the film with a knife and cook for a further 10 minutes until the fish and rice are done.
4 Stir in the parsley and lemon zest and juice. Leave to stand for 2–3 minutes before serving.

• Per serving 437 kcalories, protein 35g, carbohydrate 66g, fat 6g, saturated fat 1g, fibre 1g, added sugar none, salt 1.8g

TOP LEFT: Parmesan-crusted Fish   TOP RIGHT: Cheesy Fish Grills   BOTTOM: Fish O'Leekie

TOP: 20-minute Seafood Pasta   BOTTOM LEFT: Italian-style Roasted Fish   BOTTOM RIGHT: Easiest-ever Seafood Risotto

20-minute Seafood Pasta

For a Spanish-style version, add a pinch of saffron and a little white wine along with the tomatoes.

1 tbsp olive oil
1 onion, chopped
1 garlic clove, chopped
1 tsp paprika
400g can chopped tomatoes
1 litre/1¾ pints chicken stock
300g/10oz spaghetti, roughly broken
240g pack mixed frozen seafood, defrosted

TO SERVE
handful of parsley leaves, chopped
4 lemon wedges

Takes 20–25 minutes • Serves 4

1 Heat the oil in a wok or large frying pan, then cook the onion and garlic over a medium heat for 5 minutes until soft. Add the paprika, tomatoes and stock, then bring to the boil.
2 Turn down the heat to a simmer, stir in the pasta and cook for 7 minutes, stirring occasionally to stop the pasta from sticking.
3 Stir in the seafood, cook for 3 minutes more until it's all heated through and the pasta is cooked, then season to taste. Sprinkle with the parsley and serve with lemon wedges.

• Per serving 370 kcalories, protein 23g, carbohydrate 62g, fat 5g, saturated fat 1g, fibre 4g, added sugar none, salt 1.4g

Italian-style Roasted Fish

Let the fresh flavours of the Mediterranean into your home with this delicious one-pot dish.

4 thick, firm white fish fillets, such as cod, haddock, hoki or pollock, skin on
1 tbsp olive oil, plus extra for drizzling
500g/1lb 2oz cherry tomatoes, halved
50g/2oz pitted black olives, halved
25g/1oz pine nuts
large handful of basil leaves

Takes 25–30 minutes • Serves 4

1 Preheat the oven to 200°C/Gas 6/fan oven 180°C. Season the fish. Heat the oil in a large roasting tin on top of the stove and cook the fillets, skin side down, for 2–3 minutes or until just crisp.
2 Scatter the tomatoes, olives and pine nuts around the fish, season and roast in the oven for 12–15 minutes until the fish flakes easily with a fork. Scatter with the basil leaves and drizzle with a little olive oil before serving.

• Per serving 242 kcalories, protein 30g, carbohydrate 4g, fat 12g, saturated fat 1.5g, fibre 1.7g, added sugar none, salt 0.99g

Easiest-ever Seafood Risotto

Risottos make the perfect microwave one-pot dish. Unlike ones cooked on the hob, you don't have to stir, leaving you free to do something else.

1 onion, finely chopped
1 bulb fennel, finely sliced
1 tbsp olive oil
300g/10oz risotto rice
500ml/18fl oz fish or vegetable stock
300g bag frozen seafood mix, defrosted
100g/4oz frozen peas
3 tbsp grated parmesan cheese
grated zest and juice of 1 lemon
handful of parsley leaves, roughly chopped

Takes 25–35 minutes • Serves 4

1 Tip the onion and fennel into a large microwave bowl, toss in the oil and microwave on High for 5 minutes. Stir in the rice, pour over the stock and cover the bowl with a plate. Microwave on High for 10–15 minutes more or until the rice is just on the verge of being cooked.
2 Stir in the seafood and peas, cover and continue to microwave on High for 2–3 minutes until the rice is cooked. Stir in the parmesan and lemon juice and leave to stand for a couple of minutes while you mix the parsley with the lemon zest. Spoon the risotto into bowls and scatter over the parsley and lemon zest. Serve.

• Per serving 419 kcalories, protein 29g, carbohydrate 64g, fat 7g, saturated fat 2g, fibre 4g, added sugar none, salt 1.16g

Prawn Pilau

You can use cooked, chopped chicken instead of the prawns, if you prefer.

2 tbsp korma curry paste
1 small onion, finely chopped
300g/10oz basmati rice, rinsed and drained
700ml/1¼ pints chicken stock
150g pack cooked peeled prawns, defrosted if frozen
cupful of frozen peas
1 red chilli, sliced into rings
handful of coriander leaves, chopped
lemon wedges, to serve

Takes 25–30 minutes • Serves 4

1 Heat a large wide pan and dry fry the curry paste with the onion for 4–5 minutes until the onion begins to soften. Add the rice to the pan and stir to coat in the curry paste. Add the stock, then bring to the boil.
2 Cover the pan and turn the heat down to low. Leave the rice to simmer slowly for 12–15 minutes until the liquid has been absorbed and the rice is cooked. Turn off the heat and stir in the prawns, peas and chilli. Cover the pan and leave to stand for 5 minutes.
3 Fluff up the rice grains with a fork and season, if you want. Scatter over the coriander and serve with lemon wedges.

• Per serving 340 kcalories, protein 18g, carbohydrate 65g, fat 3g, saturated fat 1g, fibre 2g, added sugar none, salt 2.38g

Chilli Prawn Noodles

A light and aromatic dish made entirely from storecupboard ingredients.

2 tbsp olive oil
1 onion, roughly chopped
1 heaped tbsp coriander purée (from a tube)
pinch of dried chilli flakes, or to taste
400g can chopped tomatoes with garlic
1 heaped tbsp tomato purée
1 tbsp vegetable bouillon powder
150g pack straight-to-wok noodles
400g/14oz frozen prawns (large North Atlantic ones are tender and juicy)
sugar, optional

Takes 30–40 minutes • Serves 4

1 Heat the oil in a wok or deep frying pan. Toss in the onion, squeeze in the coriander purée and sprinkle over the chilli flakes to taste (go easy at this stage). Stir fry for 5 minutes until the onion is softened but not browned.
2 Pour in the tomatoes and 1½ canfuls hot water, add the tomato purée and sprinkle over the bouillon powder. Season well. Bring to a bubble, stirring, then lower the heat and let the sauce simmer gently for about 15 minutes until slightly reduced but still runny.
3 When the sauce is ready, tip in the noodles and frozen prawns. Stir well and heat through for 2 minutes only – just to defrost the prawns and heat through the noodles. Taste for seasoning before serving, and add more chilli flakes and a little sugar, if you like.

• Per serving 228 kcalories, protein 22g, carbohydrate 18g, fat 8g, saturated fat 0.8g, fibre 2.1g, added sugar none, salt 2.95g

Creamy Spiced Mussels

Fresh mussels are surprisingly quick and easy to prepare. Serve this dish with bread to mop up the delicious juices.

2kg/4lb 8oz fresh mussels
150ml/¼ pint dry white wine
2 shallots, finely chopped
25g/1oz butter
1 tsp plain flour
1–2 tsp curry paste
100g/4oz crème fraîche
chopped parsley, to serve

Takes 35 minutes • Serves 4

1 Scrub the mussels in a large bowl of cold water and discard any that are open. Put in a large pan with the wine. Bring to the boil, cover and shake the pan over a high heat until the mussels are open – about 3–4 minutes.
2 Tip the mussels into a colander set over a large bowl to catch the juices. Discard any that have not opened. Strain the cooking liquid through a sieve. Keep the mussels warm.
3 Fry the shallots in the butter in the large pan until softened. Stir in the flour and curry paste and cook for 1 minute. Add the cooking liquid (except the last little bit, which may be gritty) and season with pepper, but no salt.
4 Stir in the crème fraîche and warm over a low heat until thick and glossy. Divide the mussels between four bowls and pour over the sauce. Scatter with parsley and serve.

• Per serving 285 kcalories, protein 19g, carbohydrate 6g, fat 18g, saturated fat 10g, fibre 1g, added sugar none, salt 1.27g

TOP: Prawn Pilau   BOTTOM LEFT: Chilli Prawn Noodles   BOTTOM RIGHT: Creamy Spiced Mussels

TOP LEFT: Sizzling Summer Cod   TOP RIGHT: Smoked Haddock Stovies   BOTTOM: Fish with Lemon and Beans

Sizzling Summer Cod

You can use salmon instead of cod, if you like, in this fresh and tasty dish.

250g jar roasted mixed peppers with herbs
250g/9oz new potatoes, scrubbed and
    thickly sliced
1 red onion, cut into wedges
140g/5oz green beans, trimmed and halved
    widthways
2 × 175g/6oz chunky cod fillets, skin on
½ lemon
crusty bread, to serve

Takes 15–20 minutes • Serves 2

1 Pour all the oil from the jar of peppers into
a deep frying pan. Heat the oil until bubbling,
then tip in the potatoes and onion and toss in
the oil. Cook for 5 minutes, stirring every now
and then, until the potatoes are beginning to
turn golden.
2 Carefully pour most of the oil out of the
frying pan, leaving behind about 1 tablespoon.
Tip in the beans and drained peppers, season
and stir until well mixed. Lay the fish, skin side
down, on top of the vegetables.
3 Cover the pan and cook over a medium
heat for 5 minutes more or until the fish flakes
easily with a fork and the vegetables are
tender. Squeeze the lemon half over the
fish and serve with crusty bread to mop
up the juices.

• Per serving 337 kcalories, protein 37g, carbohydrate
32g, fat 8g, saturated fat 1g, fibre 5g, added sugar
none, salt 0.48g

Smoked Haddock Stovies

Hearty and healthy, this is comfort food at
its best – ideal for a mid-week supper in
the winter.

knob of butter
splash of vegetable oil
2 onions, thinly sliced
1kg/2lb 4oz floury potatoes, such as Maris
    Piper or King Edward, peeled and
    thickly sliced
500g/1lb 2oz skinless smoked
    haddock, cut into large chunks
handful of parsley, coarsely chopped

Takes 30–40 minutes • Serves 4

1 Heat the butter and oil in a large wide
pan, add the onions and cook for 5 minutes,
stirring until lightly coloured. Tip in the potatoes
and cook for a further 5 minutes, stirring often,
until they are also lightly coloured.
2 Pour in 425ml/¾ pint water and grind in
black pepper to taste. Stir to mix, then gently
stir in the fish and bring to the boil. Cover and
cook for 10 minutes or until the potatoes and
fish are tender. Scatter with parsley before
serving.

• Per serving 307 kcalories, protein 29g, carbohydrate
39g, fat 5g, saturated fat 2g, fibre 4g, added sugar
none, salt 2.5g

Fish with Lemon and Beans

This is a speedy supper dish that gives
you a great sense of well being. Try stirring
in capers, olives or peppers for a slightly
different taste.

400g can butter beans, drained and rinsed
3 tbsp lemon-infused olive oil or 3 tbsp olive
    oil mixed with a little lemon juice
2 handfuls of parsley leaves, roughly
    chopped
100g/4oz piece chorizo sausage, skinned
    and chopped into small chunks
2 × 175g/6oz skinless white fish fillets, such
    as cod

Takes 10–15 minutes • Serves 2

1 Tip the butter beans into a shallow
microwave dish. Stir in half the lemon oil,
half the parsley and all the chorizo. Top with
the fish fillets and the remaining oil. Cover
the dish with cling film and pierce a few times.
Microwave on High for 4–5 minutes, until the
fish looks opaque and flakes easily.
2 Remove the fish from the dish. Stir the
beans and chorizo together and spoon onto
plates. Top with the fish and scatter with the
remaining parsley.

• Per serving 523 kcalories, protein 48g, carbohydrate
17g, fat 30g, saturated fat 7g, fibre 6g, added sugar
none, salt 2g

Smoked Salmon and Celeriac Bake

This is a Sweden-inspired, rich supper dish using easily available ingredients.

juice of 1 lemon
1 small celeriac, about 650g/1lb 7oz
2 medium baking potatoes
2 × 125g packs sliced smoked salmon
small handful of dill, chopped
1 onion, finely sliced
284ml carton double cream

Takes about 2 hours • Serves 6

1 Preheat the oven to 200°C/Gas 6/fan oven 180°C. Pour the lemon juice into a large bowl. Peel and quarter the celeriac, cut into slices the thickness of a £1 coin and toss into the lemon juice. Peel and thinly slice the potatoes and toss with the celeriac.
2 Layer the celeriac, potatoes and salmon slices in a large ovenproof dish, sprinkling dill, onion and cream over each layer, together with a little salt and plenty of black pepper. You should have 3 layers of vegetables with 2 layers of salmon, onion and dill. Finish with the remaining cream.
3 Cover the dish with foil, place on a baking tray and bake for 45 minutes. Uncover and bake for 30–40 minutes more, until the vegetables feel tender when pierced and the top is golden. Cool slightly before serving.

• Per serving 328 kcalories, protein 14g, carbohydrate 13g, fat 25g, saturated fat 15g, fibre 3g, added sugar none, salt 2.19g

Kerala Prawn Curry

If you like spicy food, you'll love this curry, with its creamy consistency, crackling curry leaves and coconut flavour.

2 red chillies, seeded and quartered
   lengthways
1 small red onion, chopped
2.5cm/1in piece fresh root ginger, peeled
   and chopped
1 tbsp vegetable or sunflower oil
1 tsp black mustard seeds
½ tsp fenugreek seeds
14 curry leaves, fresh or dried
½ tsp turmeric
½ tsp cracked black peppercorns
150ml/¼ pint reduced-fat coconut milk
250g/9oz cooked and peeled jumbo prawns,
   some with their tails on

TO SERVE
squeeze of lime
chopped fresh coriander, plus a sprig or two

Takes 25–35 minutes • Serves 2

1 In a food processor, blitz the chillies, onion and ginger with 3 tablespoons water to a smoothish paste.
2 Heat the oil in a wide shallow pan or wok. Toss in the mustard and fenugreek seeds and the curry leaves – they crackle and pop – and fry for 10 seconds. Add the onion paste, lower the heat and cook without colouring for about 5 minutes. Splash in some water if it starts to catch.
3 Add the turmeric and peppercorns and stir for a few seconds. Pour in the coconut milk and bring to a simmer, stirring all the time, then lower the heat and add the prawns. Cook for 1–2 minutes until heated through. Squeeze over some lime and sprinkle with coriander before serving.

• Per serving 294 kcalories, protein 31g, carbohydrate 8g, fat 16g, saturated fat 8g, fibre none, added sugar none, salt 2.76g

Creamy Haddock and Tatties

This must be the easiest fish pie ever! There are only five ingredients and three simple steps, and the finished dish is very tasty indeed.

400g/14oz smoked haddock (undyed is best,
   but not essential), skinned and chopped
   into chunks
1 trimmed leek, finely sliced
handful of parsley, chopped
142ml carton double cream
2 medium baking potatoes, about 200g/8oz
   each, unpeeled, sliced as thinly as possible

Takes 15–20 minutes • Serves 2

1 Scatter the haddock, leek and parsley over the base of a shallow microwave dish and mix together with your fingers or a spoon. Drizzle over half the cream and 5 tablespoons water. Lay the potato slices over the fish and leek. Season with a little salt and plenty of black pepper, and drizzle over the remaining cream.
2 Cover the dish with cling film and pierce a few times. Microwave on High for 8–10 minutes until everything is bubbling away and the potatoes are tender when pierced with a knife. While the dish is in the microwave, preheat the grill to high.
3 Remove the cling film and put the dish under the grill until the potatoes are golden. Leave to stand for a minute or two before serving.

• Per serving 646 kcalories, protein 45g, carbohydrate 38g, fat 36g, saturated fat 22g, fibre 4g, added sugar none, salt 3.97g

TOP LEFT: Smoked Salmon and Celeriac Bake   TOP RIGHT: Kerala Prawn Curry   BOTTOM: Creamy Haddock and Tatties

TOP: Paneer in Herby Tomato Sauce   BOTTOM LEFT: Spicy Pea Curry   BOTTOM RIGHT: Spring Vegetable Pilau

Paneer in Herby Tomato Sauce

Paneer is a low-fat cheese often described as Indian cottage cheese, but it's firmer and keeps its shape in cooking.

½ tsp cumin seeds
1 green chilli, seeded and chopped
4cm/1½in piece fresh root ginger, peeled and chopped
150g carton Greek yogurt
1 tsp light muscovado sugar
½ tsp garam masala
2 tbsp chopped fresh coriander leaves and stems
juice of ½ lime
3 tbsp tomato purée
250g/9oz frozen peas
227g pack paneer (Indian cheese), cut into 1cm/½in cubes
2–3 firm red tomatoes, cut into wedges
handful of roasted cashew nuts, chopped, to serve

Takes 25–35 minutes • Serves 2

1 Toast the cumin seeds in a pan to darken – about 30 seconds. Crush roughly with a rolling pin, then tip into a blender with the chilli, ginger, yogurt, sugar, garam masala, coriander, lime juice, tomato purée and 200ml/7fl oz water. Blitz until smooth.
2 Pour the sauce into the pan used to toast the cumin. Cook for 5 minutes, stirring often. Add the peas and simmer for 3–5 minutes until almost cooked.
3 Stir in the paneer and tomatoes and heat through for 2–3 minutes. Scatter with cashew nuts just before serving.

• Per serving 607 kcalories, protein 44g, carbohydrate 24g, fat 38g, saturated fat 23g, fibre 8g, added sugar 3g, salt 3.26g

Spicy Pea Curry

This is a gently spiced and very tasty curry that suits all tastes. Peas are quick-frozen within a few hours of picking, so stay deliciously fresh.

2 tbsp vegetable oil
227g pack paneer (Indian cheese), torn into pieces
1 onion, thinly sliced
2 tbsp mild curry paste
450g/1lb potatoes, peeled and cut into chunks
400g can chopped tomatoes with garlic
300ml/½ pint vegetable stock
300g/10oz frozen peas
Indian bread, to serve

Takes 40–50 minutes • Serves 4

1 Heat 1 tablespoon of the oil in a large saucepan. Fry the paneer for 2–3 minutes, stirring, until crisp and golden. Remove with a slotted spoon and set aside.
2 Fry the onion in the remaining oil for 4–5 minutes until soft and just beginning to brown. Add the curry paste and fry, stirring, for 2 minutes.
3 Add the potatoes, tomatoes, stock and paneer, bring to the boil and simmer for 15 minutes. Add the peas, bring to the boil and simmer for 5 minutes longer. Season and serve with peshwari naan or other Indian bread.

• Per serving 404 kcalories, protein 20g, carbohydrate 32g, fat 22g, saturated fat 9g, fibre 7g, added sugar none, salt 2.84g

Spring Vegetable Pilau

Use whichever vegetables are in season for this light and pretty dish. To make it richer, add 100g/4oz feta when you stir in the dill.

1 tbsp olive oil
1 onion, chopped
300g/10oz basmati rice
700ml/1¼ pints vegetable stock
100g pack asparagus, cut into 2cm/¾in chunks
large handful of peas, fresh or frozen
large handful of broad beans, fresh or frozen
1 courgette, sliced
small bunch of dill, chopped

Takes 20 minutes • Serves 4

1 Heat the oil in a frying pan and cook the onion for 5 minutes until soft. Tip in the rice, pour over the stock and stir. Bring to the boil, then lower the heat to a simmer, cover and cook for 10 minutes or until the rice is almost tender.
2 Add the vegetables to the pan, cover and let them steam for 2 minutes. Take the pan off the heat and leave to stand, covered, for another 2 minutes to absorb any more liquid. Stir in the dill just before serving.

• Per serving 317 kcalories, protein 9g, carbohydrate 66g, fat 4g, saturated fat 1g, fibre 3g, added sugar none, salt 0.58g

Bean and Vegetable Chilli

Sweet red pepper sauce makes an interesting change from tomato sauces. Serve this veggie chilli with garlic bread and a salad.

3 tbsp olive oil
2 onions, chopped
2 tsp caster sugar
250g/9oz chestnut mushrooms, sliced
2 garlic cloves, sliced
2 tsp mild chilli powder
1 tbsp ground coriander
290–350g jar sweet red pepper sauce
300ml/½ pint vegetable stock
410g can chickpeas, drained and rinsed
410g can black-eye beans, drained and rinsed
garlic bread and mixed salad, to serve

Takes 40–50 minutes • Serves 4

1 Heat the oil in a large, heavy-based saucepan and fry the onions and sugar over a high heat until deep golden. Add the mushrooms, garlic, chilli powder and ground coriander and fry for 2–3 minutes.
2 Stir in the pepper sauce, stock, chickpeas and beans and bring to the boil. Reduce the heat, cover and simmer gently for 20 minutes. Season and serve, with garlic bread and a mixed salad.

• Per serving 303 kcalories, protein 14g, carbohydrate 36g, fat 13g, saturated fat 2g, fibre 8g, added sugar 5g, salt 1.4g

Roasted Vegetables with Cheese

A colourful and hearty supper dish for autumn evenings.

1 red onion
1 large butternut squash
 (600–700g/1lb 5oz–1lb 9oz), peeled, seeded and cut into large bite-sized pieces
6 tbsp olive oil
2 tbsp chopped fresh sage leaves
1 large courgette, thickly sliced
1 tbsp balsamic or sherry vinegar
100g/4oz Lancashire cheese

Takes 40–50 minutes • Serves 2

1 Preheat the oven to 200°C/Gas 6/fan oven 180°C. Halve the onion lengthways and trim the root end, leaving a little root left on to hold the segments together. Peel each half and cut into 4 wedges. Scatter the onion and squash in a large roasting tin so they have plenty of room, and toss with 5 tablespoons of the oil, the sage and seasoning to taste. Roast for 20 minutes, stirring halfway.
2 Toss the courgette slices with the remaining oil. Remove the tin from the oven and push the squash and onion to one side. Lay the courgette slices flat on the base of the tin, season and roast for 10 minutes, until all the vegetables are tender.
3 Sprinkle the vinegar over the vegetables and toss to mix, then crumble over the cheese and toss lightly so the cheese melts a little. Serve.

• Per serving 306 kcalories, protein 8g, carbohydrate 14g, fat 25g, saturated fat 7g, fibre 3g, added sugar none, salt 0.39g

Macaroni Cheese with Mushrooms

Lighter than the original, this basic pasta dish is one to experiment with.

200g/8oz macaroni
2 leeks
6 mushrooms
4 tomatoes
2 tbsp olive oil
2 × mini Le Roulé garlic and herb soft cheeses, or mini bries or blue cheeses

Takes 20–25 minutes • Serves 2

1 Fill a large sauté pan with boiling water. Tip in the macaroni and cook according to the pack instructions until tender. (It may take slightly longer than suggested.) Meanwhile, trim, slice and wash the leeks, quarter the mushrooms and roughly chop the tomatoes.
2 Drain the pasta and keep warm. Heat the oil in the pan, add the leeks and mushrooms and fry for 4–6 minutes until the leeks are tender. Toss in the tomatoes at the last minute. Season with salt if you want to, and black pepper. Stir in the macaroni and warm through, then crumble the cheese over and let it melt slightly before serving.

• Per serving 619 kcalories, protein 17g, carbohydrate 85g, fat 26g, saturated fat 10g, fibre 8g, added sugar none, salt 0.3g

TOP: Bean and Vegetable Chilli   BOTTOM LEFT: Roasted Vegetables with Cheese   BOTTOM RIGHT: Macaroni Cheese with Mushrooms

TOP LEFT: Vegetable Casserole with Dumplings   **TOP RIGHT:** Cheesy Vegetable Hotpot   **BOTTOM:** Potato and Mozzarella Tortilla

Vegetable Casserole with Dumplings

The wine really adds flavour to this warming dish, and the baby vegetables look so pretty, too.

8 shallots, halved lengthways
3 tbsp light olive oil
250g/9oz new potatoes, halved
1 chilli, seeded and chopped
200g/8oz baby carrots, scraped
500g/1lb 2oz fennel, cut into wedges
300ml/½ pint fruity white wine
600ml/1 pint vegetable stock
200g/8oz green beans, halved
250g/9oz mushrooms, halved
200g/8oz baby courgettes, chopped
1 tbsp each chopped chives and parsley

FOR THE DUMPLINGS
50g/2oz butter, cut into pieces
100g/4oz self-raising flour
50g/2oz mature cheddar cheese, grated
3 tbsp finely chopped fresh parsley

Takes 1¾–2 hours • Serves 6

1 Fry the shallots in the oil in a flameproof casserole until softened. Add the potatoes and fry for 5–7 minutes, then add the chilli, carrots and fennel and fry until coloured. Pour in the wine and stock and bring to the boil. Season, cover and simmer for 10 minutes.
2 Make the dumplings. Rub the butter into the flour, stir in the cheese, parsley and seasoning, then stir in about 2 tablespoons water to form a soft dough. Break off small pieces and form into 20–25 dumplings.
3 Add the beans to the pan and simmer for 5 minutes, then add the mushrooms and courgettes. Bring to the boil and stir well. Place the dumplings on top. Cover and simmer for 15 minutes until the dumplings have risen. Taste for seasoning and serve sprinkled with the chives and parsley.

• Per serving 285 kcalories, protein 8g, carbohydrate 28g, fat 17g, saturated fat 7g, fibre 5.6g, added sugar none, salt 0.85g

Cheesy Vegetable Hotpot

This is vegetarian food at its easiest and most comforting.

3 leeks, trimmed, roughly sliced
large knob of butter
½ small Savoy cabbage, shredded
8 chestnut mushrooms, sliced
4 tbsp crème fraîche
3 medium potatoes, peeled and thinly sliced
1 small camembert or other rinded soft cheese, sliced with the rind on
1 tbsp fresh thyme leaves

Takes 35–40 minutes • Serves 4

1 In a shallow microwavable dish, toss the leeks in half the butter and microwave on High for 5 minutes until they begin to soften. Stir in the cabbage and mushrooms and add the crème fraîche. Lay the potato slices over the vegetables, pressing them down with a fish slice.
2 Dot the potatoes with the remaining butter and microwave, uncovered, for 15–20 minutes on High until they are done. Scatter over the cheese and thyme, and either microwave on High to melt for 2 minutes, or grill until crisp and brown. Leave to stand for a few minutes before serving.

• Per serving 308 kcalories, protein 15g, carbohydrate 19g, fat 20g, saturated fat 12g, fibre 5g, added sugar none, salt 0.83g

Potato and Mozzarella Tortilla

Use your own potato leftovers if you like. Serve with a peppery rocket and watercress salad.

2 tbsp olive oil
2 × 400g packs ready-roasted potatoes (available with different flavourings from most supermarkets)
8 eggs, beaten
4 vine-ripened tomatoes, sliced
150g ball mozzarella, torn into pieces

Takes 30 minutes • Serves 6

1 Heat the oil in a large frying pan. Empty the potatoes into the pan, spread them out to cover the base, then fry for 5 minutes. Pour in the beaten eggs so they completely cover the potatoes, season well and leave the tortilla to cook on a medium heat for about 15–20 minutes, or until the base and edges have set.
2 Meanwhile preheat the grill to high. Take the tortilla off the hob and place under the grill until the top is firm, then remove from the grill and scatter over the tomatoes and mozzarella. Put the tortilla back under the grill for a further 3–5 minutes, or until the tomatoes are soft and the cheese has melted. Serve, cut into thick wedges.

• Per serving 465 kcalories, protein 28g, carbohydrate 23g, fat 32g, saturated fat 7g, fibre 3g, added sugar none, salt 0.72g

Quorn and Cashew Nut Stir Fry

A Chinese stir fry that's perfect for all the family. Get all the ingredients prepared first so you can toss them straight into the pan.

50g/2oz cashew nuts
1 tbsp vegetable oil
200g/8oz Quorn pieces
85g/3oz small broccoli florets
85g/3oz small cauliflower florets
2 tbsp hoisin sauce
1 red or yellow pepper, seeded and sliced

Takes 15 minutes • Serves 2 (easily doubled)

1 Tip the cashews into a wok or deep, non-stick frying pan and dry fry over a medium heat for a few minutes until toasted. Remove and set aside. Heat the oil in the wok, add the Quorn, broccoli and cauliflower and stir fry for 2 minutes.
2 Mix the hoisin sauce with 6 tablespoons boiling water, pour into the wok and add the sliced pepper. Toss for 3 minutes, or until the pepper is just tender. Add seasoning to taste and serve sprinkled with the cashews.

• Per serving 363 kcalories, protein 23g, carbohydrate 19g, fat 22g, saturated fat 2.6g, fibre 9g, added sugar 5g, salt 1.43g

Tomato Baked Eggs

This is such a simple recipe and is welcome at any time of day – for a weekend lunch, an easy supper or even a leisurely breakfast.

900g/2lb ripe vine tomatoes
3 garlic cloves, thinly sliced
3 tbsp olive oil
4 large free-range eggs
2 tbsp chopped parsley and/or chives
toast or ciabatta, and green salad, to serve

Takes about 1 hour • Serves 4

1 Preheat the oven to 200°C/Gas 6/fan oven 180°C. Cut the tomatoes into quarters or thick wedges, depending on their size, then spread them over the base of a fairly shallow, large, ovenproof dish. Sprinkle the garlic over the tomatoes, drizzle with the oil and season well. Stir until the tomatoes are glistening, then bake for 40 minutes until softened and tinged with brown.
2 Make 4 gaps among the tomatoes, break an egg into each gap and cover the dish with foil. Return the dish to the oven for 5–10 minutes until the eggs are set to your liking. Scatter over the herbs and serve piping hot, with thick slices of toast or warm ciabatta and a green salad on the side.

• Per serving 204 kcalories, protein 9g, carbohydrate 7g, fat 16g, saturated fat 3g, fibre 3g, added sugar none, salt 0.27g

Greek Salad Omelette

Juicy tomatoes and creamy cheese ensure a dish with flavours that will burst in your mouth.

10 eggs
handful of parsley leaves, chopped
2 tbsp olive oil
1 large red onion, cut into wedges
3 tomatoes, chopped into large chunks
large handful of black olives (pitted are easier to eat)
100g/4oz feta, crumbled

Takes 15–20 minutes • Serves 4–6

1 Preheat the grill to high. Whisk the eggs in a large bowl with the chopped parsley, pepper and salt, if you want. Heat the oil in a large, non-stick frying pan, then fry the onion wedges over a high heat for about 4 minutes until they start to brown around the edges. Add the tomatoes and olives, stir and cook for 1–2 minutes until the tomatoes begin to soften.
2 Turn the heat down to medium and pour in the eggs. Stir the eggs as they begin to set, until half cooked but still runny in places – about 2 minutes. Scatter over the feta, then slide the pan under the grill for 5–6 minutes until the omelette is puffed up and golden. Cut into wedges and serve straight from the pan.

• Per serving for four 371 kcalories, protein 24g, carbohydrate 5g, fat 28g, saturated fat 9g, fibre 1g, added sugar none, salt 2g

TOP LEFT: Quorn and Cashew Nut Stir-fry   TOP RIGHT: Tomato Baked Eggs   BOTTOM: Greek Salad Omelette

TOP: Curried Rice with Spinach   BOTTOM LEFT: Thai Red Squash Curry   BOTTOM RIGHT: Mixed Vegetable Balti

Curried Rice with Spinach

Warming and tasty, practically no preparation, superhealthy, uses storecupboard ingredients – one-pot dishes don't get better than this.

1 tbsp sunflower oil
2 garlic cloves, crushed
2 tbsp medium curry paste (Madras is a good one to use)
250g/9oz basmati rice, rinsed
450ml/16fl oz vegetable stock
400g can chickpeas, drained and rinsed
handful of raisins
175g/6oz frozen leaf spinach, thawed
handful of cashew nuts
natural yogurt, to serve (optional)

Takes 20 minutes • Serves 4

1 Heat the oil in a large, non-stick pan that has a lid, then fry the garlic and curry paste over a medium heat for 1 minute, until it smells toasty.
2 Tip the rice into the pan with the stock, chickpeas and raisins and stir well with a fork to stop the rice from clumping. Season with salt and pepper, then cover and bring to the boil. Reduce to a medium heat and cook for 12–15 minutes or until all the liquid has been absorbed and the rice is tender.
3 Squeeze the excess water from the spinach with your hands. Tip it into the pan along with 2 tablespoons hot water, then fluff up the rice with a fork, making sure the spinach is mixed in well. Toss in the cashews. Serve drizzled with natural yogurt, if you like.

• Per serving 380 kcalories, protein 12g, carbohydrate 66g, fat 9g, saturated fat 1g, fibre 4g, added sugar none, salt 1.02g

Thai Red Squash Curry

You can vary the vegetables – try sweet potatoes, sugarsnap peas and bamboo shoots – and scatter over cashew nuts.

1 small butternut squash, about 700g/1lb 9 oz
200g pack mixed mangetout and baby corn
2 tbsp sunflower oil
1–2 tbsp Thai red curry paste, to taste
400ml can coconut milk
150ml/¼ pint vegetable stock
2 tbsp soy sauce
1 tbsp light muscovado sugar
juice of ½ lime
naan bread or chapatis, to serve

Takes 30 minutes • Serves 4

1 Cut off the ends of the squash, quarter lengthways, then scoop out the fibres and seeds. Peel, then cut into chunks. Halve the baby corn lengthways.
2 Heat the oil in a saucepan and fry the paste gently for 1–2 minutes. Add the coconut milk, stock, soy sauce and sugar and bring to the boil.
3 Add the squash and baby corn, and salt to taste, cover and simmer for 10–12 minutes. Add the lime juice and mangetout, and simmer for 1 minute. Serve hot, with naan bread or chapatis.

• Per serving 283 kcalories, protein 4.4g, carbohydrate 16.2g, fat 22.6g, saturated fat 14.6g, fibre 2.2g, added sugar 5.3g, salt 1.95g

Mixed Vegetable Balti

Serve with warm mini naan breads. Alternatively, this curry mixture makes a great low-fat filling for baked potatoes.

1 tbsp vegetable oil
1 large onion, thickly sliced
1 large garlic clove, crushed
1 eating apple, peeled, cored and chopped into chunks
3 tbsp balti curry paste
1 medium butternut squash, peeled and cut into chunks
2 large carrots, thickly sliced
200g/8oz turnips, cut into chunks
1 cauliflower, about 500g/1lb 2oz, broken into florets
400g can chopped tomatoes
425ml/¾ pint vegetable stock
4 tbsp chopped coriander, plus extra to serve
150g carton low-fat natural yogurt

Takes 1¼–1½ hours • Serves 4

1 Heat the oil in a large pan and cook the onion, garlic and apple gently, stirring occasionally, until the onion softens – about 5–8 minutes. Stir in the curry paste.
2 Tip the fresh vegetables, tomatoes and stock into the pan. Stir in 3 tablespoons of the coriander. Bring to the boil, lower the heat, cover and cook for 30 minutes.
3 Remove the lid and cook for another 20 minutes until the vegetables are soft and the liquid has reduced a little. Season with salt and pepper.
4 Mix the remaining coriander into the yogurt to make a raita. Ladle the curry into bowls, drizzle over some raita and sprinkle with extra coriander. Serve with the remaining raita.

• Per serving 201 kcalories, protein 11g, carbohydrate 25g, fat 7g, saturated fat 1g, fibre 7g, added sugar none, salt 1.13g

Steak and Mushroom Goulash

For a vegetarian crowd, swap the meat for two 400g cans of chickpeas (drained and rinsed), and increase the mushrooms to 400g/14oz.

750g/1lb 10oz rump or sirloin steak, trimmed and cut into thin strips against the grain
3 tbsp vegetable oil
200g/8oz chestnut mushrooms, quartered
1 tbsp paprika
900g/2lb potatoes, peeled and cut into small chunks
500g jar passata (sieved tomatoes)
about 850ml/1½ pints beef stock
150g carton natural yogurt
handful of parsley leaves, roughly chopped

Takes 50–60 minutes • Serves 8

1 Season the steak well. Heat 1 tablespoon of the oil in a large flameproof casserole over a medium-high heat. Add about a third of the steak and fry for 2–3 minutes until all the strips are browned, stirring once. Transfer the meat to a plate with a slotted spoon. Repeat with the remaining oil and meat.
2 Tip the mushrooms into the pan, lower the heat a little and fry, stirring occasionally, until they begin to colour (about 5 minutes). Sprinkle in the paprika and stir fry briefly, then tip in the potatoes and passata and enough stock to cover the potatoes. Stir well, cover and simmer for 20 minutes or until the potatoes are tender.
3 Return the meat to the pan with its juices, stir well and simmer for 5 minutes or until tender. Taste for seasoning and serve topped with the yogurt and parsley.

• Per serving 279 kcalories, protein 26g, carbohydrate 25g, fat 9g, saturated fat 2.2g, fibre 2g, added sugar 0.9g, salt 0.87g

Spicy Lamb with Chickpeas

Good-quality canned tomatoes really make a difference to the flavour of this dish.

1.25kg/2lb 8oz boneless lamb fillet or leg, cubed
2 × 400g cans tomatoes in rich juice
1 tbsp harissa paste, or to taste
2 × 410g cans chickpeas, drained and rinsed
large handful of coriander, roughly chopped

Takes 1½–1¾ hours • Serves 8

1 Put the lamb and tomatoes in a large pan. Fill one of the tomato cans with water, pour into the pan and stir in the harissa with a good sprinkling of salt and pepper. Bring to the boil, then reduce the heat and cover the pan. Simmer gently, stirring occasionally, for 1¼–1½ hours or until the lamb is tender.
2 Tip in the chickpeas, stir well and heat through for 5 minutes. Taste for seasoning, adding more harissa if you like. Serve scattered with coriander.

• Per serving 406 kcalories, protein 36g, carbohydrate 13g, fat 24g, saturated fat 10.8g, fibre 3.5g, added sugar none, salt 0.82g

Fragrant Chicken Curry

Impress your friends with this sensational curry, which delivers a full rich flavour and authentic spiciness without the usual high-fat content.

3 onions, quartered
4 fat garlic cloves
5cm/2in piece fresh root ginger, peeled and roughly chopped
3 tbsp moglai (medium) curry powder
1 tsp turmeric
2 tsp paprika
2 fresh red chillies, seeded and roughly chopped
2 × 20g packs fresh coriander
1 chicken stock cube
6 large boneless, skinless chicken breasts, cubed
2 × 410g cans chickpeas, drained and rinsed
natural low-fat yogurt, naan bread or poppadums, to serve

Takes 60–70 minutes • Serves 8

1 Tip the onions, garlic, ginger, curry powder, ground spices, chillies and half the coriander into a food processor. Add 1 teaspoon salt and blend to a purée (you may need to do this in 2 batches). Tip the mixture into a large saucepan and cook over a low heat for 10 minutes, stirring frequently.
2 Crumble in the stock cube, pour in 750ml/1¼ pints boiling water and return to the boil. Add the chicken, stir, then lower the heat and simmer for 20 minutes or until the chicken is tender.
3 Chop the remaining coriander, then stir all but about 2 tablespoons into the curry with the chickpeas. Heat through. Serve topped with the reserved coriander and the natural yogurt, with naan bread or poppadums on the side.

• Per serving 227 kcalories, protein 32g, carbohydrate 17g, fat 4g, saturated fat 0.4g, fibre 4.6g, added sugar none, salt 1.72g

TOP: Steak and Mushroom Goulash   BOTTOM LEFT: Spicy Lamb with Chickpeas   BOTTOM RIGHT: Fragrant Chicken Curry

TOP LEFT: Chicken with Spring Vegetables   TOP RIGHT: Hob-to-table Moussaka   BOTTOM: Moroccan Lamb Harira

Chicken with Spring Vegetables

Play around with this recipe. If you don't feel like using asparagus and broad beans, you could try broccoli sprigs and green beans instead.

2 tbsp olive oil
25g/1oz butter
8 large boneless, skinless chicken breasts, each cut into 3 pieces
8 shallots, halved
2 garlic cloves, roughly chopped
450g/1lb baby new potatoes, halved
450g/1lb baby carrots, scrubbed
3 tbsp plain flour
1½ tbsp Dijon mustard
425ml/¾ pint dry white wine
425ml/¾ pint chicken stock
225g/8oz asparagus tips, trimmed
225g/8oz shelled broad beans, thawed if frozen
1 tbsp lemon juice
100ml/3½fl oz double cream
handful chopped fresh parsley and tarragon
crusty bread, to serve

Takes 1¼–1½ hours • Serves 8

1 Heat the oil and butter in a large sauté pan and cook the chicken in batches for 3–4 minutes until golden. Remove from the pan and set aside. Toss together the shallots, garlic, potatoes and carrots in the pan. Cook for about 5 minutes until turning golden. Sprinkle over the flour, stir in the mustard and toss well, then pour over the white wine and gently simmer until reduced by about half.
2 Pour in the stock, bring to a simmer, then return the chicken to the pan. Cover and simmer for about 15 minutes.
3 Scatter over the asparagus and broad beans, without stirring, cover and simmer for a further 8 minutes. Stir in the lemon juice, cream, parsley and tarragon and heat through gently. Serve with crusty bread.

• Per serving 414 kcalories, protein 42g, carbohydrate 23g, fat 14g, saturated fat 6g, fibre 5g, added sugar none, salt 0.92g

Hob-to-table Moussaka

This is a quick variation of the classic Greek dish. For an authentic Mediterranean meal, serve with toasted pitta bread.

2 tbsp olive oil
2 large onions, finely chopped
2 garlic cloves, finely chopped
1kg/2lb 4oz minced lamb
2 × 400g cans chopped tomatoes
3 tbsp tomato purée
2 tsp ground cinnamon
200g jar chargrilled aubergines in olive oil, drained and chopped
300g/10oz feta, crumbled
large handful of mint, chopped
green salad and toasted pitta bread, to serve

Takes 40–50 minutes • Serves 8

1 Heat the oil in a large deep frying pan or sauté pan. Toss in the onions and garlic and fry until soft. Add the mince and stir fry for about 10 minutes until browned.
2 Tip the tomatoes into the pan, add a canful of water and stir in the tomato purée and cinnamon. Season generously with salt and pepper. Leave the mince to simmer for 30 minutes, adding the aubergines halfway through.
3 Sprinkle the crumbled feta and chopped mint over the mince. Bring the moussaka to the table as the feta melts, and serve with a crunchy green salad and toasted pitta.

• Per serving 454 kcalories, protein 32g, carbohydrate 10g, fat 32g, saturated fat 14.1g, fibre 2.3g, added sugar none, salt 1.83g

Moroccan Lamb Harira

This soup is a meal in itself and it's sure to be a hit with its delicious aromas and wonderful flavours.

100g/4oz dried chickpeas, soaked overnight and drained
100g/4oz Puy lentils
750g/1lb 10oz ready-diced lamb, cut into 1cm/½in cubes
1 large Spanish onion, finely chopped
1 tsp turmeric
½ tsp ground cinnamon
¼ tsp each ground ginger, saffron strands and paprika
50g/2oz butter
100g/4oz long-grain rice
4 large ripe tomatoes, peeled, seeded and chopped
2 tbsp chopped fresh coriander
4 tbsp chopped fresh flatleaf parsley
lemon quarters, to serve

Takes 2½–2¾ hours • Serves 8

1 Tip the chickpeas and lentils into a large saucepan or flameproof casserole. Add the lamb, onion and spices and pour in about 1.5 litres/2½ pints water – enough to cover the meat and pulses. Season.
2 Bring to the boil, skimming the froth from the surface as the water begins to bubble, then stir in half the butter. Turn down the heat and simmer, covered, for 2 hours until the chickpeas are tender, adding the rice and tomatoes for the last 30 minutes, with more water if necessary.
3 To finish, stir in the remaining butter with the coriander and parsley (hold a little back for a garnish if you like) and taste for seasoning. Serve hot, with a lemon quarter for each serving so guests can squeeze over lemon juice to taste.

• Per serving 370 kcalories, protein 25g, carbohydrate 28g, fat 18g, saturated fat 9.2g, fibre 3.6g, added sugar none, salt 0.27g

Saucy Summer Lamb

Jars of artichokes in oil are a great storecupboard standby. They work beautifully with the mint and tomato in this lamb medley.

1kg/2lb 4oz ripe tomatoes
1.25kg/2lb 4oz cubed lamb (boneless neck, shoulder or leg)
3 tbsp olive oil
1 large Spanish onion, thinly sliced
290g jar artichoke hearts in oil, drained
large handful of mint leaves, roughly chopped

Takes 1¼–1½ hours • Serves 8

1 Make a cross in the bottom of each tomato with a sharp knife, then put a third of the tomatoes in a large bowl and cover with boiling water. Leave for a few minutes until the skins split, then drain and peel. Repeat with the remaining tomatoes, then chop them roughly.
2 Season the lamb. Heat 2 tablespoons of the oil in a large saucepan over a medium-high heat and fry the lamb in batches until browned. Put to one side. Lower the heat, add the remaining oil and the onion to the pan and fry for about 5 minutes until softened.
3 Return the lamb to the pan and stir in the tomatoes. Bring to the boil, lower the heat and splash in some hot water to cover the meat. Put the lid on and simmer for 50–60 minutes or until the lamb is tender. Stir in the artichokes and mint, heat through and season to taste.

• Per serving 405 kcalories, protein 31g, carbohydrate 7g, fat 28g, saturated fat 10.7g, fibre 2.3g, added sugar none, salt 0.68g

Chicken with Goat's Cheese

This dish tastes rather special for something that's so easy to make. As an alternative to goat's cheese you can use Boursin.

8 large skinless chicken breasts
20g pack fresh tarragon
2 × 150g cartons soft goat's cheese, such as Charvoux
5 vine-ripened tomatoes, sliced
3 tbsp olive oil
dressed salad leaves and bread, to serve

Takes 40–50 minutes • Serves 8

1 Preheat the oven to 200°C/Gas 6/fan oven 180°C. Make a slit down the centre of each chicken breast (taking care not to cut right through), then make a pocket with your fingers. Arrange the chicken in a single layer in a large, lightly oiled ovenproof dish.
2 Reserve 8 sprigs of tarragon, chop the rest of the leaves and beat into the cheese with plenty of black pepper. Spoon into the pockets in the chicken. Place 2 tomato slices over each cheese-filled pocket, put a tarragon sprig on top and drizzle with oil.
3 Season and bake for 25–30 minutes until the chicken is cooked, but still moist. Serve hot or cold with dressed salad leaves and bread.

• Per serving 248 kcalories, protein 34g, carbohydrate 2g, fat 12g, saturated fat 4g, fibre 1g, added sugar none, salt 0.64g

Beef and Bean Hotpot

This is a brilliant way of stretching a couple of packets of mince.

750g/1lb 10oz lean minced beef
1 beef stock cube
2 large onions, roughly chopped
450g/1lb carrots, peeled and thickly sliced
1.25kg/2lb 8oz potatoes, peeled and cut into large chunks
2 × 400g cans baked beans
Worcestershire sauce or Tabasco, to taste
large handful of parsley, roughly chopped

Takes about 1 hour • Serves 8

1 Heat a large non-stick pan, add the beef and fry over a medium-high heat until browned, stirring often and breaking up any lumps with a spoon. Crumble in the stock cube and mix well.
2 Add the vegetables, stir to mix with the beef and pour in enough boiling water (about 1.2 litres/2 pints) to cover. Bring to the boil, then lower the heat and stir well. Cover the pan and simmer gently for about 30 minutes or until the vegetables are tender.
3 Tip in the baked beans, sprinkle with Worcestershire sauce or Tabasco to taste, stir well and heat through. Taste for seasoning and sprinkle with the parsley. Serve with extra Worcestershire sauce or Tabasco, for those who like a peppery hot taste.

• Per serving 362 kcalories, protein 31g, carbohydrate 51g, fat 5g, saturated fat 1.9g, fibre 7.9g, added sugar 3.4g, salt 2.05g

TOP LEFT: Saucy Summer Lamb   TOP RIGHT: Chicken with Goat's Cheese   BOTTOM: Beef and Bean Hotpot

TOP: Pork with Celeriac and Orange   BOTTOM LEFT: Lamb and Red Pepper Stew   BOTTOM RIGHT: Beef Paprikash

Pork with Celeriac and Orange

This is the magic formula for making cheaper cuts of meat meltingly tender.

1kg/2lb 4oz boneless pork shoulder, cut into
   bite-sized chunks
3 tbsp olive oil
1 large celeriac (about 1kg/2lb 4oz), peeled
   and chopped into large chunks
4 leeks, trimmed and chopped into chunks
3 carrots, peeled and chopped into chunks
2 garlic cloves, chopped
400ml/14fl oz dry white wine
400ml/14fl oz chicken stock
2 tbsp soy sauce
finely grated zest and juice of 1 large orange
large rosemary sprig

Takes 2½–2¾ hours • Serves 8

1 Preheat the oven to 140°C/Gas 1/fan oven 120°C. Season the meat well. Heat 1 tablespoon of the oil in a large flameproof casserole over a medium-high heat. Add half the pork and leave for a couple of minutes until browned underneath, then brown the other side for 2–3 minutes. Using a slotted spoon, transfer the pork to a plate. Repeat with another spoonful of oil and the remaining meat.
2 Heat the remaining oil in the pan and fry the vegetables and garlic for 3–4 minutes until starting to brown. Tip the pork and its juices into the pan, then add the remaining ingredients. Stir well and bring to the boil.
3 Cover the pan and cook in the oven for 2–2¼ hours until the pork is very tender, stirring halfway. Leave to stand for 10 minutes, taste for seasoning and serve.

• Per serving 251 kcalories, protein 29g, carbohydrate 11g, fat 10g, saturated fat 2.3g, fibre 6.9g, added sugar 0.1g, salt 1.39g

Lamb and Red Pepper Stew

Tender neck fillets of lamb are more expensive than pre-diced casserole lamb but do cut down on cooking time.

1.25kg/2lb 8oz boneless lamb fillet, cut into
   small chunks
40g/1½oz plain flour, seasoned
3 tbsp olive oil
3 garlic cloves, crushed
300ml/½ pint dry white wine
3 large red peppers, seeded and cut into
   5cm/2in pieces
500g jar passata (sieved tomatoes)
300ml/½ pint stock (lamb, chicken or
   vegetable)
3 bay leaves
175g/6oz ready-to-eat dried prunes or
   apricots

Takes 50–60 minutes • Serves 8

1 Coat the lamb in the seasoned flour, shaking off the excess. Heat 2 tablespoons of the oil in a large saucepan until hot. Tip in a third of the lamb and fry over a medium-high heat, turning occasionally, until browned. Transfer to a plate with a slotted spoon and repeat with the remaining lamb, adding the remaining oil when necessary.
2 Return all the meat to the pan, sprinkle in the garlic and cook for 1 minute. Pour in the wine and, scraping up any residue, cook over a high heat until reduced by about a third. Stir in the remaining ingredients except the dried fruit. Cover and simmer for 30–40 minutes or until the lamb is tender.
3 Stir in the dried fruit and heat through for 5 minutes, then taste for seasoning before serving.

• Per serving 497 kcalories, protein 31g, carbohydrate 22g, fat 32g, saturated fat 14.5g, fibre 2.7g, added sugar 0.9g, salt 0.69g

Beef Paprikash

A comforting and hearty dish that's perfect for winter dinner parties.

3 tbsp sunflower oil
1.5kg/3lb braising steak or stewing beef, cut
   into 5cm/2in cubes
2 large onions, sliced
2 garlic cloves, crushed
2 rounded tbsp paprika
3 tbsp tomato purée
2 tbsp wine vinegar (red or white)
2 tsp dried marjoram or mixed herbs
2 bay leaves
½ tsp caraway seeds
2 × 400g cans chopped tomatoes or
   2 × 500g jars passata
750ml/1¼ pints beef stock
2 large red peppers, seeded and cut
   into rings
142ml carton soured cream

Takes 3–3½ hours • Serves 8

1 Preheat the oven to 160°C/Gas 3/fan oven 140°C. Heat 2 tablespoons of the oil in a large flameproof casserole until very hot. Brown the meat in 2–3 batches, removing each batch with a slotted spoon.
2 Add the remaining oil, the onions and garlic. Cook on a low heat for 10 minutes, stirring now and then, until the onions soften. Add the meat and juices and blend in the paprika, tomato purée, vinegar, herbs, bay leaves and caraway seeds.
3 Tip in the tomatoes, add the stock, season and bring to the boil, adding some water if the meat is not covered. Stir, cover, and put in the oven for 2½ hours, or until the meat is tender. Halfway through, stir in the red peppers. Serve with dollops of soured cream.

• Per serving 451 kcalories, protein 43g, carbohydrate 14g, fat 25g, saturated fat 9.7g, fibre 2.8g, added sugar none, salt 0.87g

Beaujolais Berries

Marinating the strawberries in the Beaujolais gives them a lovely flavour, but don't do it too far ahead or they will lose their texture.

700g/1lb 9oz strawberries, hulled and halved
3 tbsp golden caster sugar
handful of mint leaves, plus a few extra
½ bottle Beaujolais

Takes 5–10 minutes, plus marinating • Serves 6

1 Lay the strawberries in a bowl and sprinkle over the caster sugar. Scatter over a handful of mint leaves and let the strawberries sit for about 30 minutes so they start to release their juices.
2 Pour the Beaujolais over the strawberries and scatter over a few more fresh mint leaves. Leave for another 10 minutes before serving.

• Per serving 102 kcalories, protein 1g, carbohydrate 15g, fat 1g, saturated fat none, fibre 1g, added sugar 8g, salt 0.03g

Tropical Fruit Salad

The lovely colours and fabulous flavours of this one-pot pudding will really take you by surprise.

1 ripe papaya
1 small pineapple
12 cape gooseberries (physalis)
50g/2oz butter
4 tbsp light or dark muscovado sugar
4 tbsp coconut rum (or white or dark rum) or
    pineapple and coconut juice
seeds of 1 pomegranate
vanilla or rum and raisin ice cream, to serve

Takes 25–30 minutes • Serves 4

1 Halve the papaya lengthways and scoop out the seeds, then peel the fruit and cut into slim wedges. Cut off the top, bottom and skin of the pineapple, and remove all the eyes from the flesh. Cut the pineapple lengthways into wedges and slice the core off the edge of each wedge. Cut each wedge crossways into chunks. Remove the papery husks from the cape gooseberries.
2 Melt the butter and sugar in a wide deep pan, add the prepared fruit and toss until coated and glistening. Sprinkle over the rum or fruit juice and the pomegranate seeds, and shake the pan to distribute evenly. Serve hot, with ice cream.

• Per serving 308 kcalories, protein 2g, carbohydrate 45g, fat 11g, saturated fat 6.5g, fibre 4.8g, added sugar 15.2g, salt 0.22g

Simple Summer Pudding

To make small puddings, simply tear the bread roughly and layer up with the fruit in individual ramekins. Turn out or serve as they are.

450g/1lb summer berries, defrosted if frozen
4 tbsp blackcurrant cordial or crème
    de cassis
225g carton chilled red fruits compote
6 medium slices white bread, crusts cut off

Takes 40–50 minutes • Serves 4

1 Mix the berries, cordial and compote and leave for 5–10 minutes. If you are using defrosted fruit, mix in some of the juice.
2 Line a 1.2 litre/2 pint pudding bowl with cling film, letting it hang over the sides. Cut a circle from one of the slices of bread to fit the base of the bowl, then cut the remaining slices into quarters.
3 Drain the juice from the fruit into a bowl and dip the bread into it until soaked. Layer the fruit and bread in the bowl and pour over the remaining juice. Cover with the overhanging cling film. Put a small plate or saucer on top to fit inside the rim of the bowl, then stand a couple of heavy cans on top to press it down. Chill in the refrigerator for at least 10 minutes, or until you are ready to eat (it will keep for up to 24 hours).

• Per serving 201 kcalories, protein 5g, carbohydrate 46g, fat 1g, saturated fat 0.2g, fibre 5g, added sugar 11g, salt 0.6g

TOP: Beaujolais Berries   BOTTOM LEFT: Tropical Fruit Salad   BOTTOM RIGHT: Simple Summer Pudding

TOP LEFT: Cookie-dough Crumble TOP RIGHT: Plum and Marzipan Tarte Tatin BOTTOM: Spicy Steamed Fruit Pudding

Cookie-dough Crumble

To make this tasty pudding extra fruity, slice up a couple of pears or a cooking apple (with a sprinkling of sugar) and stir into the fruit.

500g bag mixed frozen fruit
350g pot fresh cookie dough (chocolate chip is good)
cream, ice cream or custard, to serve

Takes 20–25 minutes • Serves 4

1 Preheat the oven to 220°C/Gas 7/fan oven 200°C. Tip the frozen fruit into a shallow baking dish and tear pieces of dough all over the top.
2 Bake for 20 minutes until crisp and golden. Serve with cream, ice cream or custard.

• Per serving 457 kcalories, protein 8g, carbohydrate 57g, fat 24g, saturated fat 13g, fibre 6g, added sugar 9g, salt 1.2g

Plum and Marzipan Tarte Tatin

Choose firm plums for this recipe – if they are overripe they will ooze too much juice and you will have a flood on your kitchen worktop.

25g/1oz butter
25g/1oz golden caster sugar
800g/1lb 12oz firm plums, not too ripe, halved and stoned
100g/4oz golden marzipan
40g/1½oz ground almonds
500g pack puff pastry, thawed if frozen
pouring cream (single or double), to serve

Takes about 1–1¼ hours • Serves 6–8

1 Preheat the oven to 200°C/Gas 6/fan oven 180°C. Melt the butter in a 28cm/11in tarte tatin tin over a medium heat. Tip in the sugar and 1 tablespoon water and stir for a few minutes until lightly browned. Remove from the heat and put in the plums, cut side up.
2 Chop the marzipan into as many chunks as there are plum halves, put a chunk into each plum and sprinkle over the ground almonds.
3 Roll out the pastry and trim to 4cm/1½in larger than the tin all round. Lift the pastry onto the tin and tuck it down between the plums and the inside of the tin. Bake for 30–35 minutes until the pastry is risen, crisp and golden. Cool for 10 minutes, then place a large flat plate with a rim over the tin. Holding it over the sink in case of drips, invert the tarte onto the plate. Serve with cream.

• Per serving for six 511 kcalories, protein 8g, carbohydrate 58g, fat 29g, saturated fat 3g, fibre 3g, added sugar 13g, salt 0.75g

Spicy Steamed Fruit Pudding

This special treat of a dessert makes a good alternative to Christmas pudding. Serve it with crème fraîche or vanilla ice cream.

1 cup raisins
1 cup sultanas
1 cup self-raising flour
1 cup finely grated cold butter (about 100g/4oz), plus extra at room temperature for greasing
1 cup fresh brown breadcrumbs (from around 4 thick slices bread)
1 cup light muscovado sugar
1 cup mixed nuts, chopped (optional)
1 tsp ground cinnamon
1 tsp ground mixed spice
1 cup milk
1 large egg

TO SERVE (OPTIONAL)
butterscotch or caramel sauce
handful of mixed nuts

Takes 2½–3 hours • Serves 8–10

1 Using a 300ml/½ pint coffee mug as your cup measure, empty the first 6 cups and the nuts, if using, into a bowl with the spices, then stir in the milk and egg until well combined. Tip into a buttered 1.5 litre/2¾ pint pudding bowl.
2 Cover with a double layer of buttered foil, making a pleat in the centre to allow the pudding to rise. Tie with string, then place in a steamer or large pan with enough gently simmering water to come halfway up the sides of the bowl. Cover and steam for 2½ hours, adding more water as necessary.
3 To serve, unwrap the pudding and invert onto a deep plate, then drizzle with sauce and decorate the top with nuts, if using.

• Per serving for eight 423 kcalories, protein 6g, carbohydrate 75g, fat 13g, saturated fat 7.9g, fibre 1.8g, added sugar 28.5g, salt 0.66g

Tiramisu Trifle

Everyone will fall in love with this recipe! It's hard to believe that something that tastes this good can take so little time and effort to make.

300ml/½ pint strong, good-quality black coffee
175ml/6fl oz Disaronno (amaretto) liqueur
500g carton mascarpone
500g/1lb 2oz good-quality fresh custard
250g/9oz Savoiardi biscuits (Italian sponge fingers) or sponge fingers
85g/3oz good-quality dark chocolate, roughly chopped

TO DECORATE
4 tbsp toasted slivered almonds
chopped dark chocolate

Takes 10–15 minutes, plus chilling • Serves 8–10

1 Mix the coffee and liqueur in a wide dish. Beat the mascarpone and custard together in a bowl with a hand blender or whisk.
2 Take a third of the biscuits and dip each one into the coffee mix until soft but not soggy. Line the bottom of a glass trifle dish with the biscuits and drizzle over more of the coffee mixture.
3 Sprinkle a third of the chocolate over the biscuits, then follow with a layer of the mascarpone mixture. Repeat twice more. Chill in the fridge for at least 2 hours (preferably overnight). Sprinkle with the almonds and chocolate before serving.

• Per serving for eight 624 kcalories, protein 8g, carbohydrate 54g, fat 39g, saturated fat 23g, fibre 1g, added sugar 35g, salt 0.38g

Grilled Summer Berry Pudding

This recipe has all the elements of a summer pudding, but is much simpler, and served hot. The jammy smells as it cooks are wonderful.

4 slices white sliced bread, crusts removed
85g/3oz golden caster sugar
2 tsp cornflour
200g carton low-fat fromage frais
300g/10oz mixed summer berries (such as raspberries, blueberries, redcurrants, sliced strawberries) or 300g/10oz frozen berries, defrosted

Takes 20–30 minutes • Serves 4

1 Preheat the grill to high. Lay the slices of bread slightly overlapping in a shallow flameproof dish. Sprinkle about 2 tablespoons of the sugar over the bread and grill for about 2 minutes until the bread is toasted and the sugar is starting to caramelise. Mix the cornflour into the fromage frais.
2 Pile the fruit down the middle of the bread and sprinkle with 1 tablespoon of the sugar. Drop spoonfuls of the fromage frais mixture on top, then sprinkle over the rest of the sugar.
3 Put the dish as close to the heat as you can and grill for 6–8 minutes until the fromage frais has browned and everything else is starting to bubble and turn juicy. Leave for a minute or two before serving.

• Per serving 211 kcalories, protein 7g, carbohydrate 47g, fat 1g, saturated fat none, fibre 2g, added sugar 22g, salt 0.45g

Cherry Vanilla Clafoutis

Serve the clafoutis barely warm to get the best from the subtle flavours.

650g/1lb 7oz fresh cherries (dark, juicy ones)
4 tbsp golden caster sugar
4 tbsp kirsch
3 large eggs
50g/2oz plain flour
150ml/¼ pint milk
200ml carton crème fraîche (full- or half-fat)
1 tsp vanilla extract
icing sugar, for dusting

Takes 1–1¼ hours • Serves 6

1 Preheat the oven to 190°C/Gas 5/fan oven 170°C. Stone the cherries, but try to keep them whole.
2 Scatter the cherries over the base of a buttered shallow ovenproof dish, about 1 litre/1¾ pints capacity. Sprinkle the cherries with 1 tablespoon each of sugar and kirsch.
3 Whisk the eggs with an electric beater or hand whisk until they are soft and foamy – about 1–2 minutes. Whisk in the flour and remaining sugar, then add the remaining kirsch, the milk, crème fraîche and vanilla extract.
4 Pour the batter over the cherries and bake for 35–40 minutes until pale golden. Leave to cool to room temperature, then dust lightly with icing sugar and serve just warm.

• Per serving 309 kcalories, protein 7g, carbohydrate 35g, fat 14g, saturated fat 7g, fibre 1g, added sugar 15g, salt 0.23g

TOP LEFT: Tiramisu Trifle TOP RIGHT: Grilled Summer Berry Pudding BOTTOM: Cherry Vanilla Clafoutis

Low-fat Feasts

Roasted Tomato Soup

Try this soup, cooked only to the end of step one, as a sauce for freshly cooked pasta too.

1 large onion, chopped
2 tbsp olive oil
1–2 garlic cloves
900g/2lb tomatoes, chopped
1 red pepper, seeded and chopped
4 carrots, chopped
600ml/1 pint vegetable stock
crusty bread, to serve

Takes 50 minutes • Serves 4

1 Preheat the oven to 200°C/Gas 6/fan oven 180°C. Toss together the onion, oil, garlic, tomatoes, pepper and carrots in a large roasting tin. Season with plenty of salt and freshly ground black pepper and roast for 40 minutes.
2 Pour over the stock and stir, scraping the bottom of the pan to release the scorched vegetable juices.
3 Transfer to a food processor and process until smooth. Transfer to a pan and gently reheat. Adjust the seasoning to taste and serve with toasted crusty bread.

• Per serving 155 kcalories, protein 4g, carbohydrate 21g, fat 7g, saturated fat 1g, fibre 6g, added sugar none, salt 0.61g

Cream of Pumpkin Soup

To make deep-fried sage leaves, drop clean dry leaves into deep hot oil for a few seconds until crisp, but still green.

1.3kg/3lb pumpkin, peeled, sliced and seeded
3 tbsp olive oil
1 large onion, chopped
2 garlic cloves, chopped
2 tsp cumin seeds
1 potato, peeled and chopped
6 fresh thyme sprigs or 1 tsp dried
700ml/1¼ pints vegetable stock
crème fraîche, to serve
deep-fried sage leaves, to garnish

Takes 45 minutes • Serves 6

1 Cut the pumpkin into chunks. Heat the oil in a large pan, then fry the onion, garlic and cumin for 2–3 minutes. Add the pumpkin and potato and fry, stirring for 5–6 minutes. Add the leaves from the thyme sprigs (or use dried) to the pan.
2 Pour in the stock and simmer for about 15 minutes until the pumpkin and potato are soft. Whizz in a blender until smooth, then pour into a pan, heat through and season.
3 Serve each portion with crème fraîche, lightly stirred in. Garnish with fried sage leaves.

• Per serving 122 kcalories, protein 2g, carbohydrate 11g, fat 8g, saturated fat 1g, fibre 2g, added sugar none, salt 0.4g

Chilled Fresh Pea Soup

Out of season, frozen peas work really well in this soup. Serve with Italian-style crusty bread.

25g/1oz butter
300g/10oz floury potatoes, cut into cubes
bunch of spring onions, thinly sliced
850ml/1½ pints vegetable stock
900g/2lb peas in pods, podded, or 225g/8oz fresh or frozen podded peas
200g carton natural Greek yogurt
handful of fresh chives, snipped

Takes 30 minutes, plus chilling • Serves 6

1 Melt the butter in a pan, then add the potatoes and stir well. Cover and cook gently for 5 minutes. Stir in the spring onions, then add the stock and bring to the boil.
2 Cover and cook for 10 minutes until the potatoes are just tender. Add the peas and cook for 3 minutes, then purée the soup in a food processor or blender.
3 Pour into a bowl and whisk in the yogurt, then leave to cool. When cool, cover with plastic film and chill until ready. Stir in the chives when ready to serve.

• Per serving 143 kcalories, protein 7g, carbohydrate 14g, fat 7g, saturated fat 4g, fibre 3g, added sugar none, salt 0.64g

TOP: Roasted Tomato Soup   BOTTOM LEFT: Cream of Pumpkin Soup   BOTTOM RIGHT: Chilled Fresh Pea Soup

TOP LEFT: Vegetable and Pesto Soup   TOP RIGHT: Sweet Potato and Lentil Soup   BOTTOM: Meal-in-a-bowl Noodle Soup

Vegetable and Pesto Soup

A simple soup that allows the flavour of fresh summer vegetables to shine through.

1 tbsp olive oil
1 onion, chopped
225g/8oz new potatoes, sliced
1 vegetable stock cube
100g/4oz runner beans, sliced
450g/1lb courgettes, sliced then halved
2–3 tbsp pesto

Takes 30 minutes • Serves 4

1 Heat the oil in a large pan and fry the onion for 8 minutes until golden. Add the potato slices and mix well. Dissolve the stock cube in 1.2 litres/2 pints boiling water, then add to the pan. Bring to the boil then simmer for 7 minutes until the potatoes are just cooked.
2 Add the runner beans to the pan and continue to cook for 5 minutes, adding the courgettes for the last 2 minutes of cooking time.
3 Season with plenty of salt and pepper. Remove from the heat and stir in two tablespoons of the pesto. Taste and add more pesto if necessary. Serve hot.

• Per serving 159 kcalories, protein 5g, carbohydrate 14g, fat 10g, saturated fat 2g, fibre 3g, added sugar none, salt 1.54g

Sweet Potato and Lentil Soup

This is a mildly spiced soup perfect for chilly evenings. Reheat leftovers for lunch next day.

100g/4oz red lentils (no need to soak)
1 onion, chopped
knob of butter
1 garlic clove, finely chopped
2 tbsp curry paste
450g/1lb orange sweet potatoes, peeled and cubed
450g/1lb floury potatoes, peeled and cubed
1.2 litres/2 pints hot vegetable stock
2 tbsp chopped fresh mint (optional)
142ml carton natural yogurt
naan bread, to serve

Takes 40 minutes • Serves 4

1 Cook the lentils in boiling water for 15 minutes. Cook the onion in the butter for 8 minutes until softened and beginning to brown. Stir in the garlic, curry paste and cubed potatoes. Cook for 5 minutes, stirring.
2 Drain the lentils. Add to the potatoes with the stock and cook for 12–15 minutes until the potatoes are fully cooked. Whizz in a blender until smooth. Return to the pan, season to taste and heat through.
3 Stir the mint, if using, into the yogurt and season to taste. Ladle the soup into bowls and swirl in the yogurt. Serve with naan bread.

• Per serving 330 kcalories, protein 14g, carbohydrate 63g, fat 4g, saturated fat 1g, fibre 6g, added sugar none, salt 1.53kg

Meal-in-a-bowl Noodle Soup

Look for fresh Japanese udon or yakisoba noodles in the ethnic section of the supermarket.

1 tsp vegetable oil
4–5 mushrooms, sliced
1 garlic clove, finely chopped
½ red pepper, seeded and cut into strips
small stalk of broccoli, broken into florets
211g pack fresh soupy udon or yakisoba noodles

Takes 15 minutes • Serves 1 (easily doubled)

1 Heat the oil in a medium pan. Add the mushrooms, garlic, red pepper and broccoli and stir fry until the vegetables are beginning to soften, about 4 minutes.
2 Add the noodles. Stir in the contents of the flavouring sachet from the noodle pack and pour over 300ml/½ pint boiling water.
3 Cook the noodles for 2 minutes until they are tender and piping hot.

• Per serving 457 kcalories, protein 16g, carbohydrate 84g, fat 9g, saturated fat 0.2g, fibre 5g, added sugar none, salt 0.02g

Chunky Fish Chowder

A meal-in-a-bowl soup, full of colour and flavour. You can freeze it for up to 1 month.

1 large onion, thinly sliced
500g/1lb 2oz potaotes, peeled and cut into
    small chunks
1.2 litres/2 pints milk
1 garlic clove, crushed
300g can sweetcorn kernels, drained
450g/1lb skinless smoked haddock
2 tbsp chopped fresh parsley
crusty brown bread, to serve

Takes 30–40 minutes • Serves 4

1 Put the onion and potatoes into a large saucepan, pour the milk over and season well with freshly ground black pepper. Bring to the boil, cover and simmer for 10 minutes, stirring occasionally.
2 Stir in the garlic, sweetcorn and fish, bring back to the boil, cover and simmer for 5 minutes.
3 Flake the fish into bite-sized pieces with a fork. Stir in the parsley and season to taste. Serve with crusty brown bread.

• Per serving 417 kcalories, protein 36g, carbohydrate 57g, fat 7g, saturated fat 3g, fibre 3g, added sugar 5g, salt 3.04g

Tomato Salsa Soup

A quick and easy no-cook soup made from supermarket ingredients. It makes an ideal packed lunch.

8 tomatoes (about 650g/1lb 7oz), roughly
    chopped
½ medium or 1 small red onion, roughly
    chopped
good handful of fresh coriander
500g carton passata (Italian tomato sauce)
410g can cannellini beans, drained
handful of chopped fresh coriander and
    tortilla chips, to serve

Takes 10 minutes • Serves 4

1 Put the tomatoes, onion and coriander in a food processor and pulse briefly to chop.
2 Tip into a large bowl with the passata and beans, then add 150ml/¼ pint water. Season and mix well.
3 Sprinkle with chopped coriander and serve with tortilla chips.

• Per serving 141 kcalories, protein 8g, carbohydrate 26g, fat 1g, saturated fat none, fibre 5g, added sugar 2g, salt 0.84g

Asian Vegetable Broth

Vary the combination of vegetables to suit yourself; even a bag of prepared stir-fry vegetables from the supermarket would do.

1 stalk lemon grass, thinly sliced
2.5cm/1in piece fresh ginger, sliced
2 garlic cloves, sliced
4 tbsp soy sauce
2 tbsp saké or dry sherry
finely grated zest and juice of 1 lime
1 tsp caster sugar
2 tbsp vegetable oil
2 carrots, cut into matchsticks
100g/4oz baby corn, halved
1 large red chilli, sliced
100g/4oz oyster mushrooms, sliced
50g/2oz baby spinach leaves
85g/3oz beansprouts

Takes 20 minutes • Serves 4

1 Place the lemon grass, ginger and garlic in a large pan with the soy sauce, saké or sherry, lime zest and juice and caster sugar. Add 850ml/1½ pints water and bring to the boil. Cover and simmer for 10 minutes. Strain and keep the broth warm.
2 Heat the oil in a large frying pan or wok, add the carrots, corn and chilli and stir fry for 2 minutes. Add the mushrooms, spinach and beansprouts and remove from the heat.
3 Divide the vegetables between four serving bowls, pour over the hot broth and serve immediately.

• Per serving 130 kcalories, protein 4g, carbohydrate 9g, fat 8g, saturated fat 1g, fibre 3g, added sugar 1g, salt 2.3g

TOP LEFT: Chunky Fish Chowder   TOP RIGHT: Tomato Salsa Soup   BOTTOM: Asian Vegetable Broth

TOP: Roast Asparagus with Garlic   BOTTOM LEFT: Baked Buttery Squash   BOTTOM RIGHT: Potato Wedges with Tuna

Roast Asparagus with Garlic

To prepare asparagus snap off the woody bottom then boil, steam or roast. Parboiling then roasting only works for young asparagus.

350g/12oz asparagus
2 tbsp olive oil
1 large garlic clove, cut into very thin slices
1 tbsp large capers in brine, rinsed and
    drained
juice of ½ orange

Takes 20 minutes • Serves 4 as a starter

1 Preheat the oven to 200°C/Gas 6/fan oven 180°C. Bring a large pan of water to the boil. Add the asparagus and boil for 2 minutes until crisp, but beginning to go tender.
2 Drain and refresh under cold water. Dry on kitchen paper. Pour the oil into a shallow roasting tin and roll the asparagus in it to coat.
3 Scatter over the garlic slivers and capers and roast for 8–10 minutes until the asparagus is tinged browned and cooked through – test by inserting a knife into a few spears. Sprinkle with orange juice, season with sea salt and serve warm.

• Per serving 79 kcalories, protein 3g, carbohydrate 3g, fat 6g, saturated fat 1g, fibre 2g, added sugar none, salt 0.06g

Baked Buttery Squash

Butternut squash has a lovely delicate flavour. This recipe has a buttery taste without being high in fat.

1 butternut squash, about 675g/1lb 8oz
    in weight
½ tsp paprika
3 tbsp snipped fresh chives
3 tbsp low-fat crème fraîche
1 thick slice of white bread, crust removed,
    crumbled into breadcrumbs
generous knob of butter, melted
25g/1oz grated parmesan

Takes 1 hour 10 minutes • Serves 2

1 Preheat the oven to 200°C/Gas 6/fan oven 180°C from cold. Halve the squash lengthways, then scoop out the seeds and fibres and discard. Season the squash well and put in a roasting tin half full of water. Cover with foil and bake for about 40 minutes until tender.
2 Drain, then transfer the squash to a board until cool enough to handle. Scrape the flesh into a bowl, leaving a thin border of flesh on the skin. Mix the paprika, chives and crème fraîche with the flesh and season.
3 Pile the mixture into the squash shells. Mix the breadcrumbs with the butter and parmesan and sprinkle on top. Bake for 15 minutes until lightly browned.

• Per serving 271 kcalories, protein 13g, carbohydrate 35g, fat 10g, saturated fat 6g, fibre 5g, added sugar none, salt 0.78g

Potato Wedges with Tuna

Everyone loves jacket potato wedges and this saucy version is especially popular with children.

3 large baking potatoes
3 tbsp olive oil
1 leek, sliced
200g can tuna in brine, drained
2 × 400g cans chopped tomatoes with chilli
    in tomato juice

Takes 35 minutes • Serves 4

1 Preheat the oven to 220°C/Gas 7/fan oven 200°C. Cut the potatoes into wedges and put in a roasting tin. Drizzle over two tablespoons of the oil, making sure all the potatoes are covered. Bake for 30 minutes until crispy on the outside and soft inside.
2 Meanwhile, heat the remaining oil in a pan and fry the leek until softened. Tip in the tuna and the chilli tomatoes, breaking the tuna down until well combined with the tomatoes.
3 Cook for a few minutes until hot. Season and spoon over the potatoes in the roasting tin, mixing gently. Serve immediately.

• Per serving 264 kcalories, protein 16g, carbohydrate 32g, fat 9g, saturated fat 1g, fibre 5g, added sugar none, salt 0.76g

Pepper and Egg Sauté

A healthy and colourful alternative to eggs on toast.

1 tbsp olive oil
1 large onion, finely chopped
2 garlic cloves, crushed
2 yellow peppers, seeded and finely sliced
300g/10oz French beans, cut into 5cm/2in pieces
8 tbsp white wine
4 ripe tomatoes, diced
4 medium eggs
4 tbsp chopped fresh flatleaf parsley
crusty bread, to serve

Takes 25 minutes • Serves 4

1 Heat the olive oil in a large frying pan and fry the onion and garlic for 2 minutes until softened. Add the yellow peppers, French beans and white wine. Fry, stirring for a further 2–3 minutes.
2 Add the diced tomatoes and cook for 1–2 minutes until warmed through. Make four hollows in the vegetable mixture with the back of a spoon.
3 Crack an egg into each one and cook over a medium heat for 3–4 minutes until the egg is set to your liking. Sprinkle over the parsley and season well. Serve with crusty bread.

• Per serving 187 kcalories, protein 10g, carbohydrate 11g, fat 10g, saturated fat 2g, fibre 4g, added sugar none, salt 0.23g

Trout, Beetroot and Bean Salad

A good-looking salad, and good for you too. Horseradish is delicious with both trout and beetroot.

225g/8oz fine green beans, trimmed
120g bag watercress and rocket salad
2 tsp balsamic vinegar
250g pack cooked smoked trout fillets
4 cooked beetroot, diced
6 tbsp 0% fat fromage frais
1–2 tbsp fresh lemon juice
2 tsp creamed horseradish

Takes 15 minutes • Serves 4

1 Cook the green beans in a pan of lightly salted boiling water for 3–4 minutes until just tender. Drain and refresh in cold water.
2 Put the salad leaves in a large bowl and season. Pour in the balsamic vinegar and toss well to coat. Arrange the dressed leaves on a serving dish. Flake the trout on to the leaves and top with the cooked beans and diced beetroot.
3 Mix the fromage frais, lemon juice and creamed horseradish and season to taste. Drizzle over the salad just before serving.

• Per serving 140 kcalories, protein 17g, carbohydrate 10g, fat 4g, saturated fat 1g, fibre 3g, added sugar none, salt 1.52g

Jackets with Tuna and Chives

Don't let the lengthy cooking time put you off. The actual work takes only 10 minutes.

4 baking potatoes
250g tub 'virtually fat-free' cottage cheese with onions and chives
200g can good-quality tuna in water, drained
1 celery stick, sliced
3 spring onions, trimmed and sliced
Tabasco sauce and green salad, to serve

Takes 1½ hours • Serves 4

1 Preheat the oven to 180°C/Gas 4/fan oven 160°C. Prick the potatoes with a fork. Put them straight on to a shelf in the hottest part of the oven for 1–1¼ hours, or until they are soft inside.
2 Meanwhile, mix the cottage cheese with the tuna, celery and spring onions. Season.
3 To serve, cut a deep cross in each baked potato and spoon the filling on top. Sprinkle a few drops of Tabasco sauce over and serve with a green salad.

• Per serving 237 kcalories, protein 20g, carbohydrate 39g, fat 1g, saturated fat none, fibre 3g, added sugar none, salt 0.61g

TOP: Pepper and Egg Sauté   BOTTOM LEFT: Trout, Beetroot and Bean Salad   BOTTOM RIGHT: Jackets with Tuna and Chives

TOP LEFT: Warm Potato and Spinach Salad   TOP RIGHT: Tuna, Bean and Corn Salad   BOTTOM: Japanese Salad with Rice

Warm Potato and Spinach Salad

This is a hearty salad, packed with interesting textures and flavours.

700g/1lb 9oz new potatoes, scrubbed
   and halved
225g bag of baby spinach leaves
4 rashers of smoked back bacon, trimmed
   of fat
175g/6oz button mushrooms, thinly sliced
410g can butter beans, drained

FOR THE DRESSING
1 garlic clove, crushed
2 tsp wholegrain mustard
2 tsp balsamic vinegar
1 tbsp olive oil

Takes 30 minutes • Serves 4

1 Cook the potatoes in salted boiling water
for 8–10 minutes until just tender. Drain and
immediately toss with the spinach leaves
so they wilt very slightly. Set aside.
2 Grill the bacon for 5–6 minutes until the
rashers are very crisp. Drain on kitchen paper.
Mix all the dressing ingredients in a large
bowl. Add the mushrooms and butter beans,
season and leave to stand for 5 minutes.
3 Add the potatoes, spinach and bacon to
the mushrooms, then toss together. Serve
at once.

• Per serving 282 kcalories, protein 14g, carbohydrate
39g, fat 9g, saturated fat 2g, fibre 7g, added sugar
none, salt 1.94g

Tuna, Bean and Corn Salad

An easy salad made from storecupboard
ingredients, perfect when you suddenly
fancy a snack.

125g can tuna slices or 185g can tuna
   chunks, drained
165g can sweetcorn with peppers, drained
½ red onion, finely chopped
200g can red kidney beans, drained
2 handfuls mixed salad leaves
1 tbsp olive oil
2 tsp fresh lemon juice
pinch of mild chilli powder
toasted crusty bread, to serve

Takes 10 minutes • Serves 2 (easily doubled)

1 In a large bowl, mix the tuna lightly with
the sweetcorn, onion and kidney beans.
Season well.
2 Divide the salad leaves between two plates,
season lightly, then pile the tuna salad on top.
3 Drizzle over the olive oil and lemon juice
and sprinkle with the chilli. Serve with toasted
crusty bread.

• Per serving 277 kcalories, protein 21g, carbohydrate
33g, fat 8g, saturated fat 1g, fibre 6g, added sugar 5g,
salt 1.63g

Japanese Salad with Rice

A simple salad of crunchy vegetables
in a warm dressing, served with sticky
sushi rice.

225g/8oz sushi rice
1 mooli (large white radish), peeled
2 carrots, peeled
1 small cucumber (about 250g/9oz)
3 tbsp mirin (Japanese sweet rice wine) or
   dry sherry
2 tbsp rice wine vinegar
2 tbsp Japanese soy sauce
2 tsp caster sugar
coriander sprigs, to serve

Takes 20 minutes, plus standing • Serves 4

1 Rinse the rice in a sieve in cold water
until the water runs clear. Place in a pan and
pour over 300ml/½ pint cold water, cover,
then bring to the boil. Simmer for 10 minutes
without removing the lid. Leave to stand,
covered, for 10 minutes.
2 Meanwhile, cut the mooli, carrots and
cucumber into matchsticks and place in a
bowl. Put the remaining ingredients in a small
pan and heat gently until steam starts to rise.
Pour over the vegetables and marinate for
15 minutes.
3 Divide the rice between four serving plates,
spoon the vegetables on top, then drizzle the
dressing over. Serve immediately, topped with
the coriander.

• Per serving 254 kcalories, protein 5g, carbohydrate
57g, fat 1g, saturated fat 0.03g, fibre 1g, added sugar
3g, salt 1.15g

Falafel Pittas

Spicy chickpea cakes make a tasty filling for a hot pitta bread sandwich.

2 × 400g cans chickpeas, drained
1 small onion, roughly chopped
2 carrots, roughly chopped
1 large garlic clove, roughly chopped
1 tsp ground coriander
1 tsp ground cumin
small handful of parsley sprigs
oil, for brushing
6 pitta breads
crispy lettuce, cucumber slices and natural
    yogurt, to serve

Takes 25 minutes • Serves 6

1 Preheat the grill to medium. Put the chickpeas into a food processor with the onion, carrots, garlic, coriander, cumin, parsley, salt and pepper. Whizz briefly to retain some of the chunky texture in the chickpeas. Shape the mixture into six round cakes.
2 Carefully place the falafels on a grill pan lined with foil. Brush with a little oil. Grill for 4–5 minutes on each side. Meanwhile, toast the pitta breads and tear the lettuce into strips.
3 Stuff the hot falafels into the pitta breads. Add a small handful of torn lettuce, a few slices of cucumber and a drizzle of natural yogurt. Serve straightaway.

• Per serving 281 kcalories, protein 12g, carbohydrate 53g, fat 4g, saturated fat 0g, fibre 6g, added sugar none, salt 1.3g

Chicory, Bean and Chilli Crostini

This is a modern version of beans on toast. Try it topped with stir-fried garlicky greens too.

2 tbsp olive oil
1 red onion, thinly sliced
2 garlic cloves, thinly sliced
1 red chilli, halved, seeded and sliced
2 tbsp balsamic vinegar
420g can cannellini beans, drained
    and rinsed
4 tbsp dry white wine
handful flatleaf parsley, roughly torn
4 thick slices crusty Italian bread
2 red chicory heads, halved lengthways

Takes 20 minutes • Serves 4

1 Heat one tablespoon of the oil in a frying pan and fry the onion, garlic and chilli for 5 minutes until softened. Stir in the vinegar, beans and wine and cook for 3–4 minutes until all the liquid has evaporated. Stir in the parsley and season.
2 Meanwhile, brush the remaining oil over a griddle and heat until starting to smoke. Arrange the bread and chicory, cut-side down, on top and cook for 1 minute. Remove the chicory. Turn the bread over and brown the other side.
3 Divide the bread between serving plates and spoon the beans over. Place the chicory on top and season with freshly ground black pepper. Serve immediately.

• Per serving 302 kcalories, protein 11g, carbohydrate 38g, fat 12g, saturated fat 1g, fibre 8g, added sugar none, salt 1.15g

Ham and Pear Open Sandwiches

A no-cook lunch packed with vitamins. Eat straightaway, while the pears and watercress are fresh and crisp.

3 tbsp thick honey
1 tbsp Dijon mustard
2 tsp soft dark brown sugar
4 thick slices of sourdough rye bread
1 ripe but firm Conference or William pear
4 slices Parma ham
large handful of watercress

Takes 10 minutes • Serves 2

1 Mix together the honey, mustard and soft dark brown sugar to a smooth paste.
2 Spread the honey mixture over the bread slices. Cut the pear in half lengthways without peeling it, and core and discard the pips. Cut it into thick slices.
3 Cover each piece of bread with slices of pear and top with slices of Parma ham. Add a pile of watercress leaves and grind pepper over the top. Serve straightaway.

• Per serving 315 kcalories, protein 13g, carbohydrate 58g, fat 5g, saturated fat 1g, fibre 4g, added sugar 23g, salt 2.75g

TOP LEFT: Falafel Pittas   TOP RIGHT: Chicory, Bean and Chilli Crostini   BOTTOM: Ham and Pear Open Sandwich

TOP: Tomato and Olive Spaghetti   BOTTOM LEFT: Summer Veggie Pasta   BOTTOM RIGHT: Tuna and Tomato Rice

Tomato and Olive Spaghetti

Take a few storecupboard basics and you can have supper on the table in around 15 minutes.

350g/12oz spaghetti
1 tbsp olive oil
2 garlic cloves, finely chopped
4 anchovy fillets in oil, drained
400g can plum tomatoes
100g/4oz pitted black olives, roughly
   chopped
3 tbsp capers, rinsed and roughly chopped
2 tbsp chopped fresh parsley

Takes 15 minutes • Serves 4

1 Stir the spaghetti into a large pan of salted boiling water and cook for 12–15 minutes until just tender.
2 Meanwhile, heat the oil in a pan and cook the garlic and anchovies for 2 minutes. Tip in the tomatoes and cook for 5 minutes, breaking them lightly with a wooden spoon. Stir in the olives and capers and cook for a further 5 minutes. Season to taste and stir in the parsley.
3 Drain the pasta well and return to the pan. Stir in the sauce, divide between warmed bowls and serve.

• Per serving 377 kcalories, protein 13g, carbohydrate 68g, fat 8g, saturated fat 1g, fibre 4g, added sugar none, salt 1.98g

Summer Veggie Pasta

This makes a great vegetarian family supper, but it can easily be halved to serve two.

225g/8oz pasta bows
175g/6oz fresh or frozen broad beans
   (about 650g/1lb 7oz in their pods)
1 tbsp good-quality olive oil
1 large onion, finely chopped
2 garlic cloves, chopped
2 large courgettes, cut into sticks
6 ripe plum tomatoes, cut into wedges
generous dash of Tabasco
handful of shredded basil

Takes 30 minutes • Serves 4

1 Cook the pasta according to the packet instructions, adding the fresh broad beans for the last 3 minutes (frozen ones for the last 2 minutes).
2 While the pasta is cooking, heat the oil in a large frying pan. Add the onion and cook over a medium heat for 1–2 minutes. Stir in the garlic and courgettes, toss over a medium heat for 2–3 minutes, then stir in the tomatoes and shake in the Tabasco. Stir for 2–3 minutes to soften the tomatoes a little (not too much or they will go mushy). Drain the pasta and beans.
3 Toss the vegetables and basil into the pasta and season. Serve hot (or cold as a salad with a low-fat dressing).

• Per serving 284 kcalories, protein 12g, carbohydrate 51g, fat 5g, saturated fat 1g, fibre 7g, added sugar none, salt 0.1g

Tuna and Tomato Rice

This filling meal, ready in just 25 minutes, uses mostly storecupboard ingredients, keeping shopping to a minimum.

225g/8oz long grain rice
1 tbsp olive oil
2 garlic cloves, finely chopped
1 onion, finely chopped
2 smoked streaky bacon
   rashers, chopped
175g/6oz chestnut mushrooms, sliced
2 × 400g cans chopped tomatoes
200g can tuna, drained
generous handful of fresh parsley, finely
   chopped
garlic bread, to serve

Takes 25 minutes • Serves 4

1 Cook the rice in salted boiling water for 10–12 minutes, or as directed on the packet.
2 Meanwhile, heat the oil in a pan and fry the garlic, onion and bacon for 5 minutes, stirring often. Add the mushrooms and cook for another 2–3 minutes. Stir in the tomatoes and tuna and season well. Heat through for 5 minutes.
3 Drain the rice, stir it into the tomato sauce with the parsley, mixing gently. Serve with garlic bread.

• Per serving 346 kcalories, protein 19g, carbohydrate 57g, fat 6g, saturated fat 2g, fibre 6g, added sugar 3g, salt 3.52g

Creamy Tomato and Pepper Pasta

This simple recipe uses just five ingredients and is excellent for using up tomatoes that are too soft for salad.

900g/2lb ripe tomatoes
1 red pepper
2 garlic cloves
350g/12oz pasta quills or shells
4 tbsp crème fraîche
grated parmesan, to serve

Takes 50 minutes • Serves 4

1 Preheat the oven to 200°C/Gas 6/fan oven 180°C. Quarter the tomatoes, roughly chop the pepper (discarding the seeds) and finely chop the garlic. Put them in a roasting tin and drizzle over three tablespoons of olive oil. Season well.
2 Roast for 30–35 minutes, stirring halfway through, until softened and slightly browned. Meanwhile, cook the pasta in a large pan of salted boiling water for 10–12 minutes until just tender (follow the packet instructions if you are using fresh pasta).
3 Remove the vegetables from the oven and stir in the crème fraîche a spoonful at a time. Bubble up on the stove to reheat, taste and season if necessary. Stir in the drained pasta and serve with grated parmesan.

• Per serving 419 kcalories, protein 13g, carbohydrate 77g, fat 9g, saturated fat 4g, fibre 6g, added sugar none, salt 0.38g

Pumpkin and Bean Spaghetti

The pasta sauce can be made up to two days in advance and chilled. Or thin it down with stock to make a tasty soup.

2 tbsp olive oil
2 onions, thinly sliced
2 garlic cloves, crushed
350g/12oz diced pumpkin or butternut
    squash
400g can chopped tomatoes
400ml/14fl oz vegetable stock
350g/12oz spaghetti
420g can mixed beans in a mild chilli sauce
small handful finely grated parmesan,
    to serve

Takes 50 minutes • Serves 4

1 Heat the oil in a pan and fry the onions for 8 minutes, until softened. Add the garlic and pumpkin or squash and fry for a further 5 minutes. Stir in the tomatoes and stock. Bring to the boil, cover and simmer for 15 minutes, until the pumpkin is tender.
2 Meanwhile, cook the spaghetti in a large pan of salted boiling water according to the packet instructions.
3 Add the beans to the pasta sauce and cook for 3–4 minutes. Season to taste. Drain the spaghetti well, return to the pan, then stir in the sauce. Divide between shallow bowls and serve sprinkled with parmesan.

• Per serving 477 kcalories, protein 19g, carbohydrate 88g, fat 8g, saturated fat 1g, fibre 9g, added sugar none, salt 2.01g

Spaghetti with Broccoli and Anchovies

If you love garlic, try adding a couple of chopped cloves to the breadcrumbs.

350g/12oz dried spaghetti
350g/12oz broccoli
5 tbsp olive oil
6 anchovies, chopped
2 fresh red chillies, seeded and finely
    chopped
100g/4oz white breadcrumbs,
    made with stale bread

Takes 25–30 minutes • Serves 4

1 Cook the spaghetti in a large pan of boiling water, according to the packet instructions. Cut the broccoli into small florets, thinly slice the thick stalks and throw into the pan of pasta for the last 3 minutes of cooking time.
2 Meanwhile, heat 3 tablespoons of olive oil in a frying pan, add the anchovies and chillies and fry briefly. Add the breadcrumbs and cook, stirring, for about 5 minutes until the crumbs are crunchy and golden.
3 Drain the spaghetti and return to the pan. Toss with three quarters of the crumb mixture, some salt and pepper and another 2 tablespoons of olive oil. Serve each portion sprinkled with the remaining crumbs.

• Per serving 400 kcalories, protein 17g, carbohydrate 78g, fat 4g, saturated fat 0.5g, fibre 5g, added sugar none, salt 0.8g

TOP: Creamy Tomato and Pepper Pasta   BOTTOM LEFT: Pumpkin and Bean Spaghetti   BOTTOM RIGHT: Spaghetti with Broccoli and Anchovies

TOP LEFT: Seafood Spaghetti   TOP RIGHT: Pasta with Tuna and Tomato   BOTTOM: Roast Tomato and Pepper Gnocchi

Seafood Spaghetti

There's more to spaghetti than Bolognese. Try this low-fat sauce made with a jar of cockles.

175g/6oz spaghetti
1 tbsp olive oil
2 garlic cloves, finely chopped
400g can chopped tomatoes
200g jar of cockles in vinegar, drained
pinch of dried chilli flakes
2 tbsp chopped fresh parsley

Takes 15 minutes • Serves 2 (easily doubled)

1 Cook the spaghetti in a pan of salted boiling water for 10–12 minutes until tender.
2 Meanwhile, heat the oil in a frying pan, then fry the garlic for 30 seconds. Add the tomatoes and bubble for 2–3 minutes. Add the cockles and chilli flakes, season, then stir to heat through.
3 Drain the spaghetti and return to the pan. Stir in the sauce and serve sprinkled with chopped parsley.

• Per serving 424 kcalories, protein 21g, carbohydrate 71g, fat 8g, saturated fat 1g, fibre 5g, added sugar none, salt 1.39g

Pasta with Tuna and Tomato

You can rustle up the ingredients for this tasty pasta supper from cans and packets in the storecupboard.

2 tbsp olive oil
1 onion, chopped
2 garlic cloves, finely chopped
400g can chopped tomatoes with herbs
½ tsp chilli powder
1 tsp sugar
500g packet pasta bows
100g can tuna, drained
handful of basil leaves, optional

Takes 25 minutes • Serves 4

1 Heat the oil in a pan, add the onion and cook for a couple of minutes. Stir in the garlic, tomatoes, chilli and sugar. Season and bring to the boil. Stir, then reduce the heat and simmer for 5 minutes.
2 Meanwhile, bring a large pan of salted water to the boil. Add the pasta and cook according to the packet instructions.
3 Flake the tuna into the sauce and heat through. Drain the pasta, return to the pan and stir in the sauce and basil leaves. Serve with a generous grinding of pepper.

• Per serving 553 kcalories, protein 21g, carbohydrate 102g, fat 10g, saturated fat 1g, fibre 5g, added sugar 1g, salt 0.52g

Roast Tomato and Pepper Gnocchi

Tangy goat's cheese goes wonderfully with the smoky peppers. Try it with spaghetti or pasta shapes too.

450g/1lb ripe tomatoes, halved
2 red peppers, cut into strips
2 garlic cloves, unpeeled
2 tbsp olive oil
500g pack fresh gnocchi
100g/4oz goat's cheese
fresh basil leaves and a green salad, to serve

Takes 25 minutes • Serves 4

1 Preheat oven to 220°C/Gas 7/fan oven 200°C. Put the tomatoes, peppers and garlic and oil in a roasting tin. Sprinkle with salt and stir to coat. Roast for 20 minutes. Just before the tomatoes and peppers are done, cook the gnocchi in salted boiling water for 2–3 minutes or according to the packet instructions.
2 Remove the tomatoes, peppers and garlic from the oven. Squeeze the garlic from its skin and put in a food processor with the tomatoes, peppers and pan juices. Season. Whizz for a few seconds for a rough sauce.
3 Drain the gnocchi and transfer to a bowl. Pour the sauce over the gnocchi and mix gently. Divide between plates, crumble over the cheese and scatter over torn basil leaves. Serve with a green salad.

• Per serving 326 kcalories, protein 9g, carbohydrate 50g, fat 11g, saturated fat 1g, fibre 4g, added sugar none, salt 1.6g

Fragrant Rice with Chilli Vegetables

Simple ingredients are given a flavour boost with fresh-tasting lemongrass, coriander and the fiery heat of chopped chilli.

225g/8oz jasmine or Thai rice
1 stalk lemongrass, finely chopped
175g/6oz mangetout, halved lengthways
175g/6oz baby sweetcorn, halved lengthways
2 tomatoes, roughly chopped
25g/1oz fresh coriander, finely chopped
25g/1oz desiccated coconut, lightly toasted
1 red chilli, finely chopped
1 tbsp soy sauce
coriander sprigs, to serve

Takes 45 minutes • Serves 4

1 Half fill the base of a steamer with water. Bring to the boil and cover with the steamer layer and lid. Rinse the rice under cold running water. Drain and put into a basin (check it will fit into the steamer layer). Add the lemongrass, seasoning and 600ml/1 pint boiling water to the basin. Put into the steamer and put on the lid. Cook for 30 minutes until the rice has absorbed almost all the water.
2 Arrange the vegetables in the steamer, around the basin. Cover and steam for 2 minutes.
3 Stir the coriander, coconut and chilli into the rice and divide it between serving plates. Top with the vegetables and drizzle the soy sauce over. Serve topped with the coriander sprigs.

• Per serving 249 kcalories, protein 7g, carbohydrate 48g, fat 5g, saturated fat 3g, fibre 3g, added sugar none, salt 0.65g

Warm Thai Noodle Salad

Stretch two chicken breasts to feed four in this unusual salad with a tangy dressing.

2 large boneless skinless chicken breasts
175g/6oz dried medium egg noodles
2 good handfuls of greens, such as Chinese leaf, finely shredded
2 carrots, cut into thin strips
8 spring onions, finely sliced
1 red pepper, seeded and finely sliced
handful of fresh coriander leaves

FOR THE DRESSING
1 red chilli, seeded and finely chopped
2 garlic cloves, finely chopped
1 tbsp finely chopped fresh root ginger
2 tbsp soy sauce
juice of 1 lime
2 tbsp olive oil

Takes 30 minutes • Serves 4

1 Preheat the grill to high. Put the chicken on a baking sheet and grill for 10–12 minutes without turning, until cooked through. Meanwhile, cook the noodles according to the packet instructions. Drain and rinse in cold running water to stop them sticking together.
2 Mix the vegetables in a bowl. Thinly slice the chicken and add to the bowl, along with the noodles and coriander leaves.
3 Mix the dressing ingredients together with two tablespoons of water, pour over the salad and toss well. Serve immediately.

• Per serving 336 kcalories, protein 24g, carbohydrate 40g, fat 10g, saturated fat 1g, fibre 2g, added sugar none, salt 1.7g

Zesty Noodle Stir Fry

You'll find flat rice noodles with the oriental foods in the supermarket. Change the vegetables to suit your taste.

140g/5oz flat rice noodles
6 tbsp soy sauce
5 tbsp fresh orange juice
½ tsp finely grated orange zest
1 tsp sugar
½ tsp cornflour
1 tbsp of vegetable or sunflower oil
½ tbsp grated fresh root ginger
2 garlic cloves, finely chopped
2 tbsp dry sherry
2 red peppers, seeded and sliced
2 carrots, peeled, cut into fine strips
2 courgettes cut into fine strips
100g/4oz mangetout, sliced
220g can water chestnuts, sliced
1 bunch spring onions, shredded

Takes 40 minutes • Serves 4 (easily halved)

1 Put the noodles in a large bowl, cover with boiling water for 4 minutes, then drain and rinse under cold water.
2 Mix the soy sauce, orange juice and zest, sugar and cornflour. Heat the oil in a wok, add the ginger and garlic and fry for 1 minute. Add the sherry and peppers and fry for 1 minute. Add the carrots, courgettes and mangetout and fry for 3 minutes. Stir in the water chestnuts and spring onions and fry for a minute.
3 Add the soy sauce mix and noodles and stir fry until hot. Serve straightaway.

• Per serving 240 kcalories, protein 6g, carbohydrate 47g, fat 3g, saturated fat 0g, fibre 4g, added sugar 1.6g, salt 2.77g

TOP LEFT: Fragrant Rice with Chilli Vegetables   TOP RIGHT: Warm Thai Noodle Salad   BOTTOM: Zesty Noodle Stir Fry

TOP: Salt and Pepper Fried Chicken   **BOTTOM LEFT:** Cajun-spiced Chicken   **BOTTOM RIGHT:** Chicken Skewers with Cucumber Dip

Salt and Pepper Fried Chicken

This tasty rub is also good on pork and lamb. Try the chicken barbecued too.

200g carton Greek yogurt
2 tbsp chopped fresh mint
juice of 1 lemon
good sprinkling of salt (sea salt is best)
1 heaped tbsp coarsely crushed peppercorns (buy them or crush your own with a rolling pin)
4 boneless skinless chicken breasts
2 tbsp oil
new potatoes and salad, to serve

Takes 20 minutes • Serves 4

1 Mix together the yogurt and mint with a squeeze of lemon juice; season and set aside. Mix together the salt and peppercorns. Drizzle the chicken breasts with a little lemon juice, then rub the salt and pepper mixture evenly over each breast.
2 Heat the oil in a large frying pan. Add the chicken and cook for 6–7 minutes on each side until the chicken is cooked through and golden.
3 Squeeze over the remaining lemon juice. Serve the chicken with the minty yogurt, new potatoes and a salad.

• Per serving 262 kcalories, protein 37g, carbohydrate 2g, fat 12g, saturated fat 4g, fibre none, added sugar none, salt 0.56g

Cajun-spiced Chicken

This spicy rub makes the skin deliciously crisp. Cajun seasoning is available in most supermarkets.

2 tbsp plain flour
2 tsp Cajun seasoning
½ tsp salt
4 boneless chicken breasts, about 140g/5oz each in weight
2 tbsp olive oil
tzatziki (yogurt and cucumber salad), mixed salad and new potatoes, to serve

Takes 20 minutes • Serves 4

1 Mix together the flour, Cajun seasoning and salt.
2 Rub both sides of the chicken breasts with a tablespoon of the olive oil. Dust each side with the seasoned flour. Heat the remaining oil in a frying pan.
3 Fry the coated chicken for 6–7 minutes on each side until cooked and the skin is golden and crispy. Serve with the tzatziki, salad and new potatoes.

• Per serving 238 kcalories, protein 35g, carbohydrate 8g, fat 8g, saturated fat 1g, fibre none, added sugar none, salt 0.84g

Chicken Skewers with Cucumber Dip

Serve these mildly flavoured tasty skewers with Thai fragrant rice and pak choi stir-fried in a little oil.

500g/1lb 2oz boneless skinless chicken breasts
4 tbsp chopped coriander
1 tsp coarsely ground black pepper
juice of 2 limes
1 tsp light muscovado sugar
2 garlic cloves, crushed
1 tbsp vegetable oil
rice and pak choi, to serve

FOR THE DIP
125ml/4fl oz rice vinegar
2 tbsp sugar
1 red chilli, seeded and finely chopped
1 shallot, thinly sliced
1 cucumber

Takes 30 minutes • Serves 4

1 Cut the chicken into thin slices. Mix the coriander, pepper, lime juice, sugar, garlic and oil. Toss the chicken in this mixture, then thread on to 12 bamboo skewers. (You can make these up to a day ahead and chill until ready to cook.)
2 Make the dip. Heat the vinegar and sugar in a small pan until the sugar has dissolved, then increase the heat and boil for 3 minutes, until slightly syrupy. Remove from the heat and stir in the chilli and shallot. Leave to cool.
3 Quarter a 5cm/2in piece of cucumber, then thinly slice and add to the dip. Cut the rest of the cucumber into thin sticks.
4 Cook the chicken under a preheated grill for 3–4 minutes each side, then serve with the dipping sauce, cucumber sticks, rice and pak choi.

• Per serving 210 kcalories, protein 31g, carbohydrate 12g, fat 4g, saturated fat 1g, fibre 1g, added sugar 9g, salt 0.22g

Thai-spiced Chicken

This recipe is based on a tikka marinade, but instead of curry powder, it uses red Thai curry paste and chopped coriander.

8 skinless chicken thighs
350g/12oz natural low fat yogurt
2–3 tbsp Thai red curry paste
4 tbsp chopped fresh coriander
7.5cm/3in piece cucumber
lime wedges and salad leaves, to serve

Takes 55 minutes, plus marinating • Serves 4 (easily doubled)

1 Preheat the oven to 200°C/Gas 6/fan oven 180°C. Put the chicken in a shallow dish in one layer. Blend a third of the yogurt, the curry paste and three tablespoons of the coriander. Season well with salt and pour over the chicken, turning the pieces until they are evenly coated. Leave for at least 10 minutes, or in the fridge overnight.
2 Lift the chicken on to a rack in a roasting tin and roast for 35–40 minutes, until golden. (To cook the chicken on the barbecue, reduce the cooking time to 25–30 minutes.)
3 Blend together the remaining yogurt and coriander. Finely chop the cucumber and stir into the yogurt mixture. Season. Serve with the chicken and garnish with wedges of lime and salad leaves.

• Per serving 266 kcalories, protein 43g, carbohydrate 8g, fat 7g, saturated fat 2g, fibre trace, added sugar none, salt 0.69g

Chicken and Broccoli Stir Fry

Adding a good splash of soy as the chicken cooks helps it turn an even brown colour, and boosts the flavour.

25g/1oz butter
450g/1lb boneless skinless chicken breasts, cut into thin strips
3 tbsp dark soy sauce
350g/12oz broccoli, broken into small florets
225g/8oz green beans, halved
1 bunch spring onions, cut into long slices
2 tsp cornflour
juice of 2 oranges
25g/1oz fresh basil, roughly torn
rice or noodles, to serve

Takes 30 minutes • Serves 4 (easily halved)

1 Heat the butter in a wok or large frying pan. Add the chicken strips and a splash of soy sauce and cook for 5 minutes, stirring, until the chicken starts to brown.
2 Stir in the broccoli, beans and half the spring onions and cook for 3 minutes until just cooked.
3 Mix the cornflour with the orange juice and remaining soy sauce. Pour into the pan and cook for about 1 minute, stirring, until just thickened. Scatter in the basil and remaining spring onions. Serve with rice or noodles.

• Per serving 273 kcalories, protein 40g, carbohydrate 11g, fat 8g, saturated fat 4g, fibre 4g, added sugar none, salt 2.4g

Glazed Lemon Pepper Chicken

This sticky glaze turns bland chicken breasts into something really special.

4 skinless boneless chicken breasts
4 tbsp clear honey
finely grated zest and juice of 1 lemon
2 garlic cloves, crushed
1 tbsp Dijon mustard
2 tsp freshly ground black pepper
750g/1lb 10oz baby salad potatoes or larger ones, halved
steamed broccoli florets, to serve

Takes 15 minutes, plus marinating • Serves 4

1 Slash each chicken breast two or three times with a sharp knife. In a shallow dish mix the honey, lemon zest and juice, garlic, mustard and black pepper.
2 Add the chicken and turn to coat. Leave to marinate for 30 minutes or preferably overnight.
3 Preheat the oven to 220°C/Gas 7/fan oven 200°C. Arrange the potatoes and chicken in a single layer in a shallow-sided roasting tin and pour any excess marinade on top. Roast for 25–30 minutes or until the potatoes are tender and the chicken is cooked. Serve with broccoli and any pan juices.

• Per serving 339 kcalories, protein 38g, carbohydrate 44g, fat 3g, saturated fat 1g, fibre 2g, added sugar 11g, salt 0.55g

TOP: Thai-spiced Chicken   BOTTOM LEFT: Chicken and Broccoli Stir Fry   BOTTOM RIGHT: Glazed Lemon Pepper Chicken

TOP LEFT: Chicken with Apples and Cider   TOP RIGHT: Spicy Chicken and Apricot Stew   BOTTOM: Spiced Plum Chicken

Chicken with Apples and Cider

This simple recipe uses only six ingredients. It also works well with pork steaks.

2 tbsp oil
4 boneless skinless chicken breasts
1 onion, cut into wedges
2 eating apples, such as Cox's, peeled, cored and each cut into 8 wedges
300ml/½ pint dry cider
150ml/¼ pint chicken stock
rice or mashed potato, to serve

Takes 35 minutes • Serves 4

1 Heat the oil in a large frying pan and fry the chicken breasts for 3–4 minutes on each side until golden. Remove from the pan and set aside. Lower the heat slightly and add the onion. Fry, stirring, for 2–3 minutes until tinged brown. Add the apple and cook over a high heat for 5 minutes until golden.
2 Still over a high heat, pour in the cider and bubble for 2 minutes to reduce slightly. Add the stock, stirring to scrape the bits from the bottom of the pan. Lower the heat.
3 Return the chicken to the pan, cover and simmer for 5 minutes until it is almost cooked. Remove lid and simmer for 3–4 minutes to thicken the sauce a little. Season and serve with rice or mashed potato.

• Per serving 269 kcalories, protein 34g, carbohydrate 12g, fat 7g, saturated fat 1g, fibre 2g, added sugar none, salt 0.36g

Spicy Chicken and Apricot Stew

There's very little shopping required for this simple recipe.

2 tbsp oil
8 boneless skinless chicken thighs, cut into chunks
1 large onion, sliced
2 tsp plain flour
2 tsp ground cumin
2 tsp ground coriander
1 tsp paprika
600ml/1 pint chicken stock
12 ready-to-eat dried apricots
rice and peas, to serve

Takes 1 hour • Serves 4

1 Heat half the oil in a large pan, add the chicken and fry for 7 minutes until golden. Remove and set aside. Add the remaining oil and the onion and cook for 5 minutes until browned. Return the chicken to the pan.
2 Sprinkle in the flour and spices and cook, stirring, for 1–2 minutes. Slowly pour in the stock, stirring, so it sizzles and the sauce turns a rich colour. Simmer for 15 minutes.
3 Stir in the apricots and simmer for a further 15 minutes. Taste and season. Serve with rice and peas.

• Per serving 349 kcalories, protein 41g, carbohydrate 20g, fat 12g, saturated fat 3g, fibre 3g, added sugar none, salt 1.59g

Spiced Plum Chicken

Mi-cuit plums are half cooked, so they are the softest juiciest plums to use in this recipe.

2 tsp olive oil
1 onion, chopped
1 garlic clove, finely chopped
1 tsp turmeric
½ tsp each ground cinnamon, coriander and ginger
3 boneless skinless chicken breasts, sliced into strips
284ml carton chicken stock
2 tbsp tomato purée
200g box mi-cuit plums, or ready-to-eat prunes, stoned and halved
250g/9oz couscous
handful of chopped fresh coriander, to serve

Takes 45 minutes • Serves 4

1 Heat the oil in a deep-sided frying pan. Add the onion and cook for 5 minutes until just golden. Add the garlic and cook for a minute only, then add the spices and stir for a minute. Add the chicken strips and cook for 4–5 minutes until browned.
2 Add the stock and purée, and season. Cook for 15–20 minutes, adding the plums for the last 5 minutes.
3 Meanwhile, cook the couscous according to the packet instructions; keep warm. Divide the chicken and plums between plates, sprinkle with coriander and serve with the couscous.

• Per serving 360 kcalories, protein 32g, carbohydrate 52g, fat 4g, saturated fat 1g, fibre 3g, added sugar 15g, salt 0.5g

Barbecue Turkey Strips

This hot turkey salad is easily doubled for a crowd. Try it in sandwiches too.

2 tbsp dark muscovado sugar
4 tbsp clear honey
4 tbsp soy sauce
450g/1lb turkey strips
2 tbsp each olive oil and lemon juice
2 tsp caster sugar
1 cos lettuce, torn into pieces
2 large carrots, cut into sticks
100g/4oz fresh beansprouts

Takes 35 minutes, plus marinating • Serves 4

1 Mix the muscovado sugar, half the honey and half the soy sauce in a shallow dish. Add the turkey strips and stir to coat. Cover and leave to marinate for 30 minutes.
2 Thread the turkey on to eight skewers (soak wooden ones for 20 minutes before using to prevent them burning) and cook under a preheated grill or barbecue for 6 minutes each side.
3 Whisk the remaining honey and soy sauce with the olive oil, lemon juice and caster sugar. Season and toss with the lettuce and vegetables. Pile on to four plates and put the turkey on top. Serve immediately.

• Per serving 318 kcalories, protein 29g, carbohydrate 37g, fat 7g, saturated fat 1g, fibre 2g, added sugar 29g, salt 2.91g

Sweet and Sour Turkey

Keep the heat high while cooking the turkey so it sizzles to a good brown colour – this dramatically enhances flavour.

1 tbsp vegetable oil
300g/10oz turkey strips, cut into smaller strips if necessary
2 × 200g pack mixed baby carrots, sweetcorn and mangetout
1 red pepper, seeded and sliced
225g/8oz beansprouts
finely grated zest and juice of 1 small orange
3 tbsp soy sauce
1 tsp clear honey
2 tsp cornflour
2 garlic cloves, finely chopped
cooked rice or noodles, to serve

Takes 20–25 minutes • Serves 4

1 Heat the oil in a wok or frying pan and fry the turkey for 3 minutes, stirring, until browned.
2 Add the baby vegetables and pepper and fry for 4 minutes. Stir in the beansprouts.
3 Mix the orange zest and juice, soy sauce, honey, cornflour and garlic together. Pour over the stir fry and let it bubble, stirring. When the sauce has thickened, serve with rice or noodles.

• Per serving 411 kcalories, protein 24g, carbohydrate 68g, fat 7g, saturated fat 1g, fibre 4g, added sugar 3g, salt 1.87g

Turkey Bolognese

Substitute turkey mince for lamb or beef to make a low-fat pasta sauce.

2 tbsp vegetable oil
1 large onion, chopped
2 garlic cloves, finely chopped
500g/1lb 2oz turkey mince
400g can chopped tomatoes
2 tbsp tomato purée
300ml/½ pint chicken or beef stock
350g/12oz spaghetti
1 large courgette, finely chopped
6 tomatoes, seeded and chopped
small handful of chopped parsley, to serve

Takes 40 minutes • Serves 4

1 Heat the oil in a large saucepan and fry the onion and garlic for 4–5 minutes over a low heat until softened. Stir in the turkey mince and cook for 5 minutes, stirring frequently. Stir in the chopped tomatoes, tomato purée and stock. Bring to the boil then simmer, uncovered, for 10 minutes.
2 Meanwhile, cook the spaghetti according to the packet instructions. Stir the courgette and fresh tomatoes into the sauce and simmer for 5–6 minutes. Season.
3 Drain the pasta and divide between four plates. Spoon the sauce over and serve, scattered with parsley.

• Per serving 546 kcalories, protein 43g, carbohydrate 76g, fat 10g, saturated fat 2g, fibre 6g, added sugar none, salt 0.75g

TOP LEFT: Barbecue Turkey Strips   TOP RIGHT: Sweet and Sour Turkey   BOTTOM: Turkey Bolognese

TOP: Lamb and Lentil Chilli   BOTTOM LEFT: Barbecued Balsamic Beef   BOTTOM RIGHT: Pork with Pine Kernels

Lamb and Lentil Chilli

A mildly spicy chilli with red lentils replacing the more usual kidney beans.

1 large onion, finely chopped
2 garlic cloves, crushed
200g can chopped tomatoes
1 small aubergine, about 300g/10oz,
    cut into 1cm/½in dice
140g/5oz red split lentils
300g/10oz lean diced lamb
1 tsp turmeric
2 tsp mild chilli powder
2 tsp ground cumin
1 tsp ground coriander
1 tsp light muscovado sugar
1 tbsp lemon juice
small bunch coriander or mint, roughly
    chopped
250ml/9fl oz very low-fat yogurt
basmati rice, to serve

Takes 1¼ hours • Serves 4

1 Put the onion and garlic into a large saucepan with 100ml/3½fl oz water. Bring to the boil and cook for 5 minutes, until softened and nearly all the water has been absorbed.
2 Add the tomatoes, aubergine, lentils, lamb, turmeric, chilli powder, cumin, coriander, sugar, lemon juice and 450ml/16fl oz water. Bring to the boil, cover and simmer for 1 hour, until tender.
3 Season well and stir in most of the coriander or mint and half the yogurt. Immediately remove from the heat. Serve with basmati rice and the remaining yogurt spooned on top. Sprinkle with the remaining coriander or mint.

• Per serving 305 kcalories, protein 28g, carbohydrate 32g, fat 8g, saturated fat 4g, fibre 4g, added sugar none, salt 0.4g

Barbecued Balsamic Beef

Skirt steak is mainly used for braising, but cooked this way you'll get succulent meat at a low price.

600g/1lb 5oz thick piece
    beef skirt or rump steak
2 shallots, very finely chopped
2 tbsp balsamic vinegar,
    plus a little extra
500g/1lb 2oz new potatoes
250g bag washed spinach
2 tbsp olive oil, plus a litte extra

Takes 30 minutes, plus marinating • Serves 4

1 Put the beef in a wide shallow dish and rub it all over with the shallots and balsamic vinegar. Season and leave to marinate for 20 minutes.
2 Slice the potatoes and cook in salted boiling water for 12–15 minutes, until just tender. Add the spinach and cover the pan for a couple of minutes to wilt it. Drain well, toss in two tablespoons of olive oil, and season. Keep warm.
3 Meanwhile, grill or barbecue the beef for 6–8 minutes on each side for skirt or 3–4 minutes each side for rump, depending on thickness. Remove and cover with foil for 5 minutes. Uncover and slice thinly across the grain. Serve piled on top of the potatoes and spinach, sprinkled with a little extra vinegar and olive oil.

• Per serving 324 kcalories, protein 37g, carbohydrate 23g, fat 10g, saturated fat 3g, fibre 2.6g, added sugar none, salt 0.49g

Pork with Pine Kernels

This is a very adaptable recipe, impressive enough to cook if you have friends visiting and you are short of time.

500g/1lb 2oz pork fillet
plain flour, for coating
good handful flatleaf parsley
2 tbsp olive oil
25g/1oz pine kernels
grated zest of ½ a lemon and juice of a
    whole lemon
1 tbsp clear honey
pappardelle or tagliatelle and salad, to serve

Takes 25 minutes • Serves 4

1 Cut the pork into 2cm/¾in thick slices. Toss in seasoned flour to coat very lightly and shake off excess. Coarsely chop the parsley. Heat one tablespoon of olive oil in a large frying pan, add the pork in a single layer and fry for 3 minutes on each side, or until browned. Remove and keep warm.
2 Add another tablespoon of oil to the pan, add the pine kernels and fry until lightly browned, then stir in the lemon zest, juice and honey. Bubble briefly, stirring to make a sauce.
3 Return the pork to the pan and scatter with parsley. Cook for 3 minutes, turning the pork, until thoroughly reheated. Serve with pappardelle or tagliatelle and salad.

• Per serving 212 kcalories, protein 28g, carbohydrate 4g, fat 9g, saturated fat 2g, fibre none, added sugar 4g, salt 0.2g

Springtime Lamb Stew

An easy one-pot meal. Be sure to choose lean lamb, trimmed of fat.

1 tbsp olive oil
12 shallots, peeled
350g/12oz trimmed diced lamb from the chump or loin fillet
350g/12oz new potatoes, scrubbed and cut into chunks
12 baby carrots, trimmed and peeled
150ml/¼ pint white wine
250ml/9fl oz vegetable stock
3 bay leaves
200g can chopped tomatoes
100g/4oz frozen peas
1 tbsp fresh chopped parsley
crusty bread, to serve

Takes 1 hour 10 minutes • Serves 4

1 Heat the oil in a large saucepan and add the shallots and lamb. Fry over a medium heat until they are starting to brown, about 8–10 minutes.
2 Add the potatoes, carrots, white wine, stock, bay leaves and tomatoes to the pan. Season and bring to the boil. Cover the pan and leave the stew to simmer gently over a medium heat for 25–30 minutes until the vegetables and lamb are tender.
3 Stir in the peas and cook for another 2–3 minutes until cooked. Scatter in the parsley, adjust the seasoning and serve with crusty bread.

• Per serving 291 kcalories, protein 23g, carbohydrate 21g, fat 11g, saturated fat 4g, fibre 6g, added sugar none, salt 0.58g

Steak with Mustard Vegetables

This recipe works really well with lean pork escalopes too.

450g/1lb new potatoes, halved lengthways
350g/12oz broccoli florets
finely grated zest and juice of 2 oranges
2 garlic cloves, crushed
1 tbsp wholegrain mustard
2 tbsp clear honey
2 small orange peppers, cored, seeded and cut into chunks
1 tsp vegetable oil
4 lean thin frying steaks

Takes 25 minutes • Serves 4

1 Cook the potatoes in lightly salted boiling water for 5–6 minutes. Add the broccoli, return to the boil, cook for 2–3 minutes or until tender. Drain well and set aside to keep warm.
2 Add the orange zest and juice to the pan, with the garlic, mustard and honey. Bring to the boil. Add the peppers. Cook on a high heat until the juices start to thicken, about 1–2 minutes. Add the vegetables and keep warm.
3 Heat a griddle pan. Brush the steaks with the oil and season on both sides. Put in the pan and press with a fish slice. Cook for 2 minutes, turn over and cook for a further 1–2 minutes. Serve with the vegetables and their pan juices.

• Per serving 317 kcalories, protein 34g, carbohydrate 31g, fat 7g, saturated fat 2g, fibre 5g, added sugar 6g, salt 0.4g

Spicy Pork and Aubergine

Pork fillet is low in fat and it cooks quickly. Here it's used in a mild curry.

1½ tbsp olive oil
2 onions, sliced
1 small aubergine (about 250g/9oz), trimmed and diced
500g/1lb 2oz lean pork, fillet, trimmed of any fat and sliced
2 sweet red peppers, seeded and cut into chunky strips
2–3 tbsp mild curry powder
400g can plum tomatoes
cooked basmati rice, to serve

Takes 35 minutes • Serves 4

1 Heat the oil in a large non-stick frying pan with a lid. Tip in the onions and aubergine and fry for 8 minutes, stirring frequently, until soft and golden brown.
2 Tip in the pork and fry for 5 minutes, stirring occasionally, until it starts to brown. Mix in the pepper strips and stir fry for about 3 minutes until soft.
3 Sprinkle in the curry powder. Stir fry for a minute, then pour in the tomatoes and 150ml/¼ pint water. Stir vigorously, cover the pan and leave the curry to simmer for 5 minutes until the tomatoes break down to form a thick sauce (you can add a drop more water if the mixture gets too thick). Season and serve with basmati rice.

• Per serving 293 kcalories, protein 31g, carbohydrate 16g, fat 11g, saturated fat 2g, fibre 6g, added sugar none, salt 0.4g

TOP: Springtime Lamb Stew   BOTTOM LEFT: Steak with Mustard Vegetables   BOTTOM RIGHT: Spicy Pork and Aubergine

TOP LEFT: Sticky Glazed Gammon   TOP RIGHT: Toad-in-the-hole   BOTTOM: Pork Skewers with Red Cabbage

Sticky Glazed Gammon

This zingy way with gammon is surprisingly healthy. Lean steaks are served with nutritious bulghar wheat and green vegetables.

85g/3oz bulghar wheat
85g/3oz fresh or frozen peas or petits pois
    (225g/8oz in the pod)
1 large leek, thinly sliced
1 orange, halved
1 tbsp Worcestershire sauce
1 tbsp clear honey
1 tsp Dijon mustard
2 lean gammon steaks
1 tbsp mint sauce

Takes 30 minutes • Serves 2

1 Preheat the grill to high. Tip the bulghar and 450ml/16fl oz cold water into a large saucepan, bring to the boil and simmer for 8 minutes. Toss in the peas and leek and bubble for 3–5 minutes more, until soft.
2 While the bulghar bubbles, make the glaze. Squeeze the juice of one orange half into a pan, stir in the Worcestershire sauce, honey and mustard and simmer for 2 minutes until sticky. Season the steaks with pepper only, put them on the grill rack and grill for 5–6 minutes each side, brushing frequently with the glaze.
3 When the bulghar is cooked, drain, season well and fork in the mint sauce. Cut each steak in half and serve on the bulghar, with the remaining orange half cut into segments.

• Per serving 465 kcalories, protein 45g, carbohydrate 55g, fat 8g, saturated fat 2g, fibre 5g, added sugar 7g, salt 6.89g

Toad-in-the-hole

A low-fat version of an old favourite. Be sure to choose the sausages carefully.

1 red onion, cut into wedges, layers
    separated
8 thick low-fat pork sausages
1 tsp olive oil

FOR THE BATTER
100g/4oz plain flour
1 medium egg
300ml/½ pint skimmed milk
2 tsp wholegrain mustard
1 tsp fresh thyme leaves
steamed carrots and cabbage, to serve

Takes 1 hour 20 minutes • Serves 4

1 Preheat the oven to 200°C/Gas 6/fan oven 180°C. Tip the onions into a small shallow non-stick tin (about 23 x 30cm/9 x 12in). Arrange the sausages on top of the onions, then add the oil and roast for 20 minutes.
2 While they are roasting, make the batter. Sift the flour into a bowl, drop the egg in the centre and beat in the milk a little at a time until it makes a smooth batter. Stir in the mustard and thyme and season.
3 Pour the batter quickly into the tin and return to the oven for 40 minutes until the batter is risen and golden. Serve with steamed carrots and cabbage.

• Per serving 293 kcalories, protein 23g, carbohydrate 36g, fat 7g, saturated fat 2g, fibre 1g, added sugar none, salt 2.36g

Pork Skewers with Red Cabbage

A colourful combination of pork, fruit and mellow spices.

FOR THE CABBAGE
450g/1lb red cabbage, shredded
150ml/¼ pint ginger wine, wine or stock
2 tbsp unrefined soft dark brown sugar
2 tbsp white wine vinegar
5cm/2in fresh root ginger, finely chopped

FOR THE PORK
400g/14oz lean pork tenderloin, cut into
    24 pieces
2 dessert apples, cut into 8 wedges
2 tbsp clear honey
2 tbsp wholegrain mustard
6 tbsp half-fat crème fraîche
sliced boiled potatoes, to serve

Takes 1 hour 20 minutes • Serves 4

1 Put the cabbage in a large pan with the other cabbage ingredients. Toss over a high heat for 5 minutes. Simmer, covered, on a low heat for 1 hour, stirring occasionally.
2 Meanwhile, thread alternately 3 pieces of pork and 2 apple wedges on eight skewers. Season. Gently heat the honey and mustard in a small pan. About 15 minutes before the cabbage is cooked, heat the grill. Cover the grill pan with foil. Arrange the skewers on top. Brush with the mustard mix and grill for 5–6 minutes. Turn, brush again and grill for 5–6 minutes until cooked.
3 Add crème fraîche to the glaze; heat gently. Arrange the cabbage on plates, with skewers on top and pan juices spooned over. Drizzle with the glaze and serve with sliced potatoes.

• Per serving 352 kcalories, protein 25g, carbohydrate 33g, fat 10g, saturated fat 10g, fibre 4g, added sugar 16g, salt 0.59g

Herby Cod Grills

Choose quite thin fish fillets so they cook quickly without the pesto burning.

4 tbsp natural low -at yogurt
2 tbsp sun-dried tomato pesto
2 tbsp chopped fresh parsley or dill
2 cod or haddock fillets (about
    175g/6oz each), skinned
salad and crusty bread, to serve

Takes 15 minutes • Serves 2 (easily doubled)

1 Preheat the grill. Mix the yogurt, pesto and one tablespoon of the parsley or dill. Season and pour over the fish fillets in a shallow ovenproof or microwaveable dish, covering them completely.
2 Grill for 4–5 minutes without turning until the fish fillets are cooked through to the middle. Or cover the dish with cling film and microwave on High for 3 minutes.
3 Sprinkle the remaining parsley or dill over the dish and serve with salad and crusty bread.

• Per serving 247 kcalories, protein 36g, carbohydrate 3g, fat 10g, saturated fat 4g, fibre 3g, added sugar none, salt 0.53g

Cod with Lemon and Parsley

Shallow-fried fish needs a light dusting of flour to protect it from the fierce heat, and it makes a tasty, golden crust.

2 cod fillets, about 175g/6oz each
seasoned flour
1 lemon
25g/1oz butter
1 heaped tbsp chopped parsley
new potatoes and greens or runner beans,
    to serve

Takes 20 minutes • Serves 2

1 Coat the cod fillets with the flour, dusting off any excess. Squeeze the juice from the lemon.
2 Heat half the butter in a frying pan. When it is bubbling, add the fish and cook over a fairly high heat until the underside is done, about 4–5 minutes. Using a fish slice, turn the fillets carefully and brown the other side. When the fish is just cooked (the flesh will start to flake and become opaque), add the remaining butter to the pan. When it is bubbling, stir in the lemon juice and season.
3 Bubble the sauce up until it is slightly thickened, then stir in the parsley. Serve with new potatoes and greens or runner beans.

• Per serving 277 kcalories, protein 34g, carbohydrate 9g, fat 12g, saturated fat 7g, fibre 1g, added sugar none, salt 0.77g

Mediterranean Cod

Mixed pepper antipasto is available in jars in most supermarkets and delicatessens.

750g/1lb 10oz floury potatoes
2 tbsp olive oil
4 cod fillets, 140g/5oz each in weight
225g/8oz chestnut mushrooms
8 tbsp mixed pepper antipasto
2 tbsp freshly grated parmesan

Takes 1 hour • Serves 4

1 Preheat the oven to 200°C/Gas 6/fan oven 180°C. Cut the potatoes into wedges and put in a roasting tin. Drizzle over the olive oil and stir well. Season. Cook in the middle of the oven for 45–50 minutes, stirring halfway through, until the potatoes are golden, crisp and cooked through.
2 Meanwhile, put the cod fillets in an ovenproof dish in a single layer. Season well. Slice the mushrooms and scatter over the fish.
3 Spread the mixed pepper antipasto over the top of the mushrooms. Put the fish in the oven on the shelf above the potato wedges 10 minutes before the wedges have finished cooking. Sprinkle the fish with the grated parmesan and serve hot with the potato wedges.

• Per serving 359 kcalories, protein 34g, carbohydrate 34g, fat 11g, saturated fat 2g, fibre 4g, added sugar none, salt 0.43g

TOP LEFT: Herby Cod Grills   TOP RIGHT: Cod with Lemon and Parsley   BOTTOM: Mediterranean Cod

TOP: Lemon-fried Mackerel   BOTTOM LEFT: Smoked Haddock Bake   BOTTOM RIGHT: Soy Salmon with Sesame Stir Fry

Lemon-fried Mackerel

This is a really simple dish that's delicious served with fried rice or noodles.

2 lemons
4 × 300g/10oz small mackerel or
   4 × 150g/5oz fish fillets
1 tbsp vegetable oil
3 tbsp soy sauce
1 sugar cube, or 1 tsp sugar
stir-fried rice or noodles, to serve

Takes 25 minutes • Serves 4

1 Thinly slice one of the lemons. Season the fish then place the lemon slices down the length of each. Tie in place with string.
2 Heat the oil in a large frying pan and cook the fish, lemon-side down, for 3–4 minutes until well browned. Turn and cook the other side for 3 minutes.
3 Add the soy sauce, four tablespoons of water and the sugar to the pan. Squeeze in the juice of the remaining lemon and simmer for 2–3 minutes until the fish is cooked through. Serve on a bed of rice or noodles, spooning over the pan juices.

• Per serving 163 kcalories, protein 28g, carbohydrate 4g, fat 4g, saturated fat 1g, fibre none, added sugar 1.5g, salt 2.27g

Smoked Haddock Bake

Use your microwave to speed up the cooking of the baked pototoes.

2 large baking potatoes
225g bag fresh baby leaf spinach
4 × 175g/6oz skinless undyed smoked
   haddock fillets
4 tbsp half-fat crème fraîche
50g/2oz extra mature cheddar, grated

Takes 45 minutes • Serves 4

1 Pierce the potatoes all over with a sharp knife. Microwave on High for 16 minutes. Leave to stand for 3 minutes, then slice thickly.
2 Scatter the fresh spinach into the base of a large microwaveable dish and arrange the potatoes on top. Place the fish on the top. Drop on spoonfuls of crème fraîche and sprinkle with cheese.
3 Cover with cling film and pierce several times. Microwave on High for 8 minutes. Stand for 2 minutes. Remove the cling film. Grill under a preheated grill for 3 minutes.

• Per serving 334 kcalories, protein 41g, carbohydrate 23g, fat 9g, saturated fat 9g, fibre 3g, added sugar none, salt 3.86g

Soy Salmon with Sesame Stir Fry

Salmon takes on the strong flavours of Chinese cooking very well.

4 salmon fillets, about 100g/4oz each
3 tbsp soy sauce
2 tbsp clear honey
finely grated zest and juice of 1 lemon
2 garlic cloves, thinly sliced
2.5cm/1in piece fresh root ginger,
   finely grated
8 spring onions, finely shredded

FOR THE STIR FRY
1 tsp sesame oil
100g/4oz mangetout
2 medium carrots, cut into matchsticks
100g/4oz baby corn, halved
2 courgettes, cut into matchsticks

Takes 30 minutes, plus marinating • Serves 4

1 Put the salmon in a shallow dish. Heat the soy sauce, honey, lemon zest and juice, garlic and ginger in a small saucepan with one tablespoon of water for 4 minutes. Pour over the salmon and scatter with most of the spring onions. Leave to marinate in the fridge for at least 30 minutes.
2 Heat the grill or a griddle pan. Remove the salmon, reserving the marinade. Grill or griddle the salmon for 8 minutes, turning once, until tender and golden.
3 Meanwhile, heat a wok or large frying pan to really hot and add the sesame oil. Add the mangetout, carrots and corn, and stir fry for 2 minutes. Add the courgettes and stir fry for 2 minutes. Add the reserved marinade and cook for 2–3 minutes. Serve with the salmon and remaining spring onion.

• Per serving 280 kcalories, protein 23g, carbohydrate 18g, fat 12g, saturated fat 2.5g, fibre 3g, added sugar none, salt 2.6g

Prawns with Tomato and Feta

Cheap cans of tomatoes are often a false economy. Better to go for a good-quality can and keep the fresh flavour.

3 tbsp olive oil
2 onions, finely chopped
2 × 400g cans chopped tomatoes in rich tomato sauce
pinch of sugar
350g/12oz large peeled prawns, thawed if frozen
100g/4oz feta
3 tbsp chopped fresh parsley
rice or pasta, to serve

Takes 20 minutes • Serves 4

1 Heat three tablespoons of olive oil in a frying pan, add the onions and fry gently for about 7 minutes, until softened and light brown. Add the tomatoes and a pinch of sugar and simmer for 5 minutes.
2 Throw in the prawns, season and cook gently for 5 minutes until the prawns are thoroughly hot.
3 Serve spooned over rice or pasta. Crumble over the feta and sprinkle with chopped parsley.

• Per serving 186 kcalories, protein 22g, carbohydrate 11g, fat 6g, saturated fat 3g, fibre 3g, added sugar trace, salt 1.54g

Quick Seafood Paella

With a bag of frozen seafood mixture in the freezer you can make a speedy version of a classic dish.

1 tbsp sunflower oil
1 onion, finely chopped
1 red pepper, seeded and sliced
2 garlic cloves, finely chopped
230g can chopped tomatoes
1 tsp turmeric
300g/10oz long grain rice
1.3 litres/2¼ pints vegetable stock
450g bag frozen mixed seafood (prawns, mussels and squid rings), thawed
175g/6oz green beans, halved
handful of chopped fresh parsley
1 lemon, cut into wedges

Takes 30 minutes • Serves 4

1 Heat the oil in a large frying pan and cook the onion and pepper for 5 minutes until softened but not brown. Stir in the garlic, tomatoes and turmeric and cook for 1 minute more, stirring occasionally.
2 Tip in the rice and cook for 1 minute, stirring to coat the grains. Pour in the stock, stir well and bring to the boil, then simmer uncovered for 8 minutes, stirring occasionally, until the rice is almost cooked and most of the stock has been absorbed.
3 Add the seafood and beans and cook for 3–4 minutes more. Stir in the parsley and season. Serve straight from the pan with lemon wedges.

• Per serving 463 kcalories, protein 32g, carbohydrate 75g, fat 6g, saturated fat 1g, fibre 3g, added sugar none, salt 1.91g

Smoked Haddock Fishcakes

Cooked peas add extra colour and flavour to these simple fishcakes.

450g/1lb peeled potatoes, cut into chunks
2 eggs
225g/8oz skinless smoked haddock
4 tbsp milk
25g/1oz butter
175g/6oz frozen peas, cooked
100g/4oz white breadcrumbs
2 tbsp vegetable oil
salad, to serve

Takes 50 minutes • Serves 2

1 Preheat the oven to 200°C/Gas 6/fan oven 180°C. Boil the potatoes and eggs in salted water for 10–12 minutes. Meanwhile put the fish, milk and butter in a pan, season, cover and simmer for 4–5 minutes. Strain and reserve the liquor. Flake the fish.
2 Drain the potatoes and eggs. Shell the eggs and mash them with the potatoes. Add the liquor, season and stir in the fish and peas. Shape into six cakes. Press into the breadcrumbs, coating evenly.
3 Pour the oil into a roasting tin. Heat for 5 minutes in the oven. Add the fishcakes, coat in the oil and cook for 25–30 minutes, turning halfway through. Serve with salad.

• Per serving 252 kcalories, protein 15g, carbohydrate 27g, fat 10g, saturated fat 3g, fibre 3g, added sugar none, salt 1.22g

TOP: Prawns with Tomato and Feta   BOTTOM LEFT: Quick Seafood Paella   BOTTOM RIGHT: Smoked Haddock Fishcakes

TOP LEFT: Vegetable and Bean Bake   TOP RIGHT: Sweet Potato and Cauliflower Curry   BOTTOM: Stuffed Peppers

Vegetable and Bean Bake

Potatoes and canned beans make this simple supper a filling meal. Serve with a leafy green salad.

1 tbsp sunflower oil
2 large onions, thinly sliced
2 garlic cloves, crushed
1 tsp paprika
2 tbsp tomato purée
410g can cannellini beans, drained
    and rinsed
2 tbsp fresh chopped parsley
2 large baking potatoes, peeled and sliced
1 large courgette, sliced diagonally
4 ripe tomatoes, sliced
150ml/¼ pint vegetable stock
25g/1oz grated parmesan

Takes 1½ hours • Serves 4

1 Preheat the oven to 220°C/Gas 7/fan oven 200°C. Heat the oil in a pan. Gently fry the onion and garlic for 10 minutes. Stir occasionally. Add the paprika and cook for 1 minute. Add the tomato purée, beans and parsley. Tip into a 3 litre/5¼ pint shallow ovenproof dish.
2 Parboil the potatoes in lightly salted boiling water for 5 minutes. Drain and spread over the beans. Top with the courgettes and tomatoes.
3 Pour over the stock. Bake for 35 minutes, until tender. Sprinkle with cheese and cook for 10 minutes until golden.

• Per serving 304 kcalories, protein 14g, carbohydrate 50g, fat 7g, saturated fat 2g, fibre 8g, added sugar none, salt 0.57g

Sweet Potato and Cauliflower Curry

Choose the brown-skinned sweet potatoes with the attractive orange flesh.

1 tbsp vegetable oil
1 onion, chopped
1 garlic clove, crushed
2 tbsp medium curry powder
4 tsp plain flour
350g/12oz orange-fleshed sweet potatoes
    (brown-skinned), cut into cubes
350g/12oz cauliflower florets
850ml/1½ pints vegetable stock
100g/4oz green beans, trimmed
1 tsp garam masala
naan bread and lime wedges, to serve

Takes 35 minutes • Serves 4

1 Heat the oil in a large pan and fry the onion for 2–3 minutes, stirring occasionally, until softened. Stir in the garlic, curry powder and flour and cook for a further minute.
2 Add the sweet potatoes to the pan along with the cauliflower and stock. Bring to the boil and simmer for 10–15 minutes until the potatoes are almost tender.
3 Stir in the green beans and garam masala and cook for 3 minutes. Serve with warm naan bread and wedges of lime.

• Per serving 257 kcalories, protein 9g, carbohydrate 44g, fat 6g, saturated fat 1g, fibre 6g, added sugar none, salt 0.81g

Stuffed Peppers

This is ideal as a starter but could also be served as an energy-rich snack, just as delicious served hot or cold.

3 small baking potatoes, peeled and cut
    into 5mm slices
½ × 425g can pimientos, drained
1 red chilli, seeded and finely chopped
25g/1oz pine nuts, toasted
2 garlic cloves, crushed
4 tbsp sun-dried tomato paste
100g/4oz brown breadcrumbs
2 large red and 2 large yellow peppers,
    seeded and halved
handful fresh basil leaves
2 tbsp rosemary-infused olive oil
crusty bread, to serve

Takes 1 hour • Serves 8 (as a starter)

1 Preheat the oven to 200°C/Gas 6/fan oven 180°C. Cook the potatoes in lightly salted boiling water for 8 minutes. Drain and set aside. Place the pimientos, chilli, pine nuts, garlic, sun-dried tomato paste and breadcrumbs in a food processor and process to form a coarse paste.
2 Place the pepper halves, skin-side down, in a large roasting tin. Sandwich the potato slices with the pimiento paste and basil leaves and arrange, on their sides, in the pepper halves. Drizzle over the rosemary-infused oil and season.
3 Bake for 30 minutes until the peppers are cooked and the potatoes are tender. Serve immediately with crusty bread.

• Per serving 173 kcalories, protein 4g, carbohydrate 24g, fat 7g, saturated fat 1g, fibre 3g, added sugar none, salt 0.32g

Gnocchi Gratin

You know when gnocchi is cooked as it rises to the surface. Vary the recipe by adding peas, beans – or anything that takes your fancy.

1 red pepper, seeded and quartered
400g pack fresh potato gnocchi
125g pack very low-fat garlic and herb
   soft cheese
75ml/2½fl oz dry white wine
large pinch of freshly grated nutmeg
85g/3oz baby spinach leaves
8 large basil leaves, roughly torn
garlic bread, to serve

Takes 20 minutes • Serves 2

1 Preheat the grill to hot. Grill the pepper quarters, skin-side up, for 7–8 minutes until charred. Place in a plastic bag, seal and leave to stand for 5 minutes to loosen the skins.
2 Bring a large pan of water to the boil and cook the gnocchi according to the packet instructions, until they rise to the surface. Meanwhile, in a separate pan warm the soft cheese, wine and nutmeg until melted and hot. Season to taste.
3 Remove the skin from the peppers and cut the flesh into strips. Toss with the gnocchi, spinach and basil, then pour the melted cheese sauce over. Serve immediately with garlic bread.

• Per serving 470 kcalories, protein 19g, carbohydrate 81g, fat 7g, saturated fat 4g, fibre 6g, added sugar none, salt 0.97g

Squash with Tomatoes and Chickpeas

A filling meal using the bottle-shaped squash. Or serve the sauce with jacket potatoes.

2 medium-sized butternut squashes, about
   700g/1lb 9oz each, halved lengthways
   and seeded
1 tbsp olive oil
1 tbsp balsamic vinegar
1 onion, roughly chopped
4 garlic cloves, peeled and very thinly sliced
400g can plum tomatoes
410g can chickpeas, drained and rinsed
300ml/½ pint vegetable stock
2 tbsp tomato purée
1 tsp caster sugar
large handful of baby spinach leaves

Takes 1 hour 20 minutes • Serves 4

1 Preheat the oven to 200°C/Gas 6/fan oven 180°C. Arrange the squash cut-side up in a large non-stick roasting tin. Brush with the oil and season generously. Drizzle with the balsamic vinegar and roast for 45 minutes until just tender.
2 Meanwhile, put the onion, garlic, tomatoes, chickpeas, stock, tomato purée and caster sugar into a large saucepan. Bring to the boil, break up the tomatoes slightly and simmer for 25 minutes, stirring occasionally until thickened.
3 Season to taste. Stir in the spinach and cook until just wilted. Serve the butternut squash with the sauce spooned over.

• Per serving 239 kcalories, protein 10g, carbohydrate 41g, fat 5g, saturated fat none, fibre 8g, added sugar 2g, salt 0.78g

Vegetable Paella

A veggie version of the traditional Spanish rice dish. Smoked paprika adds extra flavour, but ordinary paprika works too.

2 tbsp olive oil
1 onion, finely chopped
1 garlic clove, crushed
1 red pepper, seeded and finely chopped
1 green pepper, seeded and finely chopped
100g/4oz chestnut mushrooms, sliced
225g/8oz long grain rice
850ml/1½ pints vegetable stock
½ tsp smoked or ordinary paprika
large pinch of saffron strands
85g/3oz frozen peas
2 tomatoes, seeded and finely diced
2 tbsp chopped flatleaf parsley
green salad, to serve

Takes 35 minutes • Serves 4

1 Heat the oil in a frying pan and fry the onion for 2–3 minutes, stirring occasionally, until softened. Add the garlic, red and green peppers and mushrooms and cook for a further 2–3 minutes, stirring occasionally.
2 Stir in the rice and fry for 1 minute. Stir in the stock, paprika and saffron. Bring to the boil and simmer for 10–12 minutes, stirring occasionally, until the rice is just tender (top up with more water if necessary). Stir in the peas and cook for a further 2–3 minutes. Season to taste.
3 Spoon the paella on to serving plates and sprinkle over the tomato and parsley. Serve immediately with a green salad.

• Per serving 324 kcalories, protein 7g, carbohydrate 58g, fat 9g, saturated fat 1g, fibre 4g, added sugar none, salt 0.06g

TOP LEFT: Gnocchi Gratin   TOP RIGHT: Squash with Tomatoes and Chickpeas   BOTTOM: Vegetable Paella

TOP: Chargrilled Peppers with Couscous   BOTTOM LEFT: Thai Red Vegetable Curry   BOTTOM RIGHT: Beetroot and Lamb's Lettuce Risotto

Chargrilled Peppers with Couscous

A light and colourful warm salad, making use of couscous instead of rice or pasta.

50g/2oz couscous
2 tbsp sultanas or raisins
1 red pepper and ½ yellow or orange pepper, seeded and quartered
½ lemon, cut into wedges
1 tsp olive oil
2 tbsp chopped fresh parsley or coriander

Takes 10 minutes • Serves 1

1 Put the couscous and sultanas or raisins in a bowl, pour over 150ml/¼ pint boiling water and leave for 5 minutes until the water is absorbed. Preheat the grill to high.
2 Put the peppers, skin-side up, on the grill rack with the lemon wedges, brush with oil and grill for 5 minutes until the pepper skins are blackened (leave the skins on for a smoky flavour). Stir the herbs into the couscous and season.
3 Spoon the couscous on to a plate, top with the peppers and squeeze the juice from the grilled lemon over. Serve immediately.

• Per serving 326 kcalories, protein 7g, carbohydrate 63g, fat 7g, saturated fat 1g, fibre 5g, added sugar none, salt 0.05g

Thai Red Vegetable Curry

Thai curries are often thinner and hotter than Indian curries, with fantastic vivid flavours.

1 tbsp vegetable oil
1 large onion, diced
500g/1lb 2oz sweet potatoes, cubed
300g/10oz squash or marrow, cubed
250g/9oz flat green beans
2 tomatoes, diced
2 × 400g cans coconut milk
2 tsp Thai red curry paste
juice of 1 large lime
2 tbsp soy sauce
handful fresh basil or coriander
boiled rice, to serve

Takes 35 minutes • Serves 6

1 Heat the oil in a large pan and cook the onion, sweet potato and squash for 5 minutes until beginning to soften. Cut the beans into 5cm/2in lengths, then add these and the tomatoes and cook for a further 2–3 minutes until the tomatoes begin to soften.
2 Add the coconut milk and curry paste and bring to the boil. Cook the mixture for 10–12 minutes until the vegetables are tender.
3 Add the lime juice, soy sauce and fresh basil or coriander; check the seasoning. Serve with boiled rice.

• Per serving 170 kcalories, protein 4g, carbohydrate 34g, fat 3g, saturated fat trace, fibre 5g, added sugar trace, salt 1.44g

Beetroot and Lamb's Lettuce Risotto

The grated raw beetroot in the salad mix softens during heating and gives the rice pretty flecks of pink.

25g/1oz butter
1 onion, chopped
300g/10oz risotto rice
150ml/¼ pint dry white wine
850ml/1½ pints vegetable stock
50g/2oz freshly grated parmesan
150g bag beetroot and lamb's lettuce salad

Takes 30 minutes • Serves 4

1 Melt half the butter in a pan with a lid. Stir in the onion and cook for 5 minutes until softened but not brown. Add the rice and cook for 3 minutes, stirring to coat the grains. Pour in the wine and bubble away. Stir in the stock and return to the boil. Cover the pan and simmer, without stirring, for 12–15 minutes, until the rice is just tender.
2 Remove from the heat, stir in the parmesan and remaining butter and season. Tip in the salad and stir gently until the leaves are wilted; take care not to overstir or the rice will turn too pink.
3 Divide between warm serving plates and serve sprinkled with freshly ground black pepper.

• Per serving 398 kcalories, protein 13g, carbohydrate 62g, fat 10g, saturated fat 6g, fibre 2g, added sugar none, salt 1.23g

Strawberry Yogurt Brûlées

Leave the brûlée topping until up to an hour before serving as it slowly softens on standing.

500g/1lb 2oz strawberries
juice of 1 orange
500g carton natural yogurt
100g/4oz caster sugar

Takes 30 minutes, plus chilling • Serves 6

1 Slice the strawberries and divide between six serving dishes or glasses. Sprinkle over the orange juice, then spoon over the yogurt. Chill until ready to serve.
2 Tip the sugar into a small pan with two tablespoons of cold water. Heat gently, stirring to dissolve the sugar, then increase the heat and stop stirring. Boil the mixture carefully until it turns a light caramel colour, then remove from the heat and plunge the base of the pan into a sink filled with cold water to stop it cooking further.
3 When the bubbles have subsided, carefully pour a little over each dessert. Leave for 10 minutes before serving or chill for up to an hour.

• Per serving 202 kcalories, protein 7g, carbohydrate 43g, fat 1g, saturated fat 1g, fibre 1g, added sugar 26g, salt 0.26g

Melon and Ginger Sorbet

Check the melons are really ripe and fragrant for the best flavour.

2 ripe Galia melons (about 1.5kg/3lb 5oz), halved and seeded
75g/3oz caster sugar
4 pieces stem ginger in syrup, drained and chopped
1 medium egg white (uncooked eggs should be avoided by those who are very young, elderly or pregnant)

Takes 15 minutes, plus freezing • Serves 4

1 Scoop out the flesh from the melons and place in a food processor with the sugar. Blend until smooth, then stir in the ginger and transfer to a shallow freezerproof dish. Freeze for 2 hours until mushy.
2 Whisk the egg white until just stiff, but not dry. Remove the iced melon from the freezer and mash with a fork, then stir in the egg white.
3 Return to the freezer for a further 2 hours until frozen. Serve decorated with extra stem ginger, if liked.

• Per serving 173 kcalories, protein 3g, carbohydrate 42g, fat 0.4g, saturated fat 0.01g, fibre 2g, added sugar 21g, salt 0.33g

Summery Provençal Apricots

The dimpled apricots look charming left whole, but you can halve and stone them before poaching if you prefer.

175cl bottle dry, fruity rosé wine
175g/6oz golden caster sugar
1 vanilla pod, split open lengthways with a sharp knife, then cut in 4 (keep the seeds inside)
700g/1lb 9oz ripe fresh apricots
vanilla ice-cream, to serve

Takes 40 minutes • Serves 4

1 Pour the wine into a saucepan, tip in the sugar and then add the pieces of vanilla pod. Stir over a low heat until the sugar has dissolved.
2 Add the apricots. Cover and gently poach until just softened – about 15–20 minutes for whole fruit and 10–15 minutes for halves.
3 Lift the apricots out with a slotted spoon and put them in a bowl. Boil the liquid hard for 8–10 minutes to make a thin syrup. Pour over the apricots and leave to cool. Serve warm or cold, with a piece of vanilla pod to decorate and a scoop of vanilla ice cream.

• Per serving 356 kcalories, protein 2g, carbohydrate 62g, fat none, saturated fat 3g, fibre 3g, added sugar 46g, salt 0.03g

TOP: Strawberry Yogurt Brûlées   BOTTOM LEFT: Melon and Ginger Sorbet   BOTTOM RIGHT: Summery Provençal Apricots

TOP LEFT: Guilt-free Sticky Toffee Puds   TOP RIGHT: Marzipan and Mincemeat Apples   BOTTOM: Poached Pears with Blackberries

Guilt-free Sticky Toffee Puds

Date purée replaces fat in this tempting recipe, hence the title.

175g/6oz pitted dried dates
150ml/¼ pint maple syrup
1 tbsp vanilla extract
2 large eggs, separated
85g/3oz self-raising flour
0% Greek yogurt and extra maple syrup, to
    serve (optional)

Takes 1½ hours • Serves 4

1 Preheat the oven to 180°C/Gas 4/fan oven 160°C. Simmer the dates in 175ml/6fl oz water for 5 minutes. Tip into a food processor, add 6 tablespoons of maple syrup and the vanilla, and blend until smooth. Transfer to a bowl and mix in the egg yolks, followed by the flour.
2 Whisk the egg whites until stiff, and fold into the date mixture. Put one tablespoon of maple syrup into each of four 200ml/7fl oz pudding moulds. Add the mixture. Cover each tightly with foil, stand in an ovenproof dish and pour in hot water to halfway up the sides of the moulds. Cook for 1 hour, until a skewer inserted into the centre comes out clean.
3 Uncover, run a knife around the edges, and invert on to plates. Drizzle over yogurt and maple syrup to serve.

• Per serving 339 kcalories, protein 7g, carbohydrate 73g, fat 4g, saturated fat 1g, fibre 2g, added sugar 25g, salt 0.33g

Marzipan and Mincemeat Apples

A simple dessert with just four ingredients. Serve with natural yogurt.

2 medium Bramley apples
85g/3oz marzipan, chopped
8 tbsp mincemeat
finely grated zest and juice of 1 small lemon
natural yogurt, to serve

Takes 25 minutes • Serves 4

1 Cut the apples in half widthways. Remove and discard the cores, then stand the apples in a microwave-proof dish. Mix the marzipan with the mincemeat and lemon zest. Spoon into the centre of the apples and spoon over the lemon juice.
2 Cover the dish with cling film, pierce several times and microwave on High for 4½ minutes. If you don't have a turntable and the apples are not cooking evenly, turn the dish halfway through.
3 Remove the cling film and leave to stand for 5 minutes before serving with some natural yogurt.

• Per serving 200 kcalories, protein 2g, carbohydrate 41g, fat 4g, saturated fat 1g, fibre 2g, added sugar 24g, salt trace

Poached Pears with Blackberries

For a special occasion, substitute half the apple juice with 150ml/¼ pint of red wine.

4 medium pears
zest of 1 lemon (peel off with a potato peeler)
1 tbsp lemon juice
250g/9oz blackberries
300ml/½ pint unsweetened apple juice
50g/2oz golden caster sugar
8 tbsp 0% fat natural Greek yogurt

Takes 40 minutes • Serves 4

1 Peel the pears but don't remove their stalks. Place them in a saucepan with the lemon zest and juice, half the blackberries, the apple juice and caster sugar. Heat until simmering, then cover and cook gently for 20–25 minutes until the pears are tender, turning them once.
2 Remove the pears from the liquid and cool for a few minutes. Halve each, core with a teaspoon or melon baller, and transfer to four dishes.
3 Strain the liquid through a sieve, into a pan. Add the remaining blackberries and warm gently. Serve the pears and blackberries with the yogurt.

• Per serving 180 kcalories, protein 5g, carbohydrate 41g, fat 0g, saturated fat 0g, fibre 5g, added sugar 13g, salt trace

Melon with Hot Redcurrant Sauce

Choose an orange-fleshed melon for its colour and sweet flavour. If you have time, chill the melon cubes first.

finely grated zest and juice of 1 orange
2 tbsp redcurrant jelly
1 ripe orange-fleshed melon
low-fat natural yogurt, to serve

Takes 10 minutes • Serves 4

1 Put the orange zest and juice in a pan with the redcurrant jelly and a splash of water. Heat gently, stirring occasionally, until the jelly has melted to a smooth sauce.
2 Cut the melon into quarters, discarding the seeds and the skin. Cut the flesh into 2.5cm/1in cubes and put in a bowl.
3 Pour the hot redcurrant sauce over the melon, stir well and serve with spoonfuls of yogurt.

• Per serving 66 kcalories, protein 1g, carbohydrate 16g, fat trace, saturated fat none, fibre 2g, added sugar none, salt 0.04g

Tequila Sunrise Sorbet

A refreshing palate-cleansing sorbet – great after Mexican food. But watch out, as it has a kick of its own!

225g/8oz caster sugar
juice of 2 limes
juice of 2 lemons
juice of 5 oranges
100ml/3½fl oz tequila, plus extra to serve
1 medium egg white (uncooked eggs should be avoided by those who are very young, elderly or pregnant)
4 tbsp grenadine
orange and lime wedges, to serve

Takes 10 minutes, plus freezing • Serves 6

1 Put 100ml/3½fl oz water into a large pan with the sugar and fruit juices. Cook over a low heat for 3–4 minutes, stirring until the sugar has dissolved. Boil for 1 minute. Cool completely. Stir in the tequila and chill.
2 Whisk the egg white until stiff and fold into the fruit syrup. Pour half the mixture into a freezerproof container and seal. Stir the grenadine into the other half, mix well and pour into a freezerproof container. Seal. Freeze for 2 hours until slushy around the edges. Break up any ice crystals with a fork and refreeze for a further 2 hours until solid.
3 Remove the sorbets from the freezer 20 minutes before serving. Frost the serving dishes with egg white and sugar. Scoop both sorbets into each dish. Pour over a shot of tequila and decorate with citrus wedges.

• Per serving 211 kcalories, protein 1g, carbohydrate 39g, fat 0.01g, saturated fat none, fibre 0.11g, added sugar 35g, salt 0.03g

Banana and Apricot Compôte

The apricots can be cooked up to two days ahead and stored in the fridge. Try serving it for breakfast too.

250g/9oz ready-to-eat dried apricots
200ml/7fl oz apple juice
2 bananas, sliced
4 passion fruit (or a punnet of raspberries)
2 tbsp toasted flaked almonds
yogurt or crème fraîche, and biscuits, to serve

Takes 30 minutes, plus cooling • Serves 4

1 Put the apricots, apple juice and 200ml/7fl oz water in a pan. Bring to the boil, cover and simmer for 20 minutes.
2 Remove from the heat and leave to cool – you can make ahead up to this stage.
3 Tip the cooled apricots into a bowl and stir in the banana. Mix in the flesh from the passion fruit. Sprinkle the almonds over the fruit and serve with yogurt or crème fraîche, and biscuits.

• Per serving 341 kcalories, protein 7g, carbohydrate 71g, fat 5g, saturated fat trace, fibre 8g, added sugar none, salt 0.13g

TOP LEFT: Melon with Hot Redcurrant Sauce   TOP RIGHT: Tequila Sunrise Sorbet   BOTTOM: Banana and Apricot Compôte

Veggie Dishes

Saffron and Leek Soup

Saffron lends a splash of sunshine colour and flavour to a simple leek soup, topped with crispy leek rings.

4 medium leeks
50g/2oz butter
1 tbsp olive oil
good pinch of saffron strands
2 tbsp plain flour
1.2 litres/2 pints vegetable stock
oil, for shallow frying
1 tbsp cornflour
1 medium egg white, lightly beaten
2 spring onions, diagonally sliced

Takes 35 minutes • Serves 4

1 Cut a 7.5cm/3in length of leek into slices. Separate into rings and set aside. Chop the remaining leeks. Heat the butter and oil in a large pan and cook the leeks for 1 minute, stirring. Mix in the saffron and flour, then gradually stir in the stock, bring to the boil and simmer gently for 10 minutes, until thickened, stirring frequently.
2 Transfer the soup to a food processor and whizz until smooth. You may need to do this in batches. Return to the clean pan and season to taste. Heat through gently.
3 Meanwhile, heat a little oil in a frying pan. Toss the leek rings in the cornflour. Shake off the excess, then dip the rings into the egg white. Fry the leek rings until crisp and golden. Drain and serve scattered over the soup along with the spring onion.

• Per serving 219 kcalories, protein 4g, carbohydrate 12g, fat 17g, saturated fat 7g, fibre 2g, added sugar none, salt 1.34g

Spring Greens and Rice Soup

The rice will continue to absorb the stock after the soup is cooked. If you reheat the soup you may need to add more stock.

1 tbsp olive oil
1 onion, chopped
2 garlic cloves, crushed
100g/4oz risotto rice
finely grated zest and juice of 1 lemon
1.4 litres/2½ pints vegetable stock
2 large firm tomatoes, seeded and chopped
225g/8oz spring greens, stalks removed and shredded
120g jar vegetarian pesto sauce
vegetarian parmesan shavings, to garnish

Takes 35 minutes • Serves 4

1 Heat the oil in a large pan and fry the onion and garlic for 3–4 minutes until softened. Stir in the rice and cook for 1 minute, stirring occasionally.
2 Add the lemon zest and juice and stock. Bring to the boil and simmer for 15 minutes.
3 Stir the tomatoes, greens and pesto into the soup. Bring to the boil and simmer for 4–5 minutes until the rice is tender. Season to taste and serve sprinkled with the parmesan shavings.

• Per serving 409 kcalories, protein 12g, carbohydrate 33g, fat 26g, saturated fat 5g, fibre 3g, added sugar none, salt 1.93g

Spinach, Sage and Potato Soup

A velvety smooth soup with a dramatic colour but gentle flavour.

50g/2oz butter
2 red onions, chopped
3 garlic cloves, crushed
15g fresh sage, shredded, plus extra to garnish
2 large potatoes (about 500g/1lb 2oz), diced
1.4 litres/2½ pints vegetable stock
250g/9oz baby spinach leaves
4 tbsp crème fraîche, to serve (optional)

Takes 40 minutes • Serves 4

1 Melt the butter in a large pan and fry the onions for 5–6 minutes over a low heat until softened slightly. Add the garlic, sage and potatoes, cover and cook over a very low heat for 10 minutes.
2 Stir in the stock, bring to the boil and cook for 5 minutes. Add the spinach and cook for 2 minutes. Transfer the mixture to a food processor or blender and whizz until smooth (you may need to do this in batches).
3 Return to the pan and heat gently until warmed. Season to taste and serve with a spoonful of crème fraîche, if using, garnished with the extra sage.

• Per serving 265 kcalories, protein 7g, carbohydrate 28g, fat 14g, saturated fat 9g, fibre 4g, added sugar none, salt 1.67g

TOP: Saffron and Leek Soup   BOTTOM LEFT: Spring Greens and Rice Soup   BOTTOM RIGHT: Spinach, Sage and Potato Soup

TOP LEFT: Hot Sour Corn Soup   TOP RIGHT: Celery and White Bean Salad   BOTTOM: Greek Pasta Salad

Hot Sour Corn Soup

If you can't buy fresh lemongrass, most supermarkets stock it minced in jars. Substitute a teaspoon of this instead.

1 corn on the cob
1 tbsp vegetable oil
1 red chilli, seeded and sliced
1 shallot, finely chopped
2 stalks lemongrass, bruised
3 baby leeks or spring onions, sliced
1 red pepper, seeded and thinly sliced
400ml can coconut milk
850ml/1½ pints vegetable stock
2 kaffir lime leaves (optional)
175g/6oz thread egg noodles
juice of 1 lime
small bunch coriander, roughly chopped

Takes 35 minutes • Serves 4

1 Hold the corn cob upright on a board, and, using a sharp knife, slice downwards to strip the corn kernels from the cob. Heat the oil in a large pan, add the kernels, chilli, shallot, lemongrass, leeks or spring onions and red pepper, and cook for 3–4 minutes, stirring occasionally.
2 Add the coconut milk, stock and lime leaves, if using. Bring to the boil, then cover. Reduce the heat and simmer gently for 15 minutes. Discard the lemongrass stalks. Add the noodles and cook for 4 minutes until tender.
3 Remove from the heat and stir in the lime juice and coriander. Season with salt, if necessary, and serve immediately.

• Per serving 545 kcalories, protein 11g, carbohydrate 41g, fat 39g, saturated fat 27g, fibre 9g, added sugar none, salt 0.97g

Celery and White Bean Salad

The flavours of tomatoes and white wine work really well with celery in this warm salad.

50g/2oz butter
1½ heads of celery, sliced diagonally
1 tbsp chopped fresh rosemary
150ml/¼ pint dry white wine
150ml/¼ pint vegetable stock
pinch of saffron strands
450g/1lb tomatoes, skinned, seeded and cut into wedges
finely grated zest and juice of ½ lemon
410g can cannellini beans, drained and rinsed
50g/2oz pitted black olives
handful of flatleaf parsley, roughly torn
crusty bread, to serve

Takes 40 minutes • Serves 4

1 Melt the butter in a large pan and add the celery and rosemary. Cover and cook gently for 10 minutes, until soft but not browned.
2 Stir in the wine, stock and saffron. Bring to the boil and boil for 8–10 minutes, until the liquid has reduced by half.
3 Stir in the tomatoes, lemon zest and juice and cannellini beans. Bring to the boil and simmer for 5 minutes. Stir in the olives and season to taste. Allow to cool slightly. Scatter with parsley and serve with crusty bread to mop up the juices.

• Per serving 262 kcalories, protein 9g, carbohydrate 23g, fat 13g, saturated fat 7g, fibre 9g, added sugar none, salt 2.32g

Greek Pasta Salad

The traditional combination of tomatoes, olives and feta cheese is made more substantial by the addition of pasta.

300g/10oz fusilli (spirals) or farfalle (butterflies) or penne (quill tubes)
225g bag prepared fresh baby spinach leaves
250g punnet cherry tomatoes, halved
100g/4oz kalamata olives
225g/8oz feta, broken into rough chunks
3 tbsp olive oil
crusty bread, to serve

Takes 30 minutes • Serves 4

1 Tip the pasta into a large pan of salted boiling water and boil for 10 minutes. Throw in the spinach, stir well and boil for another 2 minutes. Drain into a colander or sieve and leave to drip dry.
2 Tip the tomatoes, olives and feta into a large bowl, grind lots of black pepper over and then drizzle with the olive oil.
3 Toss in the drained pasta and spinach, and serve with crusty bread.

• Per serving 418 kcalories, protein 18g, carbohydrate 37g, fat 23g, saturated fat 8g, fibre 5g, added sugar 0.1g, salt 3.48g

Hot Mushroom and Kumquat Salad

Tangy kumquats contrast with the earthy flavours of the mushrooms and sweet red onion.

5 tbsp olive oil
250g/9oz mixed mushrooms,
    (eg field, shiitake, chestnut), sliced
1 red onion, sliced
50g/2oz kumquats, sliced
pinch of dried chilli flakes
50g/2oz sliced white bread, crusts removed
    and cubed
85g/3oz rocket
1 tbsp white wine vinegar

Takes 30 minutes • Serves 2 (easily doubled)

1 Melt one tablespoon of the oil in a frying pan and fry the mushrooms for 2–3 minutes. Add the onion and kumquats and fry for a further 2–3 minutes. Set aside and keep warm.
2 Mix together the chilli flakes, bread cubes and one tablespoon of the oil. Season well. Heat one tablespoon of oil in the frying pan and fry the bread mixture until crisp and golden. Divide the rocket between serving plates and top with the mushroom and kumquat mix and the chilli croûtons.
3 Whisk together the last of the oil with the vinegar, season, and drizzle over the salad. Serve immediately.

• Per serving 488 kcalories, protein 6g, carbohydrate 19g, fat 39g, saturated fat 6g, fibre 4g, added sugar none, salt 0.46g

Two Cheese Salad with Croûtons

Use less salty Lancashire cheese in place of feta, if you prefer.

2 thick slices white bread, crusts removed
1 tsp paprika
2 tbsp olive oil
1 garlic clove, crushed
1 large cos or romaine lettuce
2 ripe avocados
2 tbsp lemon juice
1 large courgette, cut into sticks
140g/5oz feta, crumbled into chunks
25g/1oz finely grated parmesan
6 tbsp olive oil dressing (ready-made)

Takes 30 minutes • Serves 4

1 Preheat the oven to 220°C/Gas 7/fan oven 200°C. Cut the bread into 2cm/¾in cubes. Toss with the paprika, olive oil and garlic, then spread out on a baking sheet. Bake for 7–8 minutes, until crisp.
2 Tear the lettuce into large pieces. Peel and slice the avocados and toss with lemon juice and freshly ground black pepper.
3 Mix the lettuce, courgette, feta or Lancashire cheese and croûtons. Put into a large salad bowl with the avocado, and sprinkle with parmesan. Drizzle olive oil dressing over the salad to serve.

• Per serving 453 kcalories, protein 12g, carbohydrate 12g, fat 40g, saturated fat 10g, fibre 4g, added sugar none, salt 1.92g

English Garden Salad

A fresh-tasting salad made from summer vegetables, crumbly cheese and mint.

500g/1lb 2oz new potatoes, sliced thickly
350g/12oz runner beans, sliced
a bunch of spring onions, chopped
240g tub sunblush or sun-dried tomatoes,
    drained
225g/8oz Cheshire or Lancashire cheese
a good handful of fresh mint leaves, roughly
    chopped
4–5 tbsp bought honey and mustard dressing

Takes 30 minutes • Serves 4

1 Cook the potatoes in salted boiling water for 7 minutes. Add the beans to the pan and cook for a further 7–9 minutes, until the potatoes and beans are just tender.
2 Drain the vegetables and rinse under cold running water to stop them cooking. Shake the colander to get rid of as much water as possible, then tip into a large bowl. Add the onions and tomatoes, crumble in the cheese and mix well.
3 Add most of the mint and dressing and toss everything lightly together. Tip into a serving dish, drizzle with a little more dressing and scatter over the rest of the mint.

• Per serving 427 kcalories, protein 18g, carbohydrate 29g, fat 27g, saturated fat 11g, fibre 6g, added sugar none, salt 2.39g

TOP LEFT: Hot Mushroom and Kumquat Salad   TOP RIGHT: Two Cheese Salad with Croûtons   BOTTOM: English Garden Salad

TOP: Goat's Cheese Salad   BOTTOM LEFT: Feta and Griddled Peach Salad   BOTTOM RIGHT: Feta and Flageolet Salad

Goat's Cheese Salad

Choose a small soft goat's cheese. The rind is edible but discard the ends to make four matching slices.

100g/4oz soft goat's cheese
1 oval bread roll, cut into 4 slices and ends discarded
4 tsp olive oil
1 tsp lemon juice or white wine vinegar
½ tsp wholegrain or Dijon mustard
1 garlic clove, chopped
handful of mixed salad leaves

Takes 10 minutes • Serves 1 (easily multiplied)

1 Preheat the grill to high. Cut the cheese into four slices. Toast the bread slices on both sides, then top with the cheese.
2 Sprinkle with black pepper and a little of the olive oil and grill for 2–3 minutes.
3 Meanwhile, mix together the remaining olive oil, lemon juice or vinegar, mustard and garlic. Season, then toss with the salad leaves. Pile on to a plate and top with the cheese toasts.

• Per serving 509 kcalories, protein 19g, carbohydrate 16g, fat 42g, saturated fat 15g, fibre 1g, added sugar none, salt 1.84g

Feta and Griddled Peach Salad

Check the cheese counter in the supermarket for jars of marinated feta in oil. Use the oil for the dressing.

juice of 1 lime
4 fresh ripe peaches, each cut into wedges
200g bag mixed salad leaves
300g jar marinated feta in oil
1 red onion, sliced
2 tbsp chopped fresh mint

Takes 10 minutes • Serves 4

1 Heat a lightly greased griddle pan until very hot. Squeeze the lime juice over the peaches and place them on the griddle pan. Cook them for 2–3 minutes, turning, until nicely charred.
2 In a large salad bowl, mix together the salad leaves, feta, two tablespoons of the oil from the feta, the red onion and chopped mint. Season well.
3 Divide between plates and top with the charred peaches. Sprinkle over black pepper and serve.

• Per serving 272 kcalories, protein 11g, carbohydrate 11g, fat 21g, saturated fat 9g, fibre 2g, added sugar none, salt 2.32g

Feta and Flageolet Salad

Use authentic Greek feta for the best flavour. It keeps for about six months unopened in the fridge, so it's a great supper standby.

100g/4oz baby spinach leaves
300g/10oz large salad tomatoes, cut into wedges
400g can flageolet or cannellini beans, drained and rinsed
1 small red onion, finely chopped
200g pack feta
crusty bread, to serve

FOR THE DRESSING
1 garlic clove, finely chopped
1 tbsp lemon juice
1 tsp clear honey
3 tbsp olive oil

Takes 10–20 minutes • Serves 4

1 Cover a large platter or shallow dish with the spinach leaves. Scatter the tomato wedges over the spinach, followed by the beans and red onion.
2 Drain off the liquid from the pack of feta and crumble the cheese over the vegetables.
3 Tip the dressing ingredients into a small bowl, season and whisk with a fork until slightly thickened. Drizzle over the salad, and serve with crusty bread.

• Per serving 515 kcalories, protein 31g, carbohydrate 56g, fat 20g, saturated fat 8g, fibre 19g, added sugar 1g, salt 2.05g

Mini Muffin Pizzas

Muffins make instant pizza bases. Use pesto in place of pizza topping sauce if you have some handy.

1 very small courgette
1 toasting muffin
2 tbsp ready-made pizza topping or passata (sieved tomatoes)
2 sun-dried tomatoes, thinly sliced
40g/1½oz feta, cubed
1 tsp torn fresh oregano leaves
2 tsp olive oil

Takes 15 minutes • Serves 1 (easily multiplied)

1 Preheat the grill to medium. Using a potato peeler, peel the courgette lengthways into thin ribbons.
2 Split the muffin in half. Spread the cut halves with the pizza topping or passata and toast for 1–2 minutes until hot.
3 Arrange the courgettes over the muffin halves. Top with the sun-dried tomatoes, feta and oregano. Season. Drizzle with the olive oil and grill for 2 minutes.

• Per serving 448 kcalories, protein 15g, carbohydrate 39g, fat 27g, saturated fat 9g, fibre 3g, added sugar 1g, salt 1.81g

Halloumi and Tomato Pitta

Grill the halloumi cheese until just golden and eat it immediately as it becomes chewy when it cools.

2 cos lettuce leaves, shredded
1 plum tomato, sliced
1 thin slice sweet onion, separated into rings
1 sprig fresh mint, chopped
1 tsp olive oil
3 thick slices halloumi
1 pitta bread

Takes 10 minutes • Serves 1 (easily multiplied)

1 Preheat the grill to high. Put the lettuce, tomato slices, onion rings and mint in a bowl, toss together with the olive oil and season.
2 Place the halloumi slices on a baking sheet and grill for about 2 minutes until turning golden, then turn over and grill for a further minute.
3 Grill the pitta pocket for a few seconds on each side until it puffs open. Tuck the cheese and salad inside the pitta and eat immediately.

• Per serving 375 kcalories, protein 16g, carbohydrate 46g, fat 15g, saturated fat 7g, fibre 3g, added sugar none, salt 1.45g

Olive and Ricotta Pâté

You should find all these ingredients at the delicatessen counter. Buy some good bread to go with it.

450g/1lb ricotta cheese
50g/2oz vegetarian parmesan, finely grated
2 medium egg whites, lightly beaten
190g jar lemon and mint marinated green olives
185g can pitted black olives, drained
4 sun-dried tomatoes, roughly chopped
2 sprigs fresh rosemary, leaves only
bread and roasted tomatoes, to serve

Takes 40 minutes • Serves 6

1 Preheat the oven to 200°C/Gas 6/fan oven 180°C. Oil and base line a 20cm/8in sandwich tin. In a large bowl, beat together the ricotta, parmesan, egg whites and seasoning.
2 Spoon into the prepared cake tin and level the surface with the back of a wet spoon. Press the olives, sun-dried tomatoes and rosemary into the surface and bake for 25–30 minutes until firm.
3 Turn out and remove the paper. Serve in wedges with bread and roasted tomatoes.

• Per serving 227 kcalories, protein 12g, carbohydrate 3g, fat 19g, saturated fat 8g, fibre 2g, added sugar none, salt 4.07g

TOP: Mini Muffin Pizzas   BOTTOM LEFT: Halloumi and Tomato Pitta   BOTTOM RIGHT: Olive and Ricotta Pâté

TOP LEFT: Stir-fried Salad with Almonds   TOP RIGHT: Vegetable Blini Stacks   BOTTOM: Souffléd Avocado Omelette

Stir-fried Salad with Almonds

Sounds strange, but take the pan off the heat before you add the salad ingredients and you'll love the fresh-tasting result.

3 tbsp olive oil
85g/3oz whole blanched almonds
1 bunch spring onions, sliced
1 small cucumber, seeded and sliced
3 sticks celery, cut into batons
225g/8oz small tomatoes, quartered
2 little gem lettuces, torn in pieces
25g/1oz watercress
25g/1oz fresh coriander
juice of ½ lemon
½ tsp sugar
crusty bread or boiled rice, to serve

Takes 15 minutes • Serves 4

1 Heat two tablespoons of the oil in a frying pan or wok and fry the almonds for 2–3 minutes until golden. Drain on kitchen paper then chop roughly.
2 Add the remaining oil to the pan and when hot, add the spring onions, cucumber, celery and tomatoes and stir fry for 2 minutes. Remove from the heat, add the remaining ingredients and toss together until combined. Season.
3 Spoon the warm salad on to serving plates and scatter the almonds over. Spoon the pan juices over and serve with crusty bread or boiled rice, if liked.

• Per serving 247 kcalories, protein 6g, carbohydrate 6g, fat 22g, saturated fat 2g, fibre 3g, added sugar 1g, salt 0.09g

Vegetable Blini Stacks

Blinis make brilliant bases for canapés and starters. Try them with herby cream cheese, tomatoes and rocket too.

225g/8oz asparagus
    spears, trimmed
100g/4oz sugarsnap peas
140g/5oz broccoli florets
250g crème fraîche
1½ tbsp fresh vegetarian pesto
handful of fresh basil, roughly torn
8 large, ready-made blinis
    (about 10cm/4in diameter)
140g/5oz semi-dried tomatoes, drained

Takes 20 minutes • Serves 4

1 Preheat the oven to 180°C/Gas 4/fan oven 160°C. Bring a large pan of salted water to the boil. Add the asparagus, sugarsnap peas and broccoli and cook for 2 minutes until just tender. Drain and set aside. Combine the crème fraîche, pesto and half the basil. Season to taste.
2 Place four blinis on a large ovenproof dish. Top with the vegetables and tomatoes and spoon over the crème fraîche mixture.
3 Halve the remaining blinis and place on top of the vegetables. Bake for 8 minutes until heated through.

• Per serving 372 kcalories, protein 10g, carbohydrate 20g, fat 28g, saturated fat 13g, fibre 4g, added sugar none, salt 0.43g

Souffléd Avocado Omelette

Tapenade is a thick purée of olives, capers, garlic and olive oil (but watch out for hidden anchovies).

3 medium eggs, separated
1 tbsp milk
2 tbsp chopped fresh flatleaf parsley
2 tsp olive oil
2 tbsp vegetarian black olive tapenade
1 small avocado, halved, stoned and sliced
juice of ½ lemon
tomato salad, to serve (optional)

Takes 10 minutes • Serves 4

1 Place the egg whites in a large bowl and whisk to soft peaks. Place the egg yolks in a separate bowl with the milk and parsley. Season and beat together. Add a quarter of the whites to the yolks and gently stir. Fold in the remaining egg whites.
2 Preheat the grill to high. Heat the oil in a 20cm/8in non-stick frying pan. Add the egg mixture and cook for 2–3 minutes until lightly set. Place under the grill for 1–2 minutes to cook the top.
3 Spoon the olive tapenade over one half of the omelette. Top with the avocado and squeeze over the lemon juice. Fold over the other half, transfer to a plate and serve with a tomato salad, if liked.

• Per serving 717 kcalories, protein 21g, carbohydrate 21g, fat 70g, saturated fat 12g, fibre 4g, added sugar none, salt 2.39g

Spicy Vegetable Chapati Wraps

Curry can be deceivingly high in fat – this version is packed with flavour and has only 5g fat per serving.

300g/10oz sweet potatoes, peeled and
    roughly cubed
400g can peeled plum tomatoes
400g can chickpeas, drained
½ tsp dried chilli flakes
2 tbsp mild curry paste
100g/4oz baby spinach leaves
2 tbsp chopped fresh coriander
4 plain chapatis (Indian flatbreads)
4 tbsp 0% Greek yogurt

Takes 25 minutes • Serves 4

1 Cook the sweet potatoes in salted boiling water for 10–12 minutes until tender. Meanwhile, put the tomatoes, chickpeas, chilli flakes and curry paste in another pan and simmer gently for about 5 minutes, stirring all the time.
2 Preheat the grill. Drain the sweet potatoes and add to the tomato mixture. Stir in the spinach and cook for a minute until just starting to wilt. Stir in the coriander, season to taste and keep warm.
3 Sprinkle the chapatis with a little water and grill for 20–30 seconds each side. Spoon on the filling, top with yoghurt and fold in half to serve.

• Per serving 289 kcalories, protein 12g, carbohydrate 54g, fat 5g, saturated fat none, fibre 5g, added sugar none, salt 1.08g

Thai Coconut Vegetable Soup

Sounds exotic but frozen stir fry vegetables plus coconut and Thai curry paste add up to a tasty Thai-style meal.

1 tbsp vegetable oil
25g/1oz fresh root ginger, peeled and sliced
2 garlic cloves, sliced
2 lemongrass stalks, bruised
3–4 bird's eye chillies, bruised
4 kaffir lime leaves, bruised
400ml can coconut milk
200ml carton coconut cream
500g/1lb 2oz mixed
stir-fry vegetables
fresh basil and coriander leaves, to garnish

Takes 30 minutes • Serves 3

1 Heat the oil in a frying pan or wok and stir fry the ginger, garlic, lemongrass and chillies for 30 seconds.
2 Add the lime leaves to the pan and pour the coconut milk and cream over. Bring to the boil, cover and simmer gently for about 15 minutes, stirring occasionally.
3 Add the vegetables to the pan and return to the boil. Simmer for 2–3 minutes, stirring frequently, until the vegetables are just tender. Ladle into bowls and serve topped with the fresh basil and coriander.

• Per serving 917 kcalories, protein 11g, carbohydrate 20g, fat 80g, saturated fat 72g, fibre 18g, added sugar 1g, salt 0.18g

Minted Spring Vegetables

This is a wonderfully creamy mixture yet the fresh flavours of the vegetables still shine through.

25g/1oz butter
1 tbsp olive oil
225g/8oz baby onions
200ml/7fl oz dry white wine
2 medium leeks, halved and cut into 5cm/2in
    ribbons
350g/12oz frozen petits pois
3 heads of baby gem lettuce, quartered
    lengthways
200ml/7fl oz crème fraîche
2 tbsp chopped fresh mint
2 tbsp chopped fresh flatleaf parsley
bulghar wheat or couscous, to serve

Takes 35 minutes • Serves 4

1 Heat the butter and olive oil in a large non-stick frying pan until lightly foaming. Add the baby onions and cook over a low heat for 8 minutes. Add the wine and leeks and bring to the boil. Simmer for 5 minutes until the leeks are tender.
2 Add the petits pois and simmer for a further 5 minutes. Add the lettuce and simmer for a further 3 minutes.
3 Stir in the crème fraîche and herbs. Season well and warm through very gently for 2–3 minutes. Serve spooned over hot, soaked bulghar wheat or steamed couscous.

• Per serving 321 kcalories, protein 9g, carbohydrate 18g, fat 20g, saturated fat 10g, fibre 8g, added sugar none, salt 0.23g

TOP LEFT: Spicy Vegetable Chapati Wraps   TOP RIGHT: Thai Coconut Vegetable Soup   BOTTOM: Minted Spring Vegetables

TOP: Rösti with Egg and Onions   BOTTOM LEFT: Crustless Vegetable Quiche   BOTTOM RIGHT: Pizza-topped Polenta

Rösti with Egg and Onions

A simple potato cake makes a welcome change from toast with your fried egg.

4 tsp olive oil
½ red or white onion, finely sliced
50g/2oz potato, coarsely grated
1 tsp wholegrain mustard
1 medium egg
2 tomatoes, sliced
drizzle of balsamic vinegar

Takes 15 minutes • Serves 1 (easily multiplied)

1 Heat half the oil in a non-stick frying pan. Fry half the onion until crispy. Drain and reserve. Mix the potato with the rest of the onion, mustard and seasoning.
2 Add the remaining oil to the pan, add the potato mixture and press into a 12cm/4½in round. Fry for 8–10 minutes until golden, turning several times. Fry the egg alongside the rösti.
3 Arrange the tomatoes on a plate and drizzle with the balsamic vinegar. Serve the rösti on the tomatoes with the egg and crispy onion on top.

• Per serving 335 kcalories, protein 9g, carbohydrate 16g, fat 27g, saturated fat 4g, fibre 3g, added sugar none, salt 0.53g

Crustless Vegetable Quiche

As the name suggests there's no pastry, just chunky vegetables set in egg.

1 tbsp vegetable oil
1 yellow and 1 orange pepper, cut into quarters and seeded
2 courgettes, cut into chunks
2 large red onions, cut into wedges
4 medium eggs, beaten
100ml/3½fl oz milk
2 tbsp fresh vegetarian pesto sauce
green salad, to serve

Takes 40 minutes • Serves 4

1 Preheat the oven to 200°C/Gas 6/fan oven 180°C. Heat the oil in a wok or large frying pan and stir fry the peppers, courgettes and onions over a high heat for 2–3 minutes.
2 Transfer the vegetables to an oiled 2 litre/ 3½ pint ovenproof dish. In a large bowl, mix together the eggs, milk, pesto and seasoning.
3 Pour over the vegetables and bake for 25 minutes until firm to the touch in the centre. Serve warm with a crisp green leaf salad.

• Per serving 211 kcalories, protein 9g, carbohydrate 10g, fat 15g, saturated fat 3g, fibre 2g, added sugar none, salt 0.36g

Pizza-topped Polenta

Ready-made polenta is sold in large sausage or oblong shapes. Not to be confused with quick-cook polenta powder.

500g pack ready-made polenta
½ tsp dried oregano
25g/1oz freshly grated parmesan
50g/2oz cheddar, grated
4 tbsp olive oil
4 large flat mushrooms, stalks removed
400g/14oz ripe tomatoes, roughly chopped
1 garlic clove, finely chopped

Takes 55 minutes • Serves 4

1 Preheat the oven to 220°C/Gas 7/fan oven 200°C from cold. Cut the polenta into 12 slices, 1cm/½in thick, and lay in four overlapping piles in a roasting tin. Sprinkle with oregano and most of the cheese. Pour the oil in a bowl, season and brush each mushroom. Place stalk-side up on the polenta piles.
2 Tip the tomatoes and garlic into the remaining oil. Spoon the tomatoes and their juices in and around the mushrooms and polenta, then season.
3 Sprinkle over the remaining cheese. Roast for 30 minutes until the tomatoes have softened and the mushrooms are tender. Serve hot.

• Per serving 422 kcalories, protein 14g, carbohydrate 50g, fat 20g, saturated fat 6g, fibre 3g, added sugar none, salt 0.42g

Brie and Tomato Tart

This couldn't be simpler – just arrange the topping in neat rows on ready-rolled puff pastry.

250g/9oz puff pastry
225g/8oz brie
4–5 largish ripe tomatoes
225g/8oz courgettes
½ tsp dried oregano

Takes 45 minutes • Serves 4

1 Preheat the oven to 200°C/Gas 6/fan oven 180°C. Roll out the pastry to a 23 × 30cm/9 × 12in oblong, put on a damp baking sheet, and score the pastry with a knife 2.5cm/1in from the edges. Prick the base with a fork, inside the marks.
2 Slice the brie, tomatoes and courgettes into thin slices. Heat two tablespoons of olive oil in a frying pan and fry the courgettes for 1–2 minutes until softened. Add the oregano; season. Cook for 1–2 minutes; cool slightly.
3 Starting from one short end, arrange four overlapping rows of brie, tomatoes and courgettes within the cut marks. Drizzle over the pan juices; season. Bake for 25–30 minutes until the pastry is puffed up and the courgettes are tender. Serve warm.

• Per serving 419 kcalories, protein 15g, carbohydrate 27g, fat 29g, saturated fat 9g, fibre 2g, added sugar none, salt 1.41g

Cheese and Chutney Melts

This dish is perfect for easy entertaining on nights at home with friends.

4 large crusty bread rolls
2 tbsp olive oil
4 tbsp green tomato chutney
4 small, rinded goat's cheeses
4 sprigs thyme
green salad, to serve (optional)

Takes 30 minutes • Serves 4

1 Preheat the oven to 190°C/Gas 5/fan oven 170°C. Cut a deep hollow in the top of each roll. Remove the bread from the centre and brush the insides with the oil. Season. Place on a baking sheet and bake for 5 minutes until lightly crisped.
2 Spoon the chutney into the rolls. Remove the rind from the top and bottom of each cheese and place one in each of the rolls. Push a sprig of thyme into the top and season with black pepper.
3 Scrunch foil around the roll, leaving the cheese uncovered. Bake for 15–20 minutes, until the cheese is golden and bubbling, removing the foil for the last 5 minutes. Serve with a green salad, if liked.

• Per serving 399 kcalories, protein 15g, carbohydrate 45g, fat 19g, saturated fat 7g, fibre 1g, added sugar 3g, salt 1.68g

Herby Stuffed Mushrooms

Remember that the mushrooms shrink during cooking. You could use medium mushrooms and serve more.

4 very large flat mushrooms
2 tbsp olive oil

FOR THE STUFFING
3 sprigs fresh thyme
4 tbsp chopped fresh flatleaf parsley
100g/4oz roasted, shelled pistachio nuts, chopped
85g/3oz pitted black olives, chopped
finely grated zest and juice of ½ lemon
100g/4oz white breadcrumbs
140g/5oz feta, cut into small cubes
crusty bread, to serve
green salad, to serve (optional)

Takes 30 minutes • Serves 4

1 Preheat the oven to 200°C/Gas 6/fan oven 180°C. Remove the mushroom stalks and chop roughly. Brush the mushrooms with a little olive oil. Place in a roasting tin and season. Bake for 10 minutes until beginning to soften.
2 Meanwhile, mix all the stuffing ingredients with the chopped mushroom stalks and the remaining olive oil. Season.
3 Spoon the stuffing on top of the mushrooms and bake for a further 5–8 minutes, until the feta begins to soften. Serve immediately on toasted crusty bread with a green salad, if liked.

• Per serving 433 kcalories, protein 15g, carbohydrate 24g, fat 31g, saturated fat 8g, fibre 2g, added sugar none, salt 2.96g

TOP: Brie and Tomato Tart   BOTTOM LEFT: Cheese and Chutney Melts   BOTTOM RIGHT: Herby Stuffed Mushrooms

TOP LEFT: **Stuffed Mushroom Bruschettas**   TOP RIGHT: **Halloumi Vegetable Pan Fry**   BOTTOM: **Cheesy Bread Pudding**

Stuffed Mushroom Bruschettas

The big mushrooms cook to a moist firmness under their cloak of peppers and melting goat's cheese.

4 thick slices country-style loaf, white or
   brown
2 x 20g tubs garlic butter or 50g/2oz
   softened butter beaten with 1 chopped
   garlic clove
4 large flat mushrooms
olive oil, for drizzling
200g jar roasted red peppers, either strips in
   oil or whole peppers in brine
140g/5oz firm goat's cheese
mixed salad, to serve

Takes 40 minutes • Serves 2

1 Preheat the oven to 190°C/Gas 5/fan oven 170°C. Spread both sides of each slice of bread with garlic butter (no need to remove the crusts). Put the bread slices in one layer on a baking sheet.
2 Put a mushroom on top of each and drizzle with a little olive oil. Season. Drain the peppers, slice if necessary, and divide between the mushrooms.
3 Cut the goat's cheese into four slices and put one slice on top of each stack. Bake for 25–30 minutes, until the mushrooms are cooked and the cheese golden. Serve with a mixed salad.

• Per serving 679 kcalories, protein 27g, carbohydrate 45g, fat 45g, saturated fat 27g, fibre 5g, added sugar none, salt 2.9g

Halloumi Vegetable Pan Fry

Halloumi cheese can be toasted in a pan without much oil – softening the cheese rather than melting it.

3 tbsp olive oil
250g/9oz halloumi, cut into slices
2 medium onions, cut in wedges
3 courgettes, sliced
8 tomatoes, halved
420g can butter beans, drained

Takes 30 minutes • Serves 4

1 Heat two tablespoons of the oil in a roasting tin or large frying pan, add the halloumi slices and fry until golden on both sides. Lift out, cut each slice into quarters and set aside. Add the onions to the tin and fry for 5 minutes until golden.
2 Toss in the courgettes and fry until golden. Remove the onions and courgettes from the tin and set aside. Heat the remaining oil in the tin and fry the tomatoes until softened and juicy.
3 Return the onions, courgettes and halloumi to the tin with the beans. Warm through, gently tossing it all together as you go. Season and serve.

• Per serving 285 kcalories, protein 20g, carbohydrate 29g, fat 22g, saturated fat 9g, fibre 8g, added sugar none, salt 2.35g

Cheesy Bread Pudding

A simple but filling supper speeded up with help from the microwave.

25g/1oz butter, softened
6 slices white bread (day-old bread is best)
4 medium eggs, beaten
100ml/3½oz milk
50g/2oz vegetarian parmesan, finely grated
1 tbsp Dijon mustard
25g/1oz vegetarian cheddar, grated
tomato and spring onion salad, to serve

Takes 25 minutes • Serves 4

1 Spread the butter on one side of each slice of bread and cut into triangles. Arrange in a 1.5 litre/2¾ pint microwaveproof dish.
2 In a bowl, mix together the eggs, milk, parmesan and mustard and pour over the bread. Leave to stand for 5 minutes. Preheat the grill to hot. Microwave the pudding on High for 5 minutes.
3 Sprinkle over the cheddar and grill for 2–3 minutes until golden. Serve hot with a tomato and spring onion salad.

• Per serving 312 kcalories, protein 17g, carbohydrate 20g, fat 19g, saturated fat 9g, fibre 1g, added sugar none, salt 1.56g

Spaghetti Genovese

Quick and tasty and cooked in one pan so there's hardly any washing up.

300g/10oz new potatoes, sliced
300g/10oz spaghetti
225g/8oz trimmed green beans, cut in half
120g carton fresh pesto
olive oil, for drizzling

Takes 20 minutes • Serves 4

1 Pour boiling water into a very large pan until half full. Return to the boil, then add the potatoes and spaghetti, and a little salt.
2 Cook for 10 minutes until the potatoes and pasta are almost tender. Tip in the green beans and cook for 5 minutes more.
3 Drain well, reserving four tablespoons of the cooking liquid. Return the potatoes, pasta and beans to the pan, then stir in the fresh pesto and reserved cooking liquid. Season to taste, divide between four serving plates and drizzle with a little olive oil.

• Per serving 330 kcalories, protein 23g, carbohydrate 8g, fat 23g, saturated fat 9g, fibre trace, added sugar 7g, salt 0.5g

Pasta with Taleggio

Taleggio is a small rectangular Italian cheese that melts wonderfully over pasta.

2 tbsp olive oil
1 onion, sliced
1 red, 1 yellow and 1 green pepper, seeded and sliced
2 garlic cloves, sliced
300ml/½ pint passata (sieved tomatoes)
350g/12oz rigatoni (ridged pasta tubes)
pinch of sugar (optional)
handful of fresh basil, torn
250g/9oz taleggio cheese, thinly sliced

Takes 45 minutes • Serves 4

1 Heat the oil in a large frying pan and fry the onion for 2–3 minutes. Add the peppers and cook over a medium heat until lightly browned. Reduce the heat, add the garlic, and cook for 2 minutes. Stir in the passata and 150ml/¼ pint water. Bring to the boil and simmer for 15 minutes until the sauce is thickened and reduced.
2 Meanwhile, cook the pasta in salted boiling water according to the packet instructions. Preheat the grill to high. Season the sauce and add a pinch of sugar, if necessary. Add the drained pasta and half the basil and spread into a shallow, flameproof dish.
3 Arrange the cheese over the top and grill for 5 minutes until the cheese is melted. Scatter over the remaining basil and serve.

• Per serving 692 kcalories, protein 15g, carbohydrate 75g, fat 39g, saturated fat 20g, fibre 5g, added sugar 15g, salt 0.59g

Ravioli with Pumpkin

Pumpkin can be bland but here it's spiced up with chilli, sage and lemon zest.

500g/1lb 2oz packet fresh cheese ravioli
1 tbsp olive oil
1 onion, finely chopped
1 garlic clove, crushed
425g can solid pumpkin
50g/2oz vegetarian parmesan, finely grated
pinch of crushed chilli flakes
finely grated zest of 1 lemon
25g/1oz butter
85g/3oz fresh white breadcrumbs
2 tbsp chopped fresh sage
deep-fried sage leaves, to garnish (optional)

Takes 30 minutes • Serves 4

1 Cook the ravioli according to the packet instructions. Meanwhile, heat the olive oil in a small pan and fry the onion and garlic for 2–3 minutes, until softened. Add the pumpkin, 300ml/½ pint water, the grated parmesan, chilli flakes and lemon zest. Stir well and cook over a low heat for 3–4 minutes. Season.
2 In a small frying pan, melt the butter, then stir in the breadcrumbs and fry until lightly golden. Stir in the chopped sage.
3 Drain the ravioli and spoon into bowls. Pour over the pumpkin sauce and sprinkle with the toasted sage breadcrumbs. Serve with the deep-fried sage, if liked.

• Per serving 674 kcalories, protein 26g, carbohydrate 94g, fat 24g, saturated fat 12g, fibre 5g, added sugar none, salt 1.28g

TOP LEFT: Spaghetti Genovese   TOP RIGHT: Pasta with Taleggio   BOTTOM: Ravioli with Pumpkin

TOP: Fiorentina Baked Pasta   BOTTOM LEFT: Chilli Bean Open Lasagne   BOTTOM RIGHT: Spaghetti Carbonara

Fiorentina Baked Pasta

This pasta dish is perfect to have bubbling in the oven while you chat to your guests.

1 tbsp olive oil
500g/1lb 2oz chestnut mushrooms, halved
2 garlic cloves, chopped
300g carton fresh spinach and cheese sauce
300ml/½ pint milk
50g/2oz vegetarian parmesan cheese, grated
300g/10oz puntalette (rice-shaped pasta)

Takes 1 hour • Serves 4

1 Preheat the oven to 190°C/Gas 5/fan oven 170°C. Heat the oil in a large frying pan, add the mushrooms and cook over a high heat for 5 minutes until lightly golden. Reduce the heat, add the garlic and cook for 2 minutes. Season and place in a shallow 1.5 litre/2¾ pint ovenproof dish.
2 Place the spinach sauce, milk, half the parmesan and pasta in a large bowl. Stir and season to taste. Pour over the mushrooms and scatter over the remaining parmesan.
3 Bake for 45 minutes until the pasta is tender and most of the liquid has been absorbed.

• Per serving 594 kcalories, protein 27g, carbohydrate 67g, fat 26g, saturated fat 12g, fibre 4g, added sugar none, salt 1.56g

Chilli Bean Open Lasagne

Don't bother with layering the lasagne in a dish, this easy version is assembled on the plate.

1 tbsp olive oil
1 onion, chopped
2 garlic cloves, crushed
1 red chilli, finely sliced
1 small aubergine, chopped
1 large courgette, chopped
410g can borlotti beans, drained
400g can chopped tomatoes
2 tbsp tomato purée
250g pack fresh lasagne sheets
handful of basil, torn
100g/4oz vegetarian cheddar, grated
green salad, to serve

Takes 30 minutes • Serves 4

1 Heat the oil in a large frying pan. Fry the onion for 3 minutes, until softened. Add the garlic, chilli, aubergine and courgette and fry for a further 2 minutes. Stir in the beans, tomatoes and tomato purée and season. Bring to the boil and simmer for 5 minutes.
2 Meanwhile, cook the lasagne sheets in salted boiling water according to the packet instructions. Drain, then halve each sheet diagonally. Stir all but four of the basil sprigs into the bean mixture.
3 Place a spoonful of the mixture on to each plate and top with a quarter of the lasagne triangles. Top with the remaining bean mix, grated cheese and the basil sprigs. Serve with a green salad.

• Per serving 400 kcalories, protein 17g, carbohydrate 73g, fat 6g, saturated fat 1g, fibre 11g, added sugar none, salt 1.21g

Spaghetti Carbonara

Egg yolks and cream make one of the quickest and most delicious pasta sauces.

350g/12oz tricolour spaghetti
225g/8oz baby carrots, halved lengthways
fine asparagus, sliced into 3cm/1¼in lengths
1 large courgette, cut into ribbons
2 medium egg yolks
200ml/7fl oz double cream
50g/2oz vegetarian parmesan, grated
50g/2oz sun-dried tomatoes in oil, drained and sliced

Takes 25 minutes • Serves 4

1 Cook the pasta in a large pan of lightly salted boiling water according to the packet instructions. About 4 minutes before the end of cooking add the carrots.
2 After 2 minutes add the asparagus and just before draining stir in the courgette ribbons. Drain and return to the pan over a low heat. Beat together the egg yolks, cream and half the parmesan and season well.
3 Pour over the pasta and vegetables and heat very gently for 2–3 minutes, stirring constantly, until the sauce has thickened slightly – do not overheat or the eggs will scramble. Stir in the sun-dried tomatoes and serve with the remaining parmesan and plenty of black pepper.

• Per serving 651 kcalories, protein 20g, carbohydrate 71g, fat 34g, saturated fat 19g, fibre 5g, added sugar none, salt 0.51g

Lemon Butter Gnocchi

Gnocchi are small Italian dumplings, treated like pasta and served with a tasty sauce.

400g packet fresh potato gnocchi
2 tbsp olive oil
300g/10oz butternut squash, peeled, halved, seeded and roughly chopped
1 tsp sugar
finely grated zest of 1 lemon and ½ of the juice
85g/3oz butter
2 tbsp chopped fresh rosemary
green salad, to serve

Takes 20 minutes • Serves 2

1 Cook the gnocchi according to the packet instructions. Meanwhile, heat the oil in a small frying pan and fry the butternut squash for 5 minutes until tender. Sprinkle over the sugar and lemon zest and fry for a further minute until slightly caramelised.
2 Melt the butter in a small pan. Stir in the lemon juice and chopped rosemary and season to taste. Drain the gnocchi and stir into the butternut squash. Stir well to combine.
3 Spoon into warmed serving bowls, then drizzle the lemon and rosemary butter sauce over. Serve with a green salad.

• Per serving 615 kcalories, protein 8g, carbohydrate 63g, fat 39g, saturated fat 21g, fibre 5g, added sugar 3g, salt 0.97g

Cheese and Tomato Cannelloni

Using fresh pasta in this dish means there's no pre-cooking needed.

5 tbsp fruity olive oil
750g/1lb 10oz ripe cherry tomatoes
2 tsp dried oregano
2 tsp golden caster sugar
6 tbsp fresh red or green pesto
225g/8oz soft rindless goat's cheese
12 fresh lasagne sheets
350g/12oz ripe vine tomatoes, thinly sliced
3 tbsp freshly grated parmesan
basil leaves and green salad, to serve

Takes 1 hour 20 minutes • Serves 4

1 Preheat the oven to 220°C/Gas 7/fan oven 200°C. Oil a shallow baking dish. Halve 250g/9oz of the cherry tomatoes. Heat the oil in a frying pan, add the whole cherry tomatoes, cover and cook over a high heat, shaking the pan, for 5 minutes. Add the oregano and sugar. Season.
2 Beat the pesto into the goat's cheese. Lay out the lasagne and spread the cheese mixture over each sheet. Top with tomato slices and roll up like a Swiss roll. Spoon half the cherry tomato sauce into the dish. Arrange the pasta rolls on top and spoon over any remaining tomato sauce. Scatter the cherry tomato halves on top and cover with foil.
3 Bake for 25–30 minutes. Uncover, sprinkle with the cheese and bake for 10 minutes until brown. Serve with basil and a green salad.

• Per serving 635 kcalories, protein 21g, carbohydrate 57g, fat 37g, saturated fat 5g, fibre 6g, added sugar 3g, salt 1.46g

Cheddar and Tomato Rice

A simple dish, easily varied by adding peas, fried mushrooms or sweetcorn.

2 tbsp oil
1 onion, thinly sliced
1 red pepper, cored, seeded and sliced
1 garlic clove, finely chopped
300g/10oz long grain rice
1 litre/1¾ pints vegetable stock
227g can chopped tomatoes
100g/4oz mature cheddar, cubed
chives and salad leaves, to garnish

Takes 1 hour • Serves 4

1 Preheat the oven to 180°C/Gas 4/fan oven 160°C from cold. Heat the oil in a large flameproof casserole, fry the onion and red pepper over a medium heat until golden. Add the chopped garlic and cook for a further minute.
2 Stir in the rice until completely coated in oil. Add the stock and tomatoes, and season. Bring to the boil and simmer for 5 minutes until nearly all the liquid has been absorbed.
3 Scatter over the cheese, cover the casserole and cook in the oven for about 30 minutes until the rice is tender. Leave for 5 minutes before garnishing with chives and salad leaves.

• Per serving 463 kcalories, protein 14g, carbohydrate 72g, fat 15g, saturated fat 6g, fibre 2g, added sugar none, salt 1.32g

TOP: Lemon Butter Gnocchi   BOTTOM LEFT: Cheese and Tomato Cannelloni   BOTTOM RIGHT: Cheddar and Tomato Rice

TOP LEFT: Gnocchi with Broad Beans   TOP RIGHT: Leek and Mushroom Risotto   BOTTOM: Baked Spinach Risotto

Gnocchi with Broad Beans

Potato gnocchi, bought vacuum-packed, make a great fridge or freezer stand-by.

350g packet potato gnocchi
2 tbsp olive oil
250g/9oz small cup mushrooms, halved
2 garlic cloves, crushed
225g/8oz frozen baby broad beans
3 tbsp chopped fresh tarragon
250g mascarpone cheese
1 tbsp lemon juice
vegetarian parmesan shavings and pared
   lemon zest, to garnish
salad, to serve (optional)

Takes 20 minutes • Serves 4

1 Cook the gnocchi according to the packet instructions. Drain and set aside. Heat the oil in a frying pan, add the mushrooms and fry quickly over a high heat until browned. Lift out with a slotted spoon and add to the gnocchi.
2 Wipe out the pan then add the garlic, beans, tarragon and mascarpone. Heat gently, stirring, until the mascarpone has melted. Add the lemon juice, mushrooms and gnocchi to the frying pan. Heat through for 1 minute. Season to taste.
3 Divide between serving plates and scatter over the parmesan shavings and pared lemon zest. Serve with salad leaves, if liked.

• Per serving 488 kcalories, protein 10g, carbohydrate 28g, fat 38g, saturated fat 20g, fibre 5g, added sugar none, salt 0.54g

Leek and Mushroom Risotto

This version is cooked in the microwave, which cuts down the need for stirring.

25g/1oz butter
1 tbsp olive oil
1 leek, cut into thin slices
1 garlic clove, crushed
300g/10oz risotto rice
850ml/1½ pints hot vegetable stock
250g/9oz chestnut
   mushrooms, sliced
50g/2oz fresh parmesan, grated
green salad, to serve

Takes 40 minutes • Serves 4

1 Put the butter, oil, leek and garlic into a large bowl. Cover with cling film and cook on High for 5 minutes.
2 Stir the rice into the hot leeks, then stir in the stock and season. Cook, uncovered, on High for 10 minutes. Throw in the mushrooms, stir and cook on High for 6 minutes.
3 Mix in half the parmesan and leave the risotto to stand for 5 minutes. Serve with a green salad and the remaining parmesan for sprinkling.

• Per serving 397 kcalories, protein 13g, carbohydrate 60g, fat 13g, saturated fat 6g, fibre 3g, added sugar none, salt 1.22g

Baked Spinach Risotto

This oven-baked risotto works beautifully and saves effort as you don't have to stand over it.

25g/1oz butter
1 garlic clove, crushed
1 small red onion, chopped
100g/4oz risotto rice
1 tbsp chopped fresh rosemary, plus extra
   to garnish
300ml/½ pint vegetable stock
250ml/9fl oz white wine
290g jar antipasto mixed peppers in
   tomato dressing
50g/2oz spinach
25g/1oz vegetarian parmesan, grated
green salad, to serve

Takes 55 minutes • Serves 2

1 Preheat the oven to 180°C/Gas 4/fan oven 160°C. Put the butter and garlic in a 1 litre/1¾ pint ovenproof dish and place in the oven for 2 minutes until the butter has melted. Add the onion and toss to coat in the butter, then return to the oven for a further 3–4 minutes to soften.
2 Add the rice, rosemary, stock and wine and return to the oven for 30 minutes, stirring once or twice during cooking.
3 Stir in the antipasto peppers and spinach and return to the oven for another 10 minutes, until all the liquid has been absorbed. Stir in the parmesan and season to taste. Serve with a fresh green salad.

• Per serving 534 kcalories, protein 11g, carbohydrate 54g, fat 23g, saturated fat 10g, fibre 3g, added sugar none, salt 1.25g

Thai Fried Rice with Vegetables

Cook the rice earlier in the day because it stir fries better when it's cooled first.

2 tbsp sunflower oil
1 red chilli, finely sliced
1 stalk lemongrass, finely chopped
2 shallots, finely sliced
1 garlic clove, crushed
5cm/2in piece fresh root ginger, finely chopped
140g/5oz jasmine rice, cooked and cooled
1 small red pepper, seeded and sliced
1 carrot, cut into matchsticks
2 spring onions, shredded
85g/3oz mangetout, sliced
1 tbsp light soy sauce
25g/1oz coconut shavings, toasted
fresh coriander leaves

Takes 35 minutes • Serves 2

1 Heat one tablespoon of the oil in a wok or large frying pan. Stir fry the chilli, lemongrass, shallots, garlic and ginger over a low heat for 2 minutes until softened. Add the cooked rice and fry, stirring, for a further 3–4 minutes.
2 Meanwhile, heat the remaining oil in another frying pan and toss in the pepper, carrot, spring onions and mangetout. Stir fry for 2–3 minutes.
3 Stir the soy sauce into the rice and spoon into serving bowls. Top with the vegetables, coconut shavings and torn coriander leaves and serve.

• Per serving 930 kcalories, protein 17g, carbohydrate 177g, fat 22g, saturated fat 6g, fibre 5g, added sugar none, salt 1.17g

Sesame Noodle Salad

A pack of egg noodles is a useful storecupboard item. They cook quickly and are good with stir fries as well as in a warm salad.

140g pack medium egg noodles
3 tbsp sesame oil
1 tbsp dark soy sauce
2 tsp lemon juice
1 large carrot, peeled
10cm/4in piece cucumber or courgette
2 tsp sesame seeds
2 garlic cloves, finely chopped
25g/1oz fresh root ginger, peeled and finely chopped
4 spring onions, shredded
½–1 tsp Chinese five-spice powder
handful of lamb's lettuce or rocket

Takes 15 minutes • Serves 2

1 Cook the noodles according to the packet instructions. Rinse in a colander under cold water and drain well. Tip into a bowl and add the sesame oil, soy sauce and lemon juice.
2 Use a potato peeler to cut the carrot into fine ribbons. Do the same with the cucumber or courgette, discarding the central seed section. Add to the noodles.
3 Heat a small pan and dry fry the sesame seeds until pale golden. Sprinkle over the noodles. Add the oil to the pan and stir fry the garlic, ginger, spring onions and five-spice powder for 30 seconds. Stir in the lettuce or rocket leaves. Toss with the noodles, season and serve.

• Per serving 655 kcalories, protein 15g, carbohydrate 58g, fat 42g, saturated fat 5g, fibre 6g, added sugar none, salt 1.47g

Spicy Nasi Goreng

You could use leftover rice to make this tasty and colourful Indonesian fried rice mixture, if it has been kept well chilled.

300g/10oz long grain rice, rinsed
2 medium eggs, beaten
3 garlic cloves
2 red chillies, thinly sliced
2 onions, sliced
3 tbsp groundnut oil
1 yellow pepper, seeded and sliced
2 carrots, cut into matchsticks
2 tbsp dark soy sauce
4 spring onions, shredded
4 tbsp chopped fresh coriander

Takes 35 minutes • Serves 2

1 Place the rice in a wok, add 600ml/1 pint water and bring to the boil. Cover and cook over a very low heat for 15 minutes, until all the liquid has been absorbed. Tip into a shallow dish and leave to cool.
2 Meanwhile, heat the wok. Add the eggs and cook, stirring, until scrambled. Remove and set aside. Whizz the garlic, half the chilli and half the onion to a paste in a blender. Heat the oil in the wok and fry the paste for 1 minute. Add the rest of the onion and chilli, plus the vegetables and stir fry for 2 minutes.
3 Add the cold rice and stir fry for 3 minutes. Stir in the soy sauce, spring onions and eggs and fry until piping hot. Season and serve immediately.

• Per serving 445 kcalories, protein 10g, carbohydrate 72g, fat 15g, saturated fat 3g, fibre 2g, added sugar none, salt 0.16g

TOP LEFT: Thai Fried Rice with Vegetables   TOP RIGHT: Sesame Noodle Salad   BOTTOM: Spicy Nasi Goreng

TOP: Pumpkin and Apple Curry   BOTTOM LEFT: Indian Chickpea Salad   BOTTOM RIGHT: Leek and Goat's Cheese Tarts

Pumpkin and Apple Curry

Serve this saucy curry in deep bowls with spoonfuls of cooling fromage frais and warm bread for dunking.

1 tbsp sunflower oil
1 large onion, roughly chopped
3 garlic cloves, chopped
500g/1lb 2oz pumpkin, peeled, seeded and cubed
800g/1lb 12oz baking potatoes, cubed
1 medium cooking apple, peeled, cored and diced
2 tsp mild curry paste
1 tsp turmeric
2.5cm/1in fresh root ginger, chopped
2 bay leaves
1 vegetable stock cube
50g/2oz raisins
4 tbsp fromage frais, to serve
bread or rice, to serve

Takes 45 minutes • Serves 4

1 Heat the oil in a pan, add the onion and fry for 5 minutes until golden. Add the garlic, pumpkin, potatoes and apple. Stir in the curry paste, turmeric, ginger and bay leaves.
2 Add 500ml/18fl oz water, the stock cube, raisins and plenty of seasoning. Bring to the boil, stirring. Cover and simmer for 15 minutes, stirring occasionally, until the vegetables are tender.
3 Spoon into bowls and top with the fromage frais and a pinch of turmeric. Serve with bread or rice.

• Per serving 270 kcalories, protein 5g, carbohydrate 55g, fat 5g, saturated fat 1g, fibre 6g, added sugar none, salt 0.23g

Indian Chickpea Salad

A substantial main course salad with spiced canned chickpeas and naan bread croûtons.

6 tbsp olive oil
3 garlic cloves, sliced
2 red chillies, seeded and sliced
4 tsp cumin seeds, lightly crushed
2 × 400g cans chickpeas, drained and rinsed
3 tomatoes, halved, seeded and diced
pared zest and juice of 1 lemon
1 naan bread

FOR THE SALAD
25g/1oz fresh coriander
½ cucumber, cut into batons
1 medium red onion, sliced
100g/4oz baby spinach leaves

Takes 30 minutes • Serves 4

1 Put five tablespoons of the oil in a pan. Add the garlic, chillies and cumin and warm over a medium heat for 10 minutes. Take care not to burn the garlic. Add the chickpeas and heat through for 5 minutes. Meanwhile, preheat the grill to high.
2 Add the tomatoes, lemon zest and juice to the chickpeas. Season and set aside. Brush the naan bread with the remaining oil and grill both sides until crisp. Tear into bite-sized pieces.
3 Toss together the salad ingredients and divide between serving plates. Spoon the chickpeas over and top with the naan bread croûtons.

• Per serving 641 kcalories, protein 23g, carbohydrate 66g, fat 33g, saturated fat 6g, fibre 11g, added sugar 0.2g, salt 0.65g

Leek and Goat's Cheese Tarts

Choose a soft rindless goat's cheese for this recipe.

250g/9oz ready-made shortcrust pastry
1 tbsp olive oil
1 leek, halved lengthways and cut into 1cm/½in pieces
1 yellow pepper, seeded and chopped
6 pitted black olives, quartered
2 tbsp fresh thyme leaves
100g/4oz soft rindless goat's cheese, cubed
green salad or steamed winter greens, to serve (optional)

Takes 45 minutes • Serves 4

1 Preheat the oven to 180°C/Gas 4/fan oven 160°C. Roll out the pastry on a lightly floured surface and use to line four 12cm/4½in loose-bottomed, fluted tart tins. Prick the pastry bases, line with greaseproof paper and fill with baking beans. Bake for 12 minutes.
2 Meanwhile, heat the oil in a large frying pan and fry the leek and pepper until softened. Remove the paper and baking beans from the tarts. Fill each tart with the leek and pepper mixture. Scatter over the olives, thyme and goat's cheese.
3 Cook for 10–12 minutes, until the pastry is golden and the cheese is slightly melted. Serve immediately with mixed salad leaves or freshly steamed winter greens, if liked.

• Per serving 441 kcalories, protein 9g, carbohydrate 38g, fat 29g, saturated fat 11g, fibre 3g, added sugar none, salt 1.68g

Root Vegetable Bake

This layered vegetable 'cake' makes a perfect alternative to a roast joint. Serve with a veggie-friendly gravy.

100g/4oz butter, softened
finely grated zest of 1 small lemon
2 garlic cloves, crushed
3 tbsp fresh thyme leaves
85g/3oz gruyère, finely grated
750g/1lb 10oz waxy potatoes, peeled
225g/8oz celeriac, peeled
450g/1lb carrots, peeled
450g/1lb parsnips, peeled and cored
vegetarian gravy, to serve

Takes 2 hours • Serves 6

1 Preheat the oven to 190°C/Gas 5/fan oven 170°C. Use 25g/1oz butter to grease a 20cm/8in cake tin (not loose-bottomed). Mash the remaining butter with the lemon zest, garlic, thyme and gruyère. Season.
2 Very thinly slice the vegetables. Layer one third of the potatoes, then celeriac, carrots and parsnips in the tin. Dot with the butter. Repeat the layers. Finish with black pepper and dots of butter.
3 Cover the tin with foil and bake for 45 minutes. Remove the foil and bake for a further 45 minutes until the vegetables are tender. Leave for 5 minutes. Invert on to a warm plate, place a plate over the top and invert again so the crispy side is on top. Serve with vegetarian gravy.

• Per serving 483 kcalories, protein 38g, carbohydrate 46g, fat 18g, saturated fat 5g, fibre 8g, added sugar none, salt 8.3g

Roasted Vegetable Couscous

Couscous only needs to be soaked before you eat it, so it's a useful accompaniment to colourful roasted vegetables.

1 each red and yellow pepper, seeded and diced
2 courgettes, diced
1 aubergine, diced
1 red onion, chopped
2 garlic cloves, chopped
1 tbsp fresh rosemary, chopped
5 tbsp olive oil
250g/9oz couscous
400g can flageolet beans, drained and rinsed
2 tbsp balsamic vinegar
green salad, to serve

Takes 45 minutes • Serves 4

1 Preheat the oven to 220°C/Gas 7/fan oven 200°C. Place all the vegetables, the garlic and rosemary in a large roasting tin and drizzle over four tablespoons oil. Season and roast for 20 minutes, stirring after 10 minutes.
2 Meanwhile, put the couscous in a bowl and pour over 400ml/14fl oz boiling water. Season and leave for 20 minutes until all the water has been absorbed. Add the flageolet beans and vinegar to the roasting tin, mix well and roast for a further 10 minutes.
3 Fluff up the couscous grains with a fork. Divide between serving plates and top with the roasted vegetable and bean mixture. Serve with a green salad.

• Per serving 478 kcalories, protein 15g, carbohydrate 61g, fat 21g, saturated fat 3g, fibre 7g, added sugar none, salt 0.06g

Potato and Onion Tart

A filling tart, delicious served hot or cold with salads.

375g pack ready-rolled shortcrust pastry, thawed if frozen
2 tbsp olive oil
450g/1lb onions, thinly sliced
2 garlic cloves, crushed
3 tbsp fresh thyme leaves or 1 tbsp dried
750g/1lb 10oz floury potatoes, peeled and thickly sliced
2 eggs
200ml carton crème fraîche
2 tbsp wholegrain mustard salad, to serve

Takes 50 minutes • Serves 4

1 Preheat the oven to 220°C/Gas 7/fan oven 200°C. Use the pastry to line the base and sides of a Swiss roll tin about 23 × 33cm/9 × 13in. Heat the oil in a large frying pan and fry the onions for 8–10 minutes, until just beginning to caramelise. Stir in the garlic and most of the thyme and cook for a further 2 minutes. Scatter half into the pastry case.
2 Parboil the potatoes in salted boiling water for 4–5 minutes. Drain well and arrange in the case. Scatter over the remaining onions.
3 Beat together the eggs, crème fraîche and mustard. Season well and pour over the vegetables. Scatter over the rest of the thyme and bake the tart for 20 minutes, until the filling has set and is golden. Serve with a salad.

• Per serving 706 kcalories, protein 14g, carbohydrate 84g, fat 37g, saturated fat 14g, fibre 6g, added sugar none, salt 0.84g

TOP: Root Vegetable Bake BOTTOM LEFT: Roasted Vegetable Couscous BOTTOM RIGHT: Potato and Onion Tart

TOP LEFT: **Aubergines with Goat's Cheese**   TOP RIGHT: **Polenta Pizza**   BOTTOM: **Tomato and Goat's Cheese Crumble**

Aubergines with Goat's Cheese

Most melting cheeses will taste great grilled on top of aubergine slices. Try using brie for a change.

4 medium aubergines, halved lengthways
100ml/3½fl oz olive oil
2 tbsp sun-dried tomato paste
25g/1oz fresh basil leaves
4 × 60g individual, rinded goat's cheeses
1 tbsp white wine vinegar
1 tsp Dijon mustard
pinch of caster sugar
160g bag mixed salad leaves
140g/5oz couscous
85g/3oz radishes, halved
crusty bread, to serve

Takes 25 minutes • Serves 4

1 Preheat the grill to hot. Brush both sides of the aubergine halves with three tablespoons of the oil and season. Place the aubergines, cut-side up, on a baking sheet and grill for 7 minutes. Turn them over and grill for a further 5 minutes, until lightly scorched.
2 Spread the cut sides with the tomato paste and arrange basil leaves on top. Slice each cheese into four rounds and arrange on the aubergines. Season and grill until bubbling.
3 Whisk the remaining oil, vinegar, mustard and sugar in a salad bowl. Toss the vegetables in the dressing until coated. Divide between serving plates and arrange the cheesy aubergine halves on top. Serve with crusty bread.

• Per serving 416 kcalories, protein 12g, carbohydrate 10g, fat 37g, saturated fat 4g, fibre 7g, added sugar none, salt 2.36g

Polenta Pizza

Instead of using bread dough, this pizza base is made from quick-cook polenta spread on a baking tray.

250g pack quick-cook polenta
50g/2oz vegetarian parmesan, grated
1 tbsp olive oil
1 red onion, sliced
2 garlic cloves, sliced
1 courgette, sliced
100g/4oz chestnut mushrooms, sliced
4 ripe plum tomatoes, sliced
100g/4oz mozzarella, thinly sliced
1 tbsp vegetarian green pesto
green salad, to serve

Takes 50 minutes • Serves 4

1 Cook the polenta according to the packet instructions. Season well and stir in the parmesan. Pour on to an oiled baking sheet, spread out to a 28cm/11in circle and leave to firm up for 15 minutes. Meanwhile, preheat the oven to 200°C/Gas 6/fan oven 180°C.
2 Heat the oil in a large frying pan and fry the onion for 5 minutes, until softened. Add the garlic and courgettes and cook for a further 2 minutes. Season and scatter over the polenta base with the mushrooms and tomatoes.
3 Arrange the mozzarella on top and dot with the pesto. Bake for 20 minutes, until the cheese has melted. Serve cut in wedges with a green salad.

• Per serving 423 kcalories, protein 19g, carbohydrate 50g, fat 18g, saturated fat 7g, fibre 53g, added sugar none, salt 0.83g

Tomato and Goat's Cheese Crumble

This is a really tasty supper dish and it's easily doubled to feed those hungry hordes.

1kg/2lb 4oz ripe tomatoes, preferably a
    mixture, including a punnet of cherry
    tomatoes
5 tbsp olive oil
225g/8oz goat's cheese, firm or soft
50g/2oz pine nuts
100g/4oz fresh white breadcrumbs
50g/2oz parmesan, freshly grated
green salad or vegetables, to serve

Takes 55 minutes • Serves 4

1 Preheat the oven to 190°C/Gas 5/fan oven 170°C. Chop the tomatoes, keeping the cherry ones whole. Heat two tablespoons of olive oil in a pan, add the chopped tomatoes, season and cook for 10 minutes, until softened, stirring occasionally. Remove from the heat and stir in the cherry tomatoes.
2 Spoon half the tomatoes into a 1 litre/1¾ pint ovenproof dish and crumble half the goat's cheese on top. Repeat the layers.
3 Heat three tablespoons of olive oil in a frying pan and lightly fry the pine nuts and breadcrumbs. Remove from the heat and stir in half the parmesan. Scatter over the tomatoes and cheese and top with the remaining parmesan. Bake for 20–25 minutes, until golden. Serve with a green salad or vegetables.

• Per serving 431 kcalories, protein 22g, carbohydrate 28g, fat 27g, saturated fat 12g, fibre 3g, added sugar none, salt 1.78g

Red Onion, Feta and Olive Tart

Frozen puff pastry makes a quick case for a tangy, salty filling.

25g/1oz butter
2 large red onions, finely sliced
2 tbsp light muscovado sugar
2 tbsp balsamic vinegar
flour, for dusting
450g puff pastry, thawed if frozen
100g/4oz feta, crumbled
175g/6oz black olives, pitted
   and chopped
1 tbsp extra virgin olive oil
shredded basil leaves, to garnish
green salad, to serve

Takes 45 minutes • Serves 4

1 Preheat the oven to 200°C/Gas 6/fan oven 180°C. Heat the butter in a pan and add the onions. Add a pinch of salt and fry for about 10 minutes, until caramelised. Add the sugar and balsamic vinegar and cook for a further 5 minutes, until the juices are reduced and syrupy. Leave to cool.
2 Roll out the pastry on a floured surface and use to line a 30 × 22cm/12 × 8½in Swiss roll tin. Cover with the onion mixture and scatter over the feta and olives. Season and drizzle over the olive oil.
3 Bake for 15–20 minutes until the pastry is risen and golden and the base is crisp. Scatter over the basil leaves and cut into wedges. Serve with a green salad.

• Per serving 646 kcalories, protein 11g, carbohydrate 53g, fat 44g, saturated fat 18g, fibre 2g, added sugar 8g, salt 4.07g

Cheesy Spring Onion Tart

Buy a ready-made pastry case to save time. Try asparagus instead of the onions.

1 bunch spring onions, trimmed
1 tbsp olive oil
225g/8oz soft goat's cheese
   (eg, chevre), rind removed
150ml/¼ pint double cream
3 large eggs, separated
24cm/9½in ready-made shortcrust
   pastry case
tomato salad, to serve

Takes 40 minutes • Serves 6

1 Preheat the oven to 190°C/Gas 5/fan oven 170°C and preheat the grill to hot. Place the spring onions on a baking sheet and brush with the oil. Grill for 2 minutes.
2 In a bowl, beat together the goat's cheese, cream and egg yolks until smooth. Whisk the egg whites until stiff and gently fold into the cheese mixture. Spoon into the pastry case and arrange the spring onions on top.
3 Bake for 20–25 minutes until golden. Serve with a tomato salad.

• Per serving 337 kcalories, protein 11g, carbohydrate 18g, fat 25g, saturated fat 13g, fibre 1g, added sugar 3g, salt 0.64g

Creamy Egg Curry

Use your favourite curry paste, rather than grind spices for this simple supper.

2 tbsp oil
1 large, or 2 medium onions
   (about 300g/10oz in total weight),
   thinly sliced
2 heaped tbsp curry paste
230g can tomatoes
8 eggs
140g/5oz frozen peas
4 tbsp Greek-style yogurt
cooked rice and mango chutney, to serve

Takes 45 minutes • Serves 4

1 Heat the oil in a frying pan. Add the onion and cook for 10 minutes until golden. Add the curry paste and cook, stirring, for 2 minutes. Add the tomatoes, 200ml/7fl oz water and season. Bring to the boil, then simmer for 20 minutes. Add a splash of water if the curry becomes too thick.
2 Meanwhile, boil the eggs for 8 minutes.
3 Stir the peas and yogurt into the curry. Simmer for 2–3 minutes. Peel and halve each egg and gently stir into the curry. Serve with cooked rice and mango chutney.

• Per serving 302 kcalories, protein 18g, carbohydrate 12g, fat 21g, saturated fat 5g, fibre 3g, added sugar none, salt 0.84g

TOP LEFT: Red Onion, Feta and Olive Tart   TOP RIGHT: Cheesy Spring Onion Tart   BOTTOM: Creamy Egg Curry

TOP: Orange and Celery Salad   BOTTOM LEFT: Tuscan Salad   BOTTOM RIGHT: Warm Red Cabbage Salad

Orange and Celery Salad

Crisp, crunchy textures with fresh-tasting flavours will make this speedy salad a firm favourite.

2 large oranges
1 small head celery (about 350g/12oz),
    trimmed, destringed and sliced on
    the diagonal
1 small red onion, cut into very thin wedges
225g/8oz red cherry tomatoes, halved
85g/3oz lamb's lettuce
1 small garlic clove, crushed
2 tbsp chopped fresh mint
6 tbsp olive oil
1 tbsp balsamic vinegar

Takes 15 minutes • Serves 4

1 Cut away the peel and pith from the oranges. Cut each side of each membrane to remove the individual segments. Do this over a bowl to catch the juices.
2 Place the orange segments in a large serving bowl and sprinkle over the sliced celery, onion wedges, tomato halves and lamb's lettuce.
3 Add the crushed garlic, chopped fresh mint, olive oil and balsamic vinegar to the orange juice and whisk until well combined. Season to taste and pour over the salad. Toss well just before serving.

• Per serving 249 kcalories, protein 2g, carbohydrate 9g, fat 23g, saturated fat 3g, fibre 3g, added sugar none, salt 0.19g

Tuscan Salad

This rustic, peasant-style salad, traditional to southern Italy, is packed with the flavour of sun-ripened vegetables.

2 red peppers, seeded and quartered
2 yellow peppers, seeded and quartered
1 ciabatta loaf
6 tbsp extra virgin olive oil
3 tbsp red wine vinegar
2 garlic cloves, crushed
6 ripe plum tomatoes, cut into chunks
50g/2oz caper berries or capers
50g/2oz marinated black olives
handful of fresh basil leaves, roughly torn
2 tbsp pine nuts, toasted

Takes 35 minutes • Serves 4

1 Preheat the grill to hot. Grill the peppers until charred and place in a plastic bag so that the steam loosens the skins.
2 Meanwhile, tear the bread into rough chunks, toast until golden brown and place in a large bowl. Beat together the olive oil, vinegar and garlic, season and set aside.
3 Remove the skin from the peppers and cut into chunks. Toss with the toasted bread along with the tomatoes, caper berries or capers, olives, basil, pine nuts and the dressing. Serve immediately on its own or as an accompaniment to a creamy goat's cheese or ripe brie.

• Per serving 622 kcalories, protein 15g, carbohydrate 69g, fat 33g, saturated fat 4g, fibre 5g, added sugar none, salt 2.68g

Warm Red Cabbage Salad

A colourful winter salad with a deliciously nutty dressing.

1 tbsp sunflower oil
1 red onion, sliced
1 small red cabbage (about 350g/12oz), finely
    shredded
1 red apple, cored and cut into chunks
1 carrot, grated
2 tbsp balsamic vinegar
½ tsp soft light brown sugar
½ tsp wholegrain mustard
4 tbsp walnut oil
2 little gem lettuces, roughly torn
50g/2oz walnut pieces
fresh flatleaf parsley, to garnish

Takes 25 minutes • Serves 4

1 Heat the oil in a frying pan and fry the onion for 1–2 minutes. Add the cabbage and cook for a further 2–3 minutes. Remove from the heat and add the apple and carrot.
2 Meanwhile, in a small bowl whisk together the vinegar, sugar, mustard and walnut oil. Season to taste.
3 Arrange the lettuce leaves on individual serving plates. Spoon the warm cabbage salad over. Sprinkle over the walnut pieces and drizzle over the dressing. Sprinkle over the flatleaf parsley and serve.

• Per serving 304 kcalories, protein 4g, carbohydrate 10g, fat 28g, saturated fat 3g, fibre 4g, added sugar 1g, salt 0.09g

Noodle and Watercress Salad

Use buckwheat soba noodles for extra flavour and colour, although egg noodles would be good, too.

225g/8oz dried buckwheat soba noodles
2 tbsp light soy sauce
2 tbsp sesame oil
4 tbsp saké (Japanese rich wine) or dry
    white wine
2 tsp caster sugar
8 fresh mint leaves
1 large firm mango, halved, stoned
    and peeled
85g/3oz watercress, stalks removed
2 tbsp sesame seeds, toasted
squeeze of lime juice

Takes 20 minutes • Serves 4

1 Cook the noodles in lightly salted boiling water according to the packet instructions, then drain and plunge immediately into cold water to refresh and stop the cooking process. Put the soy sauce, sesame oil, saké and sugar in a small pan and heat gently. Remove from the heat and stir in the mint. Set aside and allow to infuse.
2 Meanwhile, cut the mango into fine slivers. Drain the noodles thoroughly and toss with the soy sauce dressing, mango, watercress and half the sesame seeds.
3 Divide between four serving plates and sprinkle over the remaining sesame seeds. Squeeze over a little lime juice and serve immediately.

• Per serving 388 kcalories, protein 9g, carbohydrate 53g, fat 16g, saturated fat 2g, fibre 2g, added sugar 3g, salt 0.04g

Cracked Wheat and Fennel Salad

A delicious combination of roasted fennel and zesty orange, served on a bed of herby wheat.

250g/9oz bulghar wheat
3 heads of fennel, cut into wedges
4 tbsp olive oil
pared zest and juice of 2 oranges
4 tbsp chopped fresh flatleaf parsley
2 tbsp chopped fresh mint
4 plum tomatoes, cut into wedges
140g/5oz mixed olives, drained
100g/4oz rocket

Takes 45 minutes • Serves 4

1 Preheat the oven to 200°C/Gas 6/fan oven 180°C. Place the bulghar wheat in a large bowl, cover with 1 litre/1¾ pints boiling water and allow to stand for 30 minutes. Meanwhile, place the fennel in a large roasting tin, drizzle with the olive oil and season. Add the orange zest and half the orange juice and roast in the oven for 35 minutes until softened and slightly charred.
2 Drain the bulghar wheat, add the parsley and mint and remaining orange juice. Combine well and season to taste. Place the tomatoes, olives and rocket in a large bowl, add the roasted fennel with the pan juices and toss well.
3 Divide the bulghar wheat between four serving plates, top with the fennel and tomato mixture and serve.

• Per serving 422 kcalories, protein 9g, carbohydrate 53g, fat 39g, saturated fat 5g, fibre 8g, added sugar none, salt 0.03g

Warm Crispy Noodle Salad

This salad is a riot of colours and contrasting textures and it's easily adapted to use whatever vegetables you have to hand.

sunflower oil for deep frying
50g/2oz crispy rice noodles
1 tbsp oil
2.5cm/1in piece fresh root ginger, chopped
2 garlic cloves, crushed
100g/4oz sugarsnap peas, sliced lengthways
1 carrot, cut into matchsticks
4 spring onions, sliced
175g/6oz spinach leaves, shredded
100g/4oz beansprouts
½ small cucumber, cut into matchsticks
50g/2oz roasted cashew nuts, chopped
juice of 1 lime
2 tsp chilli oil

Takes 30 minutes • Serves 2

1 Heat 5cm/2in of oil in a pan until a cube of bread browns in 30 seconds. Carefully add the noodles, a few at a time, and fry for a few seconds until puffed and crisp. Remove and drain on kitchen paper.
2 Heat one tablespoon of oil in a wok, add the ginger and garlic and stir fry for 30 seconds. Add the sugarsnap peas, carrot and spring onions and stir fry for 1 minute. Add the spinach and beansprouts and cook for a further minute, until wilted.
3 Remove from the heat, stir in the cucumber and season. Divide between serving plates and scatter the nuts and crispy noodles over. Squeeze over the lime juice, drizzle over the chilli oil and serve.

• Per serving 458 kcalories, protein 14g, carbohydrate 37g, fat 29g, saturated fat 2g, fibre 6g, added sugar none, salt 0.6g

TOP: Noodle and Watercress Salad   BOTTOM LEFT: Cracked Wheat and Fennel Salad   BOTTOM RIGHT: Warm Crispy Noodle Salad

TOP LEFT: Minty Broad Bean Pâté   TOP RIGHT: Bagels with Griddled Vegetables   BOTTOM: Stuffed Focaccia

Minty Broad Bean Pâté

So simple to make – serve this fresh-tasting pâté with crusty bread for a snack or light lunch.

500g/1lb 2oz broad beans, shelled weight, outer skins removed
1 garlic clove, very finely chopped
150ml/¼ pint extra virgin olive oil, plus extra for drizzling
pinch of ground cumin
small bunch fresh mint, chopped
8 slices crusty wholegrain bread, to serve

Takes 20 minutes, plus resting • Serves 4

1 Cook the broad beans in lightly salted boiling water for 10–12 minutes, until tender. Drain well, reserving the cooking water. Transfer the broad beans to a food processor, add the garlic and whizz to a purée, adding a few tablespoonfuls of the cooking water to give a soft consistency.
2 Preheat the grill to hot. Transfer the purée to a bowl and stir in the oil, cumin and mint. Season generously. Set aside for 30 minutes, if possible, to allow the flavours time to develop.
3 Toast each slice of bread on both sides and cut in half. Arrange on individual serving plates. Spoon the pâté on to the hot toast and drizzle over a little extra virgin olive oil.

• Per serving 413 kcalories, protein 7g, carbohydrate 9g, fat 39g, saturated fat 5g, fibre 8g, added sugar none, salt 0.03g

Bagels with Griddled Vegetables

If you haven't got a griddle pan, simply stir fry the vegetables and toast the bagel under a hot grill.

5 tbsp olive oil
2 red peppers, seeded and cut into chunks
2 courgettes, cut into thin slices on the diagonal
4 onion bagels, split
2 tbsp balsamic vinegar
½ tsp sugar
70g bag wild rocket leaves

Takes 15 minutes • Serves 4

1 Brush a preheated griddle pan with a little of the oil. Add the peppers and courgettes and cook for 4–5 minutes, turning, until pleasantly charred. Transfer to a plate.
2 Toast the bagels, cut-side down, on the hot griddle pan for 1 minute, until golden. Meanwhile, to make a dressing, whisk the vinegar, sugar and remaining oil together. Season to taste.
3 Place the bagels on individual serving plates and top with the chargrilled vegetables and a handful of rocket. Drizzle the dressing over and serve immediately.

• Per serving 330 kcalories, protein 7g, carbohydrate 32g, fat 20g, saturated fat 3g, fibre 3g, added sugar 1g, salt 0.72g

Stuffed Focaccia

Focaccia is a flat, round Italian bread, often sold flavoured with herbs, olives or sun-dried tomatoes.

400g can chickpeas, drained and rinsed
juice of 1 lemon
1 garlic clove
5 tbsp extra virgin olive oil
20cm/8in round sun-dried tomato focaccia
100g/4oz semi-dried tomatoes in oil, drained
50g/2oz marinated black olives, pitted
30g bag of mixed salad leaves
1 small ripe avocado, halved, stoned, peeled and cut into chunks

Takes 15 minutes, plus chilling • Serves 6

1 For the houmous, whizz the chickpeas, half the lemon juice and garlic in a food processor until smooth. With the processor still running, drizzle in the oil steadily until combined. Season to taste.
2 Cut the focaccia into three horizontal layers of the same thickness. Spread the houmous over the bottom two layers and then scatter over the semi-dried tomatoes, olives and salad leaves.
3 Toss the avocado with the remaining lemon juice and season. Scatter over the topping, then reassemble the loaf. Chill for at least 15 minutes before cutting into wedges to serve.

• Per serving 305 kcalories, protein 8g, carbohydrate 27g, fat 19g, saturated fat 2g, fibre 4g, added sugar none, salt 1.27g

Tom Yam Noodles

This simple Thai dish of noodles and vegetables in a tasty broth makes a satisfying supper.

1 tbsp sunflower oil
1 small onion, chopped
2 garlic cloves
140g/5oz button mushrooms, sliced
1 red pepper, seeded and sliced
2 tsp vegetarian Thai red curry paste
700ml/1¼ pints vegetable stock
1 tbsp soy sauce
zest of 1 lime and juice of ½
125g/4½oz egg noodles
220g can bamboo shoots, drained
handful of fresh coriander

Takes 35 minutes • Serves 2

1 Heat the oil in a pan and fry the onion until golden. Stir in the garlic, mushrooms and red pepper and fry for 3 minutes. Add the Thai curry paste and cook for 1 minute. Stir in the stock, soy sauce and grated lime zest. Simmer for 3 minutes.
2 Add the noodles to the pan and bring to the boil. Simmer for 4 minutes, until they are cooked. Add the bamboo shoots and most of the coriander and cook for 2 minutes.
3 Divide the noodles between two soup bowls. Add the lime juice to the broth and season to taste. Pour over the noodles, scatter the remaining coriander over and serve.

• Per serving 393 kcalories, protein 15g, carbohydrate 55g, fat 14g, saturated fat 1g, fibre 7g, added sugar none, salt 2.77g

Spicy Coconut Vegetables

A simple way to make everyday vegetables taste out of the ordinary.

1 tbsp olive oil
1 onion, cut into wedges
1 red onion, cut into wedges
1 small red chilli, seeded and chopped
2 carrots, sliced
225g/8oz small broccoli florets
1 red and 1 yellow pepper, seeded and
   cut into chunks
200ml/7fl oz coconut cream
200ml/7fl oz vegetable stock
½ tsp Tabasco sauce
Thai fragrant rice, to serve

Takes 25 minutes • Serves 4

1 Heat the olive oil in a large pan and fry the onion wedges and chilli for 1–2 minutes, stirring occasionally.
2 Add the carrots, broccoli and peppers and cook for a further 5 minutes.
3 Stir in the coconut cream, stock and Tabasco sauce, reduce the heat and simmer for 5 minutes. Serve immediately with Thai fragrant rice.

• Per serving 400 kcalories, protein 7g, carbohydrate 14g, fat 36g, saturated fat 27g, fibre 11g, added sugar none, salt 0.27g

Pasta with Spicy Peas

You can use any pasta shape, but if you don't have any fresh available, replace it with 350g/12oz dried pasta.

3 tbsp olive oil
300g/10oz shallots, halved
4 tsp cumin seeds, lightly crushed
3 garlic cloves, sliced
300g/10oz cherry tomatoes, halved
good splash of Tabasco sauce
400g/14oz frozen petits pois (or peas),
   thawed
finely pared zest and juice of ½ lemon
500g/1lb 2oz fresh penne
4 tbsp chopped parsley

Takes 25 minutes • Serves 4

1 Heat the oil in a large pan. Add the shallots and cook for about 8 minutes, until softened and lightly coloured. Add the cumin and garlic and cook for a further 2 minutes.
2 Stir in the cherry tomatoes and cook for 5 minutes, until softened. Add the Tabasco sauce, petits pois or peas and lemon zest and juice. Season and cook for 2–3 minutes.
3 Meanwhile, cook the pasta according to the packet instructions and drain. Add the pasta to the peas and stir until well combined. Stir in the parsley and serve.

• Per serving 650 kcalories, protein 23g, carbohydrate 110g, fat 16g, saturated fat 2g, fibre 11g, added sugar none, salt 0.13g

TOP LEFT: Tom Yam Noodles   TOP RIGHT: Spicy Coconut Vegetables   BOTTOM: Pasta with Spicy Peas

TOP: Peach Melba Brûlée   BOTTOM LEFT: Pineapple with Rum and Raisins   BOTTOM RIGHT: Passion Fruit Syllabub

Peach Melba Brûlée

You'll find dairy-free yogurt and cream cheese in large supermarkets or health food stores.

225g/8oz raspberries
140g/5oz icing sugar
300ml/½ pint dairy-free yogurt
227g tub dairy-free cream cheese
zest of 1 lemon
2 peaches, peeled, halved and sliced
50g/2oz demerara sugar

Takes 25 minutes • Serves 4

1 Whizz half the raspberries in a food processor with 25g/1oz of the icing sugar until smooth. Place the remaining icing sugar, dairy-free yogurt, dairy-free cream cheese and lemon zest in a bowl and beat well together.
2 Preheat the grill to high. Divide the remaining raspberries and the peach slices between four 225ml/8fl oz ramekin dishes. Spoon over the raspberry purée.
3 Top with the yogurt mixture and sprinkle over the demerara sugar. Grill until the sugar has caramelised. Cool slightly before serving.

• Per serving 461 kcalories, protein 15g, carbohydrate 62g, fat 19g, saturated fat none, fibre 2g, added sugar 52.5g, salt 0.87g

Pineapple with Rum and Raisins

Some supermarkets sell ready peeled and sliced fresh pineapple, which will help to speed up this recipe.

1 ripe pineapple, peeled
25g/1oz butter
50g/2oz light muscovado sugar
25g/1oz raisins
25g/1oz pecan nuts
50ml/2fl oz rum
vanilla ice cream, to serve (optional)

Takes 20 minutes • Serves 4

1 Remove the 'eyes' from the pineapple. Cut in half, lengthways, remove the centre core and slice into wedges. Melt the butter in a griddle pan. Add the wedges of pineapple and cook until golden – about 3 minutes on each side.
2 Sprinkle over the sugar, raisins and pecan nuts and cook until the sugar has melted and becomes syrupy.
3 Carefully add the rum and ignite it, using a long match. Allow the flames to die down. Serve the pineapple wedges with the sauce spooned over and a spoonful of vanilla ice cream, if liked.

• Per serving 286 kcalories, protein 2g, carbohydrate 43g, fat 10g, saturated fat 3g, fibre 3g, added sugar 13g, salt 0.14g

Passion Fruit Syllabub

Vary the wine and lemon cream syllabub by the addition of different fruits in season.

3 tbsp white wine
1 tbsp caster sugar
finely grated zest and juice of 1 small lemon
142ml carton double cream
1 passion fruit, cut in half
starfruit slices, to decorate
dessert biscuits, to serve (optional)

Takes 10 minutes, plus marinating • Serves 2

1 Mix together the white wine, sugar and lemon zest and juice and leave for at least 30 minutes to marinate.
2 Pour the cream into the white wine mixture and, using an electric whisk, whip to soft peaks.
3 Scoop out the passion fruit flesh and seeds and stir lightly through the cream mixture. Spoon into two glasses or tumblers and decorate with the starfruit slices. Serve with dessert biscuits, if liked.

• Per serving 394 kcalories, protein 2.5g, carbohydrate 12g, fat 36g, saturated fat 22.5g, fibre 1g, added sugar 8g, salt 0.9g

Cappuccino Mousse

This light, frothy mousse is at its best made with a high-quality dark chocolate.

125g/4½oz plain chocolate
1 tbsp instant coffee granules
2 tbsp Tia Maria (coffee liqueur)
4 medium egg whites
140g/5oz caster sugar
300ml/½ pint double cream
cocoa powder, to dust

Takes 15 minutes, plus chilling • Serves 6

1 Melt the chocolate in a bowl set over a pan of simmering water, making sure the bowl doesn't touch the water. Remove from the heat and cool. Dissolve the coffee in two tablespoons of boiling water and stir in the Tia Maria. Stir into the chocolate.
2 In a bowl whisk the egg whites to soft peaks. Gradually whisk in the caster sugar until thick. Stir two tablespoonfuls of the meringue into the chocolate mixture to slacken it and then fold in the remainder. Spoon the mousse into six cappuccino cups and chill for at least 20 minutes.
3 Lightly whip the cream and spoon over the mousses. Dust with cocoa, to serve.

• Per serving 461 kcalories, protein 5g, carbohydrate 42g, fat 31g, saturated fat 19g, fibre 0.5g, added sugar 38g, salt 0.22g

Raspberry Crunch Fool

A light raspberry and orange mixture is layered with crunchy oat clusters to make a dairy-free dessert.

300g/10oz raspberries, plus extra for
   decorating
140g/5oz icing sugar
227g tub dairy-free cream cheese
400ml/14fl oz dairy-free yogurt
zest and juice of 1 orange
140g/5oz vegan oat clusters cereal
mint sprigs, to decorate

Takes 15 minutes, plus chilling • Serves 4

1 Put one third of the raspberries in a food processor with half the icing sugar and whizz until smooth. Strain through a sieve to remove the pips.
2 Beat the dairy-free cream cheese, dairy-free yogurt, orange zest and juice in a bowl with the remaining icing sugar until smooth. Mix in the raspberry purée and fold in the remaining whole raspberries.
3 Divide half the mixture between four glasses. Sprinkle over half the cereal and spoon over another layer of the raspberry mixture. Sprinkle over the remaining cereal and decorate with sugar-dipped raspberries and sprigs of mint. Chill for 1 hour before serving.

• Per serving 565 kcalories, protein 20g, carbohydrate 76g, fat 22g, saturated fat 1g, fibre 2g, added sugar 44g, salt 1.46g

Almond Nectarine Tart

This dessert looks spectacular, but made with just four ingredients, it has got to be one of the easiest to make.

140g/5oz white marzipan, cut into chunks
5 tbsp double cream
375g ready-made, ready-rolled puff pastry,
   thawed if frozen
4 nectarines, halved, stoned and thinly sliced
crème fraîche, to serve

Takes 30 minutes • Serves 8

1 Preheat the oven to 200°C/Gas 6/fan oven 180°C. Place the marzipan in a food processor with the cream and whizz to a thick paste. If necessary, roll the pastry out to a rectangle about 30 × 23cm/12 × 9in.
2 Lay the pastry on a baking sheet and score a line 2cm/¼in inside the edge all around. Spread the marzipan paste over the pastry inside the line and arrange the nectarine slices in rows on top.
3 Bake in the oven for 15–20 minutes, until the pastry is golden and risen. Cut into squares and serve with chilled crème fraîche.

• Per serving 311 kcalories, protein 4g, carbohydrate 34g, fat 18g, saturated fat 7g, fibre 1g, added sugar 9g, salt 0.39g

TOP: Cappuccino Mousse   BOTTOM LEFT: Raspberry Crunch Fool   BOTTOM RIGHT: Almond Nectarine Tart

TOP LEFT: Saffron Rice Pudding   TOP RIGHT: Gooseberry and Elderflower Crumble   BOTTOM: Apple and Blackberry Pudding

Saffron Rice Pudding

A simple dessert with the luxurious flavour of saffron.

large pinch of saffron strands
175g/6oz pudding rice
600ml/1 pint milk
300ml/½ pint double cream
125g/4½oz caster sugar
finely shredded zest and juice of 2 lemons
lemon curd and biscuits, to serve (optional)

Takes 35 minutes • Serves 4

1 Sprinkle the saffron over two tablespoons of hot water and leave to soak for 5 minutes.
2 Meanwhile, put the pudding rice, milk, cream, caster sugar and half the lemon zest into a large pan. Bring to the boil, then simmer gently for 20–25 minutes, until the rice is tender and the mixture has thickened. Stir in the saffron-infused water and lemon juice.
3 Spoon into serving bowls and sprinkle with the remaining shredded lemon zest. Serve with a spoonful of lemon curd and biscuits, if liked.

• Per serving 723 kcalories, protein 9g, carbohydrate 81g, fat 42g, saturated fat 26g, fibre 0.02g, added sugar 33g, salt 0.29g

Gooseberry and Elderflower Crumble

The addition of elderflower cordial to the gooseberry filling gives the crumble an extra zing.

550g/1lb 4oz gooseberries, topped and tailed
175g/6oz caster sugar
3 tbsp elderflower cordial
75g/2½oz butter, diced, at room temperature, plus extra for greasing
175g/6oz plain flour
50g/2oz pecan nuts, roughly chopped
fresh custard, ice cream or cream, to serve

Takes 55 minutes • Serves 6

1 Preheat the oven to 190°C/Gas 5/fan oven 170°C. Grease a 1.2 litre/2 pint ovenproof dish. Put the gooseberries, two-thirds of the sugar and the elderflower cordial in a pan and cook gently for 5 minutes, until the fruit is soft. Transfer to the greased dish.
2 To make the crumble, rub the butter into the flour until the mixture resembles rough breadcrumbs. Stir in the remaining sugar and pecan nuts. Sprinkle over the gooseberries and level the surface. Bake for 30–40 minutes, until the topping is golden.
3 Divide the crumble between individual serving bowls and serve immediately with fresh custard, ice cream or pouring cream.

• Per serving 381 kcalories, protein 5g, carbohydrate 57g, fat 17g, saturated fat 7g, fibre 4g, added sugar 31g, salt 0.25g

Apple and Blackberry Pudding

A lovely autumn pudding that's easily adapted to use most fruits in season. Serve with pouring cream.

75g/2½oz self-raising flour
75g/2½oz vegetable suet
100g/4oz white breadcrumbs
finely grated zest and juice of 1 large orange
5 tbsp milk
25g/1oz butter
1 large eating apple, peeled, cored and roughly chopped
100g/4oz blackberries
100g/4oz caster sugar
pouring cream, to serve

Takes 55 minutes • Serves 6

1 Preheat the oven to 200°C/Gas 6/fan oven 180°C. Sift the flour into a bowl, stir in a pinch of salt, the suet, breadcrumbs, orange zest and just enough milk to make a soft crumble mix.
2 Melt the butter in a large frying pan and cook the apple for 5 minutes, until softened. Stir into the suet mix, then spread into a 1.2 litre/2 pint dish. Sprinkle the blackberries over.
3 Put the orange juice, sugar and 125ml/4fl oz water in a pan. Heat, stirring, until dissolved, then boil rapidly until pale golden. Pour over the pudding. Leave to soak for 10 minutes, then bake for 25 minutes. Serve hot or warm with pouring cream.

• Per serving 286 kcalories, protein 5g, carbohydrate 56g, fat 6g, saturated fat 3g, fibre 2g, added sugar 22g, salt 0.57g

Mascarpone Cream with Grapes

Cut the richness of the mascarpone – Italian cream cheese – by combining it with yogurt.

150ml/¼ pint red wine
50g/2oz caster sugar
2 tsp arrowroot
350g/12oz seedless red, white or
    black grapes
250g/9oz mascarpone cheese
225g/8oz Greek-style yogurt
2 tbsp clear honey

Takes 20 minutes, plus chilling • Serves 4

1 Place the red wine and sugar in a large pan, bring to the boil and simmer, until the sugar has dissolved. Mix the arrowroot to a smooth paste with a little cold water, then stir into the wine. Boil, stirring continuously, for 1 minute, until thickened.
2 Stir the grapes into the wine mixture, bring to the boil, cover and simmer for 2 minutes. Leave to cool. Spoon into four tall glasses.
3 Put the mascarpone, yogurt and honey into a large bowl and whisk until smooth. Spoon over the grapes and chill until ready to serve.

• Per serving 487 kcalories, protein 0g, carbohydrate 35g, fat 34g, saturated fat 22g, fibre 1g, added sugar 19g, salt 0.58g

Cranberry Yogurt Ice

A creamy yogurt ice with far fewer calories than regular ice cream. You'll find dried cranberries in larger supermarkets.

100g/4oz dried cranberries
finely grated zest and juice of 1 orange
500ml/18fl oz Greek yogurt
50g/2oz caster sugar
150ml/¼ pint double cream
3 tbsp brandy

Takes 35 minutes • Serves 6

1 Put the cranberries, orange zest and juice and 150ml/¼ pint water in a pan, bring to the boil, cover and simmer for 25 minutes, until the cranberries are very soft. Allow to cool completely.
2 Beat together the yogurt, sugar and cream until the sugar has partially dissolved. Stir in the brandy and pour into a freezerproof container. Freeze for 3 hours until thickened. Stir in the cranberry mixture until well distributed.
3 Freeze until solid. Transfer to the fridge for about 20 minutes before serving. Use within 2 months.

• Per serving 263 kcalories, protein 6g, carbohydrate 12g, fat 20g, saturated fat 12g, fibre 1g, added sugar 9g, salt 0.18g

Tropical Fruit Crunch

Raid the fruit bowl and storecupboard to make this satisfying pud.

50g/2oz butter
100g/4oz rolled oats
6 tbsp demerara sugar
4 tbsp desiccated coconut
2 bananas, cut into chunks
2 ripe mangoes, peeled and cut into chunks
225g can pineapple chunks in natural juice,
    drained
fresh custard or single cream, to serve

Takes 15 minutes • Serves 4

1 Melt two-thirds of the butter in a large frying pan. Sprinkle over the oats, four tablespoons of the demerara sugar and the desiccated coconut and cook for 3–4 minutes, stirring occasionally, until crisp and golden.
2 Meanwhile, melt the remaining butter in another frying pan and add the bananas, mangoes and pineapple chunks. Sprinkle over the remaining demerara sugar and cook over a low heat for 5 minutes, until softened and caramelised.
3 Divide the fruit between four plates and sprinkle over the crunchy oat mixture. Serve with fresh custard or single cream.

• Per serving 589 kcalories, protein 7g, carbohydrate 91g, fat 25g, saturated fat 16g, fibre 11g, added sugar 16g, salt 0.41g

TOP LEFT: Mascarpone Cream with Grapes   TOP RIGHT: Cranberry Yogurt Ice   BOTTOM: Tropical Fruit Crunch

Meals for Two

Scallops with Chilli and Lime

Try this as a starter for a special meal for two.

2 tbsp olive oil
10 scallops
2 large garlic cloves, chopped
2 tsp chopped fresh red chilli
juice of 1 lime
small handful of fresh coriander, roughly
    chopped

Takes 10–15 minutes • Serves 2

1 Heat the oil in a non-stick frying pan until hot, add the scallops and pan fry for 1 minute until golden underneath. Flip them over and sprinkle with the garlic and chilli.
2 Cook for 1 minute more, then pour over the lime juice and season with salt and pepper. Serve immediately, scattered with the coriander.

• Per serving 260 kcalories, protein 34g, carbohydrate 2g, fat 13g, saturated fat 2g, fibre 0.3g, added sugar none, salt 0.99g

Prawns with Chilli Mayo

This is a brilliantly easy idea for a starter. And if you're having a barbecue, it's great to snack on while the rest of your food is cooking.

400g cooked prawns in shells
2 anchovy fillets from a can or jar
1 fresh red chilli
4 tbsp mayonnaise
1 little gem lettuce
lemon wedges, to serve

Takes 10 minutes • Serves 2

1 Divide the prawns between two glass tumblers. Finely chop the anchovies. Halve and seed the chilli, then finely chop the chilli flesh.
2 Mix the mayonnaise with the anchovies and chilli, and divide between two small dishes.
3 Cut the lettuce into wedges and serve the prawns with the mayo, lettuce and lemon wedges for squeezing over the prawns.

• Per serving 293 kcalories, protein 19g, carbohydrate 1g, fat 24g, saturated fat 4g, fibre 1g, added sugar none, salt 3.69g

Red Pepper Houmous

Whizz up this easy storecupboard dip and you have the perfect lunch for two.

410g can chickpeas
1 large garlic clove
2 roasted red peppers from a jar
1 tbsp lemon juice
2 tbsp olive oil, plus a little extra for drizzling
½ tsp chilli powder
celery sticks and radishes with the leaves on,
    and Italian breadsticks, to serve

Takes 5–10 minutes • Serves 2 generously

1 Rinse and drain the chickpeas, then tip them into a food processor. Peel the garlic and crush in with the chickpeas, along with plenty of salt and pepper. Whizz briefly.
2 Remove any stray seeds from the peppers, then add the peppers to the processor with the lemon juice, olive oil and chilli. Blitz again until really smooth. Taste and add extra seasoning and chilli for more of a kick, if you like.
3 Spoon into a bowl, drizzle with olive oil and serve with celery sticks, radishes and a stack of breadsticks for dipping.

• Per serving 407 kcalories, protein 11g, carbohydrate 27g, fat 29g, saturated fat 3g, fibre 7g, added sugar none, salt 2.23g

TOP: Scallops with Chilli and Lime   BOTTOM LEFT: Prawns with Chilli Mayo   BOTTOM RIGHT: Red Pepper Houmous

TOP LEFT: Chicory and Pear Salad   TOP RIGHT: Lamb and Orange Salad   BOTTOM: Cheese and Cranberry Salad

Chicory and Pear Salad

Serve this zingy salad before or after a warming winter casserole – it's really refreshing.

1 head of red chicory, or white if not
    available, trimmed
1 ripe red Williams pear
handful of rocket leaves
small handful of hazelnuts, toasted and
    chopped

FOR THE DRESSING
½ tsp green peppercorns in brine (optional)
1 tbsp hazelnut or olive oil
1 tbsp mild salad oil, such as sunflower
    or safflower
½ tsp sherry or cider vinegar

Takes 15–20 minutes • Serves 2

1 Make the dressing. If using green peppercorns, lightly crush them in a bowl with a wooden spoon, or use a pestle and mortar. Mix in the oils and vinegar and add salt to taste.
2 Carefully separate the chicory leaves and arrange 5–6 on two plates – if they are big, cut or tear each one into pieces.
3 Remove the stalk from the pear and quarter the pear lengthways. Core, then thinly slice the fruit. Arrange the pear slices on top of the chicory leaves and spoon over half the dressing. Pour the remaining dressing over the rocket and season with salt and pepper. Give the leaves a quick toss and pile on top of each salad. Sprinkle with the nuts and serve.

• Per serving 202 kcalories, protein 2.3g, carbohydrate 8.9g, fat 17.7g, saturated fat 1.6, fibre 3g, added sugar none, salt 0.01g

Lamb and Orange Salad

An unusual and superhealthy salad that will make a weekday meal a little bit special.

2 × 140g/5oz lamb leg steaks, trimmed of
    all fat
2 small oranges (blood oranges are good
    when in season)
1 carrot, coarsely grated
2 large handfuls winter salad leaves
small bunch fresh flatleaf parsley, leaves only

FOR THE DRESSING
1 tbsp olive oil
1 tsp balsamic or sherry vinegar
1 small garlic clove, crushed

Takes 15 minutes • Serves 2

1 Heat a cast iron ridged griddle pan until very hot. Rub the lamb steaks with a drop of oil, season, then cook for 5 minutes, turning once, for a medium steak. Cover with foil and set aside to rest.
2 Cut away the skin and pith of the oranges and thinly slice. Drain off the excess juices.
3 Whisk together the dressing ingredients and season to taste. Drain any meat and orange juices into the dressing, then toss with the carrot, oranges, salad leaves and parsley.
4 Slice the lamb and serve on top of the salad.

• Per serving 346 kcalories, protein 32g, carbohydrate 15g, fat 18g, saturated fat 5g, fibre 115g, added sugar none, salt 0.57g

Cheese and Cranberry Salad

This salad has really Christmassy flavours and is a lovely light alternative to heavy festive meals.

100g goat's cheese (round with a rind)
1 ripe pear
oil, for brushing
handful of pecan nuts, roughly broken
80g bag mixed watercress and spinach
crusty bread, to serve

FOR THE DRESSING
1 tbsp cranberry sauce
1 tbsp olive oil
1 tbsp lemon juice

Takes 20–30 minutes • Serves 2

1 Preheat the grill to high and line the grill rack with foil. Halve the cheese to make two discs. Halve and core the pear, cut each half into slices and arrange in two piles on the foil. Lightly brush the pears with oil then top each pile with a cheese disc (cut side up) and grill for a few minutes until lightly golden and bubbling. Scatter with the nuts and grill for a minute or so more.
2 For the dressing, whisk the cranberry sauce with the oil and lemon juice and season.
3 Arrange salad leaves on two plates. Put the pears and cheese on top. Spoon over the dressing, scatter over any stray nuts and eat straight away with crusty bread while the cheese is still deliciously runny.

• Per serving 327 kcalories, protein 13g, carbohydrate 12g, fat 26g, saturated fat 10g, fibre 3g, added sugar 2g, salt 0.99g

Smoked Haddock Salad

This is a bistro-style salad, using smoked haddock instead of the more usual bacon.

1 tbsp wholegrain mustard
1 tbsp cider or white wine vinegar, plus an
   extra splash
5 tbsp olive oil
½ small loaf of French bread, torn into
   bite-sized pieces
180g pack trimmed French beans
300g/10oz skinned smoked haddock
2 eggs
half a head of frisée, split into leaves

Takes 25–30 minutes • Serves 2

1 For the dressing whisk the mustard, vinegar, 3 tablespoons of oil, 1 tablespoon of water and a pinch of salt. Scatter the bread on a baking sheet, drizzle with the remaining oil and toast under a preheated grill for 8–10 minutes.
2 Meanwhile, boil the beans for 3–5 minutes until still slightly crunchy. Remove with a slotted spoon and toss in some of the dressing. Lower the heat, add the haddock and gently poach for 5 minutes. Transfer to a plate, add a splash of vinegar to the water, break in the eggs and poach for 3 minutes. Remove and drain.
3 Tip the frisée leaves into a large bowl and flake the haddock over in big chunks. Toss in the bread, beans and most of the dressing. Serve warm, topped with the eggs and drizzled with the remaining dressing.

• Per serving 627 kcalories, protein 43g, carbohydrate 32g, fat 37g, saturated fat 6g, fibre 4g, added sugar none, salt 4.2g

Devilled Mushrooms

Mustard, olive oil and Worcestershire sauce give these mushrooms a wonderful spicy flavour, creating tasty juices during cooking.

1 tbsp wholegrain mustard
1 tbsp olive oil
1 tbsp Worcestershire sauce
1 garlic clove, crushed
4 large flat mushrooms
½ tsp paprika
½ × 140g bag mixed salad leaves, with ruby
   chard and watercress
French or crusty bread, to serve

Takes about 20 minutes • Serves 2

1 Preheat the oven to 200°C/Gas 6/fan oven 180°C. In a large bowl, mix together the mustard, oil, Worcestershire sauce and garlic, then season with salt and freshly ground black pepper.
2 Add the mushrooms to the mixture and toss well to coat them evenly. (You can do this ahead and let them marinate while you prepare the rest of the meal.) Place them stalk-side up in a roasting tin and sprinkle over the paprika. Bake for 8–10 minutes.
3 Divide the salad leaves between two serving plates. Put two mushrooms on each plate and spoon over the juices. Serve straight away, with French or crusty bread.

• Per serving 102 kcalories, protein 5g, carbohydrate 3.7g, fat 7.6g, saturated fat 1g, fibre 3g, added sugar 0.3g, salt 0.57g

Roasted Tomato Bruschetta

This starter is incredibly simple – the cooking is minimal and the taste fresh, light and summery.

2 slices of bread from a close-textured loaf
1 tbsp extra-virgin olive oil
175g/6oz small or cherry vine tomatoes
2 garlic cloves, peeled
little balsamic vinegar
few fresh basil leaves

Takes 20–25 minutes • Serves 2

1 Preheat the oven to 200°C/Gas 6/fan oven 180°C. Brush the bread on both sides with half the oil. Grill on both sides until toasted.
2 Put the vine tomatoes and garlic in an ovenproof dish in one layer, and drizzle with the remaining oil and some salt and pepper. Bake for 10 minutes until lightly charred and softened. Leave to cool to room temperature.
3 Put a slice of bread on each serving plate. Squash one garlic clove onto each slice and top with the tomatoes along with their cooking juices. Sprinkle each with a few drops of balsamic vinegar and scatter with some roughly torn basil leaves.

• Per serving 207 kcalories, protein 6.2g, carbohydrate 30.1g, fat 7.7g, saturated fat 0.8g, fibre 2.2g, added sugar none, salt 0.7g

TOP LEFT: Smoked Haddock Salad   TOP RIGHT: Devilled Mushrooms   BOTTOM: Roasted Tomato Bruschetta

TOP: Warm Chicken Noodle Salad   BOTTOM LEFT: Mediterranean Couscous Salad   BOTTOM RIGHT: Warm Mediterranean New Potato Salad

Warm Chicken Noodle Salad

A fantastic way to use up leftovers. For extra crunch, add some baby corn or beansprouts.

50g or 1 bundle of rice noodles (such as Thai stir-fry noodles)
100g/4oz sugar snaps, halved lengthways
1 small red pepper, seeded and thinly sliced
handful of fresh basil
2 cooked boneless, skinless chicken breasts

FOR THE DRESSING
3 tbsp olive oil
finely grated zest and juice of ½ lemon
1 heaped tbsp mayonnaise

Takes 15–20 minutes • Serves 2

1 Boil the kettle and tip the rice noodles into a heatproof bowl. Pour over boiling water to cover. Leave the noodles to soak for 4 minutes.
2 Meanwhile, make the dressing. Whisk together the olive oil, lemon zest and juice and mayonnaise, then season to taste. Drain the noodles and return to the bowl. Throw in the sugar snaps, red pepper and basil. Pour in half the dressing and gently toss.
3 Divide the noodles between two bowls. Slice the chicken breasts and arrange on top of the noodles. Drizzle over the remaining dressing and serve.

• Per serving 577 kcalories, protein 40g, carbohydrate 28g, fat 35g, saturated fat 6g, fibre 2g, added sugar none, salt 0.40g

Mediterranean Couscous Salad

There's no need to cook the couscous – just soak it and mix in the tasty bits.

100g/4oz couscous
200ml/7fl oz hot vegetable stock
5 sun-dried or sunblush tomatoes, quartered
1 medium avocado, peeled, stoned and cut into large chunks
50g/2oz black olives
handful of nuts, such as pine nuts, cashews or almonds
100g/4oz feta, roughly crumbled
½ × 130g bag green salad leaves

FOR THE DRESSING
2½ tbsp olive oil
1 tbsp lemon juice

Takes 10–20 minutes • Serves 2

1 Tip the couscous into a large bowl, stir in the hot stock, cover and leave to soak for 5 minutes.
2 Make a dressing with the olive oil, lemon juice and some salt and pepper. Stir 1 tablespoon into the couscous, then gently mix in the tomatoes, avocado, olives, nuts and feta. Taste for seasoning.
3 Toss the salad leaves with the remaining dressing, divide between two plates and spoon the couscous on top.

• Per serving 608 kcalories, protein 16g, carbohydrate 33g, fat 46.6g, saturated fat 11g, fibre 4.4g, added sugar none, salt 4.79g

Warm Mediterranean New Potato Salad

Swap the mozzarella for blue cheese and the basil for chives for a totally different taste.

1 tbsp olive oil
2 garlic cloves
500g bag baby new potatoes
500ml/18fl oz vegetable stock
125g ball mozzarella, torn into bite-sized pieces
500g pack cherry tomatoes, halved
50g/2oz pine nuts, toasted
handful of fresh basil leaves, sliced

Takes 30 minutes • Serves 2

1 Heat the oil in a large frying pan and fry the garlic and potatoes for 1–2 minutes. Pour over the stock and simmer, uncovered, for 20 minutes or until the potatoes are cooked. Turn the heat up and let the stock reduce to about 2 tablespoons of sticky glaze.
2 Throw in the mozzarella, tomatoes, pine nuts and basil and give it a stir. When the cheese starts to melt, remove the pan from the heat and share between two plates. Serve with crisp lettuce leaves on the side.

• Per serving 615 kcalories, protein 23g, carbohydrate 50g, fat 37g, saturated fat 11g, fibre 6g, added sugar none, salt 1.6g

Posh Cheese on Toast

Goat's cheese is great for grilling – it browns nicely without toughening. For those with big appetites, you can simply double the quantities.

1 small ciabatta (about 175g/6oz), split in half, or 2 thick slices of sourdough bread
50g/2oz marinated peppers or 2 heaped tbsp tomato or onion relish
8 pitted black olives, sliced
100g/4oz semi-soft goat's cheese, such as chèvre
2 tsp aged balsamic vinegar (optional)
few leaves of watercress or rocket
extra-virgin olive oil

Takes 12–15 minutes • Serves 2

1 Heat the grill to medium. Toast the bread, lightly, on the rounded side. Spread the other, flat side with the peppers or relish and scatter over the olives.
2 Crumble over the cheese and return to the grill until the cheese softens and starts to brown.
3 Remove from the grill and drizzle with the balsamic vinegar, if using. Serve, topped with a small handful of watercress or rocket and a drizzle of olive oil over the top, while the cheese is still hot and bubbling.

• Per serving 485 kcalories, protein 20g, carbohydrate 48g, fat 25g, saturated fat 10g, fibre 3g, added sugar none, salt 3.48g

Mozzarella, Ham and Pesto Pizzas

A creative way of using Italian ingredients that's speedy and easy too – perfect for people on the go.

4 mini pitta breads
150g pack mozzarella
4 tsp pesto
85g/3oz smoked wafer-thin ham

Takes 10 minutes • Serves 2

1 Heat the grill to high, put the pittas on the grill rack and heat for about 1 minute while you slice the mozzarella into 5.
2 Turn the pittas over and spread each one with 1 teaspoon pesto, then top with a mozzarella slice. Pile the ham on top, so it looks quite ruffled, then tear the final mozzarella slice into 4, put it on top of the ham and grind over some black pepper.
3 Return to the grill for 3–4 minutes more until melted and starting to turn golden.

• Per serving 491 kcalories, protein 36g, carbohydrate 41g, fat 21g, saturated fat 12g, fibre 1.6g, added sugar none, salt 3.34g

Steak and Caramelised Onion Sandwich

Instead of caramelised onions, try a few roasted peppers from a jar.

4 minute steaks or 2 × 1cm thick sirloin steaks
olive oil, for frying and drizzling
1 small ciabatta loaf
4 tbsp caramelised onions from a jar
½ × 85g bag watercress

Takes 10–15 minutes • Serves 2 generously

1 Heat the grill to medium. Heat a little oil in a frying pan. Season both sides of the steaks with salt, then fry for 1–2 minutes on each side. Meanwhile, slice the ciabatta in half lengthways and grill the cut sides until golden.
2 Drizzle the toasted ciabatta with olive oil, spread the bottom half with the onions and sit the steaks on top.
3 Cover with the watercress and close the sandwich with the other half of the ciabatta. Cut into four sandwiches and serve two per person. Serve hot.

• Per serving 525 kcalories, protein 52g, carbohydrate 33g, fat 21g, saturated fat 5g, fibre 2g, added sugar 2g, salt 1.85g

TOP: Posh Cheese on Toast   BOTTOM LEFT: Mozzarella, Ham and Pesto Pizzas   BOTTOM RIGHT: Steak and Caramelised Onion Sandwich

TOP LEFT: Hot Pastrami Bagels   TOP RIGHT: Open Turkey BLT   BOTTOM: Roasted Pepper and Halloumi Wraps

Hot Pastrami Bagels

A New York deli snack for two that microwaves in minutes.

2 onion bagels
butter, for spreading
American mustard
120g pack pastrami (cured beef brisket)
2 dill pickles
handful of torn iceberg lettuce leaves

Takes 15 minutes • Serves 2

1 Split the bagels and spread each of the cut sides with butter and a little mustard. Separate the slices of pastrami, sandwich them between the bagels and put them on a sheet of double-thickness kitchen paper on a microwave-proof plate – the paper stops the bread from becoming soggy underneath and sticking to the plate. Microwave on medium for 1 minute.
2 While the bagels are warming, slice the dill pickles lengthways.
3 Take the bagels from the microwave and lift off their tops. Pile in the lettuce and sliced pickles, squirt in some more mustard and enjoy straight away while they're still warm.

• Per serving 241 kcalories, protein 17g, carbohydrate 27g, fat 8g, saturated fat 3g, fibre 2g, added sugar none, salt 3.04g

Open Turkey BLT

For a spicy hit, sprinkle the turkey with Cajun seasoning before grilling.

2 turkey steaks, about 140g/5oz each
4 rashers smoked streaky bacon
2 slices melting cheese, such as cheddar or Gruyère
half a loaf of ciabatta, cut in half horizontally
2 tbsp mayonnaise
1 medium tomato, sliced
½ avocado, peeled, stoned and thinly sliced
4 lettuce leaves (little gem is good)

Takes 15–20 minutes • Serves 2

1 Heat the grill to high. Lay the turkey steaks and bacon on a large baking tray and grill for 3 minutes on each side or until cooked through. Set the bacon aside and top the turkey steaks with the cheese slices.
2 Put the ciabatta slices next to the turkey in the pan and return them both to the grill until the bread is toasted and the cheese is melted.
3 Spread the toast with the mayonnaise and top with the cheesy turkey steaks, tomato, avocado, lettuce and bacon.

• Per serving 685 kcalories, protein 54g, carbohydrate 42g, fat 35g, saturated fat 9g, fibre 3g, added sugar none, salt 3g

Roasted Pepper and Halloumi Wraps

If you're a keen meat eater, use leftover chicken or lamb instead of cheese – just warm through with the peppers.

2 thick slices halloumi cheese
½ tsp dried oregano
1 tbsp olive oil
2 Arab flat breads (they look like circular pitta bread)
2 roasted red peppers from a jar
6 slices roasted aubergine from a jar
handful kalamata olives
2–4 lemon wedges
good handful fresh flatleaf parsley sprigs

Takes 10 minutes • Serves 2

1 Sprinkle both sides of the halloumi with the oregano. Heat the oil in a non-stick frying pan, then briefly fry the halloumi on both sides until golden. Remove from the pan, but leave the pan on the heat. Heat the flat breads over a naked gas flame for a few seconds on each side to warm them. (Alternatively you can do this in a large frying pan.)
2 Halve the peppers (removing any stray seeds) and thickly slice, then add to the pan with the aubergine, olives and fried halloumi. Heat through, squeeze over two of the lemon wedges and season well. To serve, divide the mixture and the parsley sprigs between the wraps, and top each with a lemon wedge for squeezing over, if you like.

• Per serving 561 kcalories, protein 14g, carbohydrate 51g, fat 35g, saturated fat 8g, fibre 5g, added sugar none, salt 0.91g

Crispy Italian Chicken and Polenta

Try using small chunks of unpeeled potato instead of the polenta.

500g pack ready-to-use polenta
25g/1oz parmesan, grated
2 boneless chicken breasts, skin on
250g pack cherry tomatoes
leaves from a few fresh rosemary sprigs, torn
1 garlic clove, sliced
2 tbsp olive oil

Takes 30 minutes • Serves 2

1 Preheat the oven to 220°C/Gas 7/fan oven 200°C. Using your fingers, roughly break up the polenta into small chunks and scatter over the bottom of a small roasting tin. Tip in the parmesan and mix.
2 Sit the chicken breasts, cherry tomatoes, rosemary and garlic on top of the polenta, drizzle with olive oil, then season to taste.
3 Roast for 25 minutes or until the chicken skin is crisp and golden, and the polenta and cheese are turning crusty around the edges. Serve with a green salad.

• Per serving 513 kcalories, protein 40g, carbohydrate 47g, fat 20g, saturated fat 5g, fibre 7g, added sugar none, salt 4.63g

Broccoli Lemon Chicken

Tenderstem broccoli is ideal for this dish as it cooks so quickly. Add a couple of minutes to the cooking time if you're using ordinary broccoli.

1 tbsp groundnut or sunflower oil
340g pack of mini chicken breast fillets
    (sometimes called goujons)
2 garlic cloves, sliced
200g pack tenderstem broccoli, stems halved
    if very long
200ml/7fl oz chicken stock
1 heaped tsp cornflour
1 tbsp clear honey or 2 tsp golden caster
    sugar
zest and juice of 1 lemon
large handful of roasted cashews
basmati rice or noodles, to serve

Takes 15–25 minutes • Serves 2

1 Heat the oil in a large frying pan or wok. Add the chicken and fry for 3–4 minutes until golden. Remove from the pan and add the garlic and broccoli. Stir fry for a minute or so then cover and cook for 2 minutes more, until almost tender.
2 Mix the stock, cornflour and honey or sugar well, then pour into the pan and stir until thickened.
3 Tip the chicken back into the pan and let it heat through, then add the lemon zest and juice, and cashew nuts. Stir, then serve straight away with basmati rice or noodles.

• Per serving 372 kcalories, protein 48g, carbohydrate 15g, fat 13g, saturated fat 2g, fibre 3g, added sugar 6g, salt 0.69g

Saucy Chicken and Spring Vegetables

A fresh and delicious dish that's good enough to eat every day.

2 boneless chicken breasts, skin on
1 tbsp olive oil
200g/8oz baby new potatoes, thinly sliced
500ml/18fl oz chicken stock
200g pack mixed spring vegetables
    (broccoli, peas, broad beans and
    sliced courgette)
2 tbsp crème fraîche
handful of fresh tarragon leaves, roughly
    chopped

Takes 25–30 minutes • Serves 2

1 Fry the chicken in the oil in a wok or large frying pan for 5 minutes on each side. Throw in the potatoes and stir to coat. Pour the chicken stock over, cover and simmer for 10 minutes until the potatoes are almost cooked through.
2 Remove the lid and turn the heat to high. Reduce the stock until it just coats the bottom of the pan and there's enough left to cook the vegetables. Scatter the vegetables into the pan, cover again and cook the veg for about 2 minutes.
3 Stir in the crème fraîche to make a creamy sauce, season with salt and pepper, if you like, then add the tarragon. Serve straight from the pan.

• Per serving 386 kcalories, protein 38g, carbohydrate 23g, fat 16g, saturated fat 6g, fibre 3g, added sugar none, salt 1.5g

TOP LEFT: Crispy Italian Chicken and Polenta   TOP RIGHT: Broccoli Lemon Chicken   BOTTOM: Saucy Chicken and Spring Vegetables

TOP: Speedy Chorizo with Chickpeas   BOTTOM LEFT: Mustardy Pork Chops   BOTTOM RIGHT: Gammon with Pineapple Salsa

Speedy Chorizo with Chickpeas

When you're feeling a bit disheartened by the long winter evenings, try this warming one-bowl wonder.

400g can chopped tomatoes
110g pack chorizo (unsliced)
140g/5oz wedge Savoy cabbage
sprinkling of dried chilli flakes
410g can chickpeas, drained
1 chicken or vegetable stock cube

Takes 10 minutes • Serves 2

1 Put a medium pan on the heat and tip in the tomatoes followed by a canful of water. While the tomatoes are heating, quickly chop the chorizo into chunky pieces and shred the cabbage.
2 Pile the chorizo and cabbage into the pan with the chilli flakes and chickpeas, then crumble in the stock cube.
3 Stir well, cover and leave to bubble over a high heat for 6 minutes until the cabbage is just tender. Ladle into two bowls and eat with crusty or garlic bread.

• Per serving 366 kcalories, protein 23g, carbohydrate 30g, fat 18g, saturated fat 5g, fibre 9g, added sugar 0.3g, salt 4.26g

Mustardy Pork Chops

Try swapping the pork chops for chicken breasts for a delicious variation.

2 pork chops
1 tsp wholegrain mustard
25g/1oz cheddar, grated
2 tsp crème fraîche or cream

Takes 25 minutes • Serves 2

1 Preheat the oven to 200°C/Gas 6/fan oven 180°C. Place the chops in a large, shallow roasting tray and bake for 15 minutes.
2 Mix together the mustard, cheddar and crème fraîche or cream. Spread over the top of the chops.
3 Return to the oven for 5 minutes until the cheese is melting and bubbling. Serve with some potato wedges (which can be cooked in the oven at the same time as the chops) and seasonal green vegetables.

• Per serving 435 kcalories, protein 44.1g, carbohydrate 0.2g, fat 28.6g, saturated fat 12.5g, fibre 0.1g, added sugar none, salt 0.58g

Gammon with Pineapple Salsa

This revival of an old family-favourite is updated as a stylish dish for two with a Thai-style pineapple salsa.

1 large gammon steak, rind on,
    about 350g/12oz (1cm/½in thick)
a little oil, for brushing
1 tsp clear honey

FOR THE SALSA
100g/4oz fresh pineapple, finely chopped
1 large fresh red chilli, seeded and finely
    chopped
1 tsp light muscovado sugar
1 tsp soy sauce
1 tbsp chopped fresh coriander

Takes 20 minutes • Serves 2

1 First, make the salsa. Mix together all of the ingredients (use ½ a chilli for a milder flavour, all of it for a pungent one). Set aside while you cook the gammon.
2 Preheat the grill to high for 3 minutes. Use a thin-bladed knife to slice the gammon into 2 steaks, then snip the rind every 2–3cm/ ¾–1¼ in. Lightly brush with oil. Grill for about 3 minutes on each side until just firm, then brush over the honey on one side and cook for 1 minute more. Remove and leave to stand for 2–3 minutes.
3 Serve the gammon with the salsa spooned over the top. This is good with a chicory salad or green beans and chunky-cut chips.

• Per serving 283 kcalories, protein 32g, carbohydrate 10g, fat 13g, saturated fat 4g, fibre 1g, added sugar 5g, salt 6.12g

Sizzled Lamb with Chilli Tomatoes

When the weather's good, try cooking these on the barbecue. The lamb will be juicy and tender – a wonderful summer treat.

140g/5oz ripe vine tomatoes
½ small red onion
½ fresh red chilli
1 tbsp chopped fresh coriander
2 lamb leg steaks
olive oil

Takes 20 minutes • Serves 2

1 Halve the tomatoes, then squeeze out and discard the seeds. Finely chop the tomato flesh and onion. Halve, seed and finely chop the chilli. Mix the tomatoes, onion and chilli in a bowl with the coriander and some salt and pepper. At this point the tomato mixture can be covered and chilled for up to 2 days, but bring it back to room temperature before serving.
2 Season the lamb steaks on both sides and rub with a little olive oil.
3 Barbecue or cook on a hot griddle pan for 3–4 minutes each side for medium, a little longer if you prefer your lamb well done. Serve each leg steak with a dollop of the chilli tomatoes, new potatoes and a big crunchy salad.

• Per serving 293 kcalories, protein 34.7g, carbohydrate 3.5g, fat 15.7g, saturated fat 7.3g, fibre 0.9g, added sugar none, salt 0.49g

Purple Sprouting Broccoli Grill

If you want a lighter version, use half-fat crème fraîche and 50g/2oz of parmesan instead of the gruyère.

500g/1lb purple sprouting broccoli, about 18 stems
200ml carton crème fraîche
1 tbsp wholegrain mustard
100g/4oz grated cheese, such as gruyère or cheddar
6 slices ham

Takes 20 minutes • Serves 2

1 Bring a pan of water to the boil, add the broccoli and blanch for 2 minutes. Drain into a colander and refresh under running cold water.
2 In a small bowl, mix the crème fraîche with the mustard and half the cheese. Preheat the grill to high.
3 Use each slice of ham to wrap up three stems of broccoli then place in a baking dish in a higgledy-piggledy fashion. Spread the creamy mixture over, sprinkle with the remaining cheese and grill for 10 minutes until golden and bubbly.

• Per serving 755 kcalories, protein 39g, carbohydrate 10g, fat 62g, saturated fat 38g, fibre 9g, added sugars none, salt 3.38g

Steak and Noodle Stir Fry

Look for stir-fry sauces and no-need-to-cook noodles in the supermarket.

225g/8oz rump steak
225g/8oz pak choi (Chinese greens)
1 red pepper, seeded
2 tbsp sunflower oil
100–120g sachet stir fry sauce
2 × 150g packs no-cook noodles

Takes 10 minutes • Serves 2

1 Trim any visible fat from the steak, then slice into thin strips. Cut each head of pak choi into four lengthways. Dice the pepper into small squares.
2 Heat two tablespoons of sunflower oil in a pan. Add the pepper and fry quickly for 1 minute. Add the beef and fry until browned all over. Add the pak choi and cook briefly until starting to wilt.
3 Tip in the stir fry sauce and 2 tablespoons of water and stir. Bring to the boil, then add the noodles and warm through, loosening them until they are all coated in sauce. Serve immediately.

• Per serving 499 kcalories, protein 32g, carbohydrate 53.8g, fat 18.9g, saturated fat 3.1g, fibre 3.8g, added sugar 1.6g, salt 2.52g

TOP: Sizzled Lamb with Chilli Tomatoes   BOTTOM LEFT: Purple Sprouting Broccoli Grill   BOTTOM RIGHT: Steak and Noodle Stir Fry

TOP LEFT: 10-minute Tortellini   TOP RIGHT: Spicy Sausage and Chilli Pizza   BOTTOM: Spaghetti with 5-minute Tomato Sauce

10-minute Tortellini

Stuffed pasta comes in a wide variety of fillings – choose your favourite for this fantastically quick and tasty recipe.

250g pack fresh spinach and ricotta tortellini
1 tbsp olive oil
250g pack cherry tomatoes
2 × 20g packs fresh flatleaf parsley leaves, roughly chopped
3 tbsp finely grated parmesan cheese

Takes 5–10 minutes • Serves 2

1 Boil the pasta for 2 minutes until just cooked. Meanwhile, heat the oil in a frying pan and sizzle the tomatoes until they start to blister.
2 When the pasta is cooked, drain it quickly, reserving some cooking water. Put the tomatoes back on a high heat.
3 Tip in the pasta, parsley, a splash of cooking water and most of the parmesan. Bubble everything together and season with salt and pepper, if liked. Serve with the remaining parmesan.

• Per serving 482 kcalories, protein 18g, carbohydrate 62g, fat 20g, saturated fat 8g, fibre 4g, added sugar none, salt 1.5g

Spicy Sausage and Chilli Pizza

Jazz up a basic shop-bought pizza with this tasty topping.

1 thin-crust bought cheese and tomato pizza
70g pack sliced chorizo
175g/6oz roasted red peppers, from a jar or the deli, drained and sliced
generous pinch crushed dried chillies
50g/2oz grated cheddar
few black olives

Takes 20–30 minutes • Serves 2

1 Preheat the oven to the temperature recommended on the pizza pack. Unwrap the pizza, then scrunch up the slices of chorizo and arrange on top of the pizza with the sliced peppers.
2 Sprinkle over the chilli flakes and cheese then scatter with the olives so all of the ingredients give a generous, even covering.
3 Bake the pizza according to the pack instructions – about 15 minutes – until the cheese is melted and golden.

• Per serving 792 kcalories, protein 36.2g, carbohydrate 59.3g, fat 47.3g, saturated fat 17.3g, fibre 5.5g, added sugar none, salt 4.14g

Spaghetti with 5-minute Tomato Sauce

A really versatile recipe – try chopped red pepper instead of the bacon.

5 large ripe tomatoes
140g/5oz spaghetti
3 tbsp olive oil
100g/4oz diced bacon or lardons
2 garlic cloves, chopped
50–85g/2–3oz soft fresh rindless goat's cheese
handful of fresh basil and/or snipped chives

Takes 20–25 minutes • Serves 2

1 Pour boiling water over the tomatoes to cover, leave for 1 minute, then drain and remove the skins. Quarter and seed the tomatoes, chop the flesh.
2 Bring a large pan of salted water to the boil, add the spaghetti and stir. Cook according to packet instructions. Meanwhile, heat 1 tablespoon of the oil in a frying pan, add the bacon and fry until starting to crisp up. Add the garlic, tomatoes, the rest of the oil and salt and pepper, if liked. Heat through for 1–2 minutes until just simmering.
3 Drain the spaghetti and add to the pan, tossing in the sauce until lightly coated. Divide between two warm soup plates, crumble over the cheese and scatter over the herbs. Serve with crusty bread and a glass of red wine.

• Per serving 637 kcalories, protein 23g, carbohydrate 63g, fat 35g, saturated fat 10g, fibre 5g, added sugar none, salt 1.98g

Herby Salmon and Couscous Parcels

You can cook the parcels in the microwave – cook each one separately for 3 minutes on High, then leave to stand for 2 minutes.

110g pack lemon and garlic couscous
200ml/7fl oz hot vegetable stock
1 tbsp olive oil
handful of chopped fresh herbs (parsley, plus thyme, tarragon or rosemary is good)
4 spring onions, thinly sliced
4 sunblush or sun-dried tomatoes, chopped
2 salmon fillets, about 140g/5oz each

Takes 25 minutes • Serves 2

1 Put the couscous into a bowl and stir in the stock and oil. Cover with cling film and leave to stand for 10 minutes, then uncover and fluff up with a fork. Keeping back some herbs, add the rest to the couscous with the spring onions and tomatoes. Season to taste.
2 Preheat the oven to 200°C/Gas 6/fan oven 180°C. Cut out two large sheets of non-stick baking paper, then divide the couscous between them. Sit each fillet on the couscous, top with the remaining herbs and season.
3 Fold the paper over, then twist the edges to seal – like a Cornish pasty. Put the parcels onto a baking sheet and bake for 15 minutes or until the fish feels firm through the paper. Serve in the bag.

• Per serving 504 kcalories, protein 36g, carbohydrate 39g, fat 24g, saturated fat 5g, fibre 1g, added sugar 5g, salt 2.71g

Griddled Fish with Avocado Salsa

Try the chunky salsa with griddled chicken breasts or steak.

1 ripe avocado
2 ripe plum tomatoes, each chopped into 6
1 small red onion, finely sliced
3 tbsp olive oil, plus some for drizzling
juice of ½ lemon or 1 lime
small bunch of fresh coriander, leaves only
2 × 140g/5oz fish fillets, such as Pacific cod or halibut, skin on

Takes 15 minutes • Serves 2

1 Halve and stone the avocado and use a teaspoon to scoop chunks of the flesh into a bowl. Gently mix all the other ingredients, except the fish, in with the avocado, then set aside.
2 Heat a cast iron ridged griddle pan until very hot. Season the fish with pepper, and salt if liked, then drizzle with a little olive oil.
3 Griddle the fillets for 2–3 minutes on each side until charred and cooked through. Serve with the avocado salsa.

• Per serving 423 kcalories, protein 28g, carbohydrate 6g, fat 32g, saturated fat 4g, fibre 3g, added sugar none, salt 0.25g

Stir-fry Prawns with Spinach

Pick up the ingredients for this speedy supper on your way home from work, throw them into the wok, then serve with instant egg noodles.

3 tbsp groundnut or sunflower oil
2 fat garlic cloves, thinly sliced
1 small red pepper, cored, seeded and thinly sliced
200g pack raw peeled tiger prawns, defrosted and patted dry if frozen
2 tbsp soy or fish sauce
100g/4oz bag baby spinach leaves

Takes 10 minutes • Serves 2

1 Heat a wok until you can feel a good heat rising. Add 2 tablespoons of oil and, a few seconds later, the sliced garlic. Stir fry until they start to turn golden, then, using a slotted spoon, spoon onto kitchen paper to drain.
2 Toss in the pepper and stir fry for 1 minute or so until softened, then scoop out and set aside. Add the remaining tablespoon of oil. Heat, then toss in the prawns and stir fry for another 2–3 minutes until cooked and beginning to brown. Splash in the soy or fish sauce.
3 Throw in the spinach and stir fry until it begins to wilt. Return the pepper and crisp garlic to the wok to warm through, then serve immediately.

• Per serving 269 kcalories, protein 21g, carbohydrate 7g, fat 18g, saturated fat 3g, fibre 2g, added sugar none, salt 3.38g

TOP LEFT: Herby Salmon and Couscous Parcels   TOP RIGHT: Griddled Fish with Avocado Salsa   BOTTOM: Stir-fry Prawns with Spinach

TOP: Pork with Frizzled Sage Roast   BOTTOM LEFT: Seared Beef with Bean Mash   BOTTOM RIGHT: Duck with Wine Sauce

Pork with Frizzled Sage

An autumn supper for a cosy night at home. Try serving with cider, which works well with the apples.

3 small parsnips, trimmed, cut into even chunks
3 tbsp olive oil
85g/3oz Gruyère cheese, cut in 2 slices
250g/9oz pork fillet (thick end), cut in half, then sliced through each half (but not all the way), so it can be opened like a book
1 tbsp chopped fresh sage, plus 6 leaves
2 knobs of butter
2 small Cox's apples, cored and sliced
½ small Savoy cabbage, cored and finely shredded
small wine glass of dry white wine or cider

Takes 1–1¼ hours • Serves 2

1 Preheat oven to 180°C/Gas 4/fan oven 160°C. Toss parsnips in 2 tablespoons of oil in a roasting tin and roast for 20 minutes. Put a slice of cheese in each opened piece of pork, sprinkle with chopped sage, season. Close pork, tying with string to make 2 parcels.
2 Heat remaining oil with half the butter in a pan, brown pork for 2–3 minutes each side. Lay pork on top of parsnips, roast for 20–25 minutes.
3 Meanwhile, heat remaining butter, fry sage leaves 30 seconds until crisp then remove. Fry apples in same pan until caramelised. Remove, add cabbage and stir fry until tender. Arrange cabbage, pork and apples on plates. Reduce the wine or cider in roasting tin for 3–4 minutes, pour around meat and scatter with sage leaves.

• Per serving 705 kcalories, protein 44g, carbohydrate 30g, fat 42g, saturated fat 16g, fibre 11g, added sugar 1g, salt 1.08g

Seared Beef with Bean Mash

This unusual bean mash, flavoured with horseradish, is the perfect accompaniment to beef. Serve with a big red wine.

4 tbsp extra-virgin olive oil
1 tbsp each chopped fresh rosemary and thyme
280g/9½oz piece beef fillet, trimmed
50g/2oz unsalted butter
1 large onion, finely chopped
2 garlic cloves, crushed
410g can cannellini beans, drained and rinsed
¼ small Savoy cabbage (about 200g/8oz), cored and shredded
3 tbsp chicken stock or water
1 tbsp finely grated horseradish (from a jar is fine)
3 tbsp chopped fresh flatleaf parsley
about 2 tbsp basil or olive oil, for drizzling

Takes 40 minutes, plus 2 hours or overnight chilling • Serves 2

1 Mix 2 tablespoons of the oil with rosemary, thyme and some pepper, in a shallow dish. Coat the beef in it, cover and chill for 2 hours or overnight.
2 Let beef come to room temperature. Heat a cast iron griddle pan until very hot. Wipe the beef, and cook 4–6 minutes on each side for rare. Rest for 15 minutes. Heat 1 tablespoon of oil and half the butter in a pan. Gently cook the onion and garlic for 8–10 minutes until soft, not brown. Add beans and cook for 1–2 minutes.
3 Heat a wok or large pan. Add remaining oil and butter. Stir fry the cabbage for 1–2 minutes. Add stock, season. Cook for a few more minutes to evaporate most of the liquid. Stir horseradish into the beans and mash. Stir in the parsley and season. Carve the beef into
4 Serve with beans and cabbage, drizzled with oil.

• Per serving 890 kcalories, protein 44g, carbohydrate 36g, fat 65g, saturated fat 21g, fibre 12g, added sugar none, salt 0.83g

Roast Duck with Wine Sauce

Duck legs are perfect for slow-roasting – the flesh falls off the bones and the fat is released into the gravy to add body and flavour.

2 duck legs
small bunch of rosemary sprigs
2 fat garlic cloves
¼ tsp five-spice powder
¼ bottle of red wine
1 tbsp redcurrant or quince jelly

Takes 1¼ hours • Serves 2

1 Preheat the oven to 190°C/Gas 5/fan oven 170°C. Put the duck legs in one layer in a small roasting tin on a bed of the rosemary sprigs and garlic cloves. Sprinkle with salt and the five-spice powder. Roast for 1 hour.
2 Bring the wine and jelly to a gentle simmer, stirring to dissolve the jelly, then continue to simmer for 4 minutes.
3 When the duck has been cooking for 1 hour remove from the oven and spoon off almost all the fat (save it for roast potatoes), then pour the wine mixture around it and return to the oven for a further 10–15 minutes to finish cooking the duck and reduce the sauce.

• Per serving 375 kcalories, protein 36.3g, carbohydrate 5g, fat 15.4g, saturated fat 4.3g, fibre none, added sugar 3.2g, salt 0.77g

Spatchcock Barbecue Chicken

Try adding lightly oiled cherry tomatoes, halved red onions and lemons to the barbecue for the last 10 minutes, to serve with the chicken.

1.3kg/3lb chicken, spatchcocked
a little beer or water, to baste
1–2 lemons, quartered, to serve

FOR THE MARINADE
3 tbsp olive oil, plus extra to serve
1 tsp paprika, plus extra to serve
1 garlic clove, crushed
zest and juice of 1 lemon

Takes 1 hour, plus marinating • Serves 2

1 Make the marinade. Mix together the oil, paprika, garlic, lemon zest and some salt and pepper. Brush this all over the skin of the spatchcock chicken and marinate in the fridge for 30 minutes.
2 To cook on a barbecue: preheat the barbecue. Cook for 5 minutes each side in the centre, then draw aside to the edges to cook on a gentler heat. Turn regularly. Baste in between with beer or water. To check that the chicken is cooked through, pierce with a knife between the thighs and breast bone: the flesh should be white and firm.
3 Remove from the heat and leave to rest, covered with foil, for 10–15 minutes. Cut into portions, drizzle over the lemon juice and seasoning, plus a little oil and pinches of paprika. Serve with lemon quarters.

• Per serving 650 kcalories, protein 59g, carbohydrate 1g, fat 45g, saturated fat 14g, fibre 1g, added sugar none, salt 0.91g

Steak with Chunky Chips

A fail-safe recipe for classic steak and chips – a real spoil-yourself supper.

500g/1lb 2oz floury potatoes
olive oil, for drizzling
2 thick sirloin steaks
100g/4oz crème fraîche
1–2 tbsp horseradish, depending on how hot you like it
2 tbsp snipped fresh chives

Takes 1 hour • Serves 2

1 Preheat the oven to 200°C/Gas 6/fan oven 180°C. Cut the potatoes into chunky chips, leaving the skin on. Dry with kitchen paper, then tip into a roasting tin. Drizzle over 2 tablespoons of olive oil and shake the tin to coat the potatoes. Sprinkle with pepper and roast for 40–45 minutes, shaking the tin halfway through the cooking time. Season with salt when they are cooked.
2 Season the steaks and rub with olive oil. Mix the crème fraîche, horseradish and half the chives, salt and pepper.
3 When the chips are almost done, heat the grill to high and grill the steaks for 2–3 minutes on each side, depending on how you like them, and on their thickness. Serve with a pile of chips, a dollop of horseradish cream and a green salad with the remaining chives.

• Per serving 417 kcalories, protein 19g, carbohydrate 47g, fat 18g, saturated fat 9g, fibre 2g, added sugar none, salt 2.17g

Succulent Sirloin and Tender Shallots

Half steak, half roast, this main course just oozes fine dining.

400g/14oz–500g/1lb 2oz sirloin steak in one piece (you can order from a butcher with some warning)
1–2 tbsp cracked black pepper
1 tbsp vegetable oil
small knob of butter
6 small shallots, peeled, halved, but still attached at root
1 fresh thyme sprig
1 bay leaf
glass of red wine (about 175ml/6fl oz)
100ml/3½fl oz beef stock
buttered green beans and roasted new potatoes with thyme, to serve

Takes 50 minutes–1 hour • Serves 2

1 Preheat oven to 220°C/Gas 7/fan oven 200°C. Season the steak with black pepper and some salt. Heat oil, then butter, in a heavy-based pan. Sear the steak for 1–2 minutes on each of its 6 sides. Remove to a shallow roasting tin, and lower heat under the pan.
2 Sizzle the shallots in the pan for 6–8 minutes until softening. Add thyme and bay, turn up the heat and add the wine. Bubble and stir for about 5 minutes until reduced to a sticky glaze. Add the stock and bring to a boil. Tip sauce into a small saucepan and set aside.
3 Tip steak juices into the sauce. Roast the steak for 15 minutes for rare, 20 for medium, 30 for well done. Rest steak on a board for 5 minutes. Pour juices from the roasting tin into the sauce and gently reheat. Carve the steak thickly. Serve with shallots, beans and potatoes.

• Per serving 496 kcalories. protein 47g, carbohydrate 6g, fat 25g, saturated fat 9g, fibre none, added sugar none, salt 0.58g

TOP: Spatchcock Barbecue Chicken   BOTTOM LEFT: Steak with Chunky Chips   BOTTOM RIGHT: Succulent Sirloin and Tender Shallots

TOP LEFT: Pork with Gin and Coriander Sauce   TOP RIGHT: Moroccan Spiced Rack of Lamb   BOTTOM: Lamb with Lemon and Dill

Pork with Gin and Coriander Sauce

An unusual, but delicious, treat for two. Choose a highly aromatic gin to complement the simplicity of the pork.

4 tbsp gin, warmed
2 juniper berries, crushed
1 garlic clove, finely chopped
1 sprig fresh rosemary, finely chopped
1 tsp coriander seeds
3 tbsp olive oil
2 × 175g/6oz thick, boneless pork steaks, trimmed
150ml/¼ pint English apple juice, (the cloudy varieties have more flavour)
4 tbsp crème fraîche
mashed potato and buttered Savoy cabbage, to serve

Takes 35–45 minutes, plus soaking and marinating time • Serves 2

1 Pour the warm gin over the juniper berries. Soak for 20 minutes, then drain, reserving the gin. Pound the garlic, rosemary, coriander seeds, juniper berries and 2 tablespoons of olive oil. Spread this mixture over the pork. Cover and marinate (preferably overnight).
2 Heat the remaining oil in a small non-stick frying pan until very hot. Cook the pork quickly on both sides until golden. Pour in the gin – boil fast until it disappears. Pour in the apple juice. Scrape the pan to loosen any bits.
3 Simmer for 10 minutes until the pork is cooked and the sauce reduced but not too thick. Remove the pork to a warm plate. Swirl the crème fraîche into the sauce and boil rapidly for 1–2 minutes until syrupy, then season. Serve with mashed potatoes and buttered Savoy cabbage with sliced garlic.

• Per serving 557 kcalories, protein 41g, carbohydrate 10g, fat 32g, saturated fat 10g, fibre none, added sugar none, salt 0.35g

Moroccan Spiced Rack of Lamb

A rack of lamb is a great idea for two people – you can buy a ready-trimmed rack from the chilled section of larger supermarkets.

5 tbsp olive oil
1–1½ tbsp harissa paste
¼ tsp cumin
¼ tsp turmeric
¼ tsp paprika
¼ tsp ground coriander
20g pack fresh flatleaf parsley, chopped
juice of ½ small lemon
1 rack of lamb (6–8 cutlets)
2 carrots, peeled and cut into chunks
100g/4oz couscous
150ml/¼ pint vegetable stock
juice of 1 satsuma
¼ tsp ground allspice
½ × 20g pack fresh mint, chopped
½ red onion, finely chopped
Greek yogurt and 50g/2oz flaked almonds, toasted, to serve

Takes 40–45 minutes • Serves 2

1 Preheat oven to 220°C/Gas 7/fan oven 200°C. Mix 2 tablespoons of the oil with the harissa, cumin, turmeric, paprika, coriander, half the parsley, lemon juice and a pinch of salt. Season lamb, spread with spice mix then roast for 15–20 minutes for rare–medium, 25 minutes for well done.
2 Meanwhile, toss carrots in a small roasting tin, with a pinch of salt and 1 tablespoon of the oil. Roast for 15 minutes. Meanwhile, tip couscous into bowl, pour over hot stock and let stand for 5 minutes. Stir and cool. Stir in remaining oil, parsley, satsuma juice, allspice, mint, onion, carrots and season.
3 Rest lamb for 5 minutes. Slice in half to give 3–4 cutlets each, then halve again. Serve with the yogurt and couscous scattered with almonds.

• Per serving 888 kcalories, protein 34g, carbohydrate 40g, fat 67g, saturated fat 18g, fibre 5g, added sugar none, salt 1.22g

Lamb with Lemon and Dill

When the winter winds are howling, shut out the cold, light the fire and cosy up with this one-pot feast that's ideal for sharing.

350g/12oz ready-diced lamb
2 tsp plain flour
1 tbsp sunflower oil
1 onion, chopped
300ml/½ pint hot chicken or vegetable stock (a cube or powder is fine)
3 tbsp chopped fresh dill
1 bay leaf
300g/10oz salad potatoes, thickly sliced
zest and juice of ½ lemon
2 tbsp crème fraîche (half-fat is fine)

Takes 1¼ hours • Serves 2

1 Toss the lamb in the flour with a little salt and plenty of freshly ground black pepper. Heat the oil in a heavy-based pan, add the onion and fry for about 5 minutes until softened. Add the lamb and stir well until tinged brown.
2 Stir in the stock, 2 tablespoons of the dill and the bay leaf. Bring to the boil, then simmer for 30 minutes.
3 Add the potatoes and lemon juice and cook for a further 30 minutes until the potatoes are tender. Serve in soup plates or individual dishes with a spoonful of crème fraîche and a scattering of lemon zest and dill on each serving. Some crusty bread on the side will be useful for mopping up all the juices.

• Per serving 531 kcalories, protein 41g, carbohydrate 34g, fat 27g, saturated fat 11g, fibre 3g, added sugar none, salt 0.86g

Pepper Chicken Potato Crush

So simple, but packed with flavour, this dish is great for two people to prepare and eat together.

3 plump garlic cloves, peeled
3 tbsp chopped fresh flatleaf parsley
3 tbsp olive oil
2 boneless, skinless chicken breasts, preferably organic
100g goat's cheese (Capricorn is good), cut into 6 rounds
3 strips of roasted peppers in oil, drained, each cut in half
a few fresh thyme sprigs
300g/10oz small new potatoes
85g pack rocket or watercress, tough stems removed

Takes 55 minutes • Serves 2

1 Preheat oven to 200°C/Gas 6/fan oven 180°C. Soften the garlic in a little simmering water for 4–5 minutes. Drain and chop. Mix with the parsley and 1 tablespoon of oil. Make 3 deep diagonal slits across each breast. Reserve half the garlic mixture and spread the rest over the chicken and into the slits.
2 Halve each cheese slice and tuck two halves, a piece of pepper and some thyme into each slit. Season and bake in an oiled shallow dish for 30 minutes, until chicken is cooked.
3 Meanwhile, cook the potatoes for about 15 minutes. Drain, return to the pan and coarsely crush with a fork. Stir in rocket or watercress to leave to wilt. Stir remaining oil into the garlic mixture, season and stir into the potatoes. Serve with the chicken and any chicken juices.

• Per serving 562 kcalories, protein 46g, carbohydrate 30g, fat 29g, saturated fat 3g, fibre 4g, added sugar none, salt 0.88g

Chicken with Grainy Mustard Sauce

This is a substantial dish, so all you need to add to make a meal of it is tagliatelle or new potatoes.

2 boneless, skinless chicken breasts (about 300g/10oz total weight), preferably free-range
6 rashers of unsmoked streaky bacon, without rind
250g/9oz ready-washed spinach leaves, tough stalks removed
60g firm (not soft) goat's cheese, such as Crottin de Chavignol, cut in small cubes
2 tbsp olive oil
200ml/7fl oz vegetable or chicken stock
200ml/7fl oz dry white wine
½ × 200ml tub (or 4 heaped tbsp) crème fraîche
1 heaped tsp wholegrain mustard
tagliatelle or new potatoes, to serve

Takes 1–1¼ hours • Serves 2

1 Flatten each breast to 1½ times its original width. Overlap and stretch 3 bacon rashers on a board into a rectangle. Lay a breast on top, repeat with remaining bacon and chicken. Cover each with 4 spinach leaves, flatten. Put cheese along the middle. Season with pepper. Roll each one up, secure with cocktail sticks.
2 Heat half the oil in a frying pan. Cook the chicken over a high heat for 3–4 minutes until bacon is golden. Turn, cook for 3–4 minutes more. Add stock and wine. Simmer for 20 minutes, turning chicken halfway. Remove chicken, stir in crème fraîche and mustard.
3 Heat remaining oil in a large pan, add remaining spinach, season. Cover and cook for 2 minutes to wilt the spinach. Squeeze well. Serve each breast, halved, with the sauce and tagliatelle or new potatoes.

• Per serving 773 kcalories, protein 58g, carbohydrate 5g, fat 51g, saturated fat 23g, fibre 3g, added sugar none, salt 3.59g

Mediterranean Salad Tarts

A fresh and tasty idea for bringing summer into your home at any time of year – perfect for a candlelit supper.

2 large onions, thinly sliced
knob of butter
2 tbsp olive oil, plus extra
1 tsp light muscovado sugar
6 medium new potatoes
250g ready-made puff pastry, thawed if frozen
200g/8oz cherry tomatoes on the vine
100g/4oz camembert, cut into slices
6 anchovy fillets
6 black olives, not pitted
1 tbsp good-quality pesto
50g/2oz rocket leaves
100g/4oz green beans, lightly steamed
good squeeze of lemon juice
a few fresh basil leaves, roughly torn

Takes 55 minutes • Serves 2

1 Fry onions slowly in butter and half the oil for 15–20 minutes until soft and golden. Stir in the sugar, cook 3–4 minutes. Remove and cool.
2 Cook potatoes in boiling water for 10 minutes or until tender. Drain, cool and slice.
3 Preheat the oven to 220°C/Gas 7/fan oven 200°C. Halve the pastry, roll into 2 18cm/7in rounds. Put each round on a baking sheet and spread the onions over. Reserve 2 sprigs of tomatoes and halve the others. Lay the cheese, sliced potatoes, tomatoes and anchovies over the onions. Top each tart with a tomato sprig, olives and an extra drizzle of oil. Bake for 15–20 minutes until golden.
4 Mix pesto with remaining oil. Toss rocket and beans with lemon juice and extra oil. Season. Drizzle pesto over the tarts, scatter with basil leaves. Serve with the rocket salad.

• Per serving 1025 kcalories, protein 28g, carbohydrate 93g, fat 63g, saturated fat 13g, fibre 7g, added sugar 3g, salt 3.49g

TOP LEFT: Pepper Chicken Potato Crush   TOP RIGHT: Chicken with Grainy Mustard Sauce   BOTTOM: Mediterranean Salad Tarts

TOP: Mussels with Wine and Smoky Bacon   BOTTOM LEFT: Salmon Teriyaki with Crispy Ginger   BOTTOM RIGHT: Baked Trout with Chicory and Bacon

Mussels with Wine and Smoky Bacon

Fresh mussels are surprisingly quick and easy to prepare. Serve this dish with bread to mop up the delicious juices.

200g/8oz new potatoes, halved
350g/12oz, about ½ small Savoy cabbage, cored and shredded
1 tbsp olive or sunflower oil
1 small onion, finely chopped
1 plump garlic clove, crushed
200ml/7fl oz dry white wine
2 fresh thyme sprigs
1 bay leaf
1kg/2lb 4oz fresh mussels, well scrubbed and beards removed (discard any that are open or don't close when tapped)
100g/4oz smoked streaky bacon, chopped
2 tbsp double cream

Takes about 50 minutes • Serves 2

1 Cook potatoes in boiling salted water for 10–12 minutes until tender, adding the cabbage for the last 2 minutes. Meanwhile, heat oil in a saucepan, fry the onion and garlic for 2 minutes. Add wine and herbs, season with pepper. Bring to the boil, tip in mussels and cover tightly. Cook for 5–8 minutes, shaking the pan often, until they open.
2 Meanwhile, dry-fry bacon until crisp. Drain on kitchen paper. Drain the potatoes and cabbage. When mussels open, put a colander over a saucepan and tip in the mussels and liquid. Discard herbs and any unopened mussels.
3 Warm the cooking liquid and stir in the cream. Season. Spoon the potatoes and cabbage into bowls, top with the mussels and bacon, then the cooking liquid.

• Per serving 553 kcalories, protein 32.4g, carbohydrate 34.3g, fat 29.3g, saturated fat 10.4g, fibre 7g, added sugar 0.7g, salt 2.78g

Salmon Teriyaki with Crispy Ginger

Try this creative oriental salmon supper when you want a treat.

1 tbsp vegetable or groundnut oil, plus extra
2 salmon fillets, each about 140g/5oz, preferably organic (skin on or off)
8 × 5cm/2in long slices fresh root ginger, cut into very thin strips
149g/5oz Thai or basmati rice
1 tsp sesame oil
250g/9oz asparagus, trimmed
1 tbsp sesame seeds, toasted (in a dry pan over a medium heat for about a minute, shaking often)

FOR THE MARINADE
3 tbsp Japanese soy sauce
1 tbsp clear honey
2 tbsp dry sherry
1 small garlic clove, crushed

Takes 30–35 minutes, plus one hour marinating • Serves 2

1 Mix marinade ingredients in shallow dish. Coat salmon in marinade, cover, chill for 1 hour.
2 Heat about 1cm/½in oil in a small pan. Fry the ginger for about 1 minute until crispy. Remove and drain on paper towels. Set aside.
3 Ten minutes before serving, cook the rice in unsalted boiling water. Meanwhile, heat the tablespoon of vegetable oil in a frying pan. Reserving the marinade, fry the salmon for 3–5 minutes on each side. Mix the sesame oil with a teaspoon of vegetable oil. Steam the asparagus for 3–5 minutes, then toss in the oil mixture. Simmer the marinade in a pan for less than a minute to reduce slightly. Drain the rice, stir in the sesame seeds. Sit the salmon on the asparagus, pour over the sauce, top with the ginger and serve with the rice.

• Per serving 682 kcalories, protein 40g, carbohydrate 71g, fat 27g, saturated fat 4g, fibre 3g, added sugar 8g, salt 6.96g

Baked Trout with Chicory and Bacon

Baking the trout in a foil parcel keeps it nice and moist and the chicory infuses it with a slightly nutty taste.

4 trout fillets, skin on (about 140g/5oz each)
50g/2oz butter, softened
1 tbsp Dijon mustard
20g pack fresh flatleaf parsley, chopped
2 shallots, finely chopped
6 garlic cloves, crushed
juice of 1 lemon
3 heads of chicory
50g/2oz dry-cured streaky bacon, chopped
25g/1oz roasted, skinned hazelnuts, chopped
olive oil and lemon wedges, to serve

Takes 35–40 minutes • Serves 2

1 Preheat oven to 200°C/Gas 6/fan oven 180°C. Make 3 slashes in skin of each fillet. Mix half the butter with mustard, parsley, shallots, garlic and lemon juice. Rub over fish and into the slashes.
2 Keeping a few chicory leaves back, divide the rest between 2 large sheets of foil. Lay one fillet, skin-side down, on each pile of chicory. Top with second fillet, skin-side up. Season. Loosely wrap foil around, seal the edges. Put parcels on a baking sheet. Bake 15 minutes.
3 Meanwhile, melt remaining butter in small frying pan. Fry bacon and hazelnuts until golden. Transfer fish and chicory to plates, drizzling over the juices and a splash of oil. Garnish with reserved chicory scattered with bacon and hazelnuts. Serve with lemon wedges.

• Per serving 707 kcalories, protein 63g, carbohydrate 9g, fat 47g, saturated fat 19g, fibre 4g, added sugar none, salt 2.26g

Oriental Rice Express

Microwaving the rice is a fantastic short-cut option for stress-free cooking.

2 tbsp olive oil
1 large onion, chopped into chunks
½ tsp Chinese five-spice powder or
   ground ginger
300–340g pack fresh stir-fry
   vegetables (such as sliced water
   chestnuts, mushrooms and pak choi)
2 × 250g packets ready-cooked
   express basmati rice
2 tbsp soy sauce, or more to taste

Takes 15–25 minutes • Serves 2

1 Heat the wok, pour in the oil and heat it up.
Add the onion and cook, stirring occasionally,
until it starts to brown. Sprinkle in the five-
spice powder or ginger and stir fry for 30
seconds. Stir in the vegetables, keeping
the heat quite high. Stir fry for 4–5 minutes
until the vegetables begin to soften, but
stay crunchy.
2 While the vegetables cook, make a
2.5cm/1in tear in the top of each rice
packet. Microwave each packet separately
for 2 minutes on high. (If you don't have a
microwave, cook the rice according to the
pack instructions before you heat up the wok.)
3 Splash in the soy sauce, and remove from
the heat. For more sauce, splash in 1–2
tablespoons of water. Serve rice topped with
the vegetables.

• Per serving 503 kcalories, protein 12g, carbohydrate
85g, fat 15g, saturated fat 2g, fibre 5g, added sugar
none, salt 2.75g

Feta-stuffed Roasty Onions

These stuffed onions make an excellent
vegetarian main course with a rice or
couscous pilaf and a crisp salad.

2 medium onions
2 tbsp olive oil, plus extra for drizzling
4 thyme sprigs

FOR THE STUFFING
200g block of feta, crumbled
50g/2oz white or brown breadcrumbs
1 fresh red chilli, seeded and finely chopped
6 pieces of sun-dried tomato in olive oil,
   drained and chopped
large pinch chopped fresh thyme leaves
2 tbsp chopped fresh parsley
50g/2oz walnut pieces, chopped
1 medium egg, beaten

Takes about 1½ hours • Serves 2

1 Preheat oven to 190°C/Gas 5/fan oven
170°C. Keeping them whole, peel the onions,
discarding the first layer as you peel. Halve
the onions widthways and spoon out several
layers from each centre. Use bits of the centre
layers (sliced) to fill any holes. Put onions,
cut side up, in a small ovenproof dish. Add
a splash of water, brush them with some oil.
Cover, bake for 40–45 minutes until tender.
2 Meanwhile, chop the inner layers.
Heat remaining oil, fry the onion, stirring
occasionally, for 10 minutes until softened.
Cool, then mix in a bowl with half the feta and
remaining stuffing ingredients. Season.
3 Increase oven to 200°C/Gas 6/fan oven
180°C. Divide stuffing between onions.
Scatter over remaining cheese and thyme
sprigs. Drizzle with oil and cook for 25
minutes.

• Per serving 742 kcalories, protein 28g, carbohydrate
35g, fat 55g, saturated fat 17g, fibre 5g, added sugar
none, salt 5g

Spiced Butternut Squash with Cheese

The sweet squash partners the chilli,
spinach and cheese deliciously.

1 heaped tsp coriander seeds
½ tsp crushed dried chilli flakes
½ tsp coarse sea salt
½ tsp black peppercorns
1 large butternut squash, peeled, seeded and
   cut into chunks
3 tbsp olive oil
4 garlic cloves, unpeeled and whole
225g bag baby spinach
225g/8oz Ardrahan (or other strong
semi-soft cheese, rind removed), cut into
   slices

Takes 1¼ hours • Serves 2

1 Preheat the oven to 200°C/Gas 6/fan oven
180°C. Roughly crush the spices, salt and
peppercorns using a pestle and mortar. Mix
the squash and oil in a roasting tin, sprinkle
over half the spice mix and tuck in the garlic.
2 Roast for 20 minutes, turn the squash over
and dust with the rest of the spice mix. Roast
for another 20 minutes.
3 Remove and peel the garlic, then return
the cloves to the tin and stir in the spinach.
Scatter over the cheese and return to the
oven for 2–3 minutes or until the spinach has
wilted and the cheese melted.

• Per serving 331 kcalories, protein 6.2g, carbohydrate
39g, fat 17.8g, saturated fat 2.4g, fibre 7.2g, added
sugar none, salt 1.3g

TOP: Oriental Rice Express   BOTTOM LEFT: Feta-stuffed Roasting Onions   BOTTOM RIGHT: Spiced Butternut Squash with Cheese

TOP LEFT: Tamarind Chickpeas   TOP RIGHT: Griddled Halloumi with Spiced Couscous   BOTTOM: Indian Beans on Toast

Tamarind Chickpeas

The different flavours in each mouthful make this dish irresistible. Serve for supper or for lunch as an alternative to soup or a sandwich.

1 tbsp vegetable or sunflower oil
¼ tsp nigella seeds (look for these in supermarkets)
1½ tsp fennel seeds
1 medium onion, chopped
400g can chopped tomatoes
3 fresh green chillies, seeded and cut into quarters lengthways
2–3 tsp light muscovado sugar
1 tsp paprika
1 tsp turmeric
410g can chickpeas, drained and rinsed
1 tbsp tamarind paste
1 tbsp chopped fresh coriander
½ × 250g bag baby spinach leaves
natural yogurt and chapatis, to serve

Takes 25–35 minutes • Serves 2

1 Heat the oil in a saucepan and fry the nigella and fennel seeds for about 10 seconds. Add the onion and cook gently for 8–10 minutes until golden.
2 Mix in the tomatoes, chillies, sugar, paprika, turmeric and chickpeas. Bring to the boil, then simmer for 10 minutes.
3 Stir in the tamarind and coriander. Add the spinach leaves and stir gently until they've just wilted. Serve with yogurt and chapatis.

• Per serving 334 kcalories, protein 16g, carbohydrate 45g, fat 11g, saturated fat 1g, fibre 9g, added sugar 5g, salt 1.34g

Griddled Halloumi with Spiced Couscous

Any leftovers are delicious served cold for lunch.

1 head of broccoli
handful of sugar snap peas
175g/6oz couscous
½ tsp each cinnamon, cumin and coriander
300ml/½ pint hot vegetable stock
250g pack halloumi cheese
handful of cherry tomatoes, halved
juice of ½ lemon
drizzle of olive oil
small handful of fresh coriander leaves, chopped

Takes 20 minutes • Serves 2

1 Cut the broccoli into florets and thickly slice the stalk. Pour boiling water into a steamer. Steam the broccoli for 6 minutes. Add the peas and steam for 2 minutes more.
2 Meanwhile, mix the couscous with the spices in a bowl, pour over the hot stock, then cover and leave to stand for 5 minutes.
3 Heat a non-stick frying pan or griddle pan. Cut the halloumi into 6–8 slices and cook quickly on each side for 2 minutes until lightly tinged brown.
4 Mix the vegetables and tomatoes into the couscous, fork in the lemon juice, oil and coriander. Pile onto two plates and top with the halloumi.

• Per serving 711 kcalories, protein 40g, carbohydrate 52g, fat 39g, saturated fat 19g, fibre 5g, added sugar none, salt 5.12g

Indian Beans on Toast

If you want a break from bread, serve the beans with rice instead.

1 tbsp vegetable oil
1 medium onion, cut into thin wedges
½ tsp turmeric
½ rounded tsp ground cumin
2 medium tomatoes, cut into rough chunks
½ × 410g can green lentils, drained
1 plain or garlic and coriander naan
handful of fresh coriander leaves, roughly torn
yogurt and lemon wedges, to serve

Takes 20–30 minutes • Serves 2

1 Heat the oil in a frying pan. Tip in the onion and cook, stirring occasionally, until really golden (5–8 minutes). Stir in the turmeric and cumin for 1 minute to release their flavour. Add the tomatoes and cook briefly, gently stirring, until they just start to soften but don't lose their shape.
2 Tip the lentils into the pan and heat through. While they are warming, tear the naan bread roughly in half and toast under the grill or in the toaster just to warm through, but not brown.
3 Stir 2 tablespoons of water into the lentils to make a little sauce, then warm through. Add the coriander to the lentils, season with salt and serve spooned over the naan while hot, with a dollop of yogurt and a lemon wedge.

• Per serving 376 kcalories, protein 12.2g, carbohydrate 57.4g, fat 12.4g, saturated fat 3.3g, fibre 4.9g, added sugar 1.8g, salt 2.08g

Potato Wedge Tortilla

Try to buy mature cheddar for this dish –
it has loads of flavour so you don't have to
use very much.

1 tbsp sunflower oil
1 large potato, cut into 8 wedges (no need
    to peel)
1 small onion, halved and sliced
1 red pepper, seeded and cut into chunks
6 eggs
handful of grated cheddar cheese, preferably
    mature

Takes 30–40 minutes • Serves 2

1 Heat the oil in a non-stick frying pan. Add
the potato wedges and fry gently for 15–20
minutes, turning occasionally until golden
and cooked through. Take the potato out of
the pan, add the onion and fry until soft and
golden. Add the red pepper and cook until
softened. Return potatoes to the pan.
2 Beat the eggs with plenty of seasoning,
then pour over the potato, pepper and onion.
Push the egg mix around in the pan to make
space for the uncooked egg to flow into.
3 When the egg looks quite set, throw the
grated cheese over and put under a hot grill
for a few minutes until the cheese is golden.
Cut into wedges and serve. (Salad is good
with this.)

• Per serving 467 kcalories, protein 28g, carbohydrate
23g, fat 30g, saturated fat 9g, fibre 2g, added sugar
none, salt 0.89g

Greek Salad Tortillas

With just six ingredients, these tortilla
wraps are perfect picnic food.

2 very large soft tortilla wraps
1 large vine-ripened tomato, roughly chopped
5cm/2in piece of cucumber, cut into sticks
6 kalamata olives, stoned (optional)
50g/2oz feta cheese
2 heaped tbsp houmous

Takes 10 minutes • Serves 2

1 Heat the tortillas. If you have gas, put each
one for 10 seconds on a lit gas ring – you
have to be a little bit brave – then turn it over
quickly, using tongs, and heat the other side
for another 8 seconds or so. The tortillas will
be slightly charred in places.If you don't have
gas, warm a pan to a medium heat before
quickly tossing in your tortillas one at a time.
You don't need any oil.
2 Make a row of tomato, cucumber, feta and
olives down the centre of each warm tortilla.
Spread the houmous around the top and
sides of the tortillas. Fold in the sides to seal
in the ingredients and roll up tightly to make
a big cigar. Cut each in half and eat with
your fingers.

• Per serving 297 kcalories, protein 10g, carbohydrate
25g, fat 18g, saturated fat 5g, fibre 3g, added sugar
none, salt 2.08g

Storecupboard Minestrone

Adapt this tasty and substantial winter
soup according to what you've got in the
freezer – try adding frozen broad beans,
sweetcorn or spinach.

2 tbsp olive oil
1 onion, roughly chopped
2 × 400g cans chopped tomatoes
1 tbsp vegetable bouillon powder (such as
    Marigold Swiss vegetable bouillon)
1 tbsp pesto, plus extra to serve
pinch of sugar
50g/2oz dried mini pasta shapes for soup
    (such as farfalline), or spaghetti or other
    pasta, broken into small pieces
410g can mixed pulses, drained and rinsed
200g/8oz frozen green vegetables, such as
    sliced green beans and peas

Takes 30 minutes • Serves 2

1 Heat the oil in a large saucepan and cook
the onion over a low heat until softened.
Pour in the tomatoes and 4 canfuls of water.
Sprinkle in the bouillon powder, then stir in the
pesto, sugar and seasoning to taste.
2 Increase the heat and bring to the boil. Add
the pasta and simmer for 10 minutes or until
just tender, stirring occasionally.
3 Tip in the pulses and frozen vegetables,
stir well and bring to the boil again. Cover and
simmer for 10 minutes, stirring occasionally.
Taste for seasoning. Serve with extra pesto.

• Per serving 256 kcalories, protein 12g, carbohydrate
33g, fat 9g, saturated fat 2g, fibre 9g, added sugar 1g,
salt 2.16g

TOP LEFT: Potato Wedge Tortilla   TOP RIGHT: Greek Salad Tortillas   BOTTOM: Storecupboard Minestrone

TOP: Spring-into-summer Pasta   BOTTOM LEFT: Rigatoni with Roasted Squash   BOTTOM RIGHT: Spinach with Coriander Couscous

Spring-into-summer Pasta

The lemon and mint make this a perfect dish for a summer meal.

175g/6oz tagliatelle
250g/9oz courgettes
½ × 190g pack fresh shelled peas, or
    use frozen
zest and juice of ½ lemon
small handful of fresh mint leaves, chopped
½ × 250g tub ricotta
olive oil, for drizzling

Takes 15 minutes • Serves 2

1 Cook the tagliatelle according to the pack instructions. Meanwhile, cut the courgettes into thin finger-length sticks.
2 When the pasta has 2 minutes left to cook, tip the courgettes and peas into the pan, then cook until just tender. Drain and return to the pan.
3 Toss in the lemon zest and juice, most of the mint, then season to taste. Divide between two bowls, spoon small dollops of ricotta over each, sprinkle with the remaining mint and serve with a drizzle of oil and a grind of pepper.

• Per serving 486 kcalories, protein 22.1g, carbohydrate 75.6g, fat 12.7g, saturated fat 5.4g, fibre 6.1g, added sugar none, salt 0.19g

Rigatoni with Roasted Squash

Roasting the squash brings out its sweet nutty flavour and the onions add a savoury note.

1 butternut squash, about 700g/1lb 9oz
2 red onions
2 garlic cloves, sliced
2 tbsp olive oil
175g/6oz rigatoni or penne
3 rounded tbsp crème fraîche
freshly grated vegetarian parmesan cheese,
    to serve (optional)

Takes 50 minutes • Serves 2 generously

1 Preheat the oven to 200°C/Gas 6/fan oven 180°C. Peel, halve and seed the squash, then cut into bite-sized chunks and tip into a roasting tin. Peel the onions, leaving the roots intact, then cut each one lengthways into 8 wedges and add them to the tin with the garlic, oil and some seasoning. Toss until all the ingredients are glistening, then roast for 30 minutes.
2 Meanwhile, cook the pasta in salted boiling water for 8–10 minutes, or according to the pack instructions, until tender. Drain, reserving 4 tablespoons of the water.
3 Remove the tin from the oven and stir in the 4 tablespoons water and the crème fraîche, then toss in the pasta. Serve sprinkled with black pepper and parmesan if you like.

• Per serving 572 kcalories, protein 16.7g, carbohydrate 102g, fat 13.8g, saturated fat 7.6g, fibre 9.2g, added sugar none, salt 0.16g

Spinach with Coriander Couscous

A substantial, well-balanced and delicious supper full of healthy ingredients.

1 tbsp olive oil
1 onion, roughly chopped
2 tsp ground coriander
½ tsp ground cumin
3 garlic cloves, crushed
2 tbsp tomato purée
410g can chickpeas in unsalted water,
    drained
175g/6oz couscous
small bunch of fresh coriander, finely
    chopped
300ml/½ pint hot vegetable stock
175g/6oz cherry tomatoes
250g bag baby leaf spinach

Takes 30–40 minutes • Serves 2

1 Heat the oil in a large saucepan and fry the onion until softened. Stir in the ground spices and garlic and fry for 2 minutes more. Stir in the tomato purée, chickpeas and 150ml/¼ pint water. Bring to the boil, cover and cook gently for 5 minutes.
2 Meanwhile, put the couscous and chopped coriander in a large heatproof bowl, pour the hot stock over and cover tightly with cling film. Leave for 10 minutes to absorb the liquid.
3 Tip the cherry tomatoes and spinach into the chickpeas. Stir until the spinach has wilted and the tomatoes softened, but still have their shape. Season with pepper. Fluff up the couscous grains with a fork. Taste and add salt only if needed (the stock is salty). Serve topped with the chickpeas and spinach.

• Per serving 624 kcalories, protein 26.3g, carbohydrate 96g, fat 17.3g, saturated fat 4g, fibre 15.7g, added sugar none, salt 0.95g

Chilli Prawns

Jumbo king prawns are ideal for quick cooking – just wrap in foil and cook on the side of the barbecue until piping hot.

300g/10oz jumbo king prawns
2 lemongrass stalks, bruised

FOR THE MARINADE
½ large fresh red chilli, seeded and finely chopped
2 tsp olive oil
1 tsp fish sauce or soy sauce
1 plump garlic clove, crushed
1 tsp grated fresh root ginger
½ tsp ground cumin

Takes 15 minutes • Serves 2

1 Mix the marinade ingredients and add to the prawns, rubbing it all over to coat. Leave for 5 minutes.
2 To cook on a barbecue: thread the prawns on metal skewers, place in the centre of the preheated grill on the lemongrass stems for fragrance, and cook for 2–3 minutes, turning once until opaque.
3 Discard the lemongrass before eating.

• Per serving 122 kcalories, protein 26.6g, carbohydrate 0.2g, fat 1.7g, saturated fat 0.3g, fibre none, added sugar none, salt 0.85g

Thai-style Steamed Fish

Serve with Thai jasmine rice. And if you have some sesame seeds, toast a handful and toss into the rice just before serving.

2 trout fillets, each weighing about 140g/5oz
small knob of fresh root ginger, peeled and chopped
1 small garlic clove, chopped
1 small fresh red chilli (not bird's eye), seeded and finely chopped
grated zest and juice of 1 lime
3 baby pak choi, each quartered lengthways
2 tbsp soy sauce

Takes 25–30 minutes • Serves 2

1 Nestle the fish fillets side by side on a large square of foil and scatter the ginger, garlic, chilli and lime zest over them. Drizzle the lime juice on top, then scatter the pieces of pak choi around and on top of the fish.
2 Pour the soy sauce over the pak choi and loosely seal the foil to make a package, making sure you leave space at the top for the steam to circulate as the fish cooks.
3 Steam for 15 minutes. (If you haven't got a steamer, put the parcel on a heatproof plate over a pan of gently simmering water, cover with a lid and steam.)

• Per serving 199 kcalories, protein 29g, carbohydrate 4g, fat 7g, saturated fat 2g, fibre none, added sugar none, salt 3.25g

Teriyaki Chicken Noodle Broth

Sensational for a light meal, this broth is packed with flavour.

1.3 litres/2¼ pints hot vegetable stock (using Marigold Swiss vegetable bouillon)
½ tsp grated fresh root ginger
1 tbsp teriyaki marinade or light soy sauce
¼ tsp Chinese five-spice powder
50g/2oz fine egg or rice noodles
140g/5oz fresh stir-fry vegetables
50g/2oz mushrooms (any type), halved or sliced
85g/3oz skinless roast chicken, torn into shreds
½ tsp sesame seeds
chilli sauce, to serve

Takes 15–20 minutes • Serves 2

1 Pour the stock into a large pan and heat until just simmering. Stir in the ginger and teriyaki marinade or soy sauce and then add the five-spice powder.
2 Add your chosen noodles and cook for 3–4 minutes, giving them a gentle stir to loosen them up every now and then. Tip in the stir-fry vegetables and mushrooms. Cook for a couple of minutes, then add the cooked chicken and simmer for a further 1–2 minutes.
3 Season the soup to taste and ladle into warmed bowls. Sprinkle with sesame seeds. Serve with the chilli sauce.

• Per serving 238 kcalories, protein 18.2g, carbohydrate 25.3g, fat 7.8g, saturated fat 1.3g, fibre 2.4g, added sugar 0.2g, salt 2.07g

TOP: Chilli Prawns   BOTTOM LEFT: Thai-style Steamed Fish   BOTTOM RIGHT: Teriyaki Chicken Noodle Broth

TOP LEFT: Sizzling Pepper Chicken Salad   TOP RIGHT: Honeyed Pork with Rosy Apples   BOTTOM: Plaice in a Hot Vinaigrette

Sizzling Pepper Chicken Salad

This is such a tasty salad that you'll find it hard to believe it's low fat. It's good with turkey escalopes, too.

200g/8oz small new potatoes (Jersey Royals if you can get them), scrubbed and halved
2 celery sticks, sliced diagonally
1 red pepper, seeded and sliced
¼ cucumber, chopped
2 spring onions, finely sliced diagonally
2 small boneless, skinless chicken breasts, total weight about 300g/10oz
1 tsp freshly ground black pepper (more if you like)
1 tbsp olive oil
4 tbsp fat-free Italian-style salad dressing

Takes 25–35 minutes • Serves 2

1 Put the potatoes into a pan of boiling salted water, boil for 8–10 minutes until tender. Drain. Toss the other vegetables in a bowl.
2 Cut the chicken breasts into finger-length strips and toss them with pepper and a little salt to coat them. Heat the olive oil in a frying pan or wok over a medium heat. Tip in the chicken and stir fry for 4–6 minutes, until golden brown and no longer pink in the middle – cut a piece in half to check.
3 Add the potatoes to the chicken and heat. Pour over the dressing (it will sizzle furiously), and immediately tip the contents of the pan over the vegetables. Toss together and serve.

• Per serving 349 kcalories, protein 40g, carbohydrate 30g, fat 8g, saturated fat 1g, fibre 3g, added sugar none, salt 0.57g

Honeyed Pork with Rosy Apples

This simple recipe works well with pork chops, too.

1 generous tbsp clear honey
5 tbsp apple juice
2 tbsp chopped fresh sage or 1 rounded tsp dried
1 tsp olive oil
2 pork steaks, about 100g/4oz each, trimmed of fat
1 red-skinned dessert apple (Empire are good), cut into 8 wedges and cored
lemon juice, to taste
boiled rice and green beans, to serve

Takes 25–35 minutes, plus marinating time • Serves 2

1 In a non-metallic bowl, mix the honey with the apple juice, sage and oil; season generously. Add the steaks and swish them about until they're coated in the marinade. Leave for 20 minutes.
2 Preheat the grill to medium. Grill the steaks for 3–4 minutes, basting them with the marinade every so often. Toss the apple wedges in the rest of the marinade. Turn the steaks over and tuck the apple wedges in next to them. Grill for another 3–4 minutes until the pork is tender and the apples are turning brown.
3 While the pork and apples are grilling, pour the remaining marinade into a small saucepan and bring to the boil. Simmer until reduced by about a third, season and add lemon juice to your taste. Serve with rice and green beans.

• Per serving 313 kcalories, protein 33g, carbohydrate 25g, fat 10g, saturated fat 2g, fibre 1g, added sugar 11g, salt 0.25g

Plaice in a Hot Vinaigrette

All you need to serve with the plaice is a bowl of hot buttered new potatoes.

2 large plaice fillets, about 140g/5oz each, skin on
1½ tbsp olive oil
1 garlic clove, thinly sliced
1 leek, washed, trimmed and shredded into very thin strips
juice of ½ lemon, plus wedges
boiled new potatoes, to serve

Takes 25–35 minutes • Serves 2

1 Preheat the grill to high. Lay the plaice fillets, skin-side down, on an oiled baking sheet, season with salt and freshly ground black pepper and drizzle with ½ tablespoon of the oil. Grill the fish for 2–3 minutes (no need to turn).
2 While the plaice is grilling, heat the remaining oil in a small frying pan. Add the garlic and leek and fry over a gentle heat until soft and golden. Pour in the lemon juice, then take the pan off the heat.
3 Remove the fish from under the grill and put on warm plates. Using a slotted spoon, top the fish with the garlicky leeks. Heat the vinaigrette left in the pan for a minute until piping hot, then pour it over the fish and season with pepper. Serve with lemon wedges and boiled new potatoes.

• Per serving 203 kcalories, protein 24.6g, carbohydrate 2.6g, fat 10.5g, saturated fat 1.5g, fibre 1.5g, added sugar none, salt 0.68g

Risotto with Fresh Minted Peas

This creamy risotto makes a delicious backdrop for sweet, new-season peas.

2 tsp vegetable bouillon powder (such as
  Marigold Swiss vegetable bouillon)
½ tbsp olive oil
1 onion, finely chopped
2 garlic cloves, peeled and finely chopped
140g/5oz arborio rice
2 tsp lemon juice
175g/6oz fresh or frozen peas,
  shelled weight (you will need 450g/1lb
  peas in their pods)
2 tbsp finely grated vegetarian parmesan
1 tbsp chopped fresh mint

Takes 30–40 minutes • Serves 2

1 Make the bouillon powder up to 600ml/
1 pint with boiling water for stock. Heat the
oil in a wide, shallow pan and fry the onions
until soft. Add the garlic and rice and cook,
stirring, for a few minutes until the rice turns
translucent. Stir in the lemon juice until most
of the liquid has evaporated.
2 Pour in enough stock to just cover the rice.
Cook, stirring, over a moderate heat for 20
minutes. As the liquid evaporates, gradually
add more stock. When the rice is done,
virtually all the liquid should be absorbed.
3 After the rice has cooked for 15 minutes,
add the peas, bring to a simmer, and cook for
the remaining 5 minutes. Season with black
pepper, stir in three quarters of the parmesan
and mint. Serve scattered with the remaining
cheese and mint.

• Per serving 412 kcalories, protein 16.8g,
carbohydrate 71.8g, fat 8.4g, saturated fat 2.9g,
fibre 6.3g, added sugar none, salt 0.44g

Herby Mushroom Pasta

To make a creamier version, stir 100g/4oz ricotta or quark into the pasta along with the cooked mushrooms.

250g/9oz flat or Portobello mushrooms,
  thickly sliced
2 tsp wholegrain mustard
3 garlic cloves, sliced or crushed
150ml/¼ pint vegetable stock (from a cube
  is fine)
250g/8oz penne pasta (or other tube shapes)
3 tbsp chopped fresh flatleaf parsley
finely grated zest of 1 lemon

Takes 20 minutes • Serves 2

1 Put the mushrooms, mustard, garlic and
vegetable stock into a frying pan, bring to
the boil and simmer for 5 minutes or until
the stock has nearly all evaporated and the
mushrooms are soft.
2 Meanwhile, cook the pasta according to
the pack instructions.
3 Drain and toss with the mushrooms,
parsley and lemon zest. Season to taste and
serve straight away.

• Per serving 235 kcalories, protein 9g, carbohydrate
49g, fat 2g, saturated fat 0.2g, fibre 3g, added sugar
2g, salt 0.25g

Spaghetti alle Vongole

A glass of cold white wine, such as Sancerre, is the perfect accompaniment to this light supper dish.

145g/5oz spaghetti
500g/1lb 2oz fresh clams in shells
2 ripe tomatoes
2 tbsp olive oil
1 fat garlic clove, chopped
1 small fresh red chilli, finely chopped
splash white wine (about half a small glass)
2 tbsp chopped parsley

Takes 20–25 minutes • Serves 2

1 Put the water for the spaghetti on to boil.
Rinse the clams in several changes of cold
water. Discard any that are open or damaged.
Cover the tomatoes with boiling water, leave
for 1 minute, then drain and slip off their skins.
Remove the seeds and chop the flesh.
2 Cook spaghetti according to pack
instructions. Meanwhile, heat the oil in a large
pan, add the garlic and chilli, then fry gently
for a few seconds. Stir in the tomatoes, then
add the clams and splash of wine, salt and
pepper, and bring to the boil. Cover and cook
for 3–4 minutes, until clams open.
3 Drain pasta, then tip into pan with the
parsley and toss together. Serve in bowls with
bread for mopping up juices.

• Per serving 409 kcalories, protein 16g, carbohydrate
56g, fat 13g, saturated fat 2g, fibre 3g, added sugar
none, salt 0.10g

TOP LEFT: Risotto with Fresh Minted Peas   TOP RIGHT: Herby Mushroom Pasta   BOTTOM: Spaghetti alle Vongole

TOP: Maple Pears with Cranberries   **BOTTOM LEFT:** Choc-mel Muffins   **BOTTOM RIGHT:** Tropical Crème Brûlées

Maple Pears with Cranberries

Try this microwave pud idea for a special treat in just 10 minutes.

2 ripe pears
small handful of dried cranberries
1 tbsp maple syrup, plus extra to serve
25g/1oz pecan nuts, roughly broken
Greek yogurt, to serve

Takes 10 minutes • Serves 2

1 Peel and halve the pears and scoop out the cores with a teaspoon. Lay the halves in a shallow microwaveable dish, cut side down, along with the cranberries. Pour 1 tablespoon of the maple syrup over and cover with cling film.
2 Microwave on High for 3 minutes until softened, stirring halfway through. Uncover and leave to cool for a few minutes. Stir the pecan nuts through the syrup.
3 Spoon into serving dishes, drizzle extra maple syrup over, if you like, and serve with yogurt.

• Per serving 193 kcalories, protein 1.6g, carbohydrate 27.9g, fat 9.1g, saturated fat 0.8g, fibre 4.2g, added sugar 4.6g, salt 0.02g

Choc-mel Muffins

Use good-quality vanilla ice cream to make the most of this oozingly delicious chocolate dessert.

50g chocolate caramel bar
2 tbsp double cream
2 chocolate muffins
4 scoops of vanilla ice cream

Takes 10 minutes • Serves 2

1 Break the chocolate bar in pieces into a small pan. Spoon in the cream and heat gently, stirring over a low heat until just melted.
2 Scoop a little bit from the middle of each muffin to make a small hole.
3 Drop a couple of scoops of ice cream onto each muffin, then drizzle the chocolate sauce over the top.

• Per serving 486 kcalories, protein 6.7g, carbohydrate 52.3g, fat 29.3g, saturated fat 16.1g, fibre 0.6g, added sugar 38.8g, salt 0.43g

Tropical Crème Brûlées

Impress your guests with this sensational dessert — a real special-occasion pudding.

½ medium ripe mango
1 passion fruit
½ × 200ml carton crème fraîche
1 tsp rum
2 scant tbsp golden caster sugar

Takes 10–15 minutes • Serves 2

1 Peel the mango, cut the flesh into small chunks and divide evenly between two 175ml/6fl oz ramekin dishes. Halve the passion fruit and scoop the contents of each half over the mango.
2 Mix the crème fraîche and rum together and spoon over the fruit to cover. Chill well.
3 To serve, sprinkle a spoonful of the sugar over the top of each dish and brûlée until the sugar has caramelised. This is best done with a blowtorch, as it is hard to get them to caramelise under a grill. Leave for about 5 minutes to harden before serving. (If you don't have a blowtorch, just sprinkle the tops with dark muscovado sugar and leave for about 10 minutes for the sugar to dissolve and give a brulée look.)

• Per serving 289 kcalories, protein 1.8g, carbohydrate 25.3g, fat 20.2g, saturated fat 12.9g, fibre 2.2g, added sugar 13.1g, salt 0.04g

Strawberry Mess

Turn a tub of ice cream into an indulgent treat.

200g/8oz strawberries
1 ready-made meringue nest
scoops of strawberry ice cream

Takes 10 minutes • Serves 2

1 Hull the strawberries. Roughly mash half of them with a fork and slice the rest.
2 Divide the strawberries between two bowls.
3 Break the meringue nest into rough pieces, then scatter over the strawberries. Top with scoops of ice cream.

• Per serving 197 kcalories, protein 3.9g, carbohydrate 32.7g, fat 6.5g, saturated fat 4.3g, fibre 1.1g, added sugar 20g, salt 0.16g

Warm Peaches with Basil and Honey

The fragrance of the basil works really well with the scented peaches in this special, easy and low-fat dessert.

knob of unsalted butter
1 ripe peach or nectarine, stoned and thickly sliced
1 tbsp clear honey
juice of ½ orange
4–5 fresh basil leaves, shredded
vanilla or white chocolate ice cream, to serve

Takes 10 minutes • Serves 2

1 Melt the butter in a frying pan, add the peach or nectarine slices, then cook on both sides until slightly softened (about 3 minutes).
2 Add the honey and stir to make a sauce, then pour in the orange juice and allow to bubble briefly.
3 Stir in the basil and serve warm with scoops of ice cream.

• Per serving 76 kcalories, protein 0.7g, carbohydrate 11.4g, fat 3.3g, saturated fat 2.1g, fibre 0.8g, added sugar 5.7g, salt 0.01g

Iced Summer Berries with White Chocolate Sauce

In mid-summer, try using fresh berries rather than frozen.

200g/4oz mixed frozen berries, such as raspberries, blueberries, strawberries (or fresh)

FOR THE SAUCE
½ × 142ml carton double cream
85g/3oz white chocolate

Takes 5 minutes • Serves 2

1 Let the frozen berries thaw slightly – they should be icy but not solidly frozen. (If using fresh berries, freeze briefly until they are icy, but not solid.)
2 Make the sauce. Pour the cream into a small pan and break in the chocolate. Heat gently, stirring, until the chocolate melts and the sauce is smooth. If the heat gets too high, the chocolate will seize.
3 Pile the berries into shallow dishes and pour the hot chocolate sauce over, so they start to soften in the warmth of the sauce.

• Per serving 609 kcalories, protein 5.4g, carbohydrate 33.1g, fat 51.5g, saturated fat 29.2g, fibre 2.7g, added sugar 20.2g, salt 0.19g

TOP: Strawberry Mess   BOTTOM LEFT: Warm Peaches with Basil and Honey   BOTTOM RIGHT: Iced Summer Berries with White Chocolate Sauce

TOP LEFT: Berry Daiquiri   TOP RIGHT: Chocolate Berry Cups   BOTTOM: Raspberry and Mango Salad

Berry Daiquiri

Strawberries make the easiest daiquiries because they blend really smoothly.

350g/12oz ripe strawberries or 400g/14oz
    raspberries (or use a mix of 200g/8oz
    strawberries and 200g/8oz raspberries)
about 12 ice cubes
juice of 1 lime
2 tbsp lemon juice
200ml/7fl oz white rum
2 small lime slices, to serve

Takes 10 minutes • Serves 2

1 If using raspberries, blend these first to a purée then rub through a sieve to extract the pips.
2 Put a handful of ice cubes in a powerful blender and crush. Add the berries or pulp, plus the lime and lemon juice and rum.
3 Whizz again and pour into two chilled cocktail glasses straight away. Decorate each with a lime slice.

• Per serving 271 kcalories, protein 1.5g, carbohydrate 10.9g, fat 0.2g, saturated fat none, fibre 2g, added sugar none, salt 0.03g

Chocolate Berry Cups

Perfect served with a glass of Asti Spumante at the end of a summer meal.

148ml carton double cream
50g/2oz dark chocolate, broken into pieces
1 tbsp icing sugar
280g/10oz mixed summer fruits (raspberries,
    strawberries,
cherries, blueberries), stoned and halved if
    necessary

Takes 15–20 minutes • Serves 2

1 Heat the cream in a saucepan until just coming to the boil. Remove from the heat, drop in the chocolate pieces, then stir until melted. Cool slightly.
2 Tip the icing sugar and most of the fruit into the pan and mix gently.
3 Spoon into two glasses or cups, top with the remaining fruit, then chill in the fridge until needed (up to 3 hours ahead of serving).

• Per serving 580 kcalories, protein 3.8g, carbohydrate 37.6g, fat 47g, saturated fat 26.3g, fibre 3.7g, added sugar 28.6g, salt 0.06g

Raspberry and Mango Salad

For a special occasion, add a dash of vodka to the syrup before pouring over the fruit.

100ml/3½oz cranberry juice
1½ tsp caster sugar
1 medium ripe mango
150g punnet raspberries
vanilla ice cream or yogurt, to serve

Takes 10 minutes • Serves 2

1 In a small pan, bring the cranberry juice and sugar to a rolling boil, then remove from the heat and leave to cool.
2 Meanwhile, peel and thinly slice the mango, then tip into a large bowl with the raspberries.
3 Pour the cranberry syrup over, then spoon into bowls. Serve with scoops of ice cream or spoonfuls of yogurt.

• Per serving 142 kcalories, protein 2.1g, carbohydrate 34.4g, fat 0.5g, saturated fat none, fibre 5.8g, added sugar 8.3g, salt 0.03g

Valentine's Molten Chocolate Pots

Prepare these exquisite puds up to 4 hours ahead and keep in the fridge. If cooking from cold, give them an extra 2–3 minutes in the oven.

50g/2oz butter, plus extra for greasing
1 tbsp ground almonds, plus extra for dusting
100g/4oz dark chocolate, broken in pieces
1 medium egg yolk
1 medium egg
2 tbsp golden caster sugar
4 tbsp Baileys
icing sugar to dust

Takes 25–30 minutes • Serves 2

1 Preheat oven to 230°C/Gas 8/fan oven 210°C. Make the stencils by up-ending a ramekin or coffee cup (whichever you are using) and tracing a circle round it on to paper. Draw a smaller heart shape within the circle. Cut out the circle, then cut the heart from it, to make two stencils.
2 Butter two large ramekins or heatproof coffee cups and dust with ground almonds. Melt the chocolate and butter together.
3 Whisk the yolk, whole egg and sugar until light and pale then gently fold in the chocolate-butter mixture, ground almonds and Baileys. Divide between the ramekins. Bake for 10 minutes until puffed up and just set.
4 Place a stencil over each cooked pudding. Dust the puddings with icing sugar, remove the paper and serve immediately.

• Per serving 735 kcalories, protein 9g, carbohydrate 60g, fat 50g, saturated fat 23g, fibre 2g, added sugar 58g, salt 0.66g

Hot Passion Pina Coladas

This tasty pud is the perfect end to an exotic feast.

1 passion fruit
2 slices of fresh pineapple
icing sugar, to coat
4 tsp rum or Malibu
2 big scoops of coconut ice cream

Takes 15 minutes • Serves 2

1 Halve the passion fruit and scoop out the pulp. Set aside.
2 Coat the pineapple slices in icing sugar. Heat a small non-stick heavy-based frying pan, add the pineapple slices and cook for a few minutes until caramelised on each side, turning once.
3 Lay each pineapple slice on a plate, drizzle with the rum or Malibu, then top with scoops of the ice cream. Spoon the passion fruit pulp over and serve.

• Per serving 233 kcalories, protein 2.9g, carbohydrate 32.8g, fat 8.5g, saturated fat 6g, fibre 1.6g, added sugar 22.8g, salt 0.11g

Sticky Cinnamon Figs

Splash a few tablespoons of armagnac or brandy over the figs before grilling to make a boozy pudding.

4 ripe figs
knob of butter
2 tbsp clear honey
small handful of shelled pistachio nuts or almonds
½ tsp ground cinnamon or mixed spice
mascarpone or Greek yogurt, to serve

Takes 10 minutes • Serves 2

1 Preheat a grill to medium-high. Cut a deep cross in the top of each fig, then ease the top apart so it opens like a flower.
2 Sit the figs in a small baking dish and drop a piece of butter into the centre of each fruit. Drizzle the honey over the figs, then sprinkle with the nuts and spice.
3 Grill for 5 minutes until the figs are softened and the honey and butter make a sticky sauce in the bottom of the dish. Serve warm with dollops of mascarpone or yogurt.

• Per serving 186 kcalories, protein 3.6g, carbohydrate 24.1g, fat 9.1g, saturated fat 2.8g, fibre 1.7g, added sugar 11.5g, salt 0.08g

TOP LEFT: Valentine's Molten Chocolate Pots   TOP RIGHT: Hot Passion Pina Coladas   BOTTOM: Sticky Cinnamon Figs

Cheap Eats

Potato, Spinach and Cheese Melt

Double Gloucester adds attractive colour to the softened spinach.

650g/1lb 7oz new potatoes, cut into
   long wedges
1 tbsp oil
250g pack ready-washed
   baby spinach leaves
100g/4oz Double Gloucester
1–2 tbsp snipped fresh chives
100g/4oz wafer-thin smoked ham

Takes 25 minutes • Serves 4

1 Bring a large pan of salted water to the boil. Add the potatoes and boil for 12–15 minutes until tender.
2 Drain the potatoes well, then return to the pan. Add the oil and lightly toss the potatoes. Put the pan over a medium heat, add the spinach, cover and shake the pan occasionally until the spinach has wilted.
3 Cut the cheese into cubes or crumble it straight into the pan. Season well and add the chives. When the cheese starts to melt, spoon on to hot serving plates. Using scissors, snip strips of ham over the top and serve straight away.

• Per serving 289 kcalories, protein 16g, carbohydrate 27g, fat 14g, saturated fat 6g, fibre 3g, added sugar none, salt 1.31g

Tomato Salsa Salad

A chunky and satisfying salad, easily doubled for a crowd.

650g/1lb 7oz tomatoes
4 spring onions, chopped
2 tbsp chopped fresh parsley
1 garlic clove, finely chopped
4 tbsp olive oil
1 tbsp lemon juice
650g/1lb 7oz new potatoes, halved
4 rashers unsmoked bacon
4 hard-boiled eggs
lettuce, to serve

Takes 30 minutes • Serves 4

1 Finely chop 225g/8oz of the tomatoes and combine with the spring onions, parsley, garlic, oil and lemon juice to make a salsa. Season to taste. Cook the new potatoes in lightly salted boiling water until just tender. Drain and refresh under cold running water. Thickly slice.
2 Preheat the grill to high and cook the bacon for 3–4 minutes until crisp. Allow to cool slightly then break into bite-sized pieces. Cut the remaining tomatoes and the eggs into eighths.
3 Toss the potatoes, egg, tomato slices and tomato salsa in a serving bowl. Season to taste. Scatter over the bacon and serve on a bed of lettuce.

• Per serving 362 kcalories, protein 14g, carbohydrate 32g, fat 21g, saturated fat 4g, fibre 4g, added sugar none, salt 1.05g

Warm Chickpea Salad

Cubed feta cheese sold in jars of olive oil is ideal for this recipe. Use the oil to make the dressing.

1 red onion, cut into wedges
2 courgettes, thickly sliced
1 red pepper, seeded and cut into
   large chunks
375g/13oz ripe tomatoes, halved
5 tbsp olive oil
juice of ½ a lemon
3 tbsp chopped fresh mixed herbs, (chives,
   parsley and mint) or 3 tbsp chopped
   fresh parsley
2 × 400g cans chickpeas, drained
100g/4oz feta, cut into cubes
pitta bread, to serve

Takes 45 minutes • Serves 4

1 Preheat the oven to 220°C/Gas 7/fan oven 200°C. Put the onion, courgettes, red pepper and tomatoes into a shallow roasting tin and season with black pepper. Drizzle with two tablespoons of the olive oil and toss well. Roast for 30 minutes, stirring halfway through, until the vegetables are tender.
2 Meanwhile, mix together the lemon juice and remaining olive oil and season. Stir in the herbs.
3 Allow the vegetables to cool for 5 minutes, then tip into a bowl with the chickpeas, feta and lemon and olive oil dressing. Toss lightly before serving with pitta bread.

• Per serving 375 kcalories, protein 15g, carbohydrate 29g, fat 23g, saturated fat 5g, fibre 8g, added sugar none, salt 1.62g

TOP: Potato, Spinach and Cheese Melt   BOTTOM LEFT: Tomato Salsa Salad   BOTTOM RIGHT: Warm Chickpea Salad

TOP LEFT: Warm Potato and Broccoli Salad   TOP RIGHT: Ham, Potato and Feta Salad   BOTTOM: Salami, Bean and Avocado Salad

Warm Potato and Broccoli Salad

This salad looks most attractive when you use Desirée or Romano potatoes.

700g/1lb 9oz potatoes, cut into chunks
350g/12oz broccoli, cut into florets
5 tbsp olive oil
1 onion, peeled and cut into thin wedges
12 rashers rindless streaky bacon, smoked or unsmoked
1 tbsp white wine vinegar
1 tbsp wholegrain mustard

Takes 40 minutes • Serves 4

1 Parboil the potatoes in salted boiling water for 5 minutes, adding the broccoli for the last 3 minutes. Drain the potatoes and broccoli.
2 Heat two tablespoons of oil in a pan. Add the onion and potatoes only and cook for 8–10 minutes until golden. Meanwhile, grill the bacon until crisp, then drain on kitchen paper. Add the broccoli to the pan with the onion and potatoes and warm through. Tip the vegetables into a bowl.
3 Add the remaining olive oil, vinegar and mustard to the pan the onion was cooked in, stirring until warm. Pour over the vegetables, toss gently and season with pepper. Serve with the bacon rashers on top.

• Per serving 492 kcalories, protein 19g, carbohydrate 34g, fat 32g, saturated fat 9g, fibre 5g, added sugar none, salt 2.82g

Ham, Potato and Feta Salad

A substantial main meal salad for all the family to enjoy. It is good served warm or cold.

1kg/2lb 4oz new potatoes, halved if large
175g/6oz feta cheese cubes in oil
1 tsp dried oregano
8 tomatoes, roughly chopped
100g/4oz pitted black olives
225g/8oz (about 4 slices) thick-sliced ham, cut into large pieces
handful of chopped fresh parsley

Takes 30 minutes • Serves 4

1 Bring a large pan of water to the boil (no need to add salt). Add the potatoes and cook for 15 minutes until tender.
2 Meanwhile, heat two tablespoons of the feta oil in a pan. Add the oregano and tomatoes and cook over a medium heat for 3–4 minutes, until slightly softened. Stir in the olives, feta cubes and ham, and stir well. Drain the potatoes and return to the pan.
3 Tip the olive and tomato mixture into the potato pan and season. Sprinkle over the parsley and toss lightly. Serve warm or cold.

• Per serving 408 kcalories, protein 23g, carbohydrate 47g, fat 16g, saturated fat 7g, fibre 5g, added sugar none, salt 4.47g

Salami, Bean and Avocado Salad

Mix the ingredients, minus the avocado, the night before eating for maximum flavour.

150g pack button mushrooms, sliced
8 radishes, sliced
½ small red onion, thinly sliced
400g can haricot or cannellini beans, drained
4 tbsp light olive oil
1 tbsp wine vinegar or cider vinegar
1 garlic clove, crushed
1 avocado
90g pack peppered salami, each slice cut into eighths

Takes 15 minutes • Serves 4

1 In a bowl, toss the mushrooms, radishes, red onion and beans.
2 In a separate bowl, mix together the olive oil, vinegar and garlic. Season.
3 Peel and stone the avocado and cut the flesh into chunks. Gently stir into the bean mixture with the salami and the dressing. Check the seasoning and serve straight away.

• Per serving 362 kcalories, protein 11g, carbohydrate 14g, fat 29g, saturated fat 6g, fibre 6g, added sugar 2g, salt 1.24g

Tomato Pizza Toasties

Cheese on toast for grown-ups, but child's play to make.

4 thick slices of bread
120g carton pesto sauce
8 tomatoes, weighing about 650g/1lb 7oz, thinly sliced
100g/4oz cheddar, grated

Takes 15 minutes • Serves 4

1 Preheat the grill to high. Toast the bread slices on one side. Turn over and spread a thin layer of pesto on the untoasted side.
2 Arrange the tomato slices over the top to cover. Season well.
3 Sprinkle over the cheese and grill for 5 minutes, until the cheese is golden and bubbling. Serve immediately.

• Per serving 380 kcalories, protein 17g, carbohydrate 25g, fat 24g, saturated fat 10g, fibre 2g, added sugar none, salt 1.36g

BLT Burgers

Kids will love these and they're brilliant for barbecues too.

500g pack minced lamb, pork or turkey
2 tbsp Worcestershire sauce
4 rashers smoked streaky bacon
tomato slices, lettuce leaves, mayonnaise and 4 burger buns, to serve

Takes 30 minutes • Serves 4

1 Preheat the grill to high, or light the barbecue. Season the mince well and stir in the Worcestershire sauce. Shape the mince into four burgers.
2 Cook the burgers under the grill or on the barbecue for 7–8 minutes on each side, until completely cooked through. Cook the bacon alongside the burgers for the last 8 minutes of cooking time, turning once, until crisp. Drain on kitchen paper.
3 Fill the buns with sliced tomatoes and lettuce leaves, then top with a burger. Lay a slice of bacon on top and finish with a spoonful of mayonnaise.

• Per serving 433 kcalories, protein 32g, carbohydrate 27g, fat 23g, saturated fat 10g, fibre 1g, added sugar none, salt 1.76g

Bacon Kebabs on Mushroom Rice

These kebabs make a lovely, lazy Sunday brunch. Prepare them the evening before, then next day just grill them and cook the rice.

2 medium leeks, each cut into 4
4 flat mushrooms
14 rashers rindless streaky bacon, halved
4 herby sausages, halved vertically
300g/10oz long grain rice
50g/2oz butter, melted
1 tsp dried thyme
squeeze of lemon juice
200ml carton crème fraîche

Takes 35 minutes • Serves 4

1 Blanch the leeks in boiling water for 3–4 minutes, then drain. Chop one mushroom and the stems of all the mushrooms, and keep to one side. Cut the other mushrooms into quarters. Stretch the bacon with the back of a knife, then wrap around each piece of leek, mushroom quarter and sausage. Thread on to skewers.
2 Preheat the grill to high. Cook the rice. Melt half the butter with half the thyme and the lemon juice. Brush over the kebabs. Grill for 10 minutes, turning, until cooked.
3 Melt the remaining butter in a pan. Cook the reserved chopped mushrooms and remaining thyme until softened. Stir in the crème fraîche and season. Drain the rice and stir into the sauce. Stir the kebab pan juices into the rice. Serve immediately.

• Per serving 1023 kcalories, protein 27g, carbohydrate 73g, fat 71g, saturated fat 35g, fibre 1g, added sugar none, salt 4.72g

TOP LEFT: Tomato Pizza Toasties   TOP RIGHT: BLT Burgers   BOTTOM: Bacon Kebabs on Mushroom Rice

TOP: Pepperoni Pizza Tart   BOTTOM LEFT: Baked Potatoes with Cracked Eggs   BOTTOM RIGHT: Corn-stuffed Tomatoes

Pepperoni Pizza Tart

If you find anchovies a bit too salty, rinse them in milk before adding them.

250g/9oz ready-made shortcrust pastry
3 tbsp olive oil
450g/1lb onions, thinly sliced
2 garlic cloves, crushed
2 x 425g cans chopped tomatoes, drained
1 tsp dried oregano
25g/1oz thinly sliced pepperoni
85g/3oz mature cheddar, grated
50g can anchovy fillets in oil, drained and
    halved lengthways
12 black olives
salad, to serve

Takes 1¼ hours • Serves 6

1 Roll out the pastry and line a 23cm/9in flan tin. Chill while you make the filling. Heat the oil in a pan and fry the onions and garlic for 15 minutes until soft. Cool for 10 minutes, then spread over the pastry.
2 Preheat the oven to 220°C/Gas 7/fan oven 200°C. Spread the tomatoes over the onions, sprinkle with oregano and top with the pepperoni. Sprinkle over the cheese and arrange the anchovies and olives on top.
3 Bake for 25–30 minutes until the pastry is cooked. Serve hot or cold with a salad.

• Per serving 376 kcalories, protein 10g, carbohydrate 28g, fat 25g, saturated fat 10g, fibre 4g, added sugar none, salt 1.68g

Baked Potatoes with Cracked Eggs

You can bake the potatoes in the microwave for 20 minutes first, but cook the eggs in the oven.

4 large baking potatoes (about450g/1lb each
    in weight)
25g/1oz butter
140g/5oz broccoli, cut into small florets
100g/4oz mushrooms, sliced
8 medium eggs

Takes 1½ hours • Serves 4

1 Preheat the oven to 200°C/Gas 6/fan oven 180°C from cold. Bake the potatoes for 1–1¼ hours until they are cooked through and the skins are crisp. About 5 minutes before the end of the potatoes' cooking time, melt the butter in a frying pan. Add the broccoli and mushrooms and cook, stirring, for about 3 minutes, then set aside.
2 When the potatoes are cooked, cut each in half and scoop most of the flesh into a bowl. Stir in the broccoli, mushrooms and pan juices. Season well. Spoon back into the potato skins and make a well in the middle. Set the potatoes on a baking tray.
3 Carefully crack an egg into each well. (Don't worry if the egg white spills over a little.) Return to the oven and cook for 15 minutes until the eggs have just set.

• Per serving 358 kcalories, protein 19g, carbohydrate 35g, fat 17g, saturated fat 6g, fibre 4g, added sugar none, salt 0.52g

Corn-stuffed Tomatoes

Huge tomatoes make tasty containers for a scrumptious stuffing.

4 large beef tomatoes
sprinkling of caster sugar
2 tbsp olive oil
1 leek, thinly sliced
4 rashers streaky bacon, chopped
½ tbsp chopped fresh rosemary
3 slices day-old white bread
85g/3oz frozen or canned sweetcorn
175g/6oz gruyère, diced
2 tbsp chopped fresh parsley

Takes 45 minutes • Serves 4

1 Preheat the oven to 200°C/Gas 6/fan oven 180°C. Cut the tops off the tomatoes and discard. Using a spoon, scoop out the seeds to leave a hollow shell. Lightly season inside with a little sugar, salt and pepper, then put in a greased shallow baking dish.
2 Heat the oil in a frying pan and cook the leek, bacon and rosemary for 7 minutes, stirring occasionally. Meanwhile, cut the bread into cubes, then cook in the pan for 3 minutes, stirring to brown all over. Season, then add the corn, cheese and parsley.
3 Divide the stuffing between the tomatoes and bake for 20 minutes until the filling is golden.

• Per serving 321 kcalories, protein 15g, carbohydrate 22g, fat 20g, saturated fat 8g, fibre 3g, added sugar none, salt 1.46g

Goat's Cheese and Tomato Tart

Choose a mild soft cheese that doesn't overpower the flavour of the tomatoes.

1 medium floury potato, peeled
85g/3oz cold butter, cut into pieces
1 onion, finely chopped
7 fresh thyme sprigs or 1 tsp dried
140g/5oz plain flour
450g/1lb ripe tomatoes, thickly sliced
1 tbsp red wine vinegar
100g/4oz soft goat's cheese
olive oil, for drizzling
green salad, to serve

Takes 55 minutes • Serves 4

1 Preheat the oven to 200°C/Gas 6/fan oven 180°C. Chop the potatoes, then cook in salted boiling water for 10–12 minutes. Drain and mash. Meanwhile, melt 25g/1oz butter in a small pan and cook the onion until beginning to brown. Strip the leaves from four thyme sprigs and add to the pan, or add half the dried thyme.
2 In a bowl, rub the remaining butter into the flour. Add the onion, pan juices and mashed potatoes, and season. Mix to a soft dough, then press into a 23cm/9in round on a greased baking sheet.
3 Arrange the tomatoes on the dough and drizzle over the vinegar. Sprinkle over the remaining thyme and season. Crumble the cheese over and drizzle with oil. Bake for 35–40 minutes. Serve with a green salad.

• Per serving 434 kcalories, protein 11g, carbohydrate 39g, fat 27g, saturated fat 16g, fibre 3g, added sugar none, salt 0.89g

Cheesy Potato Jackets

Choose large floury potatoes, such as King Edward or Maris Piper and serve for a light lunch or supper.

4 baking potatoes, about 350g/12oz each in
   weight, scrubbed
50g/2oz butter
4 tbsp milk
100g/4oz cheddar, grated
2 eggs, beaten
splash of Tabasco

Takes 1½ hours • Serves 4

1 Preheat the oven to 200°C/Gas 6/fan oven 180°C from cold. Rub the potatoes with a little salt, then transfer to a baking sheet and cook for 1–1¼ hours, until tender. Remove from the oven and leave until cool enough to handle.
2 Using a sharp knife, cut the tops off the potatoes and scoop the insides into a bowl, leaving the shells intact. Mash the potato flesh with a fork, beat in the butter, milk, 85g/3oz of the cheese, the eggs and Tabasco. Season. Pile back into the potato shells.
3 Scatter the remaining cheese over the top and bake for a further 20 minutes, until fluffy and golden.

• Per serving 509 kcalories, protein 18g, carbohydrate 61.1g, fat 23g, saturated fat 13.1g fibre 4.6g, added sugar none, salt 0.89g

Tuna Pizza Squares

Use packets of pizza-base mix to keep preparation to a minimum.

2 × 145g packets pizza-base mix
2 tbsp olive oil, plus extra for brushing
2 onions, thinly sliced
200g can chopped tomatoes
½ tsp dried oregano
200g can tuna, drained
85g/3oz stoned black olives
50g/2oz cheddar, grated
green salad, to serve

Takes 35 minutes • Serves 4

1 Grease a 33 × 28cm/13 × 11in Swiss roll tin. Put the pizza-base mixes in a bowl, add 250ml/9fl oz warm water and mix together to make a smooth dough. Knead for 5 minutes, then roll out on to a floured surface to the same size as the tin. Put the dough in the tin and brush with olive oil.
2 Preheat the oven to 200°C/Gas 6/fan oven 180°C. Heat the oil in a frying pan and fry the onions until golden. Set aside. Spread the tomatoes on to the dough base. Scatter over the oregano and season.
3 Break the tuna into chunks and arrange on the base with the olives. Scatter the onions and cheese on top and bake for 15–20 minutes, until the dough is risen, golden and cooked through. Cut into squares and serve with a salad.

• Per serving 633 kcalories, protein 28g, carbohydrate 91g, fat 18g, saturated fat 5g, fibre 6g, added sugar 3g, salt 3.52g

TOP: Goat's Cheese and Tomato Tart   BOTTOM LEFT: Cheesy Potato Jackets   BOTTOM RIGHT: Tuna Pizza Squares

TOP LEFT: Herbed Cheese Puffs TOP RIGHT: Bubble and Squeak Cakes BOTTOM: Spinach and Ham Tart

Herbed Cheese Puffs

Cheesy, herby choux pastry puffs are good with tomato sauce or with smoked haddock.

70g/2½oz plain flour
pinch of English mustard powder
50g/2oz butter, cubed
100g/4oz mature cheddar, grated
2 eggs, beaten
3 tbsp chopped fresh mixed herbs
steamed broccoli or leeks, to serve

FOR THE TOMATO SAUCE
1 tbsp olive oil
1 garlic clove, chopped or crushed
400g can tomatoes
1 tbsp tomato purée

Takes 50 minutes • Serves 4

1 Preheat the oven to 220°C/Gas 7/fan oven 200°C. Grease a baking sheet. Sift the flour, mustard powder and a pinch of salt on to a sheet of greaseproof paper. Bring the butter and 150ml/¼ pint water to the boil. Tip in the flour, remove from the heat and beat to a smooth thick paste. Beat in 85g/3oz of the cheese. Leave to cool for 5 minutes.
2 Gradually beat the eggs into the paste, then stir in the herbs. Drop spoonfuls on to the baking sheet spaced slightly apart, to form a 20cm/8in ring. Sprinkle over the remaining cheese.
3 Bake for 25–30 minutes until puffed up and crisp. Meanwhile, put the tomato sauce ingredients in a small pan. Season. Bring to the boil, stirring, then simmer for 10 minutes until thickened. Cut the puff into wedges. Serve with the sauce and broccoli or leeks.

• Per serving 340 kcalories, protein 13g, carbohydrate 18g, fat 25g, saturated fat 13g, fibre 2g, added sugar none, salt 0.88g

Bubble and Squeak Cakes

You can make one big cake by pressing the mix into a frying pan instead. Grill the top.

700g/1lb 9oz floury potatoes, such as
    Maris Piper, cut into chunks
4 carrots, sliced
350g/12oz green cabbage, shredded
50g/2oz cheddar, grated
175g/6oz thick slice of ham, cubed
1 bunch spring onions, finely sliced
1–2 tbsp wholegrain mustard
25g/1oz butter
2 tbsp oil

FOR THE SAUCE
400g can chopped tomatoes
1 tbsp tomato purée
1 tsp sugar

Takes 40 minutes, plus chilling • Serves 4

1 Cook the potatoes and carrots in salted water for 15 minutes until tender. Steam the cabbage over the pan for 8 minutes. Drain well. Return the potatoes and carrots to the pan and mash.
2 Stir in the cabbage, cheese, ham, half the spring onions and mustard to taste. Divide the mixture into eight and shape into 10cm/4in cakes. Chill for 30 minutes. To make the sauce, cook the tomatoes, remaining spring onions, purée, sugar and seasoning for 10 minutes.
3 Heat half the butter and oil in a frying pan. Fry four cakes at a time for 3–4 minutes on each side until golden. Keep them warm while frying the others in the rest of the butter and oil. Serve with the sauce.

• Per serving 423 kcalories, protein 21g, carbohydrate 45g, fat 19g, saturated fat 8g, fibre 9g, added sugar 1g, salt 2.03g

Spinach and Ham Tart

Ready-made puff pastry and cheese sauce make this quick to assemble.

250g/9oz frozen leaf spinach
2 eggs
300g carton ready-made cheese sauce
150ml/¼ pint milk
225g/8oz wafer-thin ham
375g sheet ready-rolled puff pastry, thawed
    if frozen

Takes 40 minutes • Serves 6

1 Preheat the oven to 200°C/Gas 6/fan oven 180°C. Thaw the spinach in the microwave for 8 minutes on defrost. Pat really dry with kitchen paper. Beat the eggs into the cheese sauce with the milk and some freshly ground black pepper. Roughly tear each ham slice in half.
2 Unroll the pastry and roll it out a bit more to line a 35 × 23cm/14 × 9in Swiss roll tin. Scatter the spinach over the pastry base, then the ham in rough folds. Pour over the cheese sauce mixture.
3 Bake the tart for 25–30 minutes until set and golden on top.

• Per serving 414 kcalories, protein 18g, carbohydrate 30g, fat 26g, saturated fat 5g, fibre 1g, added sugar none, salt 2.21g

Fettucine with Watercress Pesto

This contemporary variation on traditional fresh pesto sauce is made from watercress, walnuts and lime.

350g/12oz fettucine
85g/3oz watercress
100g/4oz walnuts, chopped
50g/2oz parmesan, grated
1 garlic clove
finely grated zest and juice of 2 limes
100ml/3½fl oz olive oil
Italian bread and tomato salad, to serve

Takes 15 minutes • Serves 4

1 Cook the pasta in lightly salted boiling water according to the packet instructions.
2 Meanwhile, put the watercress, half the walnuts, the parmesan, garlic and lime zest and juice in a food processor and whizz to a paste. With the motor still running, gradually drizzle in the olive oil. Season.
3 Drain the pasta and return to the pan. Stir in the pesto, then divide the pasta between serving bowls. Scatter over the remaining walnuts and serve with Italian bread and a tomato salad.

• Per serving 763 kcalories, protein 20g, carbohydrate 67g, fat 48g, saturated fat 8g, fibre 4g, added sugar none, salt 0.42g

Tagliatelle with Smoked Salmon

Look for smoked-salmon trimmings to keep costs down.

1 tbsp vegetable oil
250g/9oz chestnut or button mushrooms, quartered
375g/13oz dried or fresh tagliatelle
125g pack smoked salmon (trimmings are fine), chopped
3 tbsp chopped fresh parsley
200ml carton half-fat crème fraîche
juice of ½ lemon
salad, to serve

Takes 20 minutes • Serves 4

1 Heat the oil in a frying pan. Add the mushrooms and cook for 8 minutes until beginning to brown.
2 Meanwhile, bring a large pan of salted water to the boil. Add the pasta and cook according to the packet instructions.
3 Stir the salmon, parsley, crème fraîche and lemon juice into the mushrooms and season. Drain the pasta and quickly toss with the creamy sauce. Serve immediately with a salad.

• Per serving 484 kcalories, protein 22g, carbohydrate 72g, fat 14g, saturated fat 6g, fibre 4g, added sugar none, salt 1.64g

Herby Pasta with Peas and Bacon

Soft cheese with herbs and garlic makes an almost instant pasta sauce.

350g/12oz pasta, such as penne
350g/12oz frozen peas
1 large red pepper, seeded and cut into chunks
8 rashers rindless streaky bacon
150g pack soft cheese with herbs and garlic
300ml/½ pint milk

Takes 20 minutes • Serves 4

1 Cook the pasta according to the packet instructions. About 5 minutes before the end of the cooking time, add the frozen peas and red pepper. Bring back to the boil and cook for 5 minutes.
2 Meanwhile, preheat the grill to high and grill the bacon until crispy. Snip into bite-sized pieces.
3 Put the soft cheese and milk into a large saucepan. Warm through, stirring continuously until smooth and thickened. Drain the pasta and vegetables, and toss with the cheese sauce and bacon. Season with freshly ground black pepper.

• Per serving 686 kcalories, protein 26g, carbohydrate 81g, fat 31g, saturated fat 16g, fibre 8g, added sugar none, salt 1.71g

TOP LEFT: Fettucine with Watercress Pesto   TOP RIGHT: Tagliatelle with Smoked Salmon   BOTTOM: Herby Pasta with Peas and Bacon

TOP: Tomato and Salmon Pasta   BOTTOM LEFT: Minted Chicken Rigatoni   BOTTOM RIGHT: Roasted Vegetable Pasta

Tomato and Salmon Pasta

Roast the tomatoes to emphasise their sweetness and concentrate the flavour.

2 tbsp fresh oregano leaves, or 1 tsp dried
900g/2lb small ripe tomatoes
2 onions, sliced
1 garlic clove, finely chopped
2 tbsp olive oil
350g/12oz spaghetti
450g/1lb boneless skinless salmon fillet
garlic bread, to serve

Takes 40 minutes • Serves 4

1 Preheat the oven to 200°C/Gas 6/fan oven 180°C. If using fresh oregano, strip the leaves from the stems. Tip half the oregano leaves, or all the dried oregano, into a roasting tin with the tomatoes, onions and garlic. Drizzle over the oil. Season, then stir well. Roast for 30 minutes, stirring occasionally, until the tomatoes have softened.
2 Cook the spaghetti in salted boiling water for 10–12 minutes, stirring occasionally. Meanwhile, cut the salmon into bite-sized cubes. Add to the roasting tin for the last 5 minutes of cooking time.
3 Drain the pasta and spoon into the tomatoes and salmon. Sprinkle over the remaining fresh oregano, if using, and serve hot with garlic bread.

• Per serving 615 kcalories, protein 36g, carbohydrate 77g, fat 20g, saturated fat 4g, fibre 6g, added sugar none, salt 0.19g

Minted Chicken Rigatoni

Ready-made stock (fresh or in cubes) can be quite salty, so don't season this dish until the sauce is cooked.

350g/12oz rigatoni
225g/8oz fresh or frozen peas
knob of butter
1 tbsp vegetable oil
1 red pepper, seeded and sliced
4 boneless skinless chicken breasts, cut into 2.5cm/1in cubes
1 onion, finely chopped
1 garlic clove, finely chopped
200ml/7fl oz chicken stock
4 tbsp chopped fresh mint, plus a few leaves to garnish
1 tbsp wholegrain mustard
200ml carton crème fraîche

Takes 35 minutes • Serves 4

1 Cook the pasta in salted boiling water for 10–12 minutes, adding the peas for the last 3 minutes.
2 Heat the butter and oil in a large frying pan. Add the red pepper and cook for 5 minutes until starting to brown. Transfer to a plate. Add the chicken and onion to the pan and cook over a high heat for 8 minutes, until the chicken is browned. Stir in the garlic for the last minute.
3 Add the stock, bring to the boil, then cook for 3 minutes to reduce by half. Stir in the red pepper, mint, mustard and crème fraîche. Season with pepper – add salt if necessary. Drain the pasta, stir into the chicken and serve.

• Per serving 718 kcalories, protein 51g, carbohydrate 80g, fat 23.8g, saturated fat 11.8g fibre 6.3g, added sugar none, salt 0.72g

Roasted Vegetable Pasta

Roasting the vegetables makes them sweet-tasting, rich and satisfying.

2 courgettes, cut into sticks
1 red pepper, seeded and cut into strips
2 garlic cloves, finely sliced
3 tbsp olive oil
300g/10oz pasta shells
200ml carton half-fat crème fraîche
2 tsp wholegrain mustard
85g/3oz cheddar, grated

Takes 30 minutes • Serves 4

1 Preheat the oven to 220°C/Gas 7/fan oven 200°C. Put the courgettes and red pepper in a roasting tin and sprinkle over the sliced garlic.
2 Drizzle with olive oil, then season and toss to make sure all the vegetables are coated with oil. Roast for 15–20 minutes, until the vegetables are tender and just beginning to brown.
3 Bring a large pan of salted water to the boil. Add the pasta and cook for 10–12 minutes until just cooked. Drain, then stir into the roasted vegetables with the crème fraîche, mustard and grated cheddar. Serve immediately.

• Per serving 490 kcalories, protein 19g, carbohydrate 62g, fat 20g, saturated fat 9g, fibre 4g, added sugar none, salt 0.58g

Spaghetti with Tomato and Brie

Ring the changes by using blue cheese, or for non-veggies, top with strips of crispy bacon.

300g/10oz spaghetti
500g/1lb 2oz courgettes, halved lengthways
3 tbsp olive oil
2 garlic cloves, thinly sliced finely grated zest and juice of 1 lemon
6 ripe tomatoes, roughly chopped
140g/5oz brie, diced

Takes 35 minutes • Serves 4

1 Cook the spaghetti in salted boiling water for 10–12 minutes until tender or according to the packet instructions. Meanwhile, slice the courgettes. Heat the oil in a large frying pan, then fry the courgettes and garlic for 3–4 minutes until softened.
2 Add the lemon zest, tomatoes and about three tablespoons of the pasta water (enough to make a sauce). Cook for a further 2–3 minutes until the tomatoes begin to soften. Remove from the heat and stir in the brie so it just starts to melt. Season and add lemon juice to taste.
3 Drain the spaghetti well and add to the tomato sauce mixture. Toss well together, divide between bowls and serve.

• Per serving 490 kcalories, protein 19g, carbohydrate 62g, fat 20g, saturated fat 7g, fibre 5g, added sugar none, salt 0.66g

Chicken and Spinach Pasta

You can use this all-in-one method of sauce-making in other recipes too.

350g/12oz pasta, such as penne
175g/6oz frozen leaf spinach
1 tbsp oil
4 boneless skinless chicken thighs, cut into strips
1 garlic clove, finely chopped
425ml/¾ pint semi-skimmed milk
25g/1oz plain flour
25g/1oz butter
140g/5oz mature cheddar, grated
freshly grated nutmeg, to taste

Takes 50 minutes • Serves 4

1 Cook the pasta in salted boiling water for 10 minutes, adding the spinach for the last 3–4 minutes of cooking time. Drain well. Meanwhile, heat the oil in a wok or large pan, add the chicken strips and garlic and stir fry for 3–4 minutes, until the meat is well browned and cooked through. Remove from the pan and set aside.
2 Add the milk to the pan, sprinkle in the flour, then add the butter and whisk over a medium heat until thickened and smooth. Stir in about 85g/3oz of the cheese and season with salt, pepper and nutmeg.
3 Preheat the grill to high. Mix the chicken into the sauce with the pasta and spinach. Spoon into an ovenproof dish, sprinkle with the remaining cheese and grill until golden.

• Per serving 705 kcalories, protein 44g, carbohydrate 78g, fat 27g, saturated fat 13g, fibre 4g, added sugar none, salt 1.11g

Spicy Sausage Pasta

Try a change from your usual sausage. Most supermarkets stock some exotic varieties.

2 tbsp olive oil
6 good-quality sausages
1 onion, finely chopped
1 garlic clove, chopped
400g can chopped tomatoes
1 tsp dried oregano
350g/12oz penne or rigatoni pasta
1 tbsp red pesto

Takes 35 minutes • Serves 4

1 Heat the oil in a frying pan and cook the sausages over a high heat for about 8 minutes until brown. Remove from the pan and cut into 2.5cm/1in pieces.
2 Fry the onion and garlic in the frying pan for 5 minutes. Add the tomatoes, sausage pieces and oregano, and season to taste. Cover, reduce the heat and simmer for 10 minutes. Meanwhile, cook the pasta in salted boiling water for 10–12 minutes until just tender.
3 When the sauce has thickened, stir in the pesto. Drain the pasta and return to the pan. Stir in the sauce and serve immediately.

• Per serving 652 kcalories, protein 27g, carbohydrate 77g, fat 29g, saturated fat 8g, fibre 4g, added sugar none, salt 2.17g

TOP: Spaghetti with Tomato and Brie   BOTTOM LEFT: Chicken and Spinach Pasta   BOTTOM RIGHT: Spicy Sausage Pasta

TOP LEFT: Spicy Spaghetti with Meatballs   TOP RIGHT: Pork and Ginger Noodles   BOTTOM: Leek, Pea and Ham Pasta

Spicy Spaghetti with Meatballs

Make double the amount of meatballs and sauce and freeze half for later.

15g packet mixed fresh Mediterranean herbs (basil, oregano and parsley) – leaves stripped from their stalks
500g packet pork mince
1 egg, beaten
25g/1oz fresh breadcrumbs
2 garlic cloves, crushed
2 large onions, finely chopped
2 tbsp oil
2 tbsp tomato purée
1kg/2lb 4oz ripe tomatoes, chopped
½ tsp sugar
1 tbsp Dijon mustard
350g/12oz spaghetti

Takes 1 hour 10 minutes • Serves 4

1 Chop the parsley and basil, mix with the mince, egg, breadcrumbs, garlic and half the chopped onion, then season. Shape into 20 balls. Heat the oil in a large frying pan. Fry the meatballs for 4–5 minutes, turning frequently, until browned, then remove from the pan.
2 Fry the remaining onion until golden. Add the tomato purée, tomatoes, sugar, 425ml/¾ pint water and half the oregano. Simmer for 5 minutes. Whizz in a food processor until smooth. Return to the pan.
3 Add the mustard and meatballs. Simmer, for 25 minutes, then season. Meanwhile, cook and drain the spaghetti. Divide between serving bowls and add the meatballs and sauce. Sprinkle with the remaining oregano.

• Per serving 689 kcalories, protein 41g, carbohydrate 88g, fat 22g, saturated fat 6g, fibre 7g, added sugar 1g, salt 0.77g

Pork and Ginger Noodles

Make the most of quick-cooking ingredients to create an appetising stir fry. For vegetarians, replace the pork with mushrooms.

2 tbsp sunflower oil
450g/1lb pork fillet, cut into thin strips about 1cm/½in wide
2.5cm/1in piece fresh root ginger, grated
2 garlic cloves, finely chopped
½ savoy cabbage, about 250g/9oz, shredded
300ml/½ pint vegetable or chicken stock
1 tbsp soy sauce
100g/4oz frozen peas
2 x 150g packets Straight-to-Wok noodles
2 tbsp chopped fresh coriander, to serve

Takes 25 minutes • Serves 4

1 Heat the oil in a wok over a high heat, add the pork and stir fry for 3–4 minutes until just cooked. Stir in the ginger and garlic and continue to fry for 1–2 minutes.
2 Add the cabbage and stir fry with the pork until well combined. Pour over the stock and soy sauce.
3 Add the peas and noodles, stir well, then simmer for 5 minutes, until the cabbage is cooked but still crunchy. Scatter with coriander and serve.

• Per serving 337 kcalories, protein 31g, carbohydrate 28g, fat 12g, saturated fat 2g, fibre 4g, added sugar none, salt 1.84g

Leek, Pea and Ham Pasta

A cheap and easy supper made from readily available ingredients.

300g/10oz spaghetti
175g/6oz frozen peas
25g/1oz butter
1 large leek
4 eggs
140g/5oz thick slice of smoked ham, cut into cubes
85g/3oz cheddar or Lancashire cheese, grated

Takes 15 minutes • Serves 4

1 Bring a large pan of salted water to the boil. Add the spaghetti and cook for about 10–12 minutes, adding the peas for the last 3 minutes of the cooking time.
2 Meanwhile, heat the butter in a small pan. Wash and slice the leek. Add to the pan and cook over a medium heat for 3 minutes until softened.
3 Beat the eggs in a bowl and season. Drain the pasta and immediately return to the pan. Tip in the leeks, eggs, ham and half the cheese. Stir well. Adjust the seasoning and serve sprinkled with the remaining cheese.

• Per serving 553 kcalories, protein 32g, carbohydrate 61g, fat 22g, saturated fat 10g, fibre 6g, added sugar none, salt 1.67g

Chilli Bean Tortillas

Invite everyone to assemble their own tortillas at the table.

500g pack lamb or beef mince
1 onion, chopped
1 tsp mild chilli powder
1 tsp ground cumin
400g can chopped tomatoes
200g can red kidney beans
8 flour tortillas
handful of shredded iceberg lettuce leaves
grated cheddar, soured cream and lemon
   wedges, to serve

Takes 1 hour 10 minutes • Serves 4

1 Gently heat the mince in a frying pan to release some of the fat. Increase the heat, add the onion and cook for 7 minutes, stirring occasionally to break up the mince. Add the chilli and cumin and cook for 1 minute, stirring. Tip in the tomatoes and kidney beans and bring to the boil.
2 Reduce the heat, cover and cook for 30 minutes until the mince is tender, and then season. Warm the tortillas in the microwave on High for 45 seconds or wrap in foil and put in a preheated oven at 190°C/Gas 5/fan oven 170°C for 5 minutes.
3 Top each tortilla with lettuce and spoon over some chilli mince. Sprinkle with cheese and finish with a little soured cream and a squeeze of lemon juice, then fold the edges over to enclose the filling. Eat immediately.

• Per serving 719 kcalories, protein 41g, carbohydrate 69g, fat 33g, saturated fat 18g, fibre 6g, added sugar none, salt 1.84g

Griddled Chicken Salad

A complete meal, with tender chicken and warm new potatoes.

450g/1lb new potatoes, halved
4 boneless skinless chicken breasts
5 tbsp olive oil
juice of 1 lemon
handful of fresh chives, finely snipped
4 tbsp soured cream
1 cos or romaine lettuce, shredded
250g/9oz cherry tomatoes, halved

Takes 50 minutes • Serves 4

1 Cook the potatoes in salted boiling water for 15–20 minutes until tender. Meanwhile, flatten the chicken between two sheets of cling film with a rolling pin, and then season. In a large bowl, mix together the olive oil, lemon juice and chives. Brush a third of the dressing over the chicken.
2 Heat a griddle or large frying pan. Cook the chicken for 6–8 minutes, turning halfway. (You may need to do this in batches.) Whisk the soured cream into the remaining dressing and season.
3 Drain the potatoes and leave to cool slightly, then toss with another third of the dressing. Dress the lettuce and tomatoes with half the remaining dressing. Divide between plates with the potatoes. Top with the chicken and drizzle over the remaining dressing.

• Per serving 412 kcalories, protein 37g, carbohydrate 22g, fat 20g, saturated fat 5g, fibre 2g, added sugar none, salt 0.29g

Egg and Bacon Tart

Great for lunch boxes or picnics. Vegetarians can replace the bacon with mushrooms.

shortcrust pastry made with175g/6oz plain
   flour and 85g/3oz butter bound with
   2 tbsp water
5 eggs
4 rashers streaky bacon, chopped
1 large leek, chopped
25g/1oz butter
25g/1oz plain flour
300ml/½ pint milk
2 tsp ready-made mustard
50g/2oz cheddar, grated

Takes 1¼ hours • Serves 4 (with leftovers)

1 Preheat the oven to 200°C/Gas 6/fan oven 180°C from cold. On a floured work surface, roll out the pastry to a 28cm/11in circle. Use to line a 23cm/9in flan tin and trim off the excess. Chill the case for 15 minutes, then bake blind for 15 minutes.
2 Meanwhile, hard-boil two eggs for 8 minutes. Cool, then peel and chop. Dry fry the bacon and leek for 3 minutes until the bacon is crisp. Put the butter, flour and milk in a small pan. Bring slowly to the boil, whisking until thickened. Simmer for 2 minutes. Stir in the mustard.
3 Scatter the leek, bacon and chopped egg over the pastry. Beat the remaining eggs into the sauce and season. Pour into the case, add the cheese and bake for 40 minutes until puffed and golden.

• Per serving 635 kcalories, protein 22g, carbohydrate 44g, fat 42g, saturated fat 23g, fibre 3g, added sugar none, salt 1.9g

TOP LEFT: Chilli Bean Tortillas   TOP RIGHT: Griddled Chicken Salad   BOTTOM: Egg and Bacon Tart

TOP: Chicken and Tarragon Dauphinoise   BOTTOM LEFT: Piri Piri Chicken   BOTTOM RIGHT: Chicken with Cannellini Beans

Chicken and Tarragon Dauphinoise

You can't beat fresh tarragon but frozen, available in supermarkets, will do.

900g/2lb floury potatoes, such as Maris Piper
    or King Edward
1 tbsp oil
25g/1oz butter
1 small onion, finely chopped
450g/1lb boneless skinless chicken breasts,
    cut into 1cm/½in strips
1 tbsp chopped fresh tarragon
200ml carton crème fraîche
175g/6oz gruyère, grated
green salad, to serve

Takes 55 minutes • Serves 4 (easily doubled)

1 Preheat the oven to 200°C/Gas 6/fan oven 180°C from cold. Butter a shallow ovenproof dish. Slice the potatoes thinly and cook in salted boiling water for 10 minutes until just tender. Drain well.
2 Meanwhile, heat the oil and butter. Fry the onion for 5 minutes until softened. Add the chicken and fry over a high heat until nicely browned. Lower the heat, stir in the tarragon and half the crème fraîche, then season well.
3 Spread half the potatoes in the dish. Spoon over the chicken mixture and cover with the remaining potatoes. Dot spoonfuls of the remaining crème fraîche on top and sprinkle with gruyère. Bake for 20–25 minutes until crisp and golden. Serve with a green salad.

• Per serving 700 kcalories, protein 46g, carbohydrate 42g, fat 40g, saturated fat 21g, fibre 3g, added sugar none, salt 1.2g

Piri Piri Chicken

Make extra marinade and keep chilled, ready to add a kick to your cooking.

2 red chillies
1 red pepper
3 tbsp red wine vinegar
4 tbsp olive oil
4 boneless chicken breasts (skin on)
salad leaves, to serve

Takes 30 minutes, plus marinating • Serves 4 (easily doubled)

1 Halve and seed the chillies and red pepper. Chop the chillies finely and the pepper roughly. Tip into a food processor and add the vinegar and oil, and season. Whizz, but leave chunky.
2 Slash the chicken breasts across the skin side and put in a shallow ovenproof dish. Pour over three-quarters of the marinade, turning the chicken to coat it. Marinate for at least 10 minutes, or overnight in the fridge if you have time. Reserve the remaining marinade.
3 Heat a griddle or heavy frying pan, add the chicken and cook for 5–6 minutes each side, turning once. Serve on a bed of salad leaves with the reserved marinade drizzled over.

• Per serving 393 kcalories, protein 27g, carbohydrate 3g, fat 30g, saturated fat 7g, fibre 1g, added sugar none, salt 0.26g

Chicken with Cannellini Beans

Substitute the chicken stock with the same amount of dry white wine or cider if you like.

2 tbsp olive oil
4 boneless chicken breasts, skin left on
½ tsp paprika
1 small onion, finely chopped
100g/4oz bacon, finely chopped
230g can chopped tomatoes
400g can cannellini beans, drained
150ml/¼ pint chicken stock
squeeze of lemon juice
2 tbsp chopped fresh parsley

Takes 35 minutes • Serves 4

1 Heat the oil in a large frying pan. Season the chicken and sprinkle with paprika. Fry, skin-side down, for 8–10 minutes until the skin is golden and crispy. Turn and cook for a further 5–6 minutes until the chicken is cooked. Remove the chicken and keep warm.
2 Add the onion and bacon to the pan and cook for 5 minutes, stirring until the onion is cooked and the bacon is crispy.
3 Tip in the tomatoes, beans and stock. Stir well, then return the chicken to the pan. Bring to the boil, then reduce the heat and simmer for 2–3 minutes. Season, then stir in a squeeze of lemon juice. Sprinkle over the parsley. Serve straight from the pan.

• Per serving 455 kcalories, protein 38g, carbohydrate 15g, fat 27g, saturated fat 7g, fibre 5g, added sugar 2g, salt 1.52g

New Potato and Mince Curry

There's a tendency to undercook new potatoes – be sure they're tender before draining.

450g/1lb lean minced beef or lamb
1 tbsp vegetable oil
1 small onion, chopped
3 garlic cloves, finely chopped
1 tbsp coarsely grated fresh root ginger
1 fresh red chilli, seeded, finely sliced
2 tsp ground cumin
2 tsp ground coriander
1 tbsp korma curry paste
500g/1lb 2oz new potatoes in skins, halved
100g/4oz fresh spinach leaves, thick stems removed, leaves torn if large
150ml carton Greek yogurt
chapatis or naan bread, to serve

Takes 1 hour • Serves 4

1 Heat a frying pan and add the mince. Brown it all over, stirring to break it up. Remove from the pan and set aside. Add the oil and onion to the pan and cook on a medium heat for 5 minutes.
2 Stir in the garlic, spices and curry paste. Stir fry for 1 minute. Add the mince, potatoes and 600ml/1 pint water. Bring to the boil, cover, then simmer for 30 minutes. Season with salt to taste.
3 Stir in the spinach and simmer for 1 minute, uncovered, until wilted. Swirl in the yogurt and serve with Indian bread.

• Per serving 353 kcalories, protein 32g, carbohydrate 26g, fat 14g, saturated fat 5g, fibre 2g, added sugar none, salt 0.54g

Pork, Apricot and Ginger Skewers

Soak wooden skewers in water for 30 minutes before using to stop them burning.

1 tsp oil
1 small onion, chopped
1 garlic clove, finely chopped
500g pack pork or lamb mince
5cm/2in piece fresh ginger, grated
10 ready-to-eat dried apricots, finely chopped
handful of chopped fresh parsley
300g/10oz long grain rice
½ tsp turmeric
juice of ½ lemon
142ml carton natural yogurt
rice, to serve

Takes 55 minutes • Serves 4

1 Preheat the oven to 200°C/Gas 6/fan oven 180°C, or the grill to high. Heat the oil in a pan, then fry the onion and garlic for 5 minutes. Cool slightly, then tip into a bowl with the mince, ginger, apricots and half the parsley. Season.
2 Divide the mixture into four and mould around the skewers. If cooking in the oven transfer to a roasting tin and cook for 20 minutes, otherwise put the tin under the hot grill, turning occasionally, for 10 minutes until browned.
3 Boil the rice with 600ml/1 pint water and the turmeric, covered, for about 12–15 minutes until tender and the water has been absorbed. Stir the rest of the parsley and the lemon into the yogurt and drizzle over the skewers. Serve with rice.

• Per serving 536 kcalories, protein 32g, carbohydrate 75g, fat 14g, saturated fat 5g, fibre 1g, added sugar none, salt 0.31g

Lemon and Thyme Meatballs

Pimientos are peppers that have been roasted, peeled and seeded, then packed into cans.

2 slices white bread, crusts removed and torn in pieces
2 tbsp milk
500g pack pork mince
finely grated zest of 1 lemon
2 tsp dried thyme
1 garlic clove, finely chopped
1 tbsp olive oil
1 small onion, finely chopped
250g/9oz chestnut mushrooms, sliced
285g can pimientos, drained and chopped
200ml carton crème fraîche
350g/12oz rigatoni, cooked and drained, to serve

Takes 1 hour 10 minutes • Serves 4

1 Soak the bread in the milk for 5 minutes. Squeeze out the excess milk, then put the bread in a bowl with the mince, lemon zest, thyme and garlic. Season. Mix well and shape into 20 balls.
2 Heat the oil in a frying pan. Cover and cook the meatballs for 20 minutes, turning, until they are evenly browned. Remove and keep warm.
3 Add the onion to the pan and cook for 5 minutes until softened but not brown. Add the mushrooms and cook for 8 minutes until beginning to brown. Stir in the pimientos and crème fraîche, heat through and season. Stir the pasta into the sauce, spoon on to plates and top with the meatballs.

• Per serving 753 kcalories, protein 38g, carbohydrate 73g, fat 36g, saturated fat 14g, fibre 4g, added sugar none, salt 0.67g

TOP: New Potato and Mince Curry   BOTTOM LEFT: Pork, Apricot and Ginger Skewers   BOTTOM RIGHT: Lemon and Thyme Meatballs

TOP LEFT: Leeks with Ham and Corn   TOP RIGHT: Ham and Pepper Tart   BOTTOM: Pork and Herb Meatloaf

Leeks with Ham and Corn

A colourful gratin that children will love. Serve with new or jacket potatoes.

4 leeks, trimmed and halved widthways, then washed
225g/8oz wafer-thin ham
198g can sweetcorn with peppers, drained
1 large tomato, seeded and chopped
25g/1oz butter
25g/1oz plain flour
300ml/½ pint milk
2 tsp wholegrain mustard
50g/2oz cheddar, grated

Takes 50 minutes • Serves 4

1 Preheat the oven to 200°C/Gas 6/fan oven 180°C. Blanch the leeks for 2 minutes. Drain and refresh in cold water, then drain once more really well.
2 Wrap each piece of leek in ham. Arrange them in a buttered 2.25 litre/4 pint rectangular ovenproof dish. Scatter over the sweetcorn and tomato.
3 Put the butter, flour and milk in a pan and bring to the boil, whisking continuously until thickened. Stir in the mustard, simmer for 2–3 minutes, then pour over the leeks. Sprinkle with cheese and bake for 30 minutes until golden. Serve immediately.

• Per serving 303 kcalories, protein 20g, carbohydrate 24g, fat 15g, saturated fat 8g, fibre 4g, added sugar 3g, salt 2.17g

Ham and Pepper Tart

Leftovers – if you have any – make great packed lunches.

250g/9oz bought shortcrust pastry
1 onion, finely chopped
1 garlic clove, crushed
1 red pepper, seeded and chopped
1 tbsp olive oil
230g can chopped tomatoes, drained
100g/4oz wafer-thin ham
handful of black olives (optional)
3 eggs
3 tbsp milk
salad, to serve

Takes 1 hour 10 minutes • Serves 4

1 Preheat the oven to 200°C/Gas 6/fan oven 180°C. Use the pastry to line a 23cm/9in loose-bottomed flan tin. Bake blind for 15 minutes. Remove the paper and beans and cook for 5 minutes.
2 Fry the onion, garlic and red pepper in the oil for 4 minutes until softened. Cool slightly. Lower the oven temperature to 190°C/Gas 5/ fan oven 170°C. Tip the onion mixture and tomatoes into the pastry case. Crumple the ham between the vegetables. If using olives, scatter on top.
3 Beat the eggs and milk together, and season. Pour into the case. Bake for 25–30 minutes until set. Serve hot or cold with a salad.

• Per serving 437 kcalories, protein 16g, carbohydrate 35g, fat 27g, saturated fat 10g, fibre 3g, added sugar none, salt 1.22g

Pork and Herb Meatloaf

Prepare the meatloaf, minus the topping, the night before. Press into the tin, cover and chill.

1 tbsp oil
1 onion, finely chopped
2 smoked streaky bacon rashers, rinded and chopped
500g pack pork mince
100g/4oz fresh breadcrumbs
1 medium egg, beaten
1 tsp salt
2 tbsp tomato purée
1 tbsp dried tarragon or thyme
salad and new potatoes, to serve

FOR THE TOPPING
2 smoked streaky bacon rashers
25g/1oz breadcrumbs
50g/2oz cheddar, grated

Takes 1 hour 25 minutes • Serves 4

1 Preheat the oven to 180°C/Gas 4/fan oven 160°C. Heat the oil in a frying pan and fry the onion for 3–4 minutes until softened. Transfer to a bowl. Mix in the bacon, pork, breadcrumbs, egg, salt, tomato purée and dried herbs. Press into a 450g/1lb loaf tin. Bake, uncovered, for 1 hour.
2 To make the topping, dry fry the bacon until crisp. Remove from the pan. Fry the breadcrumbs in the bacon fat for 2 minutes until just golden. Stir into a bowl with the cheese and crumble in the bacon.
3 Five minutes before the end of cooking, sprinkle the topping over the meatloaf. Return to the oven for 5 minutes to melt the cheese. Leave to stand for 10 minutes. Loosen the sides with a knife and remove. Slice and serve with a salad and new potatoes.

• Per serving 488 kcalories, protein 37g, carbohydrate 29g, fat 26g, saturated fat 10g, fibre 1g, added sugar none, salt 3.01g

Sausage and Bean Bake

A hearty dish that will appeal to the whole family. You could use other beans instead.

2 tbsp olive oil
12 quality plump herby sausages
1 large onion, cut into wedges
6 rindless streaky bacon rashers, chopped
4 celery sticks, sliced
2 garlic cloves, crushed
600ml/1 pint vegetable or chicken stock
3 tbsp tomato purée
400g can cannellini beans, drained
2 tbsp wholegrain mustard
garlic bread, to serve

Takes 40 minutes • Serves 6

1 Preheat the oven to 200°C/Gas 6/fan oven 180°C. Heat half the oil in a frying pan, then brown the sausages all over. Transfer to a roasting tin.
2 Add the remaining oil, the onion, bacon, celery and garlic to the frying pan, and fry until golden. Add the stock and tomato purée. Add the beans, scraping up any bits from the bottom of the pan. Let the stock bubble up, then pour into the roasting tin.
3 Bake, uncovered, for 15–20 minutes. Remove the tin from the oven and stir in the wholegrain mustard, then season. Serve with hot garlic bread.

• Per serving 429 kcalories, protein 23g, carbohydrate 18.2g, fat 30g, saturated fat 9.9g, fibre 3.5g, added sugar none, salt 3.41g

Pork Chops with Gorgonzola

A simple topping makes ordinary pork chops fit for a feast.

4 large boneless pork loin chops,
    140–225g/5–8oz each
1 tbsp olive oil
1 tbsp green pesto
3 small tomatoes, thinly sliced
100g/4oz gorgonzola, cut into 4 thick slices
new potatoes and salad, to serve

Takes 20 minutes • Serves 4

1 Preheat the grill to high. Brush the chops with the olive oil and season well. Lay the chops on a baking sheet and grill for 4–5 minutes. Turn over and cook for a further 4–5 minutes.
2 Remove the chops from the grill. Brush each one with the pesto. Put the tomato slices on top of the chops and add the slices of cheese.
3 Put the chops back under the grill for 2–4 minutes, until the cheese is bubbling and has melted. Serve immediately with new potatoes and a salad.

• Per serving 351 kcalories, protein 36g, carbohydrate 1g, fat 22g, saturated fat 9g, fibre none, added sugar none, salt 1.11g

Mediterranean Shepherd's Pie

Use turkey mince for a change and add pesto for a taste of the Mediterranean.

2 onions
2 carrots
1 celery stick
500g pack mince, such as turkey
100g/4oz smoked bacon, chopped
2 tsp plain flour
284ml carton vegetable or other stock
150ml/¼ pint red wine
700g/1lb 9oz potatoes, peeled
knob of butter
4 tbsp red pesto
25g/1oz parmesan, grated

Takes 1¼ hours • Serves 4

1 Preheat the oven to 200°C/Gas 6/fan oven 180°C from cold. Chop the onions, carrots and celery in a food processor. In a pan over a low heat, cook the mince until the juices start to run, stirring. Add the vegetables and bacon and cook for 15 minutes until browned. Sprinkle over the flour and cook for 1 minute, still stirring. Stir in the stock and wine and cook, covered, for 30 minutes, stirring occasionally.
2 Meanwhile, cut the potatoes into chunks and boil for 10 minutes. Drain well, and return to the pan. Stir in the butter. Season.
3 Stir the pesto into the meat, season and spoon into a shallow ovenproof dish. Spoon the potato pieces on top, sprinkle over the cheese and bake for 30 minutes until golden. Serve immediately.

• Per serving 518 kcalories, protein 42g, carbohydrate 40g, fat 19g, saturated fat 6g, fibre 4g, added sugar none, salt 2.25g

TOP LEFT: Sausage and Bean Bake   TOP RIGHT: Pork Chops with Gorgonzola   BOTTOM: Mediterranean Shepherd's Pie

TOP: Tuna Rösti   BOTTOM LEFT: Orange Crumb Salmon   BOTTOM RIGHT: Tuna and Broccoli Pasta Bake

Tuna Rösti

Rösti are small cakes of grated potato. Here, tuna is added to make a meal of one frying-pan-sized rösti.

750g/1lb 10oz potatoes, unpeeled
3 tbsp sunflower oil
1 large onion, sliced
200g can tuna, drained
4 eggs
2 × 400g cans baked beans

Takes 45 minutes • Serves 4

1 Cook the potatoes, in their skins, in salted boiling water for 10 minutes. Meanwhile, heat a tablespoon of the oil in a frying pan and fry the onion until golden. Drain the potatoes and, when cool enough to handle, peel. Grate them coarsely into a bowl. Add the onion, tuna and seasoning and mix well.
2 Heat the remaining oil in the frying pan. Press the potato mixture into it with a spatula to make a large cake. Cook very gently for 10 minutes until the underside is golden. Put a large plate on top of the pan and turn the rösti out onto it. Slide it back into the pan and cook the other side for 8–10 minutes.
3 Meanwhile, fry the eggs and heat up the beans in a pan. Slide the rösti out of the pan onto a serving plate. Cut into wedges and serve with the fried eggs and baked beans.

• Per serving 511 kcalories, protein 30g, carbohydrate 67g, fat 16g, saturated fat 3g, fibre 10g, added sugar 7g, salt 3.34g

Orange Crumb Salmon

Salmon fillets are always on special offer somewhere, but still seem luxurious.

85g/3oz fresh breadcrumbs (2 thick slices white bread)
2 tbsp olive oil, plus extra for greasing
finely grated zest and juice of 1 orange
4 tbsp chopped fresh parsley
4 boneless skinless salmon fillets, about 140g/5oz each in weight
700g/1lb 9oz new potatoes
3 tbsp mayonnaise

Takes 35 minutes • Serves 4

1 Preheat the oven to 200°C/Gas 6/fan oven 180°C. Mix together the breadcrumbs, oil, orange zest and half the parsley. Season.
2 Put the salmon fillets on a baking sheet lined with lightly greased foil. Press the orange crumbs on to each fillet so they stick. Bake for 15–20 minutes until the salmon is just cooked and the topping is golden.
3 Meanwhile, cook the potatoes in a pan of salted boiling water for 12–15 minutes until tender, then drain. Stir the remaining parsley into the mayonnaise and thin with a little bit of the orange juice, until it has the consistency of single cream. Serve the salmon with the new potatoes and the herb mayonnaise.

• Per serving 611 kcalories, protein 34g, carbohydrate 46g, fat 33g, saturated fat 6g, fibre 3g, added sugar none, salt 0.8g

Tuna and Broccoli Pasta Bake

Instead of using soup, you could use mushroom or tomato pasta sauce from the chiller cabinet.

300g/10oz penne or rigatoni
400g/14oz broccoli, cut into small florets
200g can tuna, drained
295g can condensed mushroom soup
150ml/¼ pint milk
100g/4oz cheddar, grated
1 small packet salted crisps

Takes 30 minutes • Serves 4

1 Preheat the oven to 200°C/Gas 6/fan oven 180°C. Cook the pasta in salted boiling water for 10–12 minutes. Add the broccoli for the last 3 minutes of cooking, then drain.
2 Tip the pasta and broccoli into a shallow ovenproof dish. Scatter the tuna over. Mix the soup with the milk, then pour over the pasta and toss it all together gently.
3 Scatter over two-thirds of the cheese. Lightly crush the crisps in the bag, then sprinkle over the pasta. Top with the remaining cheese. Bake for 15 minutes until the topping is golden. Serve immediately.

• Per serving 572 kcalories, protein 33g, carbohydrate 69g, fat 20g, saturated fat 8g, fibre 5g, added sugar none, salt 2.41g

Prawn and Tomato Pasta Bake

An easy supper for a crowd, this dish is cooked and served in one tin.

450g/1lb leeks, thinly sliced
900g/2lb ripe tomatoes, quartered
3 tbsp olive oil
600g/1lb 5oz pasta shapes, such as
    penne or rigatoni
225g/8oz peeled prawns, thawed if frozen
2 tbsp sun-dried tomato paste
150ml/¼ pint vegetable stock
3 tbsp roughly chopped fresh parsley
142ml carton double cream
150g ball mozzarella, grated or finely
    chopped
4 tbsp freshly grated parmesan
1 thick slice of bread, made into crumbs

Takes 1¼ hours • Serves 8

1 Preheat the oven to 200°C/Gas 6/fan oven 180°C from cold. Put the leeks and tomatoes in a large roasting tin and drizzle over the olive oil. Season and mix well. Roast for 30 minutes.
2 Meanwhile, cook the pasta for about 10–12 minutes until tender and then drain. Tip into the roasting tin along with the prawns. Season. Mix the tomato paste into the stock and stir into the pasta. Sprinkle over the parsley, then drizzle with cream. Sprinkle over the mozzarella, parmesan and the breadcrumbs.
3 Return to the oven for 15–20 minutes until the topping is crisp and golden. Serve straight from the tin.

• Per serving 506 kcalories, protein 21g, carbohydrate 65g, fat 20g, saturated fat 9g, fibre 5g, added sugar none, salt 0.65g

Salmon and Sweetcorn Casserole

Think you don't have time to make a casserole? You do in a microwave.

2 leeks, about 300g/10oz in total
700g/1lb 9oz floury potatoes, such as
    King Edward
300ml/½ pint full-fat milk
300ml/½ pint vegetable stock
200g can sweetcorn with peppers, drained
450g/1lb skinless salmon fillet cut into
    2.5cm/1in cubes
good splash of Tabasco
handful of chopped fresh parsley

Takes 25 minutes • Serves 4

1 Halve the leeks lengthways, then slice. Set aside. Peel the potatoes, cut into cubes and put in a microwave-proof bowl with the milk and stock.
2 Cook the potatoes on High for 8 minutes until they're starting to soften. Add the leeks and cook for 5 minutes. Stir well with a fork, pressing about half the potato cubes against the side of the bowl to break up and thicken the stock.
3 Stir in the sweetcorn and salmon, and season. Cook on High for 3 minutes until the salmon is just cooked through. Stir in the Tabasco and parsley. Serve immediately.

• Per serving 453 kcalories, protein 32g, carbohydrate 47g, fat 17g, saturated fat 4g, fibre 5g, added sugar 3g, salt 0.85g

Potato and Salmon Grill

A simple and filling supper made from a can of salmon.

650g/1lb 7oz new potatoes, skin on,
    sliced lengthways
100g/4oz frozen peas
200g can salmon
200ml carton crème fraîche
100g/4oz mature cheddar, coarsely grated

Takes 25 minutes • Serves 4

1 Boil the potatoes in salted water for about 10 minutes, until almost tender but not breaking up. Tip in the frozen peas and simmer for another 2–3 minutes. Drain well then tip into a mixing bowl. Preheat the grill to high.
2 Drain the salmon and flake into chunks, then gently toss with the potatoes and peas. Season to taste and spoon into a shallow flameproof dish.
3 Dollop the crème fraîche on top, roughly spread it over, and then scatter over the cheese. Grill for a few minutes until bubbling and golden.

• Per serving 465 kcalories, protein 22g, carbohydrate 31g, fat 29g, saturated fat 15g, fibre 3g, added sugar none, salt 1.10g

TOP: Prawn and Tomato Pasta Bake   BOTTOM LEFT: Salmon and Sweetcorn Casserole   BOTTOM RIGHT: Potato and Salmon Grill

TOP LEFT: Crisp Cod and Corn Cakes   TOP RIGHT: Easy Tuna Puff Pie   BOTTOM: Warm Potato and Tuna Salad

Crisp Cod and Corn Cakes

Crushed crackers make an especially crispy coating for fishcakes.

4 tbsp milk
500g/1lb 2oz cod fillet
198g can sweetcorn, drained
6 spring onions, finely chopped
750g/1lb 10oz floury potatoes, cooked and
   mashed with butter
2 eggs
12 cream crackers, crushed into fine crumbs
oil, for shallow frying
salad leaves and tomato sauce, to serve

Takes 35 minutes • Serves 4

1 Put the milk and fish in a frying pan. Bring to the boil, cover and cook for 4–5 minutes, depending on the thickness of the fish. It should flake easily. Set aside until cool enough to handle.
2 Stir the corn and onions into the mash and season. Remove the fish with a slotted spoon and stir into the mash, taking care not to break it up too much. Divide into eight and shape into round cakes.
3 Beat the eggs lightly with a fork. Dip the cakes in the egg, then in the cracker crumbs. Heat a little oil in a frying pan and cook the cakes, four at a time, for about 3 minutes. Carefully turn and cook for 2–3 minutes until crisp and golden. Serve with a salad and some tomato sauce.

• Per serving 628 kcalories, protein 33g, carbohydrate 57g, fat 31g, saturated fat 8g, fibre 3g, added sugar 3g, salt 1.3g

Easy Tuna Puff Pie

Puff pastry rectangles, cooked separately, become the pie 'lids'.

375g packet rolled ready-to-use puff pastry
25g/1oz butter
1 onion, chopped
1 small red pepper, seeded and chopped
25g/1oz plain flour
600ml/1 pint milk
700g/1lb 9oz potato, peeled and cut
   into big chunks
225g/8oz broccoli, cut into florets
185g can tuna chunks in brine, drained
handful of chopped fresh parsley

Takes 45 minutes • Serves 4

1 Preheat the oven to 200°C/Gas 6/fan oven 180°C. Cut out four 13 x 10cm/5 x 4in pastry rectangles. Place on a baking sheet, lightly slash the tops diagonally and bake for 15–18 minutes, until they are golden and puffed.
2 Meanwhile, melt the butter in a pan, then fry the onion and pepper until soft but not brown. Add the flour and cook, stirring, for 1 minute. Stir in the milk gradually. Cook, stirring, until thickened slightly.
3 Add the potatoes and simmer, covered, for 10 minutes. Add the broccoli and simmer for 10 minutes until tender. Stir the tuna into the sauce and heat through. Season, add the parsley and spoon on to serving plates. Top each serving with a pastry lid.

• Per serving 721 kcalories, protein 26g, carbohydrate 82g, fat 34g, saturated fat 7g, fibre 5g, added sugar none, salt 1.42g

Warm Potato and Tuna Salad

A tub of pesto makes an instant, tasty dressing. The spinach softens in the heat of the potatoes.

650g/1lb 7oz new potatoes, halved
   lengthways if large
2 tbsp pesto (fresh is best)
4 tbsp olive oil
8 cherry tomatoes
175g can tuna, drained
225g/8oz green beans, halved
couple of handfuls of spinach (preferably
   baby leaves), tear if larger
crusty bread, to serve

Takes 20 minutes • Serves 4

1 Put the potatoes in a pan of salted boiling water, bring back to the boil and simmer for 8–10 minutes.
2 Meanwhile, mix together the pesto and oil. Halve the tomatoes, and drain and flake the tuna. Add the beans to the potatoes for the last 3 minutes of cooking time.
3 Drain the potatoes and beans and tip into a salad bowl. Stir in the spinach so it wilts a little in the warmth from the vegetables. Season. Scatter over the tomatoes and tuna, drizzle over the pesto and toss together. Serve with crusty bread.

• Per serving 336 kcalories, protein 15g, carbohydrate 28g, fat 19g, saturated fat 3g, fibre 3g, added sugar none, salt 0.45g

Chicken with a Red Pepper Crust

Skinless chicken breasts get a colourful coating and a flavour boost.

4 boneless skinless chicken breasts
1 small red pepper, seeded
2 garlic cloves
large handful of fresh parsley
2 tbsp olive oil
pasta or new potatoes, and green salad, to serve

Takes 30 minutes • Serves 4

1 Preheat the oven to 200°C/Gas 6/fan oven 180°C. Put the chicken breasts in a roasting tin or shallow ovenproof dish. Season.
2 Roughly chop the red pepper and finely chop the garlic. Put in a food processor with the parsley and pulse a few times until coarsely chopped. Stir in the oil and season generously. Spread the crust over the chicken.
3 Spoon two tablespoons of water into the base of the dish and roast the chicken, uncovered, for 25 minutes. Serve with pasta or new potatoes and a green salad.

• Per serving 210 kcalories, protein 23g, carbohydrate 5g, fat 11g, saturated fat 2g, fibre 1g, added sugar none, salt 0.19g

Lemon and Honey Chicken

Cooked this way, the chicken develops a delicious sweet-sour, sticky coating.

3 lemons
50g/2oz butter
3 tbsp clear honey
1 garlic clove, finely chopped
4 rosemary sprigs, leaves stripped from the stalks
8 chicken pieces, such as thighs and drumsticks
750g/1lb 10oz potatoes, cut into smallish chunks
green salad, to serve

Takes 1 hour 20 minutes • Serves 4

1 Preheat the oven to 200°C/Gas 6/fan oven 180°C from cold. Squeeze the juice from two lemons and put in a small pan with the butter, honey, garlic and rosemary, and season. Heat gently until the butter melts.
2 Arrange the chicken in one layer in a shallow roasting tin. Put the potatoes around the chicken. Drizzle the lemon butter over the chicken and potatoes, turning the potatoes until evenly coated. Cut the remaining lemon into eight wedges and nestle them among the potatoes.
3 Roast the chicken for 50 minutes to 1 hour, stirring a couple of times, until the chicken is cooked and the potatoes are crisp and golden. Serve with a green salad.

• Per serving 647 kcalories, protein 39g, carbohydrate 47g, fat 35g, saturated fat 14g, fibre 3g, added sugar 12g, salt 0.06g

Moroccan Chicken

Couscous is the perfect partner for this dish and will only need soaking then fluffing up with a fork.

4 boneless skinless chicken thighs, 500g/1lb 2oz in total
300ml/½ pint chicken or vegetable stock
2 onions, finely chopped
3 tbsp olive oil
1 tbsp clear honey
1 tsp each ground cumin and coriander
good pinch each of chilli powder and ground cinnamon
225g/8oz courgettes, cut into sticks
400g can chickpeas, drained
3 tbsp chopped fresh parsley
juice of 1 lemon
couscous or cooked rice, to serve

Takes 50 minutes • Serves 4

1 Put the chicken, stock, onions, oil, honey, herbs and spices in a pan, and season. Bring to the boil, cover and cook gently for 25 minutes until the chicken is tender.
2 Add the courgettes and chickpeas and cook for 10 minutes.
3 Stir in the parsley and the lemon juice. Season to taste. Serve with couscous or rice.

• Per serving 539 kcalories, protein 39g, carbohydrate 52g, fat 21g, saturated fat 4g, fibre 6g, added sugar 3g, salt 1.12g

TOP LEFT: Chicken with a Red Pepper Crust   TOP RIGHT: Lemon and Honey Chicken   BOTTOM: Moroccan Chicken

TOP: Mustardy Sausages with Apple   BOTTOM LEFT: Chunky Ham Pie   BOTTOM RIGHT: Lamb Chop and Chip Bake

Mustardy Sausages with Apple

A straightforward recipe using affordable ingredients.

1 tbsp vegetable oil
8 plump herby sausages, about 450g/1lb
1 medium onion, cut into wedges
2 Cox's or other eating apples (skin left on), cored and each cut into 8 wedges
1 rounded tbsp redcurrant jelly
300ml/½ pint chicken stock (made from a cube is fine)
2 tbsp mustard, preferably grainy
a few rosemary twigs

Takes 25 minutes • Serves 4

1 Heat the oil in a large frying pan, add the sausages and fry for 5 minutes, turning often. Nestle in the onion wedges and continue to fry, until everything is starting to go really golden, stirring every now and then. Turn up the heat, toss in the apples and let them take on a bit of colour too, stirring carefully so that they don't break up.
2 Stir the redcurrant jelly into the stock until it dissolves, then stir in the mustard. Pour this into the frying pan so everything bubbles madly for a few minutes to make a syrupy gravy.
3 Lower the heat, throw in the rosemary and simmer, uncovered, for 10 minutes until the sausages are cooked.

• Per serving 368 kcalories, protein 16.7g, carbohydrate 21g, fat 24.7g, saturated fat 8.1g, fibre 2g, added sugar 3.2g, salt 2.68g

Chunky Ham Pie

Ham and vegetables cooked in a mustardy sauce and topped with shortcrust pastry – great for a crowd.

1 tbsp olive oil
1 onion, chopped
1 garlic clove, crushed
450g/1lb parsnips, roughly chopped
3 carrots, roughly chopped
2 celery sticks, thickly sliced
2 tbsp plain flour
450g/1lb cooked ham, cut into chunks
142ml carton double cream
425ml/¾ pint vegetable stock
2 tbsp wholegrain mustard
375g packet ready-rolled shortcrust pastry
a little milk, for brushing
vegetables, to serve

Takes 1¼ hours • Serves 8

1 Preheat the oven to 190°C/Gas 5/fan oven 170°C. Heat the oil in a large pan and cook the onion and garlic for 3–4 minutes. Stir in the parsnips and carrots and cook for 4–5 minutes, stirring frequently. Add the celery, sprinkle in the flour and cook for 1 minute, mixing thoroughly.
2 Add the ham and pour in the cream and stock. Stir in the mustard. Season. Simmer for 5 minutes until slightly thickened, then spoon into a 2 litre/3½ pint dish. Allow to cool slightly.
3 Use the pastry to cover the pie, cutting off any trimmings. Brush with milk. Cut out leaf shapes from the pastry trimmings and put on top of the pie. Brush with milk again and bake for 30 minutes, until the pastry is golden. Serve with vegetables.

• Per serving 452 kcalories, protein 17g, carbohydrate 37g, fat 27g, saturated fat 12g, fibre 5g, added sugar none, salt 2.09g

Lamb Chop and Chip Bake

Frozen oven chips and chops cooked together in one tin in the oven.

3 tbsp olive oil
2 large onions, peeled and sliced
750g bag frozen hot and spicy potato wedges
8 small lamb chops
1 tsp dried thyme
150ml/¼ pint lamb or chicken stock
1 tbsp tomato purée

Takes 40 minutes • Serves 4

1 Preheat the oven to 230°C/Gas 8/fan oven 210°C. Heat a large roasting tin on the hob, then add two tablespoons of the olive oil.
2 Put the onions in the tin and fry for about 5 minutes, stirring often, until golden. Remove from the heat. Scatter over the potato wedges. Put the chops on top, sprinkle over the thyme and drizzle over the remaining oil.
3 Bake for 20 minutes. Mix the stock with the tomato purée and pour around the chops in the tin. Bake for 10 minutes until everything is brown and crisp. Season and then serve.

• Per serving 680 kcalories, protein 33g, carbohydrate 39g, fat 45g, saturated fat 19g, fibre 4g, added sugar none, salt 0.43g

Sausage and Corn Hash

A really quick and easy meal – the perfect (lazy!) TV supper.

1 tbsp olive oil
400g/14oz sausages (use your favourite)
700g/1lb 9oz new potatoes, cut into chunks
165g can sweetcorn, drained
2 tbsp chopped fresh coriander or parsley
226g jar spicy tomato salsa, to serve

Takes 30 minutes • Serves 4

1 Heat the oil in a large frying pan. Cut the sausages into bite-sized chunks and fry in the oil until just cooked, about 10 minutes. Meanwhile, bring a large pan of salted water to the boil, add the potatoes and cook for 8–10 minutes. Drain well.
2 Tip the potatoes into the frying pan, season and fry over a medium heat until they take on a bit of colour. Stir in the sweetcorn and heat through. Season.
3 Sprinkle with coriander or parsley. Divide between serving dishes and drizzle some salsa over the hash.

• Per serving 519 kcalories, protein 17g, carbohydrate 56g, fat 27g, saturated fat 9g, fibre 4g, added sugar 4g, salt 4.09g

Lamb and Haricot Hotpot

You can make up the savoury bean mix a day ahead of cooking the chops.

2 onions, chopped
3 tbsp olive oil
2 garlic cloves, chopped
2 × 400g can haricot beans, drained (or use cannellini or flageolet beans instead)
1 tsp dried oregano
150ml/¼ pint vegetable stock
200g can chopped tomatoes
8 lamb chops or 4 lamb leg steaks

Takes 55 minutes • Serves 4

1 Preheat the oven to 200°C/Gas 6/fan oven 180°C from cold. Fry the onions in two tablespoons of the oil for 5 minutes. Add the garlic, beans and half the oregano and stir briefly. Add the stock and tomatoes, season, then bring to the boil.
2 Tip the bean mixture into an ovenproof dish that will accommodate the chops in a single layer. Lay the chops on top.
3 Sprinkle with the remaining oregano, drizzle with the remaining oil and season. Cook in the oven for 30 minutes until the chops are tender and nicely browned.

• Per serving 518 kcalories, protein 39g, carbohydrate 30g, fat 28g, saturated fat 10g, fibre 9g, added sugar none, salt 1.67g

Bacon and Tomato Cobbler

Although similar to dumplings in taste, cobblers are more like scones in texture.

12 rashers streaky or back bacon
1 large onion, chopped
1 tbsp olive oil
4 sticks celery, thickly sliced
350g jar crushed tomatoes (or 400g can of chopped tomatoes)
150ml/¼ pint chicken stock
400g can butter beans, drained

FOR THE COBBLER TOPPING
85g/3oz butter
225g/8oz self-raising flour
2 tsp dried mixed herbs
175ml/6fl oz milk

Takes 1¼ hours • Serves 4

1 Preheat the oven to 200°C/Gas 6/fan oven 180°C from cold. Cut three bacon rashers into small pieces and set aside. Cut the rest into three pieces. Fry the onion in the oil for 2–3 minutes, add the large bacon pieces for 5–6 minutes and the celery for 3–4 minutes.
2 Add the tomatoes and stock, bring to the boil, cover and simmer for 20 minutes. Add the beans, then season.
3 To make the cobbler topping, rub the butter into the flour. Stir in the herbs, a pinch of salt and the milk. Put the tomato sauce into a 1.7 litre/3 pint ovenproof dish. Spoon over the topping and scatter over the reserved bacon. Bake for 25–30 minutes until golden.

• Per serving 855 kcalories, protein 31g, carbohydrate 63g, fat 58g, saturated fat 26g, fibre 6g, added sugar none, salt 4.74g

TOP: Sausage and Corn Hash   BOTTOM LEFT: Lamb and Haricot Hotpot   BOTTOM RIGHT: Bacon and Tomato Cobbler

TOP LEFT: Pesto Rice Cake   TOP RIGHT: Summer Chilli   BOTTOM: Lamb and Date Casserole

Pesto Rice Cake

A risotto cooked as a cake and served in slices with a good, ready-made tomato sauce.

25g/1oz butter
1 large leek (175g/6oz), finely chopped
350g/12oz risotto rice
1 litre/1¾ pints vegetable stock
100g/4oz green pesto
2 eggs, beaten
150g ball mozzarella, thinly sliced
ready-made tomato sauce, to serve

Takes 1 hour • Serves 4

1 Melt the butter in a frying pan and fry the leek for 5–6 minutes, until soft. Stir in the rice. Pour in a ladleful of stock and simmer until almost all has been absorbed. Continue to add stock and simmer, stirring continuously, for 20 minutes or until the rice is creamy.
2 Stir in the pesto, eggs, and some black pepper. Spoon half the mixture into a 23cm/9in non-stick frying pan. Arrange the mozzarella slices on top and spoon over the remaining rice. Cook over a medium heat for 4 minutes.
3 Put a plate over the frying pan and carefully invert the rice cake, then slide it back into the pan. Press to reshape it and cook for 4 minutes, until golden. Serve with ready-made tomato sauce.

• Per serving 482 kcalories, protein 19g, carbohydrate 57g, fat 22g, saturated fat 9g, fibre 2g, added sugar none, salt 1.46g

Summer Chilli

A lighter version of a popular dish, using pork instead of beef and green beans in place of red kidney beans.

2 tbsp oil
1 onion, chopped
500g pork mince
2 garlic cloves, crushed
2 tsp mild chilli powder
400g can chopped tomatoes
2 tbsp tomato purée
600ml/1 pint chicken stock
1 red pepper, seeded and cut into chunks
350g/12oz new potatoes, cut into chunks
250g/9oz green beans, trimmed
warm crusty bread, to serve

Takes 50 minutes • Serves 4

1 Heat the oil in a large frying pan, then fry the onion and pork mince for 3–4 minutes, stirring occasionally.
2 Add the crushed garlic, chilli powder, tomatoes, tomato purée, chicken stock, red pepper and new potatoes. Bring to the boil, cover and simmer over a low heat for 15 minutes until the potatoes are just tender.
3 Stir in the green beans, re-cover the pan and continue to cook for 5 minutes, until the beans are tender but crisp. Serve with warm crusty bread.

• Per serving 390 kcalories, protein 30g, carbohydrate 26g, fat 19g, saturated fat 5g, fibre 4g, added sugar none, salt 0.94g

Lamb and Date Casserole

Dates and cranberry sauce add sweetness and succulence to the lamb.

550g/1lb 4oz diced lamb
1 tbsp plain flour
2 tbsp olive oil
2 onions, chopped
3 large carrots, cut into chunks
2 garlic cloves, finely chopped
600ml/1 pint chicken, lamb or
    vegetable stock
1 tbsp cranberry sauce
2 tsp tomato purée
12 pitted ready-to-eat dates
3 tbsp chopped fresh parsley
rice or steamed couscous, to serve

Takes 1 hour • Serves 4

1 Put the lamb and flour in a plastic bag and shake well, until coated. Heat the olive oil in a large frying pan. Remove the lamb from the bag and shake off any excess flour, then add to the pan with the onions and carrots. Cook over a medium to high heat for 8–10 minutes, stirring often, until golden.
2 Stir in the garlic and cook for 1 minute. Pour in the stock and bring to the boil. Reduce the heat and simmer, covered, for 20 minutes, until thickened slightly.
3 Stir in the cranberry sauce, tomato purée, dates and parsley. Season to taste. Serve with rice or steamed couscous.

• Per serving 466 kcalories, protein 32g, carbohydrate 48g, fat 18g, saturated fat 6g, fibre 5g, added sugar 1g, salt 0.81g

Chicken and Red Pepper Pie

A substantial meal in one – no accompaniments needed.

2 tbsp vegetable oil
1 small onion, chopped
3 boneless skinless chicken breasts, cut into chunks
1 red pepper, seeded and sliced
175g/6oz broccoli, cut into small florets (including stems), chopped
425g pack ready-rolled puff pastry (with 2 sheets), thawed
150g carton fresh ready-made cheese and chive dip
milk or beaten egg, to glaze

Takes 1 hour • Serves 4

1 Heat the oil in a frying pan and fry the onion for about 3 minutes, until starting to brown. Add the chicken and cook, stirring, for 5 minutes. Tip in the pepper and broccoli and fry for 8–10 minutes, until everything is just cooked. Season. Cool slightly. Preheat the oven to 200°C/Gas 6/fan oven 180°C.
2 Put a rolled pastry sheet on a dampened baking sheet. Spoon over the chicken mixture, leaving a 2.5cm/1in border all the way round. Dot spoonfuls of dip all over. Brush the pastry edges with water, top with the other pastry sheet and fold the edges of the bottom sheet over the top one, pressing to seal. Make light slashes on the surface.
3 Brush the pastry with milk or beaten egg and bake for 25–30 minutes, until the pastry is puffed and golden.

• Per serving 727 kcalories, protein 35g, carbohydrate 46g, fat 46g, saturated fat 1g, fibre 2g, added sugar none, salt 1.33g

Pork and Potato Hotpot

Pork mince is economical when feeding a crowd. Sliced potatoes make it filling.

1 tbsp olive oil
1 onion, chopped
2 garlic cloves, crushed
1kg/2lb 4oz minced pork
1 tbsp plain flour
425ml/¾ pint chicken or vegetable stock
1 tsp dried rosemary or thyme
2 tbsp Worcestershire sauce
4 tbsp tomato purée
1.5kg/3lb 5oz potatoes, peeled
25g/1oz butter
steamed green vegetables, to serve

Takes 2 hours • Serves 8

1 Preheat the oven to 190°C/Gas 5/fan oven 170°C. Heat the oil and fry the onion and garlic for 3–4 minutes. Add the mince and fry for a further 5–6 minutes.
2 Stir in the flour and cook for 1 minute. Add the stock, then stir in the rosemary or thyme, Worcestershire sauce and tomato purée. Bring to the boil, then simmer for 30 minutes. Meanwhile, cook the potatoes in salted boiling water for 10 minutes. Drain and slice thickly.
3 Spoon half the mince mixture into a 20 x 30 x 5–7cm (8 x 12 x 2–3in deep) ovenproof dish and cover with half the potatoes. Repeat the layers, dot the top with the butter and bake for 1 hour. Serve with steamed green vegetables.

• Per serving 407 kcalories, protein 29g, carbohydrate 38g, fat 17g, saturated fat 6g, fibre 3g, added sugar none, salt 0.64g

One-pot Lamb with Rice

A good supper choice for people who can't get boiled rice right.

2 tbsp olive oil
650g/1½ lb boneless lamb (leg or shoulder), cut into 2.5cm/1in cubes
2 onions, roughly chopped
2 tsp ground cumin
2 tsp ground coriander
175g/6oz long grain rice
2 tsp dried oregano
3 tbsp tomato purée
grated zest and juice of 1 lemon
2 tbsp chopped fresh parsley

Takes 55 minutes • Serves 4

1 Heat the oil in a large frying pan with a lid. Add the lamb and cook over a high heat, stirring constantly, for 5 minutes, until browned on all sides. Add the onions and cook for a further 2–3 minutes until softened. Add the cumin and coriander and fry for a further minute.
2 Stir in the rice and oregano. Mix the purée, lemon zest and juice with 850ml/1½ pints boiling water and pour into the pan. Stir well and season.
3 Bring to the boil, then simmer for 20–25 minutes until the lamb and rice are cooked. Stir in the parsley and serve straight from the pan.

• Per serving 563 kcalories, protein 36g, carbohydrate 47g, fat 27g, saturated fat 11g, fibre 1g, added sugar none, salt 0.34g

TOP LEFT: Chicken and Red Pepper Pie   TOP RIGHT: Pork and Potato Hotpot   BOTTOM: One-pot Lamb with Rice

TOP: Lemon Curd Brûlée   BOTTOM LEFT: Coffee Ricotta Creams   BOTTOM RIGHT: Apple Blackberry Ice Cream Sauce

Lemon Curd Brûlée

Just three ingredients, but still a luxurious finale to a meal.

568ml carton double cream
225g/8oz good lemon curd
4–5 tsp icing sugar

Takes 15 minutes, plus chilling • Serves 4

1 In a large bowl, whisk the cream with an electric hand whisk until it just holds its shape, then stir in the lemon curd.
2 Spoon into six 9cm/3½in ramekins and smooth the tops. Chill for at least 1 hour, or overnight if you prefer.
3 Preheat the grill. Sift a thin layer of icing sugar over each ramekin. Grill for about 2–3 minutes until the sugar has caramelised. Alternatively, you can use a blow torch. Serve straight away.

• Per serving 507 kcalories, protein 2g, carbohydrate 12g, fat 50g, saturated fat 32g, fibre none, added sugar 9g, salt 0.09g

Coffee Ricotta Creams

It sounds rich but this dessert is surprisingly light. Make it up to 4 hours ahead of serving.

4 tbsp raisins
3 tbsp rum or brandy
6 tbsp strong black coffee
50g/2oz caster sugar
250g carton ricotta
142ml carton double cream
50g/2oz dark chocolate, grated
icing sugar, for dusting

Takes 25 minutes, plus chilling • Serves 4

1 Mix together the raisins, rum or brandy, coffee and sugar. Stir well, then leave for at least 1 hour.
2 Tip the ricotta into a bowl and beat lightly to soften. Gradually beat in the raisins, rum, coffee and sugar mixture. Whip the cream into soft peaks and fold into the ricotta with half the chocolate.
3 Spoon into four glasses and sprinkle over the remaining chocolate. Chill until you are ready to serve. Dust lightly with icing sugar before serving.

• Per serving 447 kcalories, protein 8g, carbohydrate 39g, fat 28g, saturated fat 17g, fibre 1g, added sugar 22g, salt 0.23g

Apple Blackberry Ice Cream Sauce

Sharp fruits, cooked in butter and sugar, make a tempting sauce for ice cream.

85g/3oz butter
85g/3oz golden caster sugar
4 apples, such as Cox's, peeled, cored and cut into wedges
100g/4oz blackberries
juice of 1 lemon
vanilla ice cream, to serve

Takes 20 minutes • Serves 4

1 Heat the butter and sugar in a frying pan. When the butter has melted and the sugar has dissolved, stir in the apples.
2 Cook for 5–7 minutes, stirring occasionally, until the apples are tender and the sauce is beginning to caramelise and brown. Immediately remove the pan from the heat and add the blackberries.
3 Stir in the lemon juice and serve spooned over scoops of vanilla ice cream.

• Per serving 302 kcalories, protein 1g, carbohydrate 37g, fat 18g, saturated fat 11g, fibre 3g, added sugar 22g, salt 0.42g

Blueberry and Apple Cobbler

You can substitute other fruits or fruit mixtures – fruits of the forest make a nice alternative.

1 Bramley cooking apple, about 175g/6oz
250g/9oz carton blueberries
50g/2oz light muscovado sugar
250g carton mascarpone

FOR THE COBBLER TOPPING
85g/3oz butter, cut into pieces
225g/8oz self-raising flour
50g/2oz light muscovado sugar
grated zest of 1 lemon
150g carton of natural yogurt

Takes 40 minutes • Serves 6

1 Preheat the oven to 220°C/Gas 7/fan oven 200°C. Peel, core and thinly slice the apple and put into a 1.5 litre/2¾ pint ovenproof dish. Scatter over the blueberries, sprinkle with the sugar and gently stir. Spoon over the mascarpone.
2 To make the topping, rub the butter into the flour or whizz in a food processor until it looks like fine breadcrumbs. Stir in the sugar and lemon zest. Make a well in the centre and tip in the yogurt. Stir until evenly combined, but do not overmix.
3 Spoon the cobbler mixture onto the fruit and mascarpone. Bake for 20 minutes until the topping is risen and golden and the filling is bubbling.

• Per serving 323 kcalories, protein 5g, carbohydrate 49g, fat 13g, saturated fat 8g, fibre 2g, added sugar 17g, salt 0.66g

Hot Cross Bun Pudding

A rich and fruity version of bread and butter pudding using up buns or fruited loaves.

50g/2oz butter
6 hot cross buns, split in half (fresh or slightly stale)
300ml/½ pint milk
300ml/½ pint single cream
1 tsp vanilla essence
1 tsp ground cinnamon
100g/4oz light muscovado sugar
4 eggs
2 tbsp caster sugar, for sprinkling

Takes 50 minutes • Serves 6

1 Preheat the oven to 180°C/Gas 4/fan oven 160°C from cold. Butter a 30 x 24cm/ 12 x 9½in ovenproof dish, 5cm/2in deep. Butter the buns and lay them in the dish, buttered-side up, so they slightly overlap. Pour the milk and cream into a pan and add the vanilla essence and half the cinnamon. Heat gently until it just comes to the boil, then remove from the heat.
2 In a bowl, whisk together the sugar and eggs until frothy, then whisk in the warm milk mixture. Pour evenly over the buns. Leave to stand for 5 minutes.
3 Sprinkle the remaining cinnamon over the buns and bake for 30 minutes until set. Sprinkle over the caster sugar while still warm.

• Per serving 484 kcalories, protein 11g, carbohydrate 57g, fat 25g, saturated fat 14g, fibre 1g, added sugar 30g, salt 0.58g

Pancake Streudels

Look out for ready-made pancakes in supermarket chiller or freezer cabinets.

85g/3oz butter
85g/3oz light muscovado sugar
6 eating apples, such as Cox's, peeled, each cut into 12 wedges
85g/3oz pecans, roughly chopped
85g/3oz raisins
squeeze of lemon juice
6 ready-made pancakes
icing sugar, to dust

Takes 25 minutes • Serves 6

1 Heat the butter and sugar in a frying pan, stirring until dissolved. Toss in the apples and cook, stirring gently, for 3–4 minutes until softened. Add the nuts and let them brown a little.
2 Remove from the heat and stir in the raisins and lemon juice. Spoon some filling into the centre of each pancake.
3 Fold two sides of the pancake into the centre to overlap over the filling slightly. Bring the third side over, then flip the whole pancake over to make a square pouch. Cut in half diagonally and serve with a generous sprinkling of icing sugar.

• Per serving 478 kcalories, protein 6g, carbohydrate 55g, fat 27g, saturated fat 9g, fibre 4g, added sugar 16g, salt 0.41g

TOP: Blueberry and Apple Cobbler   BOTTOM LEFT: Hot Cross Bun Pudding   BOTTOM RIGHT: Pancake Streudels

TOP LEFT: Iced Ginger Cream   TOP RIGHT: Pecan Tart   BOTTOM: Choc and Ginger Nut Slice

Iced Ginger Cream

With an original flavour for an ice cream, this dessert has an unusual but elegant taste.

6 ready-made individual meringues
425ml carton double cream
grated zest of 1 lemon
3 tbsp kirsch
2 tbsp caster sugar
4 pieces of stem ginger in syrup, finely
  chopped

Takes 20 minutes, plus chilling • Serves 6

1 Line a 18cm/7in round sandwich cake tin with cling film. Break the meringues into chunks. Whisk the cream until just stiff, then fold in the lemon zest, kirsch, sugar, ginger and meringue pieces.
2 Spoon into the tin, level the top and put in the freezer for at least 4 hours.
3 Turn out of the tin 10 minutes before serving and chill. Cut into wedges and drizzle with the syrup from the jar of ginger.

• Per serving 333 kcalories, protein 2g, carbohydrate 22g, fat 26g, saturated fat 16g, none, added sugar 19g, salt 0.54g

Pecan Tart

A spin on old-fashioned treacle tart, made extra tasty with nuts.

25g/1oz self-raising flour
140g/5oz plain flour
85g/3oz cold butter, cut into pieces
pouring cream, to serve

FOR THE FILLING
85g/3oz butter, at room temperature
140g/5oz light muscovado sugar
2 eggs, well beaten
100g/4oz golden syrup
2 tbsp double cream
100g/4oz pecan nuts, roughly chopped

Takes 1 hour 10 minutes • Serves 8

1 Preheat the oven to 190°C/Gas 5/fan oven 170°C from cold. Rub both the flours and butter into fine crumbs. Add two to three tablespoons of cold water and stir with a palette knife until a dough forms.
2 Shape into a ball, roll out and line a shallow loose-bottomed 23cm/9in fluted flan tin. Bake blind for 17 minutes, then remove the beans and paper. Cook for 5 minutes.
3 To make the filling, beat the butter and sugar until pale and fluffy, then gradually beat in the eggs, syrup and cream. Mix in the nuts. Transfer to the pastry case and bake for 30–35 minutes until set. Cool in the tin and serve with cream.

• Per serving 456 kcalories, protein 5g, carbohydrate 45g, fat 30g, saturated fat 13g, fibre 1g, added sugar 28g, salt 0.58g

Choc and Ginger Nut Slice

Put the biscuits in a plastic bag and crush them with a rolling pin.

100g/4oz unsalted butter, plus extra
  for greasing
185g/7oz plain chocolate
2 tbsp golden syrup
225g/8oz ginger biscuits, crushed
100g/4oz hazelnuts, toasted and chopped

Takes 20 minutes, plus chilling • Serves 8

1 Lightly grease a 18cm/7in sandwich tin. In a heatproof bowl set over a pan of simmering water, heat the butter, 100g/4oz chocolate and the syrup, stirring occasionally, until melted.
2 Remove from the heat and stir in the biscuit crumbs and three-quarters of the nuts. Press the mixture into the tin.
3 Melt the remaining chocolate, then spoon on top and sprinkle over the remaining nuts. Chill for 1 hour before serving, cut into slices.

• Per serving 433 kcalories, protein 4g, carbohydrate 39g, fat 30g, saturated fat 13g, fibre 2g, added sugar 20g, salt 0.68g

Cakes and Bakes

Cherry and Marzipan Cake

A special-occasion cake from *Good Food* reader and baker Carrie Hill.

200g/8oz butter, softened
200g/8oz caster sugar
4 eggs, beaten
200g/8oz self-raising flour
200g/8oz glacé cherries, chopped
100g/4oz ground almonds
2–3 drops almond extract
250g/9oz marzipan
50g/2oz blanched almonds, halved
    lengthways
icing sugar, for dusting

Takes 1 hour 55 minutes • Serves 12

1 Preheat the oven to 160°C/Gas 3/fan oven 140°C. Butter and line a deep 20cm/8in round cake tin. Beat the butter and sugar in a bowl until light and creamy. Pour in the eggs a little at a time and beat well after each addition. Mix in the flour one third at a time.
2 Fold in the cherries, ground almonds and almond extract until evenly mixed. Spoon half the mixture into the tin.
3 Roll out the marzipan to a 19cm/7½in circle. Lay this on top of the cake mixture in the tin, then cover with the rest of the mixture. Level, and scatter the almonds on top.
4 Bake for 1½ hours, or until a skewer inserted comes out clean, covering with foil after 1 hour. Leave to cool in the tin for 20 minutes, then turn out on to a wire rack and cool completely. Dust with icing sugar.

• Per serving 479 kcalories, protein 8g, carbohydrate 57g, fat 26g, saturated fat 10g, fibre 2g, added sugar 35g, salt 0.57g

Devonshire Honey Cake

This cake is based on a recipe by food writer Geraldene Holt, who lived in Devon for many years.

225g/8oz unsalted butter
250g/9oz clear honey, plus about 2 tbsp
    extra to glaze
100g/4oz dark muscovado sugar
3 large eggs, beaten
300g/10oz self-raising flour

Takes 1½ hours • Serves 12

1 Preheat the oven to 160°C/Gas 3/fan oven 140°C. Butter and line a 20cm/8in round loose-bottomed cake tin. Cut the butter into pieces and drop into a medium pan with the honey and sugar. Melt slowly over a low heat. When liquid, increase the heat under the pan and boil for about one minute. Leave to cool.
2 Beat the eggs into the cooled honey mixture using a wooden spoon. Sift the flour into a large bowl and pour in the egg and honey mixture, beating until you have a smooth batter.
3 Pour the mixture into the tin and bake for 50 minutes–1 hour until the cake is well-risen, golden brown and springs back when pressed.
4 Turn the cake out on a wire rack. Warm 2 tablespoons of honey in a small pan and brush over the top of the cake to glaze, then leave to cool.

• Per serving 336 kcalories, protein 4g, carbohydrate 43g, fat 17g, saturated fat 10g, fibre 1g, added sugar 25g, salt 0.29g

Cinnamon Nutella Cake

Chuck the lot into a bowl, give it a quick beat and it's ready to bake.

175g/6oz butter, softened
175g/6oz golden caster sugar
3 eggs
200g/8oz self-raising flour
1 tsp baking powder
2 tsp ground cinnamon
4 tbsp milk
4 rounded tbsp chocolate hazelnut spread
50g/2oz hazelnuts, roughly chopped

Takes 1½ hours • Serves 12

1 Preheat the oven to 180°C/Gas 4/fan oven 160°C. Butter and line the base of a 20cm/8in round cake tin.
2 Put the butter, sugar, eggs, flour, baking powder, cinnamon and milk into a bowl. Beat until light and fluffy.
3 Tip three quarters of the mixture into the tin, spread it level, then spoon the hazelnut spread on in four blobs. Top with the remaining mixture, swirl a few times with a skewer, then smooth.
4 Sprinkle with the nuts. Bake for 1 hour–1 hour 10 minutes, until risen, nicely browned, feels firm to the touch and springs back when lightly pressed (cover with foil if it starts to brown too quickly). Cool in the tin for 10 minutes, then turn out, peel off the paper and cool on a wire rack.

• Per serving 320 kcalories, protein 5g, carbohydrate 34g, fat 19g, saturated fat 8g, fibre 1g, added sugar 20g, salt 0.63g

TOP: Cherry and Marzipan Cake   BOTTOM LEFT: Devonshire Honey Cake   BOTTOM RIGHT: Cinnamon Nutella Cake

TOP LEFT: Raisin Spice Cake   TOP RIGHT: Olive Oil Cake   BOTTOM: Pecan Ginger Cake

Raisin Spice Cake

You can store this cake for up to a week in an airtight tin.

FOR THE TOPPING
25g/1oz butter
25g/1oz demerara sugar
1 tsp mixed spice
25g/1oz chopped nuts

FOR THE CAKE
175ml/6fl oz unsweetened orange juice
175g/6oz raisins
175g/6oz butter
175g/6oz light muscovado sugar
250g/9oz self-raising flour
1 tsp mixed spice
1 tsp ground cinnamon
1 tsp ground ginger
3 eggs, beaten

Takes 1 hour 20 minutes • Serves 10–12

1 Preheat the oven to 160°C/Gas 3/fan oven 140°C. Butter a 23cm/9in ring tin or 20cm/8in round cake tin. Make the topping: chop the butter into the topping ingredients, then sprinkle in the tin.
2 Pour the juice into a pan, then add the raisins, butter and sugar. Bring to the boil, stirring, then simmer for 5 minutes.
3 Lift off the heat; cool for 10 minutes. Sift the flour, mixed spice, cinnamon and ginger into the pan, then add the eggs and mix. Pour into the tin and smooth the top.
4 Bake for 45 minutes until firm. Cool in the tin for 5 minutes, then transfer on to a wire rack to cool completely.

• Per serving (for ten) 408 kcalories, protein 6g, carbohydrate 54g, fat 20g, saturated fat 11g, fibre 1g, added sugar 20g, salt 0.75g

Olive Oil Cake

The flavour of the olive oil comes through along with the citrus fruits and the almonds.

1 orange
1 lemon
4 large eggs
115g/4oz caster sugar
175g/6oz plain flour
1 tbsp baking powder
225ml/8fl oz extra virgin olive oil
100g/4oz blanched almonds, toasted and
    finely chopped
icing sugar, for dusting

Takes 1 hour 25 minutes • Serves 12

1 Preheat the oven to 180°C/Gas 4/fan oven 160°C. Oil and line the base of a 23cm/9in loose-bottomed or springform round cake tin. Put the orange and lemon in a pan and cover with water. Bring to the boil and leave to simmer for 30 minutes until very soft. Drain and cool. Cut away the skin from the white pith and whizz the skin to a puréed paste in a food processor.
2 In a large bowl, beat the eggs with the sugar for 7–8 minutes. Sift the flour, baking powder and a pinch of salt together, then fold lightly into the egg mixture along with the olive oil. Very gently fold in the almonds and puréed fruit skin, but don't overmix.
3 Pour the batter into the tin and bake for 45 minutes. Cool on a wire rack, then dust with icing sugar.

• Per serving 333 kcalories, protein 6g, carbohydrate 25g, fat 24g, saturated fat 3g, fibre 1g, added sugar 11g, salt 0.45g

Pecan Ginger Cake

Stays soft and moist in the middle, and the icing sets to a crisp meringue-like coating.

200g/8oz self-raising flour
4 tsp ground ginger
1 tsp baking powder
½ tsp salt
200g/8oz butter
350g/12oz golden syrup
100g/4oz light muscovado sugar
4 eggs, beaten
100g/4oz pecans, roughly chopped
100g/4oz crystallized ginger, chopped

FOR THE TOPPING AND DECORATION
175g/6oz golden granulated sugar
1 egg white
pinch of cream of tartar
85g/3oz sugar
100g/4oz pecan halves

Takes 1 hour • Serves 10

1 Preheat the oven to 180°C/Gas 4/fan oven 160°C. Butter and line the base of two 20cm/8in cake tins. Sift together the flour, ginger, baking powder and salt. Rub in the butter until it resembles crumbs.
2 Beat in the syrup, sugar, eggs, pecans and ginger. Pour into the tins and bake for 45 minutes until firm. Cool in the tins for 10 minutes, then turn out on to a wire rack.
3 Put the golden sugar, egg white, cream of tartar and 2 tablespoons hot water in a bowl set over (not in) a pan of simmering water. Beat for 10 minutes. Layer the cakes with a little icing; swirl the rest over the top and sides.
4 Heat the sugar with 4 tablespoons of water until dissolved, then boil until it forms a caramel. Stir in the pecan halves, cool on an oiled baking sheet, then use to decorate.

• Per serving 659 kcalories, protein 7g, carbohydrate 90g, fat 33g, saturated fat 11g, fibre 2g, added sugar 43g, salt 1.3g

Carrot, Apple and Raisin Cake

This egg-free cake is a real teatime treat – it's packed with fruit and cinnamon.

225g/8oz self-raising flour
½ tsp baking powder
½ tsp salt
1 tsp ground cinnamon
5 tbsp vegetable oil
grated zest of 1 orange plus 4 tbsp juice
140g/5oz light muscovado sugar
140g/5oz finely grated carrot
1 medium eating apple, peeled, cored
 and grated
85g/3oz raisins
50g/2oz pumpkin seeds
icing sugar, for dusting

Takes 1 hour 40 minutes • Serves 12

1 Preheat the oven to 180°C/Gas 4/fan oven 160°C. Butter a 20cm/8in round cake tin. Mix the flour, baking powder, salt and cinnamon together in a large bowl. In a separate bowl, mix together the oil, orange juice and sugar.
2 Add the orange mixture to the flour along with the grated carrot and apple, orange zest, raisins and pumpkin seeds and stir until really well mixed. Spoon into the prepared tin.
3 Bake for 50 minutes–1 hour, until the cake pulls from the side of the tin. Cool on a rack before removing from tin. Dust with icing sugar and serve.

• Per serving 207 kcalories, protein 3g, carbohydrate 36g, fat 7g, saturated fat 1g, fibre 1g, added sugar 13g, salt 0.47g

Authentic Yorkshire Parkin

This traditional cake for Guy Fawkes' night will keep for up to two weeks.

1 egg
3 tbsp milk
175g/6oz golden syrup
100g/4oz black treacle
85g/3oz light muscovado sugar
225g/8oz butter
100g/4oz medium oatmeal
250g/9oz plain flour
2 rounded tsp ground ginger
2 tsp bicarbonate of soda

Takes 1 hour 10 minutes • Serves 16

1 Preheat the oven to 160°C/Gas 3/fan oven 140°C. Butter a deep 23cm/9in square cake tin and line. Beat the egg and stir in the milk, then set aside.
2 Put the syrup, treacle, sugar and butter in a large pan and heat gently until the sugar has dissolved and the butter has melted. Remove from the heat. Mix together the oatmeal, flour, ginger and bicarbonate of soda, then stir into the syrup mixture, followed by the egg and milk. Combine well.
3 Pour the mixture into the tin and bake for 50 minutes–1 hour until the cake feels firm and a little crusty on top. Leave to cool in the tin, then turn out and peel off the paper. Wrap the parkin in clean greaseproof paper and foil and leave it for at least three days – this allows it to become much softer and stickier.

• Per serving 261 kcalories, protein 3g, carbohydrate 36g, fat 13g, saturated fat 8g, fibre 1g, added sugar 18g, salt 0.38g

Porter Cake

A lovely moist cake that gets even better if left undisturbed in the cake tin for a couple of days.

175g/6oz butter
450g/1lb mixed dried fruit
grated zest and juice of 1 orange
175g/6oz light muscovado sugar
200ml/7fl oz porter, Guinness or Caffrey's
1 tsp bicarbonate of soda
3 eggs, beaten
300g/10oz plain flour
2 tsp mixed spice

FOR THE TOPPING
2 tbsp flaked almonds
2 tbsp demerara sugar

Takes 2 hours 25 minutes • Serves 12

1 Preheat the oven to 150°C/Gas 2/fan oven 130°C. Butter and line the base of a deep 20cm/8in round cake tin. Put the butter, dried fruit, orange zest and juice, sugar and porter in a large pan. Bring slowly to the boil, stirring until the butter has dissolved, then simmer for 15 minutes.
2 Cool for 10 minutes, then stir in the bicarbonate of soda. The mixture will foam up, but don't worry, this is normal.
3 Stir the eggs into the pan, then sift in the flour and spice and mix well. Pour into the prepared tin, smooth the top with the back of a spoon and sprinkle with the flaked almonds and demerara sugar. Bake for 1¼–1½ hours. Cool in the tin for 15 minutes, then turn out and cool on a wire rack.

• Per serving 400 kcalories, protein 6g, carbohydrate 63g, fat 15g, saturated fat 8g, fibre 2g, added sugar 17g, salt 0.69g

TOP LEFT: Carrot, Apple and Raisin Cake   TOP RIGHT: Authentic Yorkshire Parkin   BOTTOM: Porter Cake

TOP: Sticky Ginger Cake with Ginger Fudge Icing   BOTTOM LEFT: Yummy Scrummy Carrot Cake   BOTTOM RIGHT: Mocha Fudge Cake with Coffee Icing

Sticky Ginger Cake with Ginger Fudge Icing

You can make the cake a couple of days in advance, wrap well, then ice on the day of serving.

200g/8oz unsalted butter, diced
175g/6oz molasses sugar
3 tbsp black treacle
150ml/¼ pint milk
2 large eggs, beaten
4 pieces stem ginger, drained from their syrup, chopped
300g/10oz self-raising flour
1 tbsp ground ginger

FOR THE ICING
4 tbsp ginger syrup, drained from jar
300g/10oz golden icing sugar, sifted
140g/5oz unsalted butter, softened
2 tsp lemon juice

Takes 1 hour 10 minutes • Serves 16

1 Preheat the oven to 160°C/Gas 3/fan oven 140°C. Butter and line the base of a 23cm/9in round cake tin. Gently melt the butter, sugar and treacle; cool briefly, then stir in the milk. Beat in the eggs and add the chopped stem ginger. Sift the flour, ground ginger and a pinch of salt into the warm mixture. Combine thoroughly.
2 Spoon the cake mixture into the tin and level the surface. Bake for 30–35 minutes or until firm and risen. Cool in the tin for an hour, then transfer to a wire rack.
3 Skewer the top of the cooled cake all over, then pour 2 tablespoons of the syrup over. Beat together the icing sugar, butter, lemon juice and the remaining ginger syrup, and spread over the cake.

• Per serving 379 kcalories, protein 3g, carbohydrate 53g, fat 19g, saturated fat 11g, fibre 1g, added sugar 37g, salt 0.27g

Yummy Scrummy Carrot Cake

Light and enticingly moist, this cake keeps for up to a week in a tin.

175g/6oz light muscovado sugar
175ml/6fl oz sunflower oil
3 large eggs, lightly beaten
140g/5oz grated carrot (about 3 medium carrots)
100g/4oz raisins
grated zest of 1 large orange
175g/6oz self-raising flour
1 tsp bicarbonate of soda
1 tsp ground cinnamon
½ tsp grated nutmeg (freshly grated will give you the best flavour)

FOR THE FROSTING
175g/6oz icing sugar
1½–2 tbsp orange juice

Takes 1¼ hours • Serves 15

1 Preheat the oven to 180°C/Gas 4/fan oven 160°C. Oil and line the base and sides of an 18cm/7in square cake tin. Tip the sugar into a large mixing bowl, pour in the oil and add the eggs. Lightly mix, then stir in the grated carrots, raisins and orange rind.
2 Mix the flour, soda and spices, then sift into the bowl. Lightly mix all the ingredients.
3 Pour the mixture into the prepared tin and bake for 40–45 minutes, until it feels firm and springy when you press it in the centre. Cool in the tin for 5 minutes, then turn it out, peel off the paper and cool on a wire rack.
4 Beat together the frosting ingredients in a small bowl until smooth. Set the cake on a serving plate and drizzle the icing over the top. Leave to set, then cut into slices.

• Per serving 265 kcalories, protein 3g, carbohydrate 39g, fat 12g, saturated fat 2g, fibre 1g, added sugar 24g, salt 0.41g

Mocha Fudge Cake with Coffee Icing

It's big, it's rich, it's moist – and impossible to resist.

FOR THE ICING
175g/6oz plain chocolate, melted
50g/2oz unsalted butter, melted
150ml/¼ pint double-strength espresso
1 tsp vanilla extract
300g/10oz icing sugar

FOR THE CAKE
300g/10oz plain flour, plus extra
2 tsp baking powder
1 tsp vanilla extract
3 eggs, separated
125ml/4fl oz milk
4 tbsp instant coffee granules
85g/3oz unsalted butter
280g/10oz caster sugar
85g/3oz plain chocolate, melted
125ml/4fl oz soured cream

Takes 1 hour 5 minutes, plus 4 hours chilling • Serves 10

1 Whisk together the cooled icing ingredients. Cover and chill for 3–4 hours.
2 Preheat the oven to 180°C/Gas 4/fan oven 160°C. Butter and flour two 20cm/8in cake tins. Sift the flour and baking powder. Stir the vanilla into the egg yolks. Heat half the milk to boiling point, stir in the coffee to dissolve, then add the rest of the milk and cool.
3 Cream the butter and 200g/8oz of the caster sugar. Slowly whisk in the egg yolk mixture, then the melted chocolate. Fold in the sifted dry ingredients, the cooled milk and the soured cream. Whisk the egg whites until stiff; whisk in the remaining sugar to form firm peaks. Fold the egg whites into the cake mixture and pour into the tins. Bake for 30 minutes until risen. Cool, split each cake in two, and layer with the icing.

• Per serving 627 kcalories, protein 8g, carbohydrate 103g, fat 23g, saturated fat 13g, fibre 2g, added sugar 77g, salt 0.42g

Lemon Flower Cake

A perfect cake for Easter from Orlando Murrin, former editor of *Good Food*.

FOR THE SUGAR-FROSTED FLOWERS
selection of pansies, calendulas and other
    seasonal edible flowers
1 egg white, very lightly beaten
caster sugar, for coating the flowers

FOR THE CAKE
175g/6oz butter, softened
175g/6oz caster sugar
3 eggs
175g/6oz self-raising flour
1½ tsp baking powder
finely grated zest of 1 lemon

FOR THE TOPPING AND FILLING
85g/3oz caster sugar, plus extra
    for sprinkling
juice of 1½ lemons
250g tub mascarpone

Takes 50 minutes, plus 2 hours drying time •
Serves 8–10

1 Brush the flower petals with the egg white,
then sprinkle with the caster sugar. Shake off
any excess. Leave for 2 hours to dry.
2 Preheat the oven to 190°C/Gas 5/fan
oven 170°C. Lightly butter and line two
18cm/7in round sandwich tins. Put all the
cake ingredients in a large mixing bowl, add
a tablespoon of warm water and beat until
smooth. Divide the mixture between the tins,
smooth, then bake for 25–30 minutes until the
cakes spring back when pressed.
3 Mix the topping sugar with the juice of one
lemon. Prick the cakes and spoon the topping
mixture over. Cool, then transfer to a wire
rack. Add the remaining lemon juice to the
mascarpone and use this mixture to layer the
cakes. Sprinkle caster sugar lightly over the
top, then decorate with the flowers.

• Per serving (for eight) 538 kcalories, protein 6g,
carbohydrate 54g, fat 35g, saturated fat 21g, fibre 1g,
added sugar 35g, salt 1.12g

Orange and Almond Cake

This unconventionally made bittersweet cake freezes beautifully.

1 medium orange
175g/6oz butter, softened
175g/6oz light muscovado sugar
3 eggs
175g/6oz self-raising flour
½ tsp bicarbonate of soda
50g/2oz ground almonds
icing sugar, for dredging

Takes 50 minutes • Serves 12

1 Preheat the oven to 190°C/Gas 5/fan
oven 170°C. Butter and line the base of a
23cm/9in round deep cake tin. Cut the
whole orange – skin, pith, flesh, the lot –
into pieces. Remove any pips, then whizz the
orange pieces in a food processor to a finely
chopped purée.
2 Tip the butter, sugar, eggs, flour,
bicarbonate of soda and almonds into the
processor and whizz for 10 seconds, until
smooth. Pour into the prepared tin and
smooth the top.
3 Bake for 25–30 minutes, until the cake is
risen and brown. Allow to cool in the tin for 5
minutes before turning out on to a wire rack.
Dredge thickly with icing sugar before serving.

• Per serving 266 kcalories, protein 4g, carbohydrate
29g, fat 16g, saturated fat 8g, fibre 1g, added sugar
16g, salt 0.61g

Blueberry Cheesecake Gateau

This tall cake is spectacular, easy to make and keeps for up to one day in the fridge.

225g/9oz self-raising flour
1 tsp baking powder
200g/8oz caster sugar
200g/8oz butter, softened
4 large eggs
2 tsp vanilla extract
1 tbsp milk

FOR THE ICING AND DECORATION
400g/14oz medium-fat soft cheese
grated zest of 2 limes and the juice of 1
100g/4oz icing sugar
200g/8oz blueberries

Takes 1¼ hours, plus 30 minutes decorating •
Serves 12

1 Preheat the oven to 180°C/Gas 4/fan oven
160°C. Butter and line the base of a deep
18cm/7in round cake tin.
2 Put the flour, baking powder, sugar,
butter, eggs and vanilla into a large bowl
and beat with an electric mixer on low speed
until everything is mixed together. Increase
the speed and whisk for 2 minutes. Stir in
the milk.
3 Spoon the mixture into the tin and level the
top. Bake the cake for about 50–60 minutes,
until the cake springs back when lightly
pressed. Cool, then split into three layers.
4 Beat the cheese until soft, then beat in
the lime zest and juice and the icing sugar.
Sandwich the cake back together with two
thirds of the cheese mixture, and spread the
rest on the top. Arrange the blueberries in tight
circles around the top of the cake.

• Per serving 380 kcalories, protein 8g, carbohydrate
43g, fat 21g, saturated fat 9g, fibre 1g, added sugar
27g, salt 0.69g

TOP: Lemon Flower Cake   BOTTOM LEFT: Orange and Almond Cake   BOTTOM RIGHT: Blueberry Cheesecake Gateau

TOP LEFT: Rhubarb and Orange Cake   TOP RIGHT: St Lucia Banana Cake   BOTTOM: Lemon Polenta Cake with Rosemary Syrup

Rhubarb and Orange Cake

This is good warm, as a pudding with whipped cream, or cold, as a moist fruity cake.

350g/12oz prepared rhubarb, cut into
    4cm/1½in lengths
200g/8oz golden caster sugar
finely grated zest and juice of ½ small orange
140g/5oz butter, softened
2 eggs, beaten
½ tsp baking powder
85g/3oz self-raising flour
100g/4oz ground almonds

FOR THE TOPPING
25g/1oz butter, melted
25g/1oz light muscovado sugar
finely grated zest of ½ small orange
50g/2oz slivered almonds
icing sugar, for dusting

Takes 1 hour 25 minutes, plus 1 hour standing
• Serves 6–8

1 Mix the rhubarb with 50g/2oz of the caster sugar and the orange zest. Set aside for 1 hour, stirring once or twice.
2 Preheat the oven to 190°C/Gas 5/fan oven 170°C. Butter and line the base of a deep 23cm/9in round cake tin. Cream the butter and remaining caster sugar. Add the eggs, baking powder, flour and ground almonds. Beat gently, but do not overmix. Stir in the orange juice, spoon into the tin, and level. Drain the rhubarb and spoon over the mixture. Bake for 25 minutes. Meanwhile, combine the butter, sugar, zest and almonds.
3 Reduce the oven to 180°C/Gas 4/fan oven 160°C. Sprinkle the topping over the cake and return to the oven for 15–20 minutes or until firm. Cool in the tin, then transfer to a rack. Dust with icing sugar.

• Per serving (for six) 548 kcalories, protein 9g, carbohydrate 44g, fat 39g, saturated fat 16g, fibre 3g, added sugar 41g, salt 0.74g

St Lucia Banana Cake

This cake conjures up the taste of the Caribbean.

350g/12oz self-raising flour
1 tsp bicarbonate of soda
2 tsp mixed spice
175g/6oz light muscovado sugar
4 eggs
200ml/7fl oz sunflower oil
2 bananas, mashed
100g/4oz pineapple, very finely chopped
finely grated rind and juice of 1 orange
100g pack walnuts, roughly chopped

FOR THE FROSTING
2 × 200g packs medium-fat soft cheese,
    at room temperature
200g/8oz icing sugar
50g/2oz honey-coated banana chips

Takes 1 hour 5 minutes • Serves 12

1 Preheat the oven to 180°C/Gas 4/fan oven 160°C. Butter and line two 20cm/8in sandwich tins. Sift the flour into a large bowl with the soda, mixed spice and sugar.
2 Whisk the eggs and the oil until smooth. Stir the egg mixture into the flour with the bananas, pineapple, orange rind and juice and walnuts; stir well. Divide between the prepared tins. Bake for 45 minutes until risen and firm. Cool for 10 minutes, then remove from the tins, peel off the paper and leave to cool completely.
3 Beat the soft cheese until smooth. Gradually add the icing sugar to give a smooth frosting. Spread half the frosting over one cake. Put the other cake on top. Spread over the remaining icing, swirling it with a palette knife. Sprinkle over the banana chips.

• Per serving 545 kcalories, protein 10g, carbohydrate 64g, fat 30g, saturated fat 3g, fibre 2g, added sugar 32g, salt 0.66g

Lemon Polenta Cake with Rosemary Syrup

A bold, unusual dessert that marries fruit and herbs.

175g/6oz polenta
50g/2oz plain flour
1½ tsp baking powder
¼ tsp salt
5 tbsp natural yogurt
5 tbsp groundnut oil, plus extra for greasing
grated rind of 2 lemons, plus 2 tbsp fresh
    lemon juice
2 eggs, plus 2 egg whites
400g/14oz caster sugar
2 sprigs fresh rosemary, plus extra sprigs
    to decorate
fresh raspberries and Greek yogurt, to serve

Takes 1 hour 5 minutes • Serves 8–10

1 Preheat the oven to 180°C/Gas 4/fan oven 160°C. Sift the polenta, flour, baking powder and salt into a bowl. Tip the yogurt, oil, lemon rind and juice into a jug; stir to combine.
2 Beat the eggs and egg whites with half the sugar until creamy. Beat in the yogurt mixture until smooth, then fold in the dry ingredients. Pour the batter into a 1.2 litre/2 pint lightly oiled, lined loaf tin. Bake for 40–45 minutes or until a skewer inserted comes out clean.
3 Put the remaining sugar in a pan with 200ml/7fl oz of water and the rosemary sprigs. Bring to the boil, then simmer for 10 minutes. Cool completely, then strain.
4 Cool the cake on a wire rack for 15 minutes. Prick the top and drizzle over half the rosemary syrup. Serve with the rosemary sprigs, raspberries, yogurt and extra syrup.

• Per serving (for eight) 390 kcalories, protein 6g, carbohydrate 74g, fat 10g, saturated fat 2g, fibre 1g, added sugar 53g, salt 0.43g

Fresh Cherry Almond Cake

This crumbly cake is a terrific way to enjoy fresh cherries.

140g/5oz whole blanched almonds
250g/9oz self-raising flour
140g/5oz butter, cut into small pieces
    and softened
140g/5oz caster sugar
2 eggs, beaten
125ml/4fl oz milk
300g/10oz fresh cherries, stoned and
    patted dry
25g/1oz flaked almonds

Takes 1½ hours • Serves 8

1 Preheat the oven to 180°C/Gas 4/fan oven 160°C. Butter and line the base of a 20cm/8in round, deep cake tin. Put the blanched almonds in a small pan and heat gently, shaking occasionally, until golden brown (about 10 minutes). Cool, then whizz in a food processor until finely ground.
2 Tip the flour into a bowl and stir in the ground almonds. Rub in the butter until the mixture is crumbly. Stir in the sugar, then add the eggs, milk and cherries; mix until combined, but don't overmix.
3 Spoon into the prepared tin and smooth the top, then sprinkle the flaked almonds on top. Bake for 1 hour 10 minutes until the cake is golden on top and firm to the touch. Cool in the tin for 10 minutes, then turn out on to a wire rack to cool. Eat within 3 days.

• Per serving 474 kcalories, protein 10g, carbohydrate 48g, fat 28g, saturated fat 11g, fibre 2.8g, added sugar 18g, salt 0.69g

Almond Cake with Clementines

This cake is very moist and light, and the apricots add a juicy note – a brilliant special-occasion dessert.

100g/4oz ready-to-eat dried apricots
175ml/6fl oz clementine juice (about
    6–8 clementines)
100g/4oz butter, softened
100g/4oz golden caster sugar
2 eggs
50g/2oz self-raising flour
175g/6oz ground almonds
½ tsp vanilla extract
2 tbsp slivered almonds
icing sugar, for dusting
8 clementines in syrup (from a jar), to serve
thick cream or Greek yogurt, to serve

Takes 1 hour 50 minutes • Serves 8

1 Preheat the oven to 180°C/Gas 4/fan oven 160°C. Butter and line the base of a 20cm/8in round cake tin. Finely chop the apricots and put in a pan with the clementine juice. Bring to the boil, then gently simmer for 5 minutes. Leave to cool.
2 Beat the butter, sugar, eggs and flour in a bowl for 2 minutes until light and fluffy, then fold in the ground almonds, vanilla and apricots along with their juices.
3 Turn the mixture into the prepared tin and smooth. Scatter the slivered almonds on top. Bake for 40–50 minutes until firm. Cool in the tin for 5 minutes, then turn out and cool on a wire rack. Dust the cake with icing sugar. Slice, and put a wedge on each plate with a clementine. Spoon the syrup over the cake and fruit. Serve with the cream or yogurt.

• Per serving 291 kcalories, protein 6g, carbohydrate 27g, fat 19g, saturated fat 8g, fibre 2g, added sugar 15g, salt 0.36g

Mango, Banana and Coconut Cake

Buy your mangos a couple of days ahead to ensure they are fully ripe.

1 medium, ripe mango
2 ripe bananas
1 tsp vanilla extract
225g/8oz butter, softened
140g/5oz light muscovado sugar
2 eggs, beaten
50g/2oz desiccated coconut
225g/8oz self-raising flour
½ tsp bicarbonate of soda
1 tsp mixed spice

FOR THE FILLING
200g packet full-fat soft cheese
2 tsp lemon juice
25g/1oz icing sugar, plus extra for dusting

Takes 55 minutes • Serves 10

1 Preheat the oven 160°C/Gas 3/fan oven 140°C. Butter and line the bases of two round 20cm/8in sandwich tins. Peel, stone and chop the mango, then purée the flesh. Mash the bananas, then mix in half the mango purée and the vanilla.
2 Beat together the butter and sugar until light and fluffy. Beat in the eggs, a little at a time, then stir in the banana mixture, and the coconut. Sift in the flour, bicarbonate of soda and spice, then fold in lightly. Divide the mixture between the tins and smooth. Bake for 30–35 minutes. Cool in the tins for 5 minutes, then turn out on to a wire rack.
3 Beat together the filling ingredients, then stir in the reserved mango. Spread one cake with the filling. Put the other cake on top and dust lightly with icing sugar.

• Per serving 468 kcalories, protein 5g, carbohydrate 42g, fat 32g, saturated fat 21g, fibre 2g, added sugar 17g, salt 0.83g

TOP LEFT: Fresh Cherry Almond Cake   TOP RIGHT: Almond Cake with Clementines   BOTTOM: Mango, Banana and Coconut Cake

TOP: Citrus Poppy Seed Cake   BOTTOM LEFT: Soured Cream Rhubarb Squares   BOTTOM RIGHT: Strawberry and Cinnamon Torte

Citrus Poppy Seed Cake

This treat can be stored in the fridge for up to 3 days.

175g/6oz butter, softened
175g/6oz caster sugar
3 eggs, beaten
250g/9oz self-raising flour
50g/2oz poppy seeds
grated rind of 2 oranges
grated rind of 2 lemons
4 rounded tbsp natural yogurt

FOR THE TOPPING
250g tub mascarpone
grated rind and juice of 1 small orange
3 tbsp orange or lemon curd
grated rind of 1 lemon

Takes 1 hour 5 minutes • Serves 10

1 Preheat the oven to 150°C/Gas 2/fan oven 130°C. Butter and line the base of a deep 20cm/8in round cake tin. Using a wooden spoon, beat together the butter, sugar, eggs, flour, poppy seeds, citrus rinds and yogurt until smooth.
2 Spread the mixture in the tin and bake for 45–50 minutes until just firm. Cool in the tin for 10 minutes, then turn out and cool on a wire rack. Peel off the paper.
3 Meanwhile, mix the mascarpone with enough orange juice to make a spreadable icing. Lightly swirl in the curd to give a marbled effect. Roughly spread over the top and sides of the cake, and scatter the grated citrus rind over the top to decorate.

• Per serving 483 kcalories, protein 7g, carbohydrate 48g, fat 31g, saturated fat 11g, fibre 2g, added sugar 18g, salt 0.74g

Soured Cream Rhubarb Squares

These squares are really light, and delicious hot or cold.

100g/4oz butter, softened
100g/4oz golden caster sugar
100g/4oz mixed nuts, roughly chopped
1 tsp ground cinnamon
250g/9oz dark muscovado sugar
1 large egg
225g/8oz plain flour
1 tsp bicarbonate of soda
½ tsp salt
2 × 142ml cartons soured cream
300g/10oz rhubarb, cut into 1cm pieces

Takes 1 hour 20 minutes • Serves 15

1 Preheat the oven to 180°C/Gas 4/fan oven 160°C. Line a 33 × 23cm/13 × 9in deep baking tin with baking paper. Melt about 15g/½oz of the butter and stir into the caster sugar, nuts and cinnamon in a bowl. Set aside.
2 Beat together the rest of the butter with the muscovado sugar and egg. When smooth and creamy, stir in the flour, bicarbonate of soda, salt and the soured cream. Lastly, stir in the rhubarb.
3 Pour the rhubarb mixture into the prepared tin and sprinkle with the sugar and nut topping. Bake for 30–35 minutes or until a skewer inserted in the centre comes out clean. Serve immediately as a pudding, or leave to cool and cut into squares. Keeps for 4–5 days in an airtight tin.

• Per serving 277 kcalories, protein 4g, carbohydrate 37g, fat 13g, saturated fat 7g, fibre 1g, added sugar 24g, salt 0.63g

Strawberry and Cinnamon Torte

The perfect crumbly dessert for a summer Sunday lunch or dinner.

175g/6oz ground almonds
175g/6oz butter, softened
175g/6oz golden caster sugar
175g/6oz self-raising flour
1 tsp ground cinnamon
1 egg, plus 1 egg yolk
450g/1lb strawberries, hulled and sliced
icing sugar, for dusting
whipped double cream mixed with Greek
    yogurt, to serve

Takes 1¼ hours • Serves 6–8

1 Preheat the oven to 180°C/Gas 4/fan oven 160°C. Butter and line the base of a loose-bottomed 23cm/9in cake tin. In a food processor, mix the ground almonds, butter, sugar, flour, cinnamon, egg and egg yolk until evenly mixed.
2 Tip half the mixture in the tin, and smooth. Spread the strawberries on top. Top with the remaining cake mixture; spread smooth.
3 Bake for 1 hour–1 hour 5 minutes. Check after 40 minutes – if the torte is getting too brown, cover loosely with foil. When cooked, the torte should be slightly risen and dark golden brown.
4 Cool slightly, then remove from the tin. Slide on to a plate and dust with icing sugar. Serve warm, in wedges, with spoonfuls of cream and Greek yogurt.

• Per serving (for eight) 491 kcalories, protein 9g, carbohydrate 45g, fat 32g, saturated fat 13g, fibre 3g, added sugar 23g, salt 0.68g

Fresh Cherry Cake with a Hint of Cinnamon

Make this cake the day before a picnic – it's sturdy and travels well.

140g/5oz self-raising flour
½ tsp ground cinnamon
50g/2oz golden caster sugar
1 egg
4 tbsp milk
85g/3oz butter, melted
350g/12oz juicy, ripe cherries, stalks and stones removed
icing sugar, for dusting

FOR THE TOPPING
25g/1oz plain flour
¼ tsp ground cinnamon
25g/1oz golden caster sugar
25g/1oz butter, diced and softened

Takes 1 hour 5 minutes • Serves 8

1 Preheat the oven to 180°C/Gas 4/fan oven 160°C. Butter and line the base of a 20cm/8in round cake tin. Sift the flour, cinnamon and sugar into a bowl. Make a well and add the egg, milk and melted butter. Combine and beat to make a thick, smooth mixture. Spoon into the tin and smooth. Scatter the cherries over the mixture and gently press them in.
2 Tip all the topping ingredients into a bowl. Rub in the butter to make a crumb-like mixture, then work until it comes together in pea-sized pieces. Scatter this over the cherries.
3 Bake for 30–35 minutes until a skewer pushed into the centre comes out clean. Leave in the tin until cool enough to handle, then tip on to a wire rack until completely cold.

• Per serving 247 kcalories, protein 3g, carbohydrate 32g, fat 12g, saturated fat 7g, fibre 1g, added sugar 12g, salt 0.46g

Apple and Cinnamon Cake

Serve this warm from the oven as a tasty dessert, or cold for a picnic or lunchbox treat.

250g/9oz self-raising flour
1 tsp ground cinnamon
1 tsp baking powder
100g/4oz light muscovado sugar
175g/6oz sultanas or raisins
125ml/4fl oz sunflower oil
2 eggs, beaten
125ml/4fl oz apple juice
2 dessert apples (not peeled), grated
25g/1oz slivered or flaked almonds
icing sugar, for dusting

Takes 1 hour • Serves 8–10

1 Preheat the oven to 180°C/Gas 4/fan oven 160°C. Line a 23cm/9in round deep cake tin with baking paper. Sift the flour into a bowl with the cinnamon and baking powder, then stir in the sugar and sultanas. Make a well in the centre and stir in the oil, eggs, apple juice and grated apple until well mixed.
2 Pour the mixture into the tin, scatter with almonds, then bake for 40–45 minutes until firm in the centre or a skewer inserted into the middle comes out clean. Leave to cool in the tin for about 5 minutes, then turn out and cool on a wire rack. Dust with icing sugar.

• Per serving (for ten) 342 kcalories, protein 6g, carbohydrate 46g, fat 16g, saturated fat 2g, fibre 2g, added sugar 10g, salt 0.46g

Whole Orange Cake

The juicy flavour of a whole orange goes into this cake.

1 small orange
140g/5oz caster sugar
3 eggs
85g/3oz self-raising flour
100g/4oz ground almonds
50g/2oz butter, melted

FOR THE ICING
85g/3oz icing sugar
juice of 1 small sweet orange (or enough to make a smooth pouring icing)
crème fraîche, to serve (optional)

Takes 1 hour 45 minutes • Serves 8–10

1 Put the orange in a pan and cover with cold water. Bring to the boil, cover and simmer for 1 hour. Remove the orange and cool.
2 Preheat the oven to 180°C/Gas 4/fan oven 160°C. Butter and line the base of a 20cm/8in round, deep cake tin. Roughly chop the cooked orange, discarding the pips. Whizz in a food processor until smooth. Whisk the sugar and eggs until light and fluffy.
3 Sift the flour and ground almonds on to the egg mixture. Using a large metal spoon, fold gently, then add the orange purée and melted butter. Fold in gently until just mixed. Pour the cake mixture into the prepared tin. Bake for 40–45 minutes until the cake is brown and springs back when lightly pressed. Cool in the tin for 5 minutes. Mix the icing sugar and juice together, drizzle, and serve with crème fraîche.

• Per serving (for eight) 307 kcalories, protein 6g, carbohydrate 41g, fat 14g, saturated fat 4g, fibre 2g, added sugar 30g, salt 0.29g

TOP: **Fresh Cherry Cake with a Hint of Cinnamon**   BOTTOM LEFT: **Apple and Cinnamon Cake**   BOTTOM RIGHT: **Whole Orange Cake**

TOP LEFT: Prune and Chocolate Torte   TOP RIGHT: Seriously Rich Chocolate Cake   BOTTOM: Cappuccino Bars

Prune and Chocolate Torte

Rich with brandy-steeped prunes, this is a cake for real lovers of chocolate.

250g/9oz no-soak prunes, halved
4 tbsp brandy
25g/1oz cocoa powder
100g/4oz dark chocolate (at least
    70% cocoa solids), broken into pieces
50g/2oz butter
175g/6oz golden caster sugar
4 large egg whites
85g/3oz plain flour
1 tsp ground cinnamon
lightly whipped cream, or crème fraîche,
    to serve

Takes 1 hour 5 minutes, plus 30 minutes
soaking time • Serves 8

1 Soak the prunes in brandy for about
30 minutes. Preheat the oven to 190°C/
Gas 5/fan oven 170°C. Butter a 23cm/9in
loose-bottomed cake tin. Put the cocoa,
chocolate, butter and 140g/5oz of the sugar
in a pan, add 100ml/3½fl oz hot water and
gently heat until smooth. Leave to cool slightly.
2 Whisk the egg whites to soft peaks, then
gradually whisk in the remaining sugar. Sift
the flour and cinnamon over and gently fold
in with a metal spoon, until almost combined.
Add the chocolate mixture and fold in until
evenly combined.
3 Pour the mixture into the tin and arrange
the prunes over the top. Sprinkle over any
remaining brandy and bake for about 30
minutes until just firm. Serve with cream or
crème fraîche.

• Per serving 311 kcalories, protein 5g, carbohydrate
51g, fat 10g, saturated fat 6g, fibre 3g, added sugar
31g, salt 0.18g

Seriously Rich Chocolate Cake

Made with ground almonds and dark chocolate, this flourless cake is beautifully dark, rich and moist.

100g/4oz butter, diced
140g/5oz best-quality dark
    chocolate, broken into pieces
6 eggs, separated
140g/5oz ground almonds
1 tbsp kirsch or Cointreau (optional)
85g/3oz caster sugar
cocoa powder, for dusting
crème fraîche, to serve

Takes 55 minutes • Serves 8–10

1 Preheat the oven to 170°C/Gas 3/fan oven
150°C. Butter and line the base of a 23cm/9in
springform cake tin. Dust the sides with a little
flour. Melt the butter and chocolate, stir until
smooth, and leave for about 5 minutes to cool
slightly. Stir in the egg yolks, ground almonds,
and the liqueur, if using.
2 Put the egg whites into a bowl, add a
pinch of salt and whisk until soft peaks form.
Continue whisking, sprinkling in the sugar
a little at a time, until stiff peaks form. Stir 2
tablespoons of the whites into the chocolate
mixture, then carefully fold in the remainder.
3 Spoon the mixture into the prepared tin and
bake for 30–35 minutes until well risen and
just firm. Cool in the tin. Remove the cake and
peel away the paper. Dust with cocoa powder,
slice, and serve with crème fraîche.

• Per serving (for eight) 401 kcalories, protein 10g,
carbohydrate 24g, fat 30g, saturated fat 11g, fibre 2g,
added sugar 22g, salt 0.66g

Cappuccino Bars

These moreish bars can be frozen, unfrosted, for up to 2 months.

1 tsp cocoa powder, plus extra for dusting
2 rounded tbsp coffee granules
225g/8oz butter, softened
225g/8oz caster sugar
4 eggs
225g/8oz self-raising flour
1 tsp baking powder

FOR THE WHITE CHOCOLATE FROSTING
100g/4oz white chocolate, broken into pieces
50g/2oz butter, softened
3 tbsp milk
175g/6oz icing sugar

Takes 50 minutes • Makes 24

1 Preheat the oven to 180°C/Gas 4/fan oven
160°C. Butter and line the bottom of a shallow
28 × 18cm/11 × 7in oblong tin. Mix the
cocoa and coffee granules into 2 tablespoons
warm water. Put in a large bowl with the other
cake ingredients.
2 Whisk for about 2 minutes with an electric
hand blender to combine, then tip into the tin
and level out. Bake for 35–40 minutes until
risen and firm to the touch. Cool in the tin
for 10 minutes, then cool on a rack. Peel off
the paper.
3 For the frosting, melt the chocolate, butter
and milk in a bowl over a pan of simmering
water. Remove the bowl and sift in the icing
sugar. Beat until smooth, then spread over the
cake. Finish with a dusting of cocoa powder.
Cut into 24 bars.

• Per bar 219 kcalories, protein 3g, carbohydrate 27g,
fat 12g, saturated fat 6g, fibre trace, added sugar 19g,
salt 0.43g

Pear, Hazelnut and Chocolate Cake

Moist and fruity enough to serve warm with cream for pud, but just as good cold.

100g/4oz blanched hazelnuts
140g/5oz self-raising flour
175g/6oz butter, cut into small pieces
140g/5oz golden caster sugar
2 large eggs, beaten
5 small ripe Conference pears
50g/2oz dark chocolate, chopped into
    small chunks
2 tbsp apricot jam

Takes 1½ hours • Serves 8

1 Preheat the oven to 160°C/Gas 3/fan oven 140°C. Butter and line the base of a 20cm/8in round cake tin. Grind the hazelnuts in a food processor until fairly fine. Add the flour and mix briefly. Add the butter and pulse until it forms crumbs. Add the sugar and eggs and mix briefly. Peel, core and chop two of the pears. Stir the pears and chocolate lightly into the cake mixture.
2 Spoon the mixture into the prepared tin and smooth the top. Peel, core and slice the remaining pears and scatter over the top of the cake. Press down lightly and bake for 50–60 minutes, until firm to the touch. Cool in the tin for 10 minutes, then turn out and cool on a wire rack. Warm the jam and brush over the top. Serve warm or cold.

• Per serving 470 kcalories, protein 6g, carbohydrate 47g, fat 30g, saturated fat 14g, fibre 3g, added sugar 18g, salt 0.5g

Dark Chocolate and Orange Cake

Chocolate and orange is a classic combination.

1 Seville orange
3 eggs
280g/10oz caster sugar
240ml/8½fl oz sunflower oil
100g/4oz dark chocolate, broken into pieces
    and melted
25g/1oz cocoa powder
250g/9oz plain flour
1½ tsp baking powder

FOR THE CHOCOLATE GANACHE
200g/8oz dark chocolate, broken into pieces
225ml/8fl oz double cream
candied orange zest, to decorate

Takes 2 hours 10 minutes, plus 1½ hours cooling time • Serves 10

1 Pierce the orange with a skewer. Cook in a pan of boiling water for 30 minutes. Remove and whizz the whole orange in a food processor. Discard any pips and cool.
2 Preheat the oven to 180°C/Gas 4/fan oven 160°C. Butter and line the base of a 23cm/9in round cake tin. Lightly beat the eggs, sugar and oil. Gradually beat in the puréed orange and cooled, melted chocolate. Sift in the cocoa, flour and baking powder. Mix well and pour into the tin. Bake for 55–60 minutes. Cool for 10 minutes, then turn out on to a wire rack.
3 Put the ganache chocolate into a heatproof bowl. Boil the cream in a pan, pour over the chocolate, and stir until smooth. Cool, up to 1½ hours, until firm. Spread over the cake, and decorate with the candied zest.

• Per serving 703 kcalories, protein 7g, carbohydrate 73g, fat 45g, saturated fat 16g, fibre 2g, added sugar 51g, salt 0.42g

Almond and Chocolate Torte

A special treat for dessert or at teatime.

5 egg whites
200g/8oz golden caster sugar
100g/4oz ground almonds
50g/2oz toasted flaked almonds
50g/2oz dark chocolate, chopped

FOR THE APRICOT CREAM
425ml/¾ pint double cream
300g/12oz apricot compote

FOR THE DECORATION
3 tbsp toasted flaked almonds
25g/1oz dark chocolate, shaved
icing sugar, for dusting

Takes 1 hour 5 minutes • Serves 8–12

1 Preheat the oven to 180°C/Gas 4/fan oven 160°C. Butter and line the base of a deep 25cm/10in cake tin. Whisk the egg whites until stiff, then gradually whisk in the golden caster sugar, a tablespoonful at a time.
2 Lightly fold in the ground almonds, the toasted flaked almonds and the chopped chocolate. Pour the mixture into the cake tin and bake for 40–45 minutes until crisp on top and light golden. Allow to cool in the tin for 5 minutes, then turn out and leave to cool on a wire rack.
3 Whip the cream until it just holds its shape. Spoon in the apricot compote, then fold it in gently to give you swirls of apricot. Spoon over the torte and scatter with toasted flaked almonds and chocolate shavings. Dust lightly with sifted icing sugar.

• Per serving (for eight) 574 kcalories, protein 9g, carbohydrate 44g, fat 42g, saturated fat 18g, fibre 3g, added sugar 37g, salt 0.16g

TOP LEFT: Pear, Hazelnut and Chocolate Cake   TOP RIGHT: Dark Chocolate and Orange Cake   BOTTOM: Almond and Chocolate Torte

TOP: Toffee Brownies   BOTTOM LEFT: Choc Crunchies   BOTTOM RIGHT: Chunky Chocolate Nut Flapjacks

Toffee Brownies

Unrefined dark muscovado sugar gives these brownies a sticky toffee flavour.

350g/12oz dark chocolate
(preferably around 50–60% cocoa solids),
    broken into pieces
250g/9oz unsalted butter, cut into pieces
3 large eggs
250g/9oz dark muscovado sugar
85g/3oz plain flour
1 tsp baking powder

Takes 1 hour 5 minutes, plus 1 hour cooling •
Makes 16

1 Preheat the oven to 160°C/Gas 3/fan oven 140°C. Butter and line the base of a shallow 23cm/9in square cake tin. Melt the chocolate and butter together, then stir well and cool.
2 Whisk the eggs until pale, then whisk in the sugar until thick and glossy and well combined. Gently fold in the melted chocolate mixture, then sift in the flour and baking powder and gently stir until smooth.
3 Pour into the prepared cake tin and bake for 30–35 minutes, or until firm to the touch. Test by inserting a wooden cocktail stick into the middle – there should be a few moist crumbs sticking to it. The mixture will still be soft in the centre, but will firm up on cooling.
4 Cool in the tin on a wire rack for at least 1 hour, then cut into 16 squares and finish cooling on the rack.

• Per brownie 324 kcalories, protein 3g, carbohydrate 34g, fat 20g, saturated fat 12g, fibre 1g, added sugar 30g, salt 0.14g

Choc Crunchies

This no-bake treat is great for lunchboxes.

200g/8oz digestive biscuits
100g/4oz butter
3 tbsp golden syrup
2 tbsp cocoa powder
50g/2oz raisins
100g/4oz dark chocolate

Takes 50 minutes • Serves 8–10

1 Butter an 18cm/7in sandwich tin. Seal the biscuits in a strong polythene bag and bash into uneven crumbs with a rolling pin.
2 Melt the butter and syrup in a pan (or microwave on High for about 1½ minutes). Stir in the cocoa and raisins, then thoroughly stir in the biscuit crumbs. Spoon into the tin and press down firmly.
3 Melt the chocolate in a heatproof bowl over a pan of simmering water (or microwave on Medium for 2–3 minutes). Spread over the biscuit base and chill for about half an hour. Keeps for up to 1 week wrapped in foil.

• Per serving (for eight) 327 kcalories, protein 3g, carbohydrate 36g, fat 20g, saturated fat 11g, fibre 1g, added sugar 17g, salt 0.77g

Chunky Chocolate Nut Flapjacks

This flapjack, bulging with chunks of chocolate and nuts, is brilliant for lunchboxes.

200g/8oz oats
25g/1oz desiccated coconut
140g/5oz butter, cut into pieces
50g/2oz light muscovado sugar
5 tbsp golden syrup
100g/4oz brazil nuts (or cashews), cut into large chunks
50g/2oz almonds, cut into large chunks
85g/3oz good-quality dark chocolate, broken into large pieces

Takes 45 minutes • Makes 12

1 Preheat the oven to 180°C/Gas 4/fan oven 160°C. Lightly butter a 23cm/9in square tin and line the base. Mix together the oats and coconut.
2 Put the butter, sugar and syrup in a pan, cook over a low heat, stirring occasionally, until the butter has melted and the sugar dissolved. Remove from the heat and stir in the oat and coconut mixture. Spoon into the tin and press down evenly. Scatter over the nuts and press lightly into the mixture. Stick the chunks of chocolate between the nuts. Bake for 25–30 minutes, or until a pale golden colour.
3 Mark into bars or squares with the back of a knife while still warm, then allow to cool completely before cutting through and removing from the tin.

• Per flapjack 325 kcalories, protein 5g, carbohydrate 28g, fat 22g, saturated fat 10g, fibre 2g, added sugar 15g, salt 0.3g

Mincemeat and Marzipan Teabread

A treat for tea by the fire, this afternoon bake keeps moist, well-wrapped, for 4–5 days.

200g/8oz self-raising flour
100g/4oz cold butter, cut into pieces
85g/3oz light muscovado sugar
85g/3oz marzipan, cut into 1cm/½in cubes
2 eggs
300g/10oz mincemeat
2 tbsp flaked almonds
icing sugar, for dusting (optional)

Takes 1 hour 20 minutes • Serves 12

1 Preheat the oven to 180°C/Gas 4/fan oven 160°C. Butter a 1kg/2lb loaf tin and line the base with greaseproof paper. Tip the flour into a bowl, add the cold butter and rub until the mixture forms fine crumbs. Stir in the sugar and marzipan cubes.
2 In another bowl, lightly whisk the eggs, then stir in the mincemeat. Stir this into the flour mixture until evenly combined. Spoon into the prepared loaf tin, smooth, and sprinkle the flaked almonds over the top. Bake for 1 hour until the teabread is risen and golden brown, or a skewer inserted comes out clean. Lightly dust the teabread with icing sugar while it is still hot.
3 Allow to cool in the tin for 10 minutes, then tip on to a wire rack to cool completely. Peel off the lining paper and cut into slices – it's also very good spread with butter.

• Per serving 265 kcalories, protein 4g, carbohydrate 41g, fat 11g, saturated fat 5g, fibre 1g, added sugar 15g, salt 0.44g

Walnut, Date and Honey Cake

Choose a richly flavoured Greek or Mexican honey for an extra-special taste.

225g/8oz self-raising flour
½ tsp ground cinnamon
175g/6oz butter, softened
100g/4oz light muscovado sugar
3 tbsp clear honey
2 eggs, beaten
2 medium, ripe bananas, about 250g/9oz total weight in their skins
100g/4oz stoned dates
50g pack walnut pieces

Takes 1 hour 25 minutes • Serves 8–10

1 Preheat the oven to 160°C/Gas 3/fan oven 140°C. Line the base and long sides of a 1kg/2lb loaf tin with greaseproof paper, buttering the tin and paper. Tip the flour, cinnamon, butter, sugar, 2 tablespoons of the honey and the eggs into a large mixing bowl. Mash the bananas and chop the dates (kitchen scissors are easiest for this), and add to the bowl. Beat the mixture for 2–3 minutes, using a wooden spoon or hand-held mixer, until well blended.
2 Spoon into the prepared tin and smooth. Scatter the walnut pieces over the top. Bake for 1 hour, then lightly press the top – it should feel firm. If not, bake for a further 10 minutes.
3 Cool for 15 minutes, then lift out of the tin using the paper. When cold, drizzle the remaining honey over. Cut into thick slices.

• Per serving (for eight) 440 kcalories, protein 6g, carbohydrate 54g, fat 24g, saturated fat 13g, fibre 1.5g, added sugar 25g, salt 0.7g

Sticky Marmalade Tealoaf

Use a chunky marmalade to give this loaf extra texture and a pretty top.

140g/5oz marmalade (about one third of a 454g jar)
175g/6oz butter, softened
175g/6oz light muscovado sugar
3 eggs, beaten
225g/8oz self-raising flour
½ tsp baking powder
2 tsp ground ginger
1 tsp mixed spice
100g packet pecan halves

Takes 1½ hours • Serves 12

1 Preheat the oven to 180°C/Gas 4/fan oven 160°C. Butter a 1kg/2lb loaf tin and line with greaseproof paper. Set aside 1 tablespoon of the marmalade in a small pan. In a bowl, blend the remaining marmalade, butter, sugar, eggs, flour, baking powder and spices for 1–2 minutes until smooth and light. Stir in about three quarters of the pecans.
2 Tip into the prepared tin and smooth the top. Sprinkle with the reserved pecans. Bake for about 1–1¼ hours until a skewer inserted comes out clean. Cover loosely with foil after 40 minutes. Once cooked, carefully remove from the tin, and cool slightly on a wire rack.
3 Gently heat the reserved marmalade, stirring until it's smooth, and spread the glaze over the top of the warm loaf. Serve in slices.

• Per serving 339 kcalories, protein 4g, carbohydrate 40g, fat 20g, saturated fat 8g, fibre 1g, added sugar 24g, salt 0.56g

TOP: Mincemeat and Marzipan Teabread   BOTTOM LEFT: Walnut, Date and Honey Cake   BOTTOM RIGHT: Sticky Marmalade Tealoaf

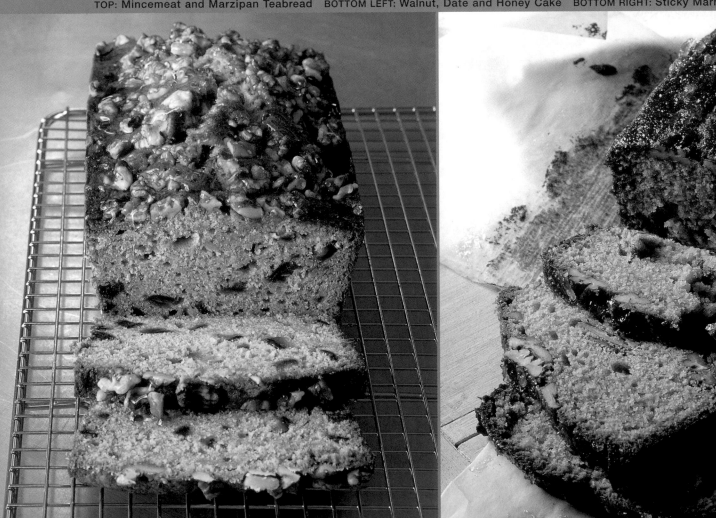

TOP LEFT: Spotted Dog   TOP RIGHT: Autumn Plum Crunch Cake   BOTTOM: Blackberry and Apple Loaf

Spotted Dog

Made in a flash, this is best cut into thick slices and spread with butter while still warm.

300g/10oz plain flour
½ tsp salt
1 tsp bicarbonate of soda
3 tbsp caster sugar
100g/4oz mixed dried fruit
1 egg, beaten
200ml/7fl oz buttermilk

Takes 50 minutes • Serves 10–12

1 Preheat the oven to 190°C/Gas 5/fan oven 170°C. Butter a 1kg/2lb loaf tin. Sift the flour, salt and bicarbonate of soda into a mixing bowl. Stir in the sugar, make a well in the centre and add the dried fruit, egg and buttermilk. Mix lightly and quickly into the flour for a soft dough.
2 Using floured hands, remove the dough from the bowl and knead very briefly. Then press the dough into the prepared tin. Bake for 35–40 minutes until the top is a dark golden colour and the loaf feels firm to the touch. Turn out and leave to cool. Serve thickly sliced and buttered.

• Per serving (for ten) 163 kcalories, protein 4g, carbohydrate 36g, fat 1g, saturated fat 0.3g, fibre 1g, added sugar 5g, salt 0.66g

Autumn Plum Crunch Cake

Moist and moreish, this rich cake has the most wonderful, crunchy sugarplum topping.

2 eggs, plus 1 egg yolk
140g/5oz butter, softened
140g/5oz golden caster sugar
140g/5oz self-raising flour
grated zest and juice of 1 orange
200g/8oz plums, stoned, half roughly
   chopped into pieces and half cut
   into wedges

FOR THE TOPPING
1½ tbsp fresh lemon juice
200g/8oz golden caster sugar
25g/1oz rough sugar pieces (or sugar cubes),
   roughly crushed

Takes 1½ hours • Serves 10

1 Preheat the oven to 160°C/Gas 3/fan oven 140°C. Butter and line the base of a 1kg/2lb loaf tin. Lightly beat the eggs and egg yolk with a pinch of salt.
2 Beat the butter and sugar in a bowl until light and fluffy. Pour in the eggs a little at a time, beating well after each addition. Fold in the flour with the orange zest and two tablespoons of the juice, then fold in the roughly chopped plums. Spoon into the prepared tin and scatter the plum wedges over. Bake for 50 minutes or until a skewer inserted comes out clean.
3 Cool for 10 minutes, then turn out on a wire rack. Mix the remaining orange juice with the lemon juice and caster sugar. Spoon over the cooling cake and sprinkle with the crushed sugar pieces. Cool until set.

• Per serving 327 kcalories, protein 3g, carbohydrate 51g, fat 14g, saturated fat 8g, fibre 1g, added sugar 38g, salt 0.45g

Blackberry and Apple Loaf

Try other fruits when in season – raspberries and tayberries would be good.

250g/9oz self-raising flour
175g/6oz butter
175g/6oz light muscovado sugar
½ tsp cinnamon
2 rounded tbsp demerara sugar
1 small eating apple, unpeeled, coarsely
   grated down to the core
2 large eggs, beaten
finely grated zest of 1 orange
1 tsp baking powder
225g/8oz blackberries

Takes 2 hours • Serves 10

1 Preheat the oven to 180°C/Gas 4/fan oven 160°C. Butter and line the base of a 1kg/2lb loaf tin. Rub the flour, butter and muscovado sugar together to make fine crumbs. Reserve 5 tablespoons of this mixture for the topping, and mix into it the cinnamon and demerara sugar. Set aside.
2 Mix the apple in with the eggs and the zest. Stir the baking powder into the rubbed-in mixture, then quickly and lightly stir in the egg mixture. Don't overmix.
3 Gently fold in three quarters of the berries. Spoon into the tin and level. Scatter the rest of the berries on top. Sprinkle over the topping and bake for 1 hour 20 minutes, testing with a skewer. After 50 minutes, cover loosely with foil. Leave in the tin for 30 minutes, then cool on a wire rack.

• Per serving 327 kcalories, protein 4g, carbohydrate 44g, fat 16g, saturated fat 10g, fibre 2g, added sugar 23g, salt 0.77g

Pumpkin and Ginger Teabread

The pumpkin adds a depth of flavour, a certain sweetness and a lusciously moist texture.

175g/6oz butter, melted
140g/5oz clear honey
1 large egg, beaten
250g/9oz raw peeled pumpkin or butternut squash, coarsely
grated (about 500g/1lb 2oz before peeling and seeding)
100g/4oz light muscovado sugar
350g/12oz self-raising flour
1 tbsp ground ginger
2 tbsp demerara sugar, plus extra for sprinkling (optional)

Takes 1½ hours • Serves 10

1 Preheat the oven to 180°C/Gas 4/fan oven 160°C. Butter and line the base and two long sides of a 1kg/2lb loaf tin with a strip of baking paper.
2 Mix the butter, honey and egg and stir in the pumpkin or squash. Then mix in the sugar, flour and ginger.
3 Pour into the prepared tin and sprinkle the top with the 2 tablespoons of demerara sugar. Bake for 50–60 minutes, until risen and golden brown. Leave in the tin for 5 minutes, then turn out and cool on a wire rack. Sprinkle more demerara sugar over the warm cake, if you wish. Serve thickly sliced and buttered.

• Per serving 351 kcalories, protein 4g, carbohydrate 52g, fat 15g, saturated fat 9g, fibre 1g, added sugar 24g, salt 0.69g

Peach and Cherry Teabread

Measuring the ingredients in a jug makes this really easy to throw together – though it does need to be started the day before baking.

300ml/½ pint ready-to-eat dried peaches, chopped
150ml/¼ pint undyed glacé cherries, halved
150ml/¼ pint raisins
300ml/½ pint light muscovado sugar
300ml/½ pint freshly made hot tea
1 egg, beaten
1 pint self-raising flour
1 tsp ground cinnamon
icing sugar, for dusting

Takes 1¾ hours, plus overnight soaking • Serves 12–14

1 Put the fruit and sugar in a bowl, pour over the tea and stir well. Cover with a tea towel and leave overnight for the fruit to plump up.
2 Preheat the oven to 160°C/Gas 3/fan oven 140°C. Butter and line the base of a 1kg/2lb loaf tin with greaseproof paper. Stir the egg into the steeped fruit mixture, then sift in the flour and cinnamon. Mix well, then turn into the prepared tin and smooth the top.
3 Bake for 1¼–1½ hours until the teabread is risen and golden. Test with a skewer (it should come out clean). Cool in the tin for 10 minutes, then turn out and cool on a wire rack. Dust the top with icing sugar.

• Per serving (for twelve) 297 kcalories, protein 4g, carbohydrate 71g, fat 1g, saturated fat 0.4g, fibre 3g, added sugar 31g, salt 0.31g

Banana and Walnut Tea Loaf

Sealed in a plastic food bag, this loaf will freeze for up to 3 months.

100g/4oz butter, softened
140g/5oz light muscovado sugar
2 eggs, lightly beaten
100g/4oz walnuts, chopped
2 ripe bananas, mashed
2 tbsp milk
225g/8oz self-raising flour

Takes 1¼ hours • Serves 12

1 Preheat the oven to 180°C/Gas 4/fan oven 160°C. Butter and line a 1kg/2lb loaf tin. Cream the butter and sugar, then add the eggs. Set aside 25g/1oz walnuts, then fold the rest into the creamed mixture with the bananas and milk. Fold in the flour. Spoon into the tin and sprinkle over the reserved walnuts.
2 Bake for 55–60 minutes until risen. Stand for 10 minutes, then turn out, remove the lining paper and cool.

• Per serving 267 kcalories, protein 4g, carbohydrate 33g, fat 14g, saturated fat 5g, fibre 1g, added sugar 12g, salt 0.37g

TOP LEFT: Pumpkin and Ginger Teabread   TOP RIGHT: Peach and Cherry Teabread   BOTTOM: Banana and Walnut Tea Loaf

TOP: Lemon and Violet Drizzle Cake   BOTTOM LEFT: Buttermilk Scones   BOTTOM RIGHT: Shortbread

Lemon and Violet Drizzle Cake

This all-in-one cake mixes easily, keeps for a week wrapped in foil, and freezes well.

100g/4oz butter, softened
175g/6oz self-raising flour
1 tsp baking powder
175g/6oz golden caster sugar
2 large eggs
6 tbsp milk
finely grated rind of 1 large lemon

FOR THE ICING AND DECORATION
juice of 1 large lemon (you need
    3 tablespoons)
100g/4oz golden caster sugar
crystallized violets and mimosa balls (or
    yellow sugar balls), to decorate

Takes 1 hour • Makes 15

1 Preheat the oven to 180°C/Gas 4/fan oven 160°C. Butter and line the base of a shallow oblong tin (about 18 × 28cm/7 × 11in) with baking paper. Tip all the cake ingredients into a large mixing bowl and beat for 2–3 minutes, until the mixture drops easily off the spoon.
2 Spoon the mixture into the prepared tin and smooth the surface with the back of a spoon. Bake for 30–40 minutes, until golden and firm to the touch. Meanwhile, make the icing: beat together the lemon juice and sugar, pour the mixture evenly over the cake while it is still hot, then leave to cool.
3 Cut the cake into 15 squares. Top each one with a crystallized violet and mimosa ball.

• Per square 175 kcalories, protein 2g, carbohydrate 29g, fat 7g, saturated fat 4g, fibre none, added sugar 19g, salt 0.3g

Buttermilk Scones

Buttermilk adds a lightness that milk alone won't give you.

350g/12oz self-raising flour
100g/4oz caster sugar
85g/3oz butter, cut into small pieces
about 175ml/6fl oz buttermilk or natural
    low-fat yogurt
whipped cream and strawberry jam, to serve

Takes 25 minutes • Makes 12

1 Preheat the oven to 200°C/Gas 6/fan oven 180°C. Mix together the flour and sugar in a bowl. Rub the butter in with your fingertips until the mixture resembles fine breadcrumbs. Make a well in the centre of the ingredients and tip in the buttermilk, all in one go, then mix lightly to form a soft dough.
2 Tip the dough out on to a lightly floured surface and knead briefly. Press the dough out to a 2.5cm/1in thickness, then stamp out 5cm/2in rounds with a cutter. Gather up the trimmings, knead again briefly and stamp out more rounds.
3 Transfer the buttermilk scones to a baking sheet, spaced a little apart, and bake for 12–15 minutes until risen and light golden. Leave the scones to cool on a wire rack and serve with the whipped cream and jam.

• Per scone 187 kcalories, protein 3g, carbohydrate 32g, fat 6g, saturated fat 4g, fibre 1g, added sugar 9g, salt 0.42g

Shortbread

Unrefined caster suga
slightly salted creamy butt_
best flavour.

150g/6oz plain flour
100g/4oz slightly salted butter, cut into
    pieces and softened
50g/2oz golden caster sugar
caster sugar, for sprinkling

Takes 50 minutes • Serves 8

1 Preheat the oven to 150°C/Gas 2/fan oven 130°C. Put the flour in a mixing bowl, add the butter and rub together to make fine crumbs. Stir in the sugar.
2 Work the mixture together until it forms a ball. Turn out on to a work surface and knead briefly until smooth. Roll and pat out on a very lightly floured surface to an 18cm/7in round. Smooth the surface with your hands. Carefully slide the dough on to an ungreased baking sheet and flute the edges. Mark the circle into eight triangles with a knife, not cutting all the way through. Prick the surface all over with a fork.
3 Bake for 30–35 minutes or until cooked. The shortbread should be very pale. While still warm, cut through the markings and sprinkle with caster sugar. Cool before eating.

• Per serving 186 kcalories, protein 2g, carbohydrate 22g, fat 10g, saturated fat 7g, fibre 1g, added sugar 8g, salt trace

arry Toffee Cake Squares

These cakes are truly scrumptious and so simple to whip together.

200g/8oz butter
200g/8oz golden syrup
300g/10oz self-raising flour
1 tsp salt
200g/8oz light muscovado sugar
3 eggs
2 tbsp milk
225g/8oz yellow marzipan
red and green food colouring
icing sugar, for dusting

Takes 1½ hours • Makes 24

1 Preheat the oven to 160°C/Gas 3/fan oven 140°C. Butter and line the base of a 32 × 23 × 2cm/13 × 9 × 1in Swiss roll tin. Gently melt the butter and syrup in a pan, stirring to combine. Cool for 15 minutes.
2 Sift the flour with the salt and stir in the muscovado sugar. Beat in the cooled syrup mixture. Beat the eggs and milk, and combine with the flour mixture until smooth. Pour into the tin and level with a spoon. Bake for 40–50 minutes until risen and firm in the centre. Leave in the tin to cool for 10 minutes. Tip on to a wire rack until cold.
3 Divide the marzipan into three; colour one piece with red and another with green colouring. Roll out and cut out star shapes. Cut the cake into 24 squares, top with marzipan stars and dust with icing sugar.

• Per square 217 kcalories, protein 3g, carbohydrate 34g, fat 9g, saturated fat 5g, fibre 1g, added sugar 22g, salt 0.37g

Simnel Muffins

Traditional simnel cake can be a bit too rich – instead, try these light little muffins with a gooey nugget of marzipan baked in the centre.

250g/9oz mixed dried fruit
grated zest and juice of 1 medium orange
175g/6oz butter, softened
175g/6oz golden caster sugar
3 eggs, beaten
300g/10oz self-raising flour
1 tsp mixed spice
½ tsp freshly grated nutmeg
5 tbsp milk
175g/6oz marzipan

FOR DECORATING
200g/8oz icing sugar
2 tbsp orange juice for mixing
sugar eggs or mini eggs

Takes 55 minutes • Makes 12

1 Tip the fruit into a bowl, add the zest and juice and microwave on Medium for 2 minutes (or leave to soak for 1 hour). Line 12 deep muffin tins with paper muffin cases. Preheat the oven to 180°C/Gas 4/fan oven 160°C. Beat together the butter, sugar, eggs, flour, spices and milk until light and fluffy, about 3–5 minutes. Stir the fruit in well.
2 Half fill the muffin cases with the mixture. Divide the marzipan into 12 equal pieces, roll into balls, then flatten with your thumb. Put one into each muffin case and spoon the rest of the mixture over. Bake for 25–30 minutes, until risen, golden and firm to the touch.
3 Beat together the icing sugar and orange juice to make icing thick enough to coat the back of a wooden spoon. Drizzle over the cooled muffins and top with a cluster of eggs.

• Per muffin 465 kcalories, protein 6g, carbohydrate 79g, fat 17g, saturated fat 8g, fibre 2g, added sugar 42g, salt 0.61g

Festive Mince Pies

Top with marzipan stars or meringue before baking to vary this festive recipe.

FOR THE PASTRY
200g/8oz plain flour
50g/2oz ground almonds
140g/5oz butter, chopped into small pieces
grated rind of 1 orange
50g/2oz caster sugar
1 egg yolk

FOR THE FILLING AND DECORATION
200g/8oz mincemeat
1 egg white, lightly whisked
caster sugar, for dusting

Takes 40 minutes, plus 30 minutes chilling time • Makes 18

1 Preheat the oven to 200°C/Gas 6/fan oven 190°C. Whizz the flour, almonds, butter, orange rind and sugar into crumbs. Add the egg yolk and a teaspoon of cold water and pulse until it forms a dough. Wrap in plastic film and chill for 30 minutes.
2 Roll out the dough thinly and stamp out eighteen 7.5cm/3in rounds. Use to line bun tins. Put a heaped teaspoon of mincemeat in each pastry case. Stamp out nine more pastry rounds. Cut out festive shapes from the centre of each round.
3 Cover the pies with the shapes and pastry rounds with the centres removed. Brush the tops with egg white and dust lightly with caster sugar. Bake for 12–15 minutes until the pastry is crisp and golden. Cool in the tins for 5 minutes, then cool on a wire rack.

• Per mince pie 164 kcalories, protein 2g, carbohydrate 20g, fat 9g, saturated fat 5g, fibre 1g, added sugar 9g, salt 0.17g

TOP: Starry Toffee Cake Squares   BOTTOM LEFT: Simnel Muffins   BOTTOM RIGHT: Festive Mince Pies

TOP LEFT: Blueberry and Lemon Friands TOP RIGHT: Cinnamon and Lemon Tarts with Berries   BOTTOM: Blackberry Fairy Cakes

Blueberry and Lemon Friands

These light-as-air cakes are sold in every self-respecting coffee shop in Sydney – try them and you too will be hooked.

100g/4oz unsalted butter
125g/4½oz icing sugar, plus extra for dusting
25g/1oz plain flour
85g/3oz ground almonds
3 egg whites
grated rind of 1 unwaxed lemon
85g/3oz blueberries

Takes 40 minutes • Serves 6

1 Preheat the oven to 200°C/Gas 6/fan oven 180°C. Generously butter six non-stick friand or muffin tins. Melt the butter and set aside to cool.
2 Sift the icing sugar and flour into a bowl. Add the almonds and mix everything between your fingers. Whisk the egg whites in another bowl until they form a light, floppy foam. Make a well in the centre of the dry ingredients, tip in the egg whites and lemon rind, then lightly stir in the butter to form a soft batter.
3 Divide the batter among the tins (a large serving spoon is perfect for this job). Sprinkle a handful of blueberries over each cake and bake for 15–20 minutes until just firm to the touch and golden brown. Cool in the tins for 5 minutes, then turn out and cool on a wire rack. To serve, dust lightly with icing sugar.

• Per friand 316 kcalories, protein 5g, carbohydrate 27g, fat 22g, saturated fat 9g, fibre 1g, added sugar 22g, salt 0.09g

Cinnamon and Lemon Tarts with Berries

These light and luscious tarts are a cross between the traditional Yorkshire curd tart and the lemony Portuguese version.

375g pack ready-rolled puff pastry
200g pack light soft cheese
grated rind of ½ lemon
100g/4oz caster sugar
2 egg yolks
1 tbsp plain flour

TO SERVE
100g/4oz each of raspberries and blueberries
cinnamon and icing sugar, for dusting
142ml carton single cream (optional)

Takes 45 minutes • Serves 6

1 Preheat the oven to 200°C/Gas 6/fan oven 180°C. Unwrap the pastry, then roll it out so you can stamp out 12 rounds using an 7.5cm/3in fluted cutter. Line 12 bun tins with the pastry and prick them with a fork all over (this is essential to stop the pastry rising up in the centre and tipping the filling out).
2 Beat the cheese until soft, then beat in the lemon rind, sugar and egg yolks. Sift in the flour and mix well. Pour into the pastry cases, almost to the top.
3 Bake the tarts for 12–15 minutes, until the pastry is golden and the filling lightly coloured. Carefully remove from the tins and leave aside on a rack to cool. To serve, place 2 tarts on a plate, scatter the berries over, dust lightly with cinnamon and icing sugar, then drizzle with a little cream, if you like.

• Per serving 411 kcalories, protein 8g, carbohydrate 48g, fat 22g, saturated fat 1g, fibre 1g, added sugar 19g, salt 0.76g

Blackberry Fairy Cakes

These little cakes are easy – fun to make and decorate with the kids.

150ml carton low-fat natural yogurt (rinse the pot and use as a measure)
1 pot of caster sugar
1 pot of sunflower oil
2 eggs
2 pots of self-raising flour
250g punnet blackberries, plus extra for decorating
finely grated rind of 1 orange

FOR THE ICING AND DECORATION
1 pot of icing sugar, plus extra for dusting
1 tbsp orange juice
orange food colouring (optional)
50g bar dark chocolate, melted

Takes 35 minutes • Makes 18

1 Preheat the oven to 190°C/Gas 5/fan oven 180°C. Line two bun tins with 18 paper cases. Tip the yogurt, sugar, oil and eggs into a bowl and whisk until combined. Tip in the flour, three quarters of the blackberries and half the orange rind; fold into the mixture with a large metal spoon – don't overwork.
2 Fill each bun case three-quarters full with the mixture and bake for 20–25 minutes until the cakes are risen and golden. Turn out and cool on a wire rack.
3 Sift the icing sugar into a bowl, add the remaining orange rind and the orange juice to make a smooth icing. Stir in a few drops of orange food colouring, if you like. Using a teaspoon, spoon a little icing on top of each cooled cake. Decorate with extra blackberries, or drizzled melted chocolate.

• Per fairy cake 177 kcalories, protein 3g, carbohydrate 29g, fat 7g, saturated fat 2g, fibre 1g, added sugar 18g, salt 0.15g

Apricot Crumb Squares

Ideal with a cup of tea at home, or to enjoy at your next picnic.

FOR THE TOPPING
175g/6oz plain flour
140g/5oz light muscovado sugar
140g/5oz butter, softened
1 tsp ground cinnamon
½ tsp salt

FOR THE CAKE
175g/6oz butter, softened
200g/8oz golden caster sugar
3 large eggs
175g/6oz plain flour
1 tsp baking powder
2–3 tbsp milk
8 fresh apricots (or canned in natural juice),
    quartered
icing sugar, for dusting

Takes 1¼ hours • Makes 16

1 Preheat oven to 180ºC/Gas 4/fan oven 160ºC, and butter a shallow 23cm/9in square cake tin. Put the five topping ingredients in a food processor and blend to make a sticky crumble.
2 In a separate bowl, blend the butter, sugar, eggs, flour and baking powder using an electric hand whisk or wooden spoon, gradually adding enough milk to make a creamy mixture that drops from a spoon. Spread in the tin and scatter with apricots. Top with the crumble and press down.
3 Bake for 45–50 minutes until golden and a skewer inserted comes out clean. Cool in the tin, cut into 16 squares and dust with icing sugar.

• Per square 332 kcalories, protein 4g, carbohydrate 42g, fat 18g, saturated fat 11g, fibre 1g, added sugar 22g, salt 0.52g

Blackcurrant Crumble Squares

These moist but crumbly squares are best eaten on the day, but will freeze for up to 3 months.

115g/4oz butter, softened
175g/6oz caster sugar
1 egg
280g/10oz self-raising flour
125ml/4fl oz milk
200g/8oz fresh blackcurrants, destalked

FOR THE CRUMBLE
115g/4oz caster sugar
85g/3oz plain flour
finely grated rind of 1 lemon
50g/2oz butter

Takes 1 hour • Makes 12

1 Preheat the oven to 180ºC/Gas 4/fan oven 160ºC. Butter a 28 × 18cm/12 × 7in oblong cake tin and line with baking paper. (You could also use a 23cm/9in square tin or a 25cm/10in round tin.)
2 Beat the butter and sugar in a large bowl with an electric hand whisk until the mixture is pale and fluffy. Whisk in the egg, then carefully fold in the flour and milk until thoroughly combined. Spoon into the tin and spread evenly. Sprinkle over the blackcurrants.
3 Mix together the sugar, flour and lemon rind. Rub in the butter until the mixture is crumbly, then sprinkle on top of the squares. Bake for 45 minutes until the topping is golden and the blackcurrants start to burst through; leave to cool in the tin. When cool, lift the cake out, and cut into squares.

• Per square 315 kcalories, protein 4g, carbohydrate 50g, fat 13g, saturated fat 8g, fibre 2g, added sugar 25g, salt 0.29g

Sticky Apricot and Almond Bars

Absolutely delicious with a cup of tea, these bars are also dairy free.

100g/4oz whole blanched almonds
250g/9oz ready-to-eat dried apricots
85g/3oz porridge oats
85g/3oz plain flour
1 tsp baking powder
250ml/9fl oz jar apple sauce
2 tbsp sunflower oil
1 egg, beaten
2 tbsp apricot jam or conserve

Takes 55 minutes • Makes 15

1 Preheat the oven to 180ºC/Gas 4/fan oven 160ºC. Oil and line the base of an 18cm/7in square tin. Roughly chop the almonds into fairly large chunks to give a good texture and finely chop the apricots to give a stickiness to the bars.
2 Put all the dry ingredients in a large bowl. Combine the apple sauce, oil and egg, and add to the dry ingredients. Mix until everything is combined and gooey. Spoon the mixture into the prepared tin, level the surface and bake for 40 minutes or until firm and springy to the touch.
3 Allow to cool in the tin for a couple of minutes, then loosen the sides and turn out on to a wire rack. Warm the apricot jam for 2–3 minutes. Then brush over the surface of the cooled bars, cut into 15 slices and enjoy.

• Per bar 145 kcalories, protein 4g, carbohydrate 19g, fat 6g, saturated fat 1g, fibre 2g, added sugar 3g, salt 0.13g

TOP LEFT: Apricot Crumb Squares   TOP RIGHT: Blackcurrant Crumble Squares   BOTTOM: Sticky Apricot and Almond Bars

TOP: Margaret's Caramel Nut Squares   BOTTOM LEFT: Sunshine Bars   BOTTOM RIGHT: Raspberry and Pine Nut Bars

Margaret's Caramel Nut Squares

Margaret Fineran, who created this recipe, was a chef at the American Embassy in London.

FOR THE PASTRY
175g/6oz plain flour
50g/2oz icing sugar
85g/3oz cold butter, cut into cubes
¼ tsp vanilla extract
1 small egg, beaten

FOR THE FILLING
85g/3oz granulated sugar
175g/6oz clear honey
50g/2oz butter
284ml carton double cream
100g/4oz pecan nuts, toasted
100g/4oz flaked almonds, toasted
100g/4oz whole hazelnuts, toasted
100g/4oz pistachios, unsalted, toasted
50g/2oz dried cranberries
whipped cream, to serve

Takes 1¼ hours, plus 4 hours freezing • Makes 9

1 Preheat the oven to 180°C/Gas 4/fan oven 160°C. Whizz together the flour, icing sugar and butter. Add the vanilla and beaten egg and pulse until the pastry comes together. Chill, wrapped in cling film, for 30 minutes.
2 Roll the pastry out on a lightly floured surface and use to line a 23cm/9in square tin. Pre-bake for 7 minutes. Bring the sugar and honey to the boil without stirring. In a separate pan, heat the butter with the cream until hot. When the sugar mixture is boiling, pour in the hot cream and butter, and simmer, stirring, for 2–3 minutes.
3 Mix in the nuts and cranberries. Spoon into the hot pastry case. Return to the oven for 7 minutes. Remove, cool, then cover and freeze for 3–4 hours. Cut into squares, thaw for 30 minutes, and serve with the cream.

• Per square 743 kcalories, protein 10g, carbohydrate 54g, fat 55g, saturated fat 19g, fibre 3g, added sugar 31g, salt 0.35g

Sunshine Bars

The solution for any picnic or open-air event – packed with good things, and easy to make.

100g/4oz dried ready-to-eat tropical medley or other mixed dried fruits
100g/4oz porridge oats
50g/2oz puffed rice cereal, such as Rice Krispies
85g/3oz desiccated coconut
50g/2oz blanched hazelnuts or shelled peanuts or other nuts
50g/2oz sunflower, sesame or pumpkin seeds
100g/4oz light muscovado sugar
125ml/4fl oz golden syrup
100g/4oz butter, cut into pieces

Takes 25 minutes, plus 2 hours setting time • Makes 18

1 Chop the tropical medley into pieces using kitchen scissors. Tip the oats, cereal, coconut and fruit into a large bowl and mix well. Put the hazelnuts and sunflower, sesame or pumpkin seeds in a large frying pan with no oil and, over a moderate heat, stir until they are lightly toasted. Leave to cool a little then tip into the bowl and mix.
2 Put the sugar, syrup and butter in a small pan and heat gently, stirring with a wooden spoon until melted, then simmer for 2 minutes until slightly thicker and syrupy. Quickly stir the syrup into the dry ingredients, mixing until well blended with no dry patches.
3 Quickly tip into a 20cm/8in square tin and press down with the back of a spoon to even out the surface. Leave to cool and set – about 2 hours. Cut the mixture into 18 bars.

• Per bar 190 kcalories, protein 2g, carbohydrate 22g, fat 11g, saturated fat 6g, fibre 2g, added sugar 11g, salt 0.26g

Raspberry and Pine Nut Bars

This easy-mix bar is the perfect bake – all you do is weigh, mix and scatter everything into the tin.

200g/8oz plain flour
200g/8oz porridge oats
250g pack butter, cut into small pieces and softened
175g/6oz light muscovado sugar
finely grated zest of 1 lemon
100g pack pine nuts
250g/9oz raspberries

Takes 1 hour • Makes 12

1 Preheat the oven to 190°C/Gas 5/fan oven 170°C. Butter a shallow 23cm/9in square tin. Tip the flour, oats and butter into a mixing bowl and work together with your fingers to make coarse crumbs. Mix in the sugar, lemon zest and three quarters of the pine nuts using your hands, then press the mixture together well so it forms large sticky clumps.
2 Drop about two thirds of the oat mixture into the tin, spread it out and press down very lightly – don't pack it too firmly. Scatter the raspberries on top, sprinkle the rest of the oat mixture over, then the rest of the pine nuts and press everything down lightly.
3 Bake for 35–40 minutes until pale golden on top. Cut into 12 bars with a sharp knife while still warm, then leave to cool in the tin before removing.

• Per bar 391 kcalories, protein 6g, carbohydrate 40g, fat 24g, saturated fat 12g, fibre 3g, added sugar 15g, salt 0.41g

Classic Flapjacks

By using different-sized tins and varying the cooking time, this recipe can be adapted to suit all tastes.

175g/6oz butter, cut into pieces
140g/5oz golden syrup
50g/2oz light muscovado sugar
250g/9oz oats

Takes 35 minutes • Makes 12

1 Preheat the oven to 180°C/Gas 4/fan oven 160°C. Line the base of a shallow 23cm/9in square tin with a sheet of baking paper if the tin is not non-stick. (Use a 20cm/8in square tin for a thicker, chewier flapjack). Put the butter, syrup and sugar in a medium pan. Stir over a low heat until the butter has melted and the sugar has dissolved. Remove from the heat and stir in the oats.
2 Press the mixture into the tin. Bake for 20–25 minutes, until golden brown on top (follow the longer cooking time for a crispier flapjack). Allow to cool in the tin for 5 minutes then mark into bars or squares with the back of a knife while still warm. Cool in the tin completely before cutting and removing – this prevents the flapjack from breaking up.

• Per flapjack 242 kcalories, protein 3g, carbohydrate 29g, fat 14g, saturated fat 8g, fibre 1g, added sugar 13g, salt 0.38g

Apple and Apricot Treacle Tart Bars

This bar is deservedly a *Good Food* favourite.

FOR THE SHORTBREAD BASE
100g/4oz butter, softened
50g/2oz light muscovado sugar
175g/6oz plain flour

FOR THE FRUIT FILLING
450g/1lb (about 2 medium) cooking apples, cored, peeled and chopped
25g/1oz caster sugar
175g/6oz ready-to-eat dried apricots, halved

FOR THE TREACLE TART TOPPING
grated rind of 1 orange, plus 1 tbsp juice
200g/8oz golden syrup
8 tbsp porridge oats

Takes 1½ hours • Makes 12

1 Preheat the oven to 160°C/Gas 3/fan oven 140°C. Beat the butter and sugar until fluffy. Stir in the flour until smooth. Tip the mixture into a 23cm/9in square tin and press down on the base. Lightly prick with a fork and bake for 15 minutes. Set aside to cool.
2 Put the apples in a pan with the sugar. Cover loosely and cook over a low heat, stirring occasionally, for about 10 minutes or until the apples are pulpy. Add the apricots and cook gently, uncovered, for a further 15 minutes, stirring. Whizz to a purée.
3 Increase the oven heat to 190°C/Gas 5/fan oven 170°C. Spread the filling over the base. Combine the topping ingredients until well mixed. Spread over the filling. Return to the oven for a further 20–30 minutes, until set and pale golden. Cool in the tin before cutting.

• Per bar 251 kcalories, protein 3g, carbohydrate 45g, fat 8g, saturated fat 5g, fibre 3g, added sugar 20g, salt 0.29g

Golden Orange and Walnut Flapjacks

This is one of those great treats that you can just sling together and bake.

250g/9oz unsalted butter, chopped into pieces
250g/9oz golden caster sugar
175g/6oz golden syrup
425g/15oz porridge oats
50g/2oz walnut pieces
finely grated zest of 1 large orange
3 tbsp fine-cut orange marmalade

Takes 55 minutes • Makes 12

1 Preheat the oven to 180°C/Gas 4/fan oven 160°C, and generously butter a 28 × 18cm/12 × 7in shallow baking tin. Melt the butter, sugar and syrup over a medium heat, stirring all the time. Take off the heat and stir in the oats, walnuts and orange zest. The mixture should be quite soft.
2 Tip the mixture into the tin and level it off. Bake for around 30 minutes, until the edges are golden brown but the centre is still a little soft. Remove from the oven and mark into 12 pieces while it is still warm, cutting halfway through with a knife. Leave to cool.
3 Heat the marmalade with 1 tablespoon of water until it becomes syrupy. Brush this glaze over the flapjack mixture and leave to cool before cutting into 12 pieces. They will keep in an airtight tin for up to a week.

• Per flapjack 455 kcalories, protein 7g, carbohydrate 60g, fat 22g, saturated fat 12g, fibre 4g, added sugar 36g, salt 0.12g

TOP: Classic Flapjacks   BOTTOM LEFT: Apple and Apricot Treacle Tart Bars   BOTTOM RIGHT: Golden Orange and Walnut Flapjacks

TOP LEFT: Breakfast Munching Muffins   TOP RIGHT: Banana and Walnut Muffins   BOTTOM: Fruitburst Muffins

Breakfast Munching Muffins

Containing marmalade, muesli, orange juice and dried apricots, these muffins make a wonderful start to your day.

100g/4oz ready-to-eat dried apricots, chopped
4 tbsp orange juice
2 large eggs
142ml carton soured cream
100ml/3½fl oz sunflower oil
85g/3oz golden caster sugar
300g/10oz self-raising flour, sifted
1 tsp baking powder
50g/2oz crunchy muesli
12 heaped tsp marmalade

FOR THE TOPPING
50g/2oz light muscovado sugar
2 tbsp sunflower oil
50g/2oz crunchy muesli

Takes 1 hour, plus 20 minutes soaking • Makes 12

1 Preheat the oven to 190°C/Gas 5/fan oven 170°C. Soak the apricots in the orange juice for 20 minutes or so to plump them up.
2 Beat the eggs in a medium bowl, then mix in the soured cream, oil and sugar. Stir into the apricot mixture. Put the flour, baking powder and muesli in a large bowl, then gently stir in the apricot mixture. Combine thoroughly but quickly – don't overmix or the muffins will be tough.
3 Spoon the mixture into 12 muffin cases (the large paper cases) in a muffin tray. Dip your thumb into a little flour, then make a fairly deep thumbprint in each muffin. Fill each with a heaped teaspoon of marmalade.
4 Combine the topping ingredients and sprinkle over the top of the muffins. Bake for 25–30 minutes, until well risen and golden.

• Per muffin 322 kcalories, protein 5g, carbohydrate 48g, fat 14g, saturated fat 3g, fibre 2g, added sugar 19g, salt 0.51g

Banana and Walnut Muffins

These deliciously moist muffins use soya flour, and also contain wholemeal flour and sunflower oil to keep them 'heart friendly'.

100g/4oz wholemeal flour
25g/1oz soya flour
3 tbsp caster sugar
2 tsp baking powder
85g/3oz walnuts, roughly chopped
1 egg, beaten
50ml/2fl oz sweetened soya milk
50ml/2fl oz sunflower oil
2 large bananas, about 200g/8oz when peeled, roughly chopped

FOR THE DECORATION
3 tbsp apricot jam
50g/2oz chopped walnuts

Takes 40 minutes • Makes 6

1 Preheat the oven to 200°C/Gas 6/fan oven 180°C. Line six muffin tins with paper muffin cases or oil the tins. Mix together the first five ingredients in a bowl with a pinch of salt and make a well in the centre.
2 In another bowl, mix together the egg, soya milk and oil. Pour this mixture into the flour and stir until just blended. Gently stir in the bananas. Spoon the mixture into the muffin cases, filling them to about two-thirds full. Bake for 25–30 minutes, until a skewer inserted comes out clean. Transfer the muffins to a wire rack.
3 Gently heat the jam and brush it on top of the muffins. Sprinkle over the walnuts and serve warm.

• Per muffin 425 kcalories, protein 9g, carbohydrate 41g, fat 26g, saturated fat 3g, fibre 3g, added sugar 17g, salt 0.89g

Fruitburst Muffins

These low-fat muffins are great to grab when you don't have time to sit down to breakfast.

225g/8oz plain flour
2 tsp baking powder
2 large eggs
50g/2oz butter, melted
175ml/6fl oz skimmed milk
100ml/3½fl oz clear honey
140g/5oz fresh blueberries
85g/3oz dried cranberries
140g/5oz seedless raisins
140g/5oz dried apricots, chopped
1 tsp grated orange zest
1 tsp ground cinnamon

Takes 50 minutes • Makes 12

1 Preheat the oven to 200°C/Gas 6/fan oven 180°C, and very lightly butter a 12-hole muffin tin. Sift the flour and baking powder into a bowl. In another bowl, lightly beat the eggs, then stir in the melted butter, milk and honey.
2 Add the egg mixture to the flour mixture with the remaining ingredients. Combine quickly without overworking (it's fine if there are some lumps left – you want it gloopy rather than fluid). Spoon the mixture into the muffin tin. Bake for 20–25 minutes until well risen and pale golden on top.
3 Leave in the tin for a few minutes before turning out. When cool, they'll keep in an airtight tin for two days. They can also be frozen for up to one month.

• Per muffin 243 kcalories, protein 5g, carbohydrate 41g, fat 8g, saturated fat 3g, fibre 2g, added sugar 6g, salt 0.59g

Triple Chocolate Chunk Muffins

No chance of keeping these for more than a day – definitely a muffin to eat while still warm and the chocolate is gooey.

250g/9oz plain flour
25g/1oz cocoa powder
2 tsp baking powder
½ tsp bicarbonate of soda
85g/3oz each dark and white chocolate, broken into chunks
100g/4oz milk chocolate, broken into chunks
2 eggs, beaten
284ml carton soured cream
85g/3oz light muscovado sugar
85g/3oz butter, melted

Takes 35 minutes • Makes 11

1 Preheat the oven to 200°C/Gas 6/fan oven 180°C. Butter 11 holes of a muffin tin. In a large bowl, combine the flour, cocoa, baking powder, bicarbonate of soda and chocolate. In a separate bowl, mix together the eggs, soured cream, sugar and butter.
2 Add the soured cream mixture to the flour mixture and stir until just combined and the mixture is fairly stiff, but don't overmix. Spoon the mixture into the holes to generously fill.
3 Bake for 20 minutes until well risen. Leave in the tins for about 15 minutes as the mixture is quite tender. Remove from the tins and cool on a wire rack.

• Per muffin 325 kcalories, protein 6g, carbohydrate 37g, fat 18g, saturated fat 11g, fibre 1g, added sugar 17g, salt 0.72g

Berry Buttermilk Muffins

Although best made with fresh blueberries, you can make these muffins using the same amount of frozen berries.

400g/14oz plain flour
175g/6oz caster sugar
1 tbsp baking powder
finely grated rind of 1 lemon
½ tsp salt
284ml carton buttermilk
2 eggs, beaten
85g/3oz butter, melted
250g/9oz fresh or frozen blueberries, or mixed summer fruits, used straight from frozen

Takes 40 minutes • Makes 12

1 Preheat the oven to 200°C/Gas 6/fan oven 180°C. Butter a 12-hole muffin tin. In a large bowl, combine the flour, sugar, baking powder, lemon rind and salt. In a separate bowl, mix together the buttermilk, eggs and butter.
2 Make a well in the centre of the dry ingredients and pour in the buttermilk mixture. Stir until the ingredients are just combined and the mixture is quite stiff, but don't overmix. Lightly fold in the berries, then spoon the mixture into the tins to fill generously.
3 Bake for about 25 minutes until risen and pale golden on top. Leave to cool in the tin for about 5 minutes before turning out on to a wire rack, as the muffins are quite delicate when hot.

• Per muffin 253 kcalories, protein 5g, carbohydrate 44g, fat 7g, saturated fat 4g, fibre 1g, added sugar 15g, salt 0.91g

Strawberry Cheesecake Muffins

Each muffin hides a surprise filling of fresh fruit and creamy cheese.

350g/12oz plain flour
1½ tbsp baking powder
140g/5oz caster sugar
finely grated rind of 2 medium oranges
½ tsp salt
2 eggs
250ml/9fl oz milk
85g/3oz butter, melted

FOR THE FILLING
175g/6oz half-fat soft cheese
3 tbsp caster sugar
6 small strawberries, halved

Takes 40 minutes • Makes 12

1 Preheat the oven to 200°C/Gas 6/fan oven 180°C. Line a muffin tin with 12 paper cases. Sift the flour and baking powder into a large bowl, then stir in the sugar, orange rind and salt. Beat the eggs and milk together in a jug or bowl, then stir in the butter and gently mix into the dry ingredients to make a loose, slightly lumpy mixture. Do not overmix or the muffins will be tough.
2 Mix together the soft cheese and sugar for the filling. Half-fill the paper cases with the muffin mixture, then push half a strawberry into each. Top with a teaspoon of sweet cheese, then spoon over the remaining muffin mixture to cover and fill the muffin cases.
3 Bake for 15 minutes until well risen and golden on top. Remove from the tin and allow to cool completely on a wire rack.

• Per muffin 293 kcalories, protein 6g, carbohydrate 42g, fat 12g, saturated fat 5g, fibre 1g, added sugar 18g, salt 1.03g

TOP LEFT: **Triple Chocolate Chunk Muffins**   TOP RIGHT: **Berry Buttermilk Muffins**   BOTTOM: **Strawberry Cheesecake Muffins**

TOP: Cranberry and Poppy Seed Muffins   BOTTOM LEFT: Squash, Cinnamon and Pumpkin Seed Muffins   BOTTOM RIGHT: Oat and Honey Muffins

Cranberry and Poppy Seed Muffins

Serve these muffins warm, drizzled with a generous helping of maple syrup.

100g/4oz unsalted butter
284ml carton soured cream
2 large free-range eggs
1 tsp vanilla extract
280g/10oz plain flour
2 tsp baking powder
1 tsp bicarbonate of soda
½ tsp salt
200g/8oz golden caster sugar
4 tsp poppy seeds
140g/5oz fresh or frozen cranberries (thawed)
maple syrup, to serve

Takes 50 minutes • Makes 10

1 Preheat the oven to 190°C/Gas 5/fan oven 170°C. Line 10 muffin tins with large discs of very loosely scrunched and lightly oiled greaseproof paper (they should come up the sides of the tin so they become paper muffin cases). Melt the butter, leave to cool for a minute or two, then beat in the soured cream, followed by the eggs and the vanilla extract.
2 In another bowl, mix the flour, baking powder, bicarbonate of soda, salt, sugar and poppy seeds together. Stir this into the soured cream mixture along with the cranberries.
3 Fill each of the prepared muffin cases generously with the mixture and bake for 20–25 minutes. Test with a skewer – it should pull out clean if muffins are done. Lift on to a cooling rack, spoon over some maple syrup and eat while they are still warm.

• Per muffin 340 kcalories, protein 6g, carbohydrate 45g, fat 16g, saturated fat 9g, fibre 1g, added sugar 21g, salt 0.98g

Squash, Cinnamon and Pumpkin Seed Muffins

This mixture will also divide between a 12-hole muffin tin for smaller muffins.

280g/10oz plain flour
1 tbsp baking powder
2 tsp ground cinnamon
1 tsp salt
3 eggs
175ml/6fl oz milk
85g/3oz butter, melted
175g/6oz light muscovado sugar
350g/12oz peeled, grated butternut squash
small handful of green pumpkin seeds

Takes 50 minutes • Makes 9

1 Preheat the oven to 200°C/Gas 6/fan oven 180°C. Lightly butter a 9-hole muffin tin or line with paper muffin cases. Sift together the flour, baking powder, cinnamon and salt and put aside.
2 In a large bowl, mix the eggs, milk and butter. Add the sugar and beat well. Add the flour mixture and beat to give a lumpy batter. Stir in the grated squash.
3 Fill the nine holes of the muffin tin (or paper cases) to the top with the mixture, sprinkle the pumpkin seeds on top. Bake for 20–25 minutes until well risen and firm to the touch. Cool slightly in the tin, turn out and cool on a wire rack.

• Per muffin 317 kcalories, protein 7g, carbohydrate 50g, fat 12g, saturated fat 6g, fibre 2g, added sugar 20g, salt 1.52g

Oat and Honey Muffins

A fluffy light muffin, ideal for lunch alongside big chunks of cheese, or as a snack spread with butter and drizzled with extra honey.

250g/9oz plain flour
85g/3oz porridge oats
1 tbsp baking powder
½ tsp cinnamon
½ tsp salt
85g/3oz raisins
2 eggs, beaten
200ml/7fl oz milk
75ml/2½fl oz vegetable oil
50g/2oz light muscovado sugar
5 tbsp clear honey

Takes 40 minutes • Makes 8

1 Preheat the oven to 200°C/Gas 6/fan oven 180°C. Butter 8 holes of a muffin tin. In a large bowl, combine the flour, oats, baking powder, cinnamon, salt and raisins. In a separate bowl, mix together the eggs, milk, oil, sugar and honey. Stir this into the flour mixture until just combined, but don't overmix – the mixture should be quite runny.
2 Spoon the mixture into the holes to fill. Bake for 20–25 minutes. Leave in the tin for a few minutes. Leave in the tin for a few minutes, then turn out on to a wire rack to cool.

• Per muffin 349 kcalories, protein 7g, carbohydrate 57g, fat 12g, saturated fat 2g, fibre 2g, added sugar 16g, salt 1.18g

Coconut and Cashew Cookies

Creamed coconut adds richness and flavour to these American-style cookies.

140g/5oz unsalted cashews, toasted
85g/3oz creamed coconut, grated
175g/6oz plain flour
½ tsp baking powder
140g/5oz butter, softened
125g/4½oz dark muscovado sugar
1 tbsp ground ginger
1 egg

Takes 35 minutes • Makes 14–16

1 Preheat the oven to 180°C/Gas 4/fan oven 160°C. Split some cashews in half; leave the rest whole. Mix with the coconut and set aside.
2 Blend the remaining ingredients in a food processor to make a smooth, stiff consistency. Set aside four tablespoonfuls of the nut mixture; stir the rest into the flour mixture.
3 Put 14–16 heaped tablespoons of the mixture in mounds, well apart, on buttered baking sheets. Flatten slightly with your fingers. Sprinkle with the reserved nut mixture and bake for 10–12 minutes until golden and set at the edges. Leave for a few minutes, then cool on a rack. The cookies will stay fresh for up to 1 week in an airtight container.

• Per cookie (for fourteen) 262 kcalories, protein 4g, carbohydrate 22g, fat 18g, saturated fat 9g, fibre 2g, added sugar 9g, salt 0.34g

Smarties Cookies

Make these treats for your next birthday party – for kids or adults.

100g/4oz butter, softened
100g/4oz light muscovado sugar
1 tbsp golden syrup
150g/6oz self-raising flour
85g/3oz Smarties (about 3 tubes)

Takes 20 minutes • Makes 14

1 Preheat the oven to 180°C/Gas 4/fan oven 160°C. Beat the butter and sugar in a bowl until light and creamy, then beat in the syrup.
2 Work in half the flour. Stir in the Smarties with the remaining flour and work the dough together with your fingers. Divide into 14 balls. Place them well apart on baking sheets. Do not flatten them.
3 Bake for 12 minutes until pale golden at the edges. Cool on a wire rack. These cookies will keep for up to 4 days in an airtight tin.

• Per cookie 167 kcalories, protein 2g, carbohydrate 23g, fat 8g, saturated fat 5g, fibre trace, added sugar 13g, salt 0.3g

Angela's All-American Chocolate Chunk Cookies

There are no clever techniques involved with Angela Nilsen's irresistible cookies – just measure, mix, stir and bake.

300g/11oz dark chocolate (about 55% cocoa solids), broken into small chunks
100g bar milk chocolate, broken into small chunks
100g/4oz light muscovado sugar
85g/3oz butter, softened
100g/4oz crunchy peanut butter
1 medium egg
½ tsp vanilla extract
100g/4oz self-raising flour
100g/4oz large salted roasted peanuts

Takes 50 minutes • Makes 12

1 Preheat the oven to 180°C/Gas 4/fan oven 160°C. Melt 100g/4oz of the dark chocolate chunks. Stir, then tip in the sugar, butter, peanut butter, egg and vanilla and beat with a wooden spoon until well mixed. Stir in the flour, all the milk chocolate chunks, the nuts and half the remaining dark chocolate chunks. The mixture will feel quite soft.
2 Drop big spoonfuls in 12 piles on to 2 or 3 baking sheets, leaving room for them to spread. Stick 2–3 pieces of the remaining dark chocolate chunks into each cookie.
3 Bake for 10–12 minutes until they are tinged very slightly darker around the edges. They will be soft in the middle, but will crisp up as they cool. Cook for longer and you'll have crisper cookies. Leave to cool for a few minutes, then transfer to a wire rack.

• Per cookie 381 kcalories, protein 7g, carbohydrate 36g, fat 24g, saturated fat 10g, fibre 2g, added sugar 27g, salt 0.42g

TOP: Smarties Cookies   BOTTOM LEFT: Coconut and Cashew Cookies   BOTTOM RIGHT: Angela's All-American Chocolate Chunk Cookies

TOP LEFT: Oaty Cherry Cookies   TOP RIGHT: Anzac Biscuits   BOTTOM: Lemon and Sultana Cookies

Oaty Cherry Cookies

Store any uncooked mixture in the fridge for up to 1 week, or freeze on the day for up to 6 months, defrosting before baking.

250g/9oz butter, softened
50g/2oz caster sugar
100g/3½oz light muscovado sugar
150g/5½oz self-raising flour
225g/8oz porridge oats
200g/7oz glacé cherries
50g/2oz raisins

Takes 30 minutes • Makes 18

1 Preheat the oven to 180°C/Gas 4/fan oven 160°C. Line 2 or 3 baking sheets with non-stick baking paper (or bake in batches). In a bowl, beat the butter and sugars together until light and fluffy. Stir in the flour and oats and mix well. Roughly chop three quarters of the cherries, then stir these and the whole cherries and raisins into the oat mixture.
2 Divide the mixture into 18 equal portions. Roughly shape each portion into a ball. Put on the baking sheets well apart to allow for spreading. Lightly flatten each biscuit with your fingertips, keeping the mixture quite rough-looking.
3 Bake for 15–20 minutes until the cookies are pale golden around the edges, but still feel soft in the centre. Cool on the baking sheets for 5 minutes, then transfer to a wire rack.

• Per cookie 249 kcalories, protein 2g, carbohydrate 33g, fat 13g, saturated fat 7g, fibre 1g, added sugar 15g, salt 0.36g

Anzac Biscuits

These delicious biscuits were made to send to the ANZACs (Australian and New Zealand Army Corps) serving in Gallipoli.

85g/3oz porridge oats
85g/3oz desiccated coconut
100g/4oz plain flour
100g/4oz caster sugar
100g/4oz butter, melted
1 tbsp golden syrup
1 tsp bicarbonate of soda

Takes 35 minutes • Makes 20

1 Preheat the oven to 180°C/Gas 4/fan oven 160°C. Put the oats, coconut, flour and sugar in a bowl. Melt the butter in a small pan or microwave and stir in the golden syrup. Add the bicarbonate of soda to 2 tablespoons boiling water, then stir into the golden syrup and butter mixture.
2 Make a well in the middle of the dry ingredients and pour in the butter and golden syrup mixture. Stir gently to incorporate the dry ingredients.
3 Put dessertspoonfuls of the mixture on to buttered baking sheets, about 2.5cm/1in apart to allow room for spreading. Bake in batches for 8–10 minutes until golden. Transfer to a wire rack to cool.

• Per biscuit 118 kcalories, protein 1g, carbohydrate 13g, fat 7g, saturated fat 5g, fibre 1g, added sugar 6g, salt 0.28g

Lemon and Sultana Cookies

Swap the sultanas for chopped nuts or other dried fruit to vary the recipe for these American-style cookies.

350g/12oz plain flour
½ tsp baking powder
½ tsp bicarbonate of soda
140g/5oz butter, cut into small pieces
175g/6oz caster sugar
85g/3oz sultanas
100g/4oz lemon curd
2 eggs, beaten

FOR THE ICING
100g/4oz sifted icing sugar
2 tbsp fresh lemon juice

Takes 30 minutes • Makes 30

1 Preheat the oven to 200°C/Gas 6/fan oven 180°C. Butter 3 baking sheets (or bake in several batches). Sift the flour, baking powder and bicarbonate of soda into a bowl. Add the butter and rub in with your fingertips until the mixture resembles fine breadcrumbs.
2 Stir in the sugar and sultanas, add the lemon curd and eggs and mix to a soft dough. Shape the dough into 30 small balls, about 2.5cm/1in wide, and put on the baking sheets, allowing plenty of space between them so they can spread. Using your fingers, gently press the top of each biscuit to flatten it slightly.
3 Bake for 12–15 minutes until risen and light golden. Leave to cool for 1 minute on the baking sheets, then transfer to a wire rack to cool completely. Blend the icing sugar and lemon juice, then drizzle over each cookie.

• Per cookie 134 kcalories, protein 2g, carbohydrate 23g, fat 5g, saturated fat 3g, fibre trace, added sugar 11g, salt 0.2g

Festive Almond Biscuits

Light biscuits with a surprise almond filling and orange-scented sugar.

75g/3oz unsalted butter, chilled and cut into pieces
115g/4oz self-raising flour
75g/3oz ground almonds
100g/4oz caster sugar
50g/2oz marzipan, cut into 20 cubes

FOR THE ORANGE SUGAR
pared rind of 2 oranges
50g/2oz icing sugar

Takes 1¼ hours • Makes 20

1 Whizz the butter with the flour and almonds to a breadcrumb consistency. Add half the caster sugar; whizz until the mixture starts to cling together, then work lightly into a ball.
2 Thinly roll out half of the dough. Use 6cm/2½in cutters to cut out crescents and stars; put 20 on a buttered baking sheet. Roll the marzipan cubes into sausage- or ball-shaped pieces and lay on the crecents and stars. Top each with matching dough shape and seal the edges. Chill for 30 minutes.
3 Preheat the oven to 160°C/Gas 3/fan oven 150°C. Put the orange rind on a baking sheet and bake for 3 minutes; cool. Mix the remaining caster sugar and the icing sugar; toss with the rind. Bake the biscuits for 18–20 minutes; cool on a wire rack. Sprinkle with the orange sugar.

• Per biscuit 109 kcalories, protein 1g, carbohydrate 14g, fat 6g, saturated fat 2g, fibre 1, added sugar 9g, salt 0.06g

Walnut Oat Biscuits

Serve with ripe Taleggio or another soft cheese, such as dolcelatte or St Andre, and a brimming bowl of fresh, juicy strawberries.

100g/4oz butter, softened
85g/3oz light muscovado sugar
1 egg, beaten
50g/2oz porridge oats
50g/2oz walnuts, finely chopped
85g/3oz plain flour
½ tsp baking powder
cheese and strawberries, to serve

Takes 25 minutes • Makes 15

1 Preheat the oven to 180°C/Gas 4/fan oven 160°C. Butter two baking sheets. In a bowl, beat the butter and sugar for 5 minutes by hand or 2 minutes in the food processor until light and fluffy. Beat in the egg, then stir in the oats, nuts, flour and baking powder.
2 Drop dessertspoonfuls of the mixture, with a little space between, on the baking sheets. Bake for 15 minutes until pale golden, then cool on a wire rack.
3 Serve as described above with the cheese and strawberries. The biscuits will keep fresh in a sealed container for up to a week.

• Per biscuit 133 kcalories, protein 2g, carbohydrate 13g, fat 9g, saturated fat 4g, fibre 1g, added sugar 6g, salt 0.15g

Pine Nut Cookies

Traditionally made with vegetable shortening, this old-fashioned type of cookie dough can also be made into a case for a fruit tart.

50g/2oz pine nuts, plus a few extra
175g/6oz butter, softened
140g/5oz golden granulated sugar, plus extra for sprinkling
seeds from 1 star anise, crushed (optional)
1 egg
250g/9oz plain flour
1 tsp baking powder

Takes 1 hour • Makes 18

1 Toast the pine nuts in a dry, heavy-based pan for 1–2 minutes. Set aside.
2 Put the butter, sugar and star anise seeds, if using, in a food processor and whizz for 1 minute. Scrape down the bowl, then whizz again briefly. Add the egg and whizz again. Tip in the flour and baking powder and whizz until the mixture forms a dough. Mix in the pine nuts (reserving enough for step 3), then chill for 30 minutes, wrapped in plastic film.
3 Preheat the oven to 180°C/Gas 4/fan oven 160°C. Take walnut-sized pieces of dough and press out into 5cm/2in rounds, level but not too neat. Put on the baking sheets and press two pine nuts on the top of each. Bake for 15 minutes until pale golden. Transfer to a wire rack to cool, sprinkle with sugar and serve.

• Per cookie 176 kcalories, protein 2g, carbohydrate 20g, fat 10g, saturated fat 5g, fibre trace, added sugar 9g, salt 0.28g

TOP LEFT: Festive Almond Biscuits   TOP RIGHT: Walnut Oat Biscuits   BOTTOM: Pine Nut Cookies

Index

almond(s)
    cake with Clementines 302–3
    and chocolate torte 310–11
    festive biscuits 342–3
    fresh almond cherry cake 302–3
    nectarine tart 172–3
    and orange cake 298–9
    and sticky apricot bars 326–7
    stir-fried salad with 134–5
anchovies and broccoli, spaghetti with 84–5
Anzac biscuits 340–1
apple(s)
    and apricot treacle tart bars 330–1
    blackberry ice cream sauce 282–3
    and blackberry loaf 316–17
    and blackberry pudding 174–5
    and blueberry cobbler 284–5
    and cider, chicken with 94–5
    and cinnamon cake 306–7
    marzipan and mincemeat 118–19
    mustardy sausages with 274–5
    and pork braise 26–7
    and pumpkin curry 154–5
    raisin and carrot cake 294–5
    rosy, honeyed pork with 222–3
apricot(s)
    and almond bars, sticky 326–7
    and apple treacle tart bars 330–1
    and banana compôte 120–1
    crumb squares 326–7
    pork, and ginger skewers 260–1
    and spicy chicken stew 94–5
    summery Provençal 116–17
Asian vegetable broth 72–3
asparagus with garlic, roast 74–5
aubergines
    with goat's cheese 158–9
    spicy pork and 100–1
avocado
    salami and bean salad 238–9
    salsa, griddled fish with 200–1
    souffléd omelette 134–5

bacon
    baked trout with chicory and 210–11
    BLT burgers 240–1
    creamy penne, chicken with 20–1
    and egg tart 256–7
    fish o'leekie 32–3
    herby pasta with peas and 248–9
    kebabs on mushroom rice 240–1

open turkey BLT 190–1
oven-baked risotto 30–1
smoky, mussels with wine and 210–11
and tomato cobbler 276–7
bagels
    with griddled vegetables 166–7
    hot pastrami 190–1
Balti, mixed vegetable 50–1
banana(s)
    and apricot compôte 120–1
    coconut and mango cake 302–3
    St Lucia cake 300–1
    and walnut muffins 332–3
    and walnut tealoaf 318–19
bangers and beans in a pan 30–1
barbecued food
    balsamic beef 98–9
    spatchcock chicken 204–5
    turkey strips 96–7
beans
    avocado and salami salad 238–9
    and bangers in a pan 30–1
    and beef hotpot 56–7
    broad, gnocchi with 150–1
    cannellini, chicken with 258–9
    chilli and chicory crostini 80–1
    chilli, open lasagne 146–7
    chilli, tortillas 256–7
    corn and tuna salad 78–9
    fish with lemon and 38–9
    flageolet, and feta salad 130–1
    and ham with orange 20–1
    haricot, and lamb hotpot 276–7
    Indian, on toast 214–15
    mash, seared beef with 202–3
    and pumpkin spaghetti 84–5
    and sausage bake 264–5
    Sunday brunch 26–7
    trout and beetroot salad 76–7
    and vegetable bake 110–11
    and vegetable chilli 44–5
    see also broad beans; white beans
Beaujolais berries 60–1
beef
    barbecued balsamic 98–9
    and bean hotpot 56–7
    paprikash 58–9
    seared with bean mash 202–3
    see also steak
beetroot
    bean and trout salad 76–7

and lamb's lettuce risotto 114–15
berries
    Beaujolais 60–1
    buttermilk muffins 334–5
    chocolate berry cups 230–1
    cinnamon and lemon tarts with 324–5
    daiquiri 230–1
    gooseberry and elderflower crumble
        174–5
    grilled summer berry pudding 64–5
    iced summer berries with white chocolate
        sauce 228–9
    see also blackberries; blueberries; cran-
        berries; raspberries; strawberries
biriyani, chicken 24–5
biscuits
    Anzac 340–1
    festive almond 342–3
    walnut oat 342–3
blackberries
    apple ice cream sauce 282–3
    and apple loaf 316–17
    and apple pudding 174–5
    fairy cakes 324–5
    poached pears with 118–19
blackcurrant crumble squares 326–7
blini stacks, vegetable 134–5
BLT
    burgers 240–1
    open turkey 190–1
blueberries
    and apple cobbler 284–5
    cheesecake gateau 298–9
    and lemon friands 324–5
bolognese, turkey 96–7
bread pudding, cheesy 142–3
breakfast munching muffins 332–3
brie
    spaghetti with tomato and 252–3
    and tomato tart 140–1
broad beans
    gnocchi with 150–1
    minty pâté 166–7
broccoli
    and anchovies, spaghetti with 84–5
    and chicken stir-fry 92–3
    lemon chicken 192–3
    and potato salad, warm 238–9
    soup with goat's cheese 12–13
    and tuna pasta bake 266–7
broth

Asian vegetable 72–3
    chunky winter 12–13
    teriyaki chicken noodle 220–1
brownies, toffee 312–13
brûlées
    lemon curd 282–3
    peach melba 170–1
    strawberry yogurt 116–17
    tropical crème 227
bruschettas
    roasted tomato 184–5
    stuffed mushroom 142–3
bubble and squeak cakes 246–7
burgers, BLT 240–1
buttermilk scones 320–1
butternut squash with cheese, spiced 212–13
buttery squash, baked 74–5

Cajun-spiced chicken 90–1
cakes
    almond with Clementines 302–3
    apple and cinnamon 306–7
    authentic Yorkshire parkin 294–5
    Autumn plum crunch 316–17
    blackberry fairy 324–5
    blueberry cheesecake gateau 298–9
    cappuccino bars 308–9
    carrot, apple and raisin 294–5
    cherry and marzipan 290–1
    cinnamon Nutella 290–1
    citrus poppy seed 304–5
    dark chocolate and orange 310–11
    Devonshire honey 290–1
    fresh cherry almond 302–3
    fresh cherry with a hint of cinnamon
        306–7
    lemon flower 298–9
    lemon polenta with rosemary syrup 300–1
    lemon and violet drizzle 320–1
    mango, banana and coconut 302–3
    mocha fudge with coffee icing 297
    olive oil 290–1
    orange and almond 298–9
    pear, hazelnut and chocolate 310–11
    pecan ginger 290–1
    porter 294–5
    raisin spice 290–1
    rhubarb and orange 300–1
    St Lucia banana 300–1
    seriously rich chocolate 308–9
    soured cream rhubarb squares 304–5

Picture and recipe credits

BBC Worldwide would like to thank the following for providing photographs. While every effort has been made to trace and acknowledge all photographers, we would like to apologise should there be any errors or omissions.

One-pot Dishes

Marie-Louise Avery p14 (tr), p25 (tl), p45 (t); Iain Bagwell p33 (tl), p34 (bl); Steve Baxter p13 (bl), p34 (br), p46 (tr); Martin Brigdale p54 (b); Carl Clemens-Gros p41 (tl), p58 (t); Ken Field p11 (2), p11 (3), p11 (5), p13 (t), p18 (br), p21 (t), p22 (b), p26 (t), p33 (tr), p37 (bl), p41 (b), p46 (b), p50 (t), p54 (tl) ; Will Heap p30 (tr); Dave King p42 (bl); Jason Lowe p11 (6), p61 (br); David Munns p14 (b), p17 (tr), p22 (tl), p25 (b), p29 (br), p37 (br), p54 (tl), p57 (tr), p65 (tr); Myles New p46 (tl); Myles New & Craig Robertson p14 (tl); Craig Robertson p61 (bl), p65 (tl); Sharon Smith p10, p49 (tl); Roger Stowell p38 (tl), p38 (tr), p41 (tr), p42 (t), p50 (bl), p50 (br), p57 (b), p58 (bl), p62 (b), p65 (b); Sam Stowell p58 (br); Simon Walton p18 (bl), p26 (bl); Philip Webb p11 (1), p13 (br), p17 (tl), p25 (tr), p26 (br), p34 (t), p37 (t), p38 (b), p42 (br), p45 (br), p49 (b), p53 (t), p62 (tl); Simon Wheeler p11 (4), p22 (tr), p45 (bl), p49 (tr), p53 (bl), p53 (br), p57 (tl), p61 (t), p62 (tr); Jonathan Whittaker p21 (bl).

Low-fat Feasts

Chris Alack p77 (t), p87 (tr), p93 (bl); Iain Bagwell p67 (6), p86 (tr), p106 (bl), 118 (b); Clive Bozzard-Hill p114 (t); Jean Cazals p69 (bl); Ken Field p77 (bl), p93 (br), p105 (tl), p117 (bl); Hulton Archive p81 (b); David Jordan p110 (b), p113 (tr); Dave King p97 (tl), 97 (b), 109 (br); Richard Kolker p67 (5), p113 (b); Steve Lee p89 (tl); David Munns p74 (t), p74 (bl), p82 (br), p105 (b); Myles New p77 (br), p89 (tr), 101 (br), 118 (tr); Nick Pope p69 (br); Bill Reavell p110 (tr); Simon Smith p114 (br); Roger Stowell p66, p67 (2), p67 (3), p70 (tl), p70 (tr), p70 (b), p73 (tr), p74 (br), p78 (tr), p82 (t), p86 (tl), p86 (b), p90 (t), 90 (bl), 90 (br), 94 (tl), 94 (b), 97 (t), 102 (b), 109 (bl), 113 (tr), 117 (t), 117 (br), 118 (tr), 121 (tl); Martin Thompson p67 (1), p69 (t), p81 (tl), p85 (br); Martin Thompson and Philip Webb p94 (tr); Simon Walton p78 (tl), p82 (bl), p89 (b), p98 (t), p101 (t), p102 (tl), p106 (br); Philip Webb p105 (tr); Simon Wheeler p85 (t), p85 (bl), p93 (t), p98 (bl), p98 (br), 102 (tr), 109 (t); Jonathan Whitaker p73 (tl), p101 (bl), p110 (tl); Frank Wieder p121 (tr); Geoff Wilkinson p67 (4), p106 (t), p114 (bl), p121 (b); BBC Worldwide p73 (b), 78 (b)

Veggie Dishes

Chris Alack p126 (tr), p149 (t), p162 (t), p166 (b), p169 (tl), p177 (b); Marie-Louise Avery p149 (bl); Iain Bagwell p145 (tl); Clive Bozzard-Hill p130 (t), p138 (t), p162 (br), p174 (tl); Peter Cassidy p137 (b), p173 (br), p174 (b); Ken Field p122, p123 (2), p125 (t), p133 (br), p150 (t), p153 (b), p154 (t); Dave King p150 (b), p173 (t); Richard Kolker p129 (tl); David Munns p129 (tr); Myles New p37 (tl); Thomas Odulate p123 (6), p133 (t), p161 (tr), p170 (t), p173 (bl), p177 (tl); William Reavell p123 (5), p133 (bl), p150 (tl), p154 (bl, p158 (tl), p161 (tl), p165 (bl), p165 (br), p170 (bl), p177 (tr); Howard Shooter p123 (1), p125 (bl), p130 (bl), p165 (t); Simon Smith p145 (b), p153 (tl), p161 (b); Roger Stowell p127 (b), p129 (b), p130 (br), p138 (br), p142 (tr), p149 (br), p157 (t); Sam Stowell p162 (bl), p166 (tl), p174 (tr); Mark Thompson p157 (br); Trevor Vaughan p123 (3), p123 (4), p134 (tr), p134 (b), p141 (bl), p146 (t), p146 (bl), p154 (br), p157 (bl), p158 (tr), p170 (br); Ian Wallace p169 (b); Simon Wheeler p140 (t), p142 (tl), p158 (b); Jonathan Whittaker p126 (tl), p137 (tr), p153 (tr); Frank Wieder p138 (bl), p141 (br), p142 (b), p145 (tr), p146 (br), p169 (tr); BBC Worldwide p134 (tl), p166 (tr)

Meals for Two

Marie-Louise Avery p209 (tr); Iain Bagwell p178, p202 (br), p217 (tl); Steve Baxter p185 (tl), p193 (tr), p201 (tr), p218 (t), p218 (br), p225 (tl), p230 (b); Peter Cassidy p210 (br), p226 (bl), p229 (t), p233 (tr); Ken Field p179 (1), p181 (br), p182 (t), p186 (bl), p190 (b), p194 (t), p206 (tr), p214 (b), p217 (b), p222 (b); Gus Filgate p179 (6), p205 (br), p233 (tl); Will Heap p179 (2), p182 (tr), p193 (tl), p233 (b); Lisa Linder p230 (tr); William Lingwood p181 (t), p186 (t), 189 (br), p214 (tr); David Munns p179 (3), p181 (bl), p185 (tr), p198 (b), p202 (t), p206 (b), p210 (t), p210 (bl), p225 (b), p229 (bl), p229 (br); Michael Paul p189 (bl), p217 (tr); Myles New & Craig Robertson p221 (bl); Craig Robertson p201 (tl), p209 (b), p221 (br), p225 (tr), p226 (t), p226 (br); Roger Stowell p179 (4), p190 (tl), p198 (tr), p202 (bl), p206 (tl), p213 (t), p213 (bl), p213 (br), p214 (tl); Simon Walton p179 (5), p194 (bl), p222 (tl), p22 (tr); Cameron Watt p189 (t), p194 (br), p201 (b), p205 (t), p221 (t); Philip Webb p186 (br), p190 (tr), p193 (b), p197 (bl), p198 (tl), p209 (tl), p230 (tl); Simon Wheeler p197 (t), p197 (br), p205 (bl), p218 (bl); Geoff Wilkinson p185 (b); Peter Williams p182 (tl).

Cheap Eats

Chris Alack p250 (bl), p257 (tr), p258 (t); Marie-Louise Avery p242 (t), p265 (tl); Jean Cazals p273 (tr), p282 (t), p282 (bl); Ken Field p262 (tr), p265 (tr); Dave King p249 (b), p274 (bl), p281 (tr); William Lingwood p285 (br); David Munns p235 (6), p242 (br), p245 (t), p245 (br), p250 (t), p261 (t), p266 (t), p266 (br), p270 (tl), p286 (tl), p266 (b); William Reavell p238 (tr); Howard Shooter p235 (2), p249 (tl); Simon Smith p242 (bl), p257 (b); Roger Stowell p234, p235 (1), p235 (4), p237 (t), 238 (tl), 238 (b), 241 (tr), 241 (b), 245 (bl), 246 (tl), 246 (b), 249 (tr), 250 (br), 253 (t), 253 (br), 254 (tr), 254 (b), 257 (tl), 258 (br), 261 (bl), 261 (br), 265 (b), 269 (t), 269 (bl), 270 (t), 270 (b), 273 (tl), 274 (t), 274 (br), 277 (t), 277 (bl), 277 (br), 278 (b), 281 (tl), 281 (b), 285 (bl); Sam Stowell p266 (bl); Martin Thompson p235 (5), p262 (b), 278 (tr); Martin Thompson and Philip Webb p253 (bl); Ian Wallace p266 (tr); Simon Wheeler p235 (3), p258 (bl); Jonathan Whitaker p285 (t); BBC Worldwide p273 (b), 278 (tl)

Cakes and Bakes

Marie-Louise Avery p292 (tr), p300 (b), p311 (b), p322 (t), p322 (br), p327 (b), p339 (bl); Steve Baxter p327 (tl); Martin Brigdale p291 (br), p304 (bl), p316 (b); Linda Burgess p289 (2), p289 (5), 295 (b), p303 (tl), p304 (br), p307 (t), p307 (br), p315 (t), p316 (tl), p327 (tr); Jean Cazals p340 (b); Gus Filgate p340 (tr); Anna Hodgson p324 (b); David Munns p291 (t), 299 (t), p332 (b); Myles New p295 (tl); Michael Paul p289 (1), p296 (t), p296 (bl), p312 (t), p315 (bl), p320 (t), p332 (tl), p339 (br); Craig Robertson p299 (br); Howard Shooter p291 (bl); Simon Smith p343 (tl; Simon Smith/Adrian Taylor p332 (tr); Roger Stowell p288, p289 (3), p299 (bl), p300 (tr), p303 (tr), p303 (b), p308 (tr), p312 (bl), p319 (tl), p320 (bl), p336 (bl), p343 (tr), p343 (b); Adrian Taylor/Bill Reavell/Niall McDiarmid p292 (tl); Martin Thompson p128; Philip Webb p289 (4), p292 (b), p296 (br), p300 (tl), p304 (t), p308 (tl), p311 (tr), p312 (tr), p316 (tr), p319 (tr), p331 (t), p331 (bl), p335 (tl), p335 (b), p336 (t); Simon Wheeler p295 (tr), p311 (tl), p315 (br), p320 (br), p322 (bl), p324 (tl), p328 (tl), p328 (br), p331 (br), p340 (tl); Jonathan Whittaker p328 (t); Geoff Wilkinson p307 (bl), p324 (tr), p335 (b); Tim Young p289 (6), p308 (b), p319 (b), p336 (bl), p339 (t)

All the recipes in this collection have been created by the editorial team on *Good Food* magazine.